Overtourism

De Gruyter Studies in Tourism

Series editor
Jillian M. Rickly

Volume 1

Overtourism

Issues, realities and solutions

Edited by
Rachel Dodds and Richard W. Butler

DE GRUYTER

ISBN 978-3-11-060408-5 (hardcover)
ISBN 978-3-11-062045-0 (paperback)
e-ISBN (PDF) 978-3-11-060736-9
e-ISBN (EPUB) 978-3-11-060570-9
ISSN 2570-1657

Library of Congress Control Number: 2019931910

Bibliographic information published by the Deutsche Nationalbibliothek
The Deutsche Nationalbibliothek lists this publication in the Deutsche Nationalbibliografie;
detailed bibliographic data are available on the Internet at http://dnb.dnb.de.

© 2019 Walter de Gruyter GmbH, Berlin/Boston
Cover image: Florence Bessand
Typesetting: Integra Software Services Pvt. Ltd
Printing and Binding: CPI books GmbH, Leck

www.degruyter.com

Overtourism. It's time for some answers

Like a volcano, overtourism has been threatening to erupt for a very long time. Many decades ago, academics recorded the first grumblings to identify concerns about the structures of tourism.

More recently, residents across the world began to see dark smoke and to raise serious concerns while ecologists started to wonder if tourism was at risk of overwhelming parts of our natural world.

Three years ago overtourism volcanoes erupted all over the world and the issues associated with the industry's unmanaged and unsustainable growth were thrust into the media and the public spotlight. A subject mostly confined to academic papers and the classroom became front page news in *The New York Times, Wall Street Journal* and *The South China Morning Post*.

The sustainability of tourism became the first issue that industry leaders were asked about, rather than the last. Tourism ministers had to confront large scale protests from residents, street graffiti saying "tourist go home", and tourists complaining of overcrowding.

Tourism essentially crossed a line, and not just in Venice and Barcelona where the protests were the loudest. Overtourism reports came in from every continent, from big cities to small island states and national parks.

While the straw that broke the camel's back in Venice might have been an extra few million tourists, even a few hundred or thousand had the same effect in smaller destinations with less capacity and little or no tourism management.

Historically the movement for more responsible and sustainable tourism has consisted of academics and activists, some progressive parts of the tourism industry (small and large) and a few enlightened destination managers.

Now local residents, and to a growing extent, tourists, are joining the fold. The late Jost Krippendorf, academic and author of *The Holiday Makers*, once said change in tourism will require "rebellious locals and rebellious tourists". Increasingly, the world has both.

Unlike the unavoidable rupture in the Earth's crust that causes volcanic eruptions, many of the issues in tourism that led to the current crisis could have been addressed.

One has to ask why they weren't, and to conclude that unmanaged growth suited an aggressive tourism industry and many destination managers whose misguided worldview was that everybody (residents, tourists, natural and cultural heritage) always benefit from tourism.

Reading industry and destination manager's responses to overtourism, it's hard not to conclude that many of them are totally unprepared to deal with the crisis on their doorstep. The challenge now is for all of us to work together to manage tourism better.

https://doi.org/10.1515/9783110607369-201

This immensely readable book edited by Rachel Dodds and Richard W. Butler, hugely experienced and expert leaders in our field, provides much of what we will need. Always rooted in practical, destination-based examples, it neatly summarises the issues, the strategies we will need to address them, and – through a range of excellent case histories from contributors – many of the solutions to overtourism.

Whether you are a destination manager, work in the tourism industry, are a community leader, or a student of tourism, there will be something for you in this book.

We need all of you to help tourism to realise its potential to be a force for good. As its best it can bring together people of different colours, faiths, ages and income levels in joyful, caring and mutually beneficial ways that support development and the conservation of natural and cultural heritage. Never has the need for more responsible tourism been greater.

Justin Francis
Responsible Travel
Lewes, England, November 2018

Acknowledgements

We would first like to acknowledge and thank the contributors in this volume, without whose efforts the book would not have been completed. We also appreciate very much the support, cooperation and quick turnaround in such a positive manner. We hope and trust they are happy with the results although we, as editors, accept responsibility for any errors or misinterpretations.

Second, we thank Ellen Meleisea for her attention to detail and diligence in copyediting the manuscript – undoubtedly making the book much better as a result of her efforts. We also acknowledge and thank the staff at De Gruyter for their assistance and cooperation.

Third, our thanks go to all those who supplied photos which have added so much to the volume, especially Florence Bessand for the fabulous cover shot.

Finally, our thanks go to our families, especially Margaret, Nick and Zoe for their patience and understanding during long periods of "computer time" and endless conversations about the topic.

https://doi.org/10.1515/9783110607369-202

Contents

Part III: **Challenges**

Rachel Dodds and Richard W. Butler

1 Introduction

The term "overtourism" has rapidly gained traction across multiple sectors, including academia, policy formulation, social movements and the media. This relatively new term, also sometimes called "loving places to death", "dealing with success" and "tourismphobia" (Goodwin, 2017; Dredge, 2017), has been defined as

> the excessive growth of visitors leading to overcrowding in areas where residents suffer the consequences of temporary and seasonal tourism peaks, which have enforced permanent changes to their lifestyles, access to amenities and general well-being. (Milano et al., 2018)

According to Goodwin (2017: 1), destinations experience overtourism when "hosts or guests, locals or visitors, feel that there are too many visitors and that the quality of life in the area or the quality of the experience has deteriorated unacceptably".

The concerns about overtourism expressed in both academic and popular literature include: too many tourists in one place, rowdy and other inappropriate behaviour by tourists, antagonism between residents and tourists, crowding, strains on infrastructure, loss of authenticity, loss of amenity and reduction in quality of life of residents and reduced enjoyment of experiences by tourists. These externalities are not all new. Throughout the past four decades, the potential and actual deteriorating relationship between hosts and guests has been the subject of much study and discussion (Doxey, 1975; Butler, 1980; Krippendorf, 1987; Boissevan, 1996). The issues related to tourism at individual destinations and resorts were discussed earlier still (Ogilvie, 1933; Christaller, 1963; Young, 1973). Plog (1973) proposed a model involving the changing characteristics of tourists themselves visiting a range of destinations as those destinations changed in character and moved from underdevelopment to development (and overdevelopment).

Although tourism and tourists have been the subject of complaints for decades, if not centuries specific term "overtourism" is relatively recent. According to Google, the word "overtourism" was first used as a search term in 2006. The term was popularized in the tourism online community by Skift, which observed that overtourism represents a hazard to destinations because

> the dynamic forces that power tourism often inflict unavoidable negative consequences if not managed well. In some countries, this can lead to a decline in tourism as a sustainable framework is never put into place for coping with the economic, environmental, and sociocultural effects of tourism. The impact on local residents cannot be understated either. (Sheivachman, 2016)

As of 2018, "overtourism" and the perils associated with it boast hashtags and are the subjects of frequent Google searches and dinner party conversations.

https://doi.org/10.1515/9783110607369-001

Researchers are questioning whether overtourism is a new phenomenon or simply "old wine in new bottles" (Dredge, 2017). Overtourism is related to other concepts familiar to tourist researchers, namely carrying capacity, resilience and sustainability. Of these, carrying capacity is the oldest. It can be expressed in environmental, economic and social-cultural terms, as well as with regard to technological limits and health and safety issues. As noted elsewhere (see Chapter 3), the concept has become unfashionable in tourism scholarship, despite its obvious relevance in discussions of overtourism. This relevance is seen in the use of the prefix "over" in the word "overtourism", with the implication that there is too much tourism in a particular destination, and that the tourism exceeds the ability, limits or capacity of the destination involved. Often overtourism is also seen as overtaxing the ability of destinations to meet desired standards and limits.

The concept of resilience – the ability of destinations to absorb shocks and disturbances (impacts) and recover – has been applied relatively recently to tourism and tourism destinations and is related to the destinations' latitude, resistance and precariousness, as well as to their vulnerability and ability to adapt to changing circumstances (Butler, 2018; Hall et al., 2016; Cheer and Lew, 2018). With regard to the concept of sustainability, the links between the level of tourism and the quality of social and environmental factors in a destination are frequently cited, with the logical conclusion that tourism levels should not exceed a point at which uncorrectable impacts occur and where tourism becomes "unsustainable" (Hunter, 1995; Briassoulis, 2002; Murphy and Price, 2005; Dodds and Butler, 2010; UNWTO, 2018). Thus, to plan for sustainability in a tourism context is to plan to operate within the carrying capacity limits of the destination and its resilience capabilities, and avoid a state of overtourism, for as Weber et al. (2017: 199) observe, it is clear that "the way tourism is managed has a direct impact on carrying capacity and the resilience to overtourism".

In any discussion of overtourism, the issue of resident dissatisfaction arises, as well as the practice, of residents and their supporters, in protesting against overtourism. In the past, excessive tourism in specific destinations was generally expressed as overuse or overdevelopment. With the exception of Doxey's (1975) oft-cited paper, what was generally absent was any discussion of resident protest. This is a key component of overtourism in the present and raises the question of whether overtourism can exist in locations devoid of local residents. This is rather like the question about a tree falling in a forest but not being witnessed and whether in such a case it makes a noise. This raises the question: Is the defining characteristic of overtourism the existence of resident protest? Certainly resident protests in Venice, Barcelona, Scotland and elsewhere, as discussed in the case studies in this volume, have attracted media and academic attention, while overcrowding and overdevelopment have generally passed without much attention beyond mild regret at an apparent inability to prevent an excess of visitation.

In order to understand overtourism and propose actions to combat it, it is important to identify the causes of overtourism. This volume begins with a discussion of the causes or, perhaps more accurately, the "enablers" of overtourism, as it is not possible to be precise in determining the specific causes of overtourism. As discussed in the next chapter, there are a number of factors that, in combination, create an environment in which overtourism can occur. Not all of these factors are new. While many have existed for many years, their influence has increased in recent years and when they are combined their effects can be dramatic for the destinations exposed to them. Thus, even though the writing has been on the wall, not everyone has chosen to read it.

After an examination of these enablers, several chapters discuss the conceptual aspects of overtourism, in particular, its relationship with the natural environment and theories such as carrying capacity, the issue of authenticity and the impact of overtourism on the social and cultural manifestations of destinations and on their residents, and in turn, on their offerings to tourists. Attention then moves to the media and its role in shaping and creating overtourism and the subsequent behaviour of tourists, and the speed and reach of social media in particular. Part 1 of the book concludes with a discussion of overtourism in the context of the Tourism Area Life Cycle model, which provided an early warning about the potential impacts of overdevelopment of destinations.

As is shown by the case studies that follow in Part 2, although each example of overtourism is specific to its particular location, most have certain features in common. One such feature is the feelings, expressed by residents of affected communities, of frustration and annoyance, if not anger, at being relatively powerless to prevent or mitigate the onset of overtourism. Even in smaller centres such as Prague and Lucerne, complaints are appearing about numbers and actions of tourists.

In general, local municipalities seem relatively ineffective at resolving the problem. Even in well publicized overtourism cities such as Barcelona, where the local government has recognized the problem for over a decade, protests are increasing visibility and frequency, with accompanying media attention. In other areas, sudden drastic actions have been taken, with locations closed to tourism in both Thailand and Philippines, reflecting concerns at higher levels of government over environmental and social problems resulting from overdevelopment and excessive visitor numbers. All of these cases are small, in terms of the numbers involved, compared to the scale of the religious ceremony of the Hajj, where the massive numbers of pilgrims are concentrated in small spaces at specific times and are engaged in rituals en masse. Here, overtourism impacts include considerable numbers of deaths, the collapse of structures and health risks, which are being tackled by the national government at great expense. In contrast, overtourism in rural areas often involves relatively small numbers of tourists but has a considerable effect on the quality of life of residents. The case studies cannot hope to be all encompassing but they do provide a level of comparison for many other destinations globally. The examples make it clear that overtourism is more of a relative problem than an absolute one in that much depends on the characteristics of affected destinations and their residents, and the relative scale of tourism in those communities. In all the examples examined, it is clear that economic priorities have taken precedence over social and environmental concerns. What is also clear is that, although relative, more and more destinations may face these issues if action is not taken.

Part 3 of the book examines the roles and responsibilities of stakeholders and, in particular, the importance of tackling overtourism at the local level, and identifies the difficulties of combining and integrating the multiple viewpoints and goals of the different groups involved. It is clear that there have been many massive failures in goal identification and establishment, policy formulation, policy implementation and, perhaps above all, incorporating local resident views into actions.

In the final chapter, the editors coordinate the examples and arguments presented in the chapters and to identify areas of common ground in terms of issues and themes, as well as suggesting some potential ways of mitigating the problem of overtourism. This book, therefore, is a compilation of work that examines the issue of overtourism from a holistic and objective perspective. While a multitude of sensationalistic media pieces exist, they are often opinionated and do not examine the contributing factors and why and how the current situation came about. This book explores these aspects.

References

Boissevain, J. (1996) Coping with Tourists: European Reactions to Mass Tourism. Providence/ Oxford: Berghahn Books.

Briassoulis, H. (2002) Sustainable Tourism and the Question of the Commons, *Annals of Tourism Research*, 29 (4): 1065–1085.

Butler, R. W. (1980) The concept of a tourist area cycle of evolution: Implications for management of resources, *The Canadian Geographer*, 24 (1): 5–12.

Butler, R.W. (2018) *Tourism and Resilience* Walliingford: CABI.

Cheer, J.M. and Lew, A.A. (2018) *Tourism, Resilience and Sustainability* London: Routledge.

Christaller, W. (1963) Some considerations of tourism location in Europe: the peripheral regions – underdeveloped countries – recreation areas, *Regional Science Association Papers*, 12, Lund Congress: 95–105.

Dodds, R. and Butler, R. W. (2010) Barriers to implementing sustainable tourism policy in mass tourism destinations, *Tourismos*, 5 (1): 35–53.

Doxey, G. V. (1975) A causation theory of visitor-resident irritants: Methodology and research inferences. In *Sixth annual conference proceedings of the Travel Research Association*. San Diego: Travel Research Association, pp. 195–198.

Dredge, D. (2017) "Overtourism" Old wine in new bottles? Linkedin, 13 September. https:// www.linkedin.com/pulse/overtourism-old-wine-new-bottles-dianne-dredge (Accessed July 2018.)

Goodwin, H. (2017) The challenge of overtourism, *Responsible Tourism Partnership Working Paper 4*. http://haroldgoodwin.info/pubs/RTP'WP4Overtourism01'2017.pdf (Accessed 23 November 2018.)

Hall, C. M. and Veer, E. (2016) The DMO is dead. Long live the DMO (or, why DMO managers don't care about post-structuralism), *Tourism Recreation Research*, 41 (3): 354–357.

Hunter, C. J. (1995) On the need to re-conceptualise sustainable tourism development, *Journal of Sustainable Tourism*, 3 (3): 155–165.

Krippendorf, J. (1987) *The holiday makers: Understanding the impact of leisure and travel*. London: Heinemann.

Milano, C, Cheer, J. M. and Novelli, M. (2018) Overtourism is becoming a major issue for cities across the globe, *The Conversation*, 18 July 2018. http://theconversation.com/overtourism-a-growing-global-problem-100029 (Accessed 20 July 2018.)

Murphy, P. E. and Price, G. G. (2005) Tourism and sustainable development. In W. F. Theobald (Ed.), *Global tourism* (3rd edition). Amsterdam: Elsevier, pp. 167–193.

Ogilvie, F.W. (1933) *The tourist movement: An economic study*. London: Staples Press.

O'Reilly, A. M. (1986) Tourism carrying capacity: concept and issues, *Tourism Management*, 7 (4): 254–258.

Plog, S.C (1973) Why destination areas rise and fall in popularity. *Cornell Hotel and Restaurant Association Quarterly* 13: 6–13.

Sheivachman (2016) Iceland and the Trials of 21st Century Tourism, *Skift*, 30 July. https://skift.com/iceland-tourism/ (Accessed 23 November 2018.)

UNWTO (2018) *'Overtourism'? Understanding and managing urban tourism growth beyond perceptions*. Madrid: UNWTO.

Weber, F., Stettler, J., Priskin, J., Rosenberg-Taufer, B., Ponnapureddy, S., Fux, S., Camp, M., Barth, M. (2017) Tourism destinations under pressure: Challenges and innovative solutions, *Working Paper*, Institute of Tourism ITW, Lucerne University of Applied Sciences and Arts. https://static1.squarespace.com/static/56dacbc6d210b821510cf939/t/5909cb282e69cf1c85253749/1493814%20076440/WTFL_study+2017_full+version.pdf (Accessed 27 September 2018.)

Young, G. (1973) *Tourism Blessing or Blight?* Harmondsworth: Penguin.

Rachel Dodds and Richard W. Butler

2 The enablers of overtourism

As noted in Chapter 1, overtourism has become a widespread issue of great concern and many governments and tourism agencies are seeking ways to address it. In order to identify appropriate measures to tackle overtourism, it is important to understand how it has come about. This chapter therefore examines the enablers of overtourism in some detail. The factors include:

- Greater numbers of tourists
- Travel has become more affordable
- New groups of tourists
- Dominance of the growth-focused mindset
- A short-term focus
- Competition for space, amenities and services
- Wider access to media and information
- Destinations lack control over tourist numbers
- Imbalance of power among stakeholders
- Tourism stakeholders are fragmented and at odds

Greater numbers of tourists

Today there are more tourists than ever before. In 1950, there were approximately 25 million international tourists and when authors such as Christaller (1963) and Krippendorf (1987) started to write about the negative impacts of tourism, international arrivals were only around 165 million (UNWTO, 2017: 2). In 2016, tourism numbers had increased almost 50-fold since 1950, reaching over a billion (UNWTO, 2017: 2). With the exception of 2001, international tourism arrivals have increased every year, and the United Nations World Tourism Organization (UNWTO) declared that international tourist arrivals had grown by 7%, with corresponding increases in domestic or internal tourism (which is estimated to be around four to five times the size of the international form of tourism). The UNWTO also has forecast continued growth at an average annual rate of 3.3%, with growth as high as 4.9% per year in the Asia-Pacific region (UNWTO, 2017: 14).

The areas that have received the most media attention regarding overtourism (Europe and South East Asia) also have the lion's share of tourism arrivals (50% and 25% respectively) (see Fig. 2.1).

https://doi.org/10.1515/9783110607369-002

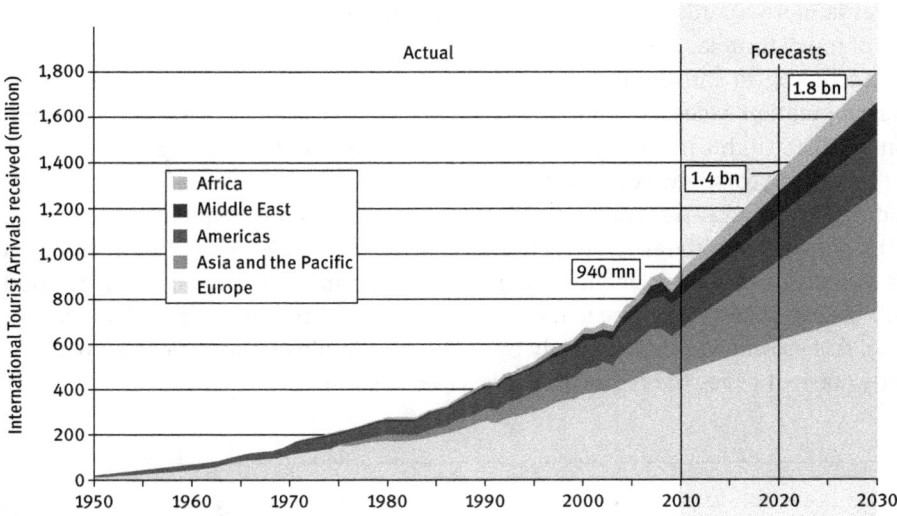

Fig. 2.1: International tourism arrivals: 1950–2030 (UNWTO, 2017: 14).

Travel has become more affordable

The rise in the number of tourists is due to both an increase in the number of people on the planet and a greater number of people who can afford to travel (Fig. 2.2).

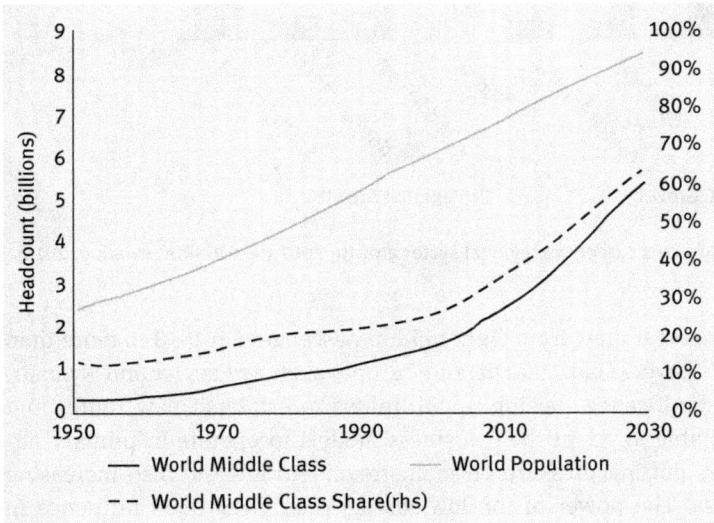

Fig. 2.2: Estimates of the size of the global middle class, 1950–2030 (Kharas, 2017: 12).

Travel is more affordable because of greater prosperity and the relative declining cost of travel (Garcia, 2017).

According to the Brookings Institution (Kharas, 2017: 12), the global middle class population exceeded 3 billion in 2015 and is forecasted to increase by 160 million by 2030. Of this increase, almost 90% will come from Asia (Kharas, 2017: 13).

In recent years, low cost carriers (LCCs) and the liberalisation of air travel have made air travel cheaper and enabled people to travel more frequently. Thompson (2013) shows that airfares fell 50% in the 30 years prior to 2013. In 2015, 1.95 billion passengers used airport facilities across Europe, up from 20.7 million in 2000 (Dobruszkes, 2006). According to the Airport Industry Connectivity Report (ACI Europe, 2016), this growth was driven largely by an increase in direct routes globally, which is partly due to the growth of low-cost carriers (see Fig. 2.3).

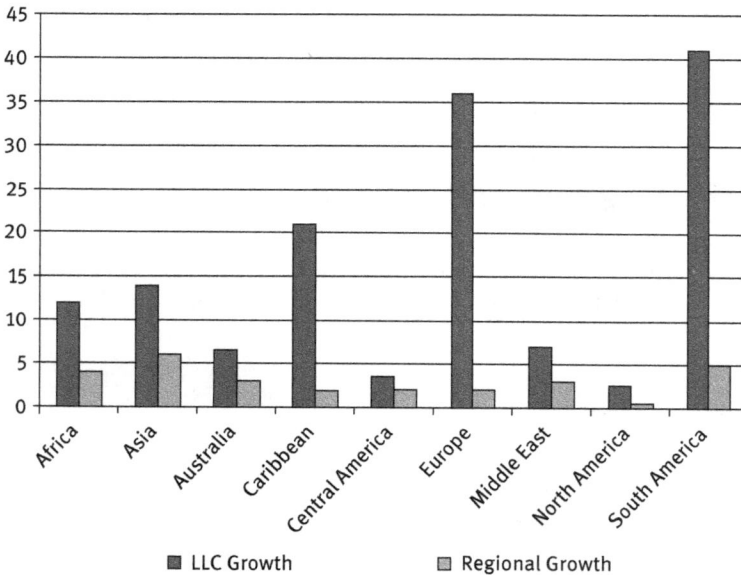

Fig. 2.3: Growth of the low cost carriers vs regional sector growth, 2007 to 2016 (RDC Aviation, 2016).

The low cost carrier sector grew from eight million passengers in 1998 to more than 100 million in 2007 (Lavery, n.d.). Carriers in Europe, such as EasyJet and Ryanair, have been of key significance, seizing opportunities to establish new routes and destinations. Being able to adapt their business models to operate in primary airports is increasingly putting pressure on mainstream carriers and also increasing cost competitiveness. The power of the low-cost carriers gives them influence in many cities. For example, carriers such as Ryanair have effectively removed cities from the destination map when airport operators refused to comply with demands for reduced landing fees, as was the case with Rimini, Italy (Lavery, n.d). Many destinations that perhaps cannot handle the large numbers of visitors brought in by low-cost carriers, can also not afford to *not* to have them (for example, Dublin, Ireland, and Krakow, Poland). Terms are therefore negotiated on the basis of potential economic performance rather than the sustainability of large tourism numbers in a destination community and low cost carriers are likely to continue to grow in size and significance.

Along with flights, cruise holidays are now also within reach of the middle class, with 33% of those who had taken cruise holidays in the previous three years having a combined household income of less than 80,000 USD (Cruise Line International Association (CLIA), 2017). The combination of a growing middle class and the declining cost of cruising have led to a major increase in cruise passenger numbers, over 20% in the five years prior to 2017. Furthermore, 27.2 million passengers were expected to cruise in 2018, an increase of almost 30% compared to 2009, when 17.8 million passengers cruised (CLIA, 2017). Not only are the numbers of passengers increasing, so too are the average ship sizes. According to Statista (n.d.), the Royal Caribbean cruise line alone ordered five additional ships, each with a capacity of nearly 5000 passengers, in the two years between 2015 and 2017. As cruise ships get larger, more people can flow into a destination at one time, thus increasing tourist numbers substantially, even if the number of ships that visit that destination remains constant.

New groups of tourists

With travel becoming more affordable and with the easing of visa restrictions for many travellers, new tourist segments are emerging, particularly in China and, to a lesser extent, India. There has been a massive growth in Chinese tourist numbers since 2000. While approximately 10.5 million overseas trips were taken by Chinese travellers in the year 2000, this figure increased to 145 million in 2017, a 1380% increase (Voellm, 2011). In 2018, over 80 countries had visa free or visa on arrival arrangements for Chinese passengers. While only 4% of the Chinese population had passports in 2018, it is predicted that this percentage will grow to 12% by 2025, which is equivalent to approximately 220 million Chinese people with passports, almost double the number (120 million) in 2015 (Goldman Sachs, 2015). Given the rapid rise in the number of passport holders, the China Outbound Tourism Research Institute (COTRI) predicts that overseas trips by China's residents will increase to more than 400 million by 2030 (Arlt, 2018). This has major implications for destinations in Europe and Asia, where overtourism issues have gained attention in recent years, as these destinations are heavily frequented by the Chinese (Chapter 12: Weber et al.). A survey of Chinese travellers found that 67% had been to Association of Southeast

Asian Nations (ASEAN) countries, 51% to Hong Kong, Macao and Taiwan, 38% to Europe, 25% to North America, and 20% to Australia and/or New Zealand (Neilson, 2017: 3). When it comes to attracting tourists, many destinations focus on attracting tourists from the highest spending countries – of which China tops the list.

Dominance of the growth-focused mindset

A key enabler of overtourism is the attitude, or mindset, of companies, governments, marketing organisations and transportation providers (e.g. airlines, cruise lines) that favour growth above all else. There have been multiple failures of forecasts and predictions about numbers and impacts – generally always too high in the case of numbers and too vague or too low regarding negative impacts. Although not new, this focus on growth is perhaps the biggest enabler of tourism expansion. Among decision makers there has historically been, and continues to be, a focus on numbers rather than yield. When yield is included in the strategic agenda, it is often just a dollar figure, rather than an objective involving job creation, poverty alleviation, increased quality of life and general community well-being.

Tourism is seen as an opportunity for employment and development by many countries that view tourism as an industry that is non-polluting compared to industries such as manufacturing and mining. It is one that cannot only create large numbers of jobs, but can also bring in much-needed foreign investment. In 2016, 9.6% of the global work force was in tourism and the industry contributed 7.6 trillion USD to the global economy (WTTC, 2017). These figures have an influence on policy makers and governments. Given these attractive figures, there is no shortage of pro-tourism reports discussing all the benefits of tourism and many countries have some sort of tourism master plan. Unfortunately, such plans are almost always focused on increasing the number of tourists rather than demonstrating how the industry can be developed sustainably and within the local limits. For example, Canada's current tourism vision (Government of Canada, 2017) lists the following targets (all solely related to growth):

- Canada will compete to be one of the Top Ten most visited countries in the world by 2025.
- The number of international overnight visits to Canada will increase by 30 per cent by 2021.
- The number of tourists from China will double, by 2021

Moreover, in accordance with the growth mindset, providers of tourism services seek to expand tourism regardless of the impacts. For example, Contiki, a well-known global tour operator, continues to promote "*The Beach*" on Thailand's island of Phi Phi Leh, as a place to see where "Leo" (Leonardo) DiCaprio hung out, even though, until its closure, the island was overrun with tourists and its ecosystem was being destroyed (Ellis-Petersen, 2018). Instead of educating their customers on why not to go there, the company still encourages tourists to go (Contiki, n.d.). They, and many other tourism companies, claim that tourists want to see the icons or bucket list attractions and that they are just meeting demand.

Because of the almost universal desire of decision makers to increase tourist numbers, most destination managers and organisations do not plan for limiting tourist numbers or slowing or halting development (Hall and Veer, 2016). Very few destination management organisations (DMOs) seek to manage tourism. Instead, they focus on promoting it as they have traditionally been, and mostly still are, generally promotion focused bodies designed and charged with at least maintaining if not increasing visitor numbers (Dredge, 2016). Destinations crowded at peak times are generally perceived as desirable, no one was thought to want to visit a half-empty resort, unless they paid far less than the normal cost. Discounted prices were used, if at all, to attract visitors at times when destinations are not full, normally early and late summer, before and after school holiday periods, in order to keep visitor numbers high. This is often justified as being necessary in order to maintain a market large enough to keep facilities open and staff employed (Butler, 2001), but it is indicative of a short-term focus (see below).

DMOs and other agencies responsible for tourism are not the only forces involved in trying to keep visitor numbers as high as possible. Transport providers have traditionally desired their services to be running as close to full as possible, and dynamic pricing is one way they have come close to achieving that goal. As visitor numbers increase, larger vehicles and/or more frequent services are required to keep pace with and promote further demand. There is, therefore, a positive feedback loop that constantly encourages further growth. All of the stakeholders involved in providing tourism goods and services, including travel agencies, on-line booking companies, transport companies, accommodation facilities and the food and beverage, car hire, facility-rental and entertainment businesses all in favour of maintaining, or preferably increasing, visitor numbers. In Canada, for example, due to a political decision, British Columbia Parks made entrance to provincial parks free. Not only has this meant that approximately 90% of the cost of running the park is now subsidized by the government, it has resulted in issues of overcrowding due to lack of monitoring and management.

A short-term focus

Related to the growth-focused mindset is the absence of a long-term view among decision makers at all levels. As discussed in multiple tourism policy papers (Bianchi, 2004; Dodds, 2007a, 2007b; Dodds and Butler, 2009; Krutwaysho and Bramwell,

2010; Waligo et al., 2013), a long-term view of development is essential and must replace the common short term focus on growth, profit and re-election. This lack of leadership has resulted in often blaming others for problems and the failure to acknowledge that issues cannot be solved overnight and often require solutions that will take long-term efforts. This issue is not helped by most government political systems where constituents rarely hold office for periods longer than three or five years. This short-term focus also ignores the longer-term impacts of tourism on local residents and the environment (see Chapter 3) and results in failures of predictions about impacts, as forecasted negative impacts are generally too vague or too low.

The growth mindset and short-term focus have resulted in market failure and a mismatch of demand and supply. It is very difficult to curb demand once established and even more difficult to reverse the process and return to an earlier state. One can easily create demand and it is relatively straightforward to accommodate supply – up to a point. Development is essentially one way and it is very difficult to curb demand once established and even more difficult to reverse the process and return to an earlier state. Although there is an expectation of the ability to manage overtourism when a destination reaches a saturation or decline stage of the life cycle, few destinations have ever dealt with this successfully. There are very few cases of de-construction (for example Calvià in Spain (Dodds, 2007a), where old hotels were destroyed to make green spaces) but even in such cases, there is no evidence that such efforts curbed demand. Few, if any, destinations really want to stop visitors, or even specific types of visitors, from coming.

Competition for space, amenities and services

With travel being inexpensive, and airlines flying to more destinations, visitors are going to places not previously frequented by tourists. This is creating problems in destinations that do not have the infrastructure and services to accommodate large numbers of tourists, particularly in rural areas and small towns (see Chapter 14; Chapter 12).

However, overtourism is also affecting established destinations and cities. Major urban centres are capable of handling large numbers of visitors (Weidenfeld et al, 2015), but even cities such as Barcelona, Prague, Venice and New York are experiencing issues, with many residents expressing their opposition to the high numbers of visitors (Chapter 10; Chapter 11; Chapter 9). In particular, residents have complained about the way in which holiday accommodation is being provided today. In essence, the problem is that tourists are competing with local residents for space, amenities and services.

More and more visitors are making use of private accommodation, which is now easily accessible via the internet and in some cases residents are becoming unhappy, both with the number of visitors arriving and the way in which holiday accommodation is being provided. In essence, the problem is a mismatch between facilities and services for visitors (and in some cases residents), such as parking, tickets for attractions and shows, space on transportation services and general amenities, and provision of often unlicensed and unregistered private accommodation. The result is that residents are being crowded out. The most successful and most criticised platform for accessing private accommodation is Airbnb, which was launched in 2008. Airbnb has doubled the number of bookings for its listed properties every year since 2008, reaching 130 million guests in 2017 (Somerville, 2018), and globally as of 2018 there were over five million Airbnb listings. These listings are not all in mainstream tourism areas. In San Francisco, for example, 72% of the Airbnb listings are located outside of the six central zip codes as compared with only 26% of the hotels (Airbnb, 2012; Lawler, 2012). This has brought tourism into residential areas, which has meant that tourism now impacts people not traditionally involved in tourism, and who have no interest in it. Impacts include having new neighbours every day in apartment buildings, long queues at local coffee shops, crowded buses and trains, and no parking spaces at local stores. While popular among travellers, Airbnb is viewed as a disruptive innovator (Christensen and Raynor, 2003).

While Airbnb and other such platforms claim that they are offering visitors a chance to experience authentic local livelihoods and local places, the presence of tourists in residential areas is distorting and changing the local way of life and neighbourhoods, thereby having the opposite effect in terms of authenticity (Chapter 4). Thus, although Airbnb and other such sharing platforms may provide additional economic opportunities for locals, they can also invade local people's sense of place and community and are wholly selfish in nature from the providers' point of view and certainly not providing an authentic experience (Lalicic and Waismayer, 2017).

Wider access to media and information

The media have always influenced travel decisions, but that influence is increasing as more and more people worldwide are gaining access to media. In recent years, films and television programmes have had a significant impact in terms of promoting the places that appear or are featured in them. Examples include *Game of Thrones*, the *Harry Potter* films, *The Beach* and *Outlander*. These and other programmes and films have resulted in large numbers of visitors both to the actual sites of filming and to places mentioned, if not actually shown, in the programmes (Chapter 14).

The internet has given travellers the ability to provide as well as receive information, and therefore as access to the internet has spread, the amount of information available about travel has grown. For example, while there were 3 million blogs in 2004, there were 164 million in 2011 (Thurm, 2014). Furthermore, digital sales of travel grew by 67% between 2014 and 2018 and are projected to grow further (Fig. 2.4).

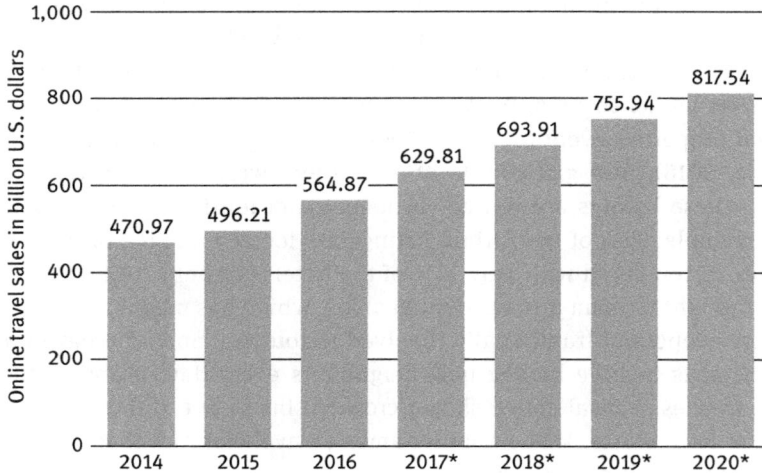

Fig. 2.4: Digital travel sales worldwide, 2014–2020 (in USD billions) (Statista, 2018a).

Changes in media technology and the emergence of new media, especially the advent of social media, are also contributing to overtourism, as such media serve as another means of promoting destinations. Facebook had 2.27 billion monthly active users as of the third quarter of 2018 (Statista, 2018b), while Twitter and Instagram had 300 million and one billion respectively (Statista, 2018c, 2018d).

More and more travel experiences are shared via social media. Social media not only allow tourists to share information with large audiences, but also allow them to share their behaviour at destinations, and such behaviour is often copied by subsequent visitors. Thus, media publicity of a location not only leads to unsustainable numbers of visitors, but also to ongoing inappropriate behaviour by some of those visitors (see Chapter 5). This often leads to dissatisfaction on the part of local residents with tourism and tourists.

Destinations lack control over tourist numbers

A key factor in enabling overtourism is that destinations are unable to control the number of tourist arrivals, as they usually have no control over transportation facilities, in particular, airports and cruise ports. For example, many airports and most cruise ports are nationally or privately controlled and therefore the destination does not have control over when, how and how many people, boats and planes arrive through these entry points. Likewise, highways and roads that lead to destinations are often not municipally controlled but are under federal or national jurisdiction, and therefore destinations cannot limit the number of people who wish to drive to that location. Many of the cities, islands, ski resorts and other destinations that are facing overtourism issues have tourists arriving via multiple transportation modes. This can cause major issues in terms of managing the flow of people.

A related issue is that in recent years, with increased affluence and leisure time, the development of second homes, condominiums and time-sharing, combined most recently, as noted earlier, with the likes of Airbnb, have seen increases in visitor investments in property at tourist destinations and rentals of those properties to other tourists, often unofficially if not illegally. Therefore, not only are more tourists going to popular destinations, but they are also becoming agents in increasing those numbers by becoming rental enterprises themselves. The fact that many of these new actors are not officially recognised, licensed or counted means that tourist numbers in some destinations are not known with any accuracy and in many cases are far exceeding comfortable numbers. In such a context, controlling numbers is next to impossible for many destinations, even if it were desired.

Imbalance of power among stakeholders

Another enabler of overtourism is the imbalance in power levels between the stakeholders. While the tourism planning and development process often faces calls for equity and inclusion of all stakeholders (Ioannides, 2001; Graci and Dodds, 2010; Getz and Timur, 2005), in reality resident and/or community voices are not paid attention to until things go wrong. These stakeholders are often not involved in planning, marketing or any other aspect of tourism, and are instead simply informed that jobs and economic benefits will be forthcoming. Tourism is often accepted by local communities because of such promises of jobs and economic benefits; promises that are eagerly accepted in areas facing economic hardship. Even when efforts are made to involve these parties, full participation is rarely achieved because some stakeholders are uninterested in the tourism process or feel divorced from decision-making and do not react or express a desire to participate until tourism reaches overtourism levels. Additionally, enterprises that address social and environmental issues in tourism and either represent communities or help to make the communities better, are often not included in mainstream tourism offerings due to their small size.

Tourism stakeholders are fragmented and at odds

A related issue is that tourism stakeholders have long lacked unity of purpose and shared goals. Despite multiple calls in recent decades for stakeholders to work together (Sautter and Leisen, 1999; Dodds, 2007a; Timur and Getz, 2008; Presenza and Cipollina, 2010; Brendehaug et al., 2016; Dodds and Butler, 2010; among others), the industry remains fragmented and power struggles are frequent. This lack of coordination and cohesion extends to the various levels of government, such that the policy of one level of government often undermines another's. Furthermore, government

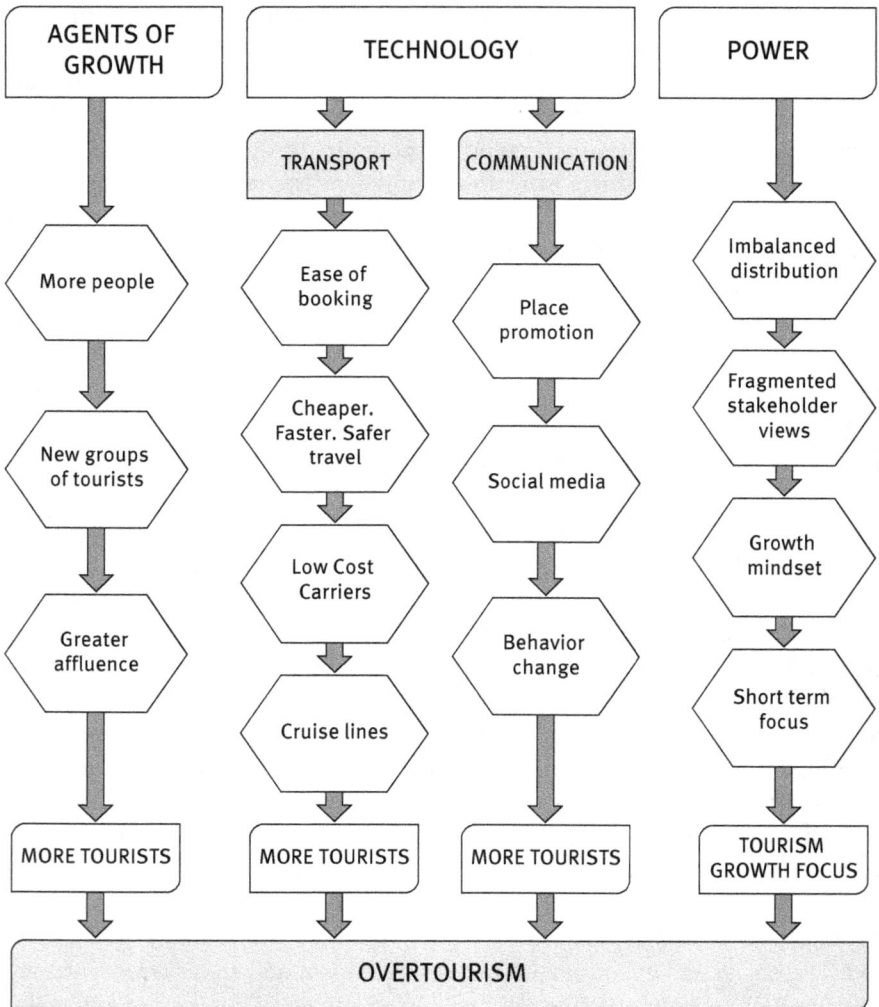

Fig. 2.5: Enablers of overtourism.

officials may say one thing, yet do another. For example, in 2017, after a sustainable tourism conference that Canada's Minister of Tourism and Small Business attended and where she gave a convincing speech about the need for sustainability in the tourism industry, the same minister issued a press release about the China-Canada year of tourism for which the priority was to increase tourist numbers. Such actions open doors to increase tourists to destinations that may not have planned for them.

All of the above enablers have come together in many destinations, resulting in a changed attitude towards tourism, particularly among residents. This change reflects political developments in many countries. For example, in March 2017, a majority voted for the United Kingdom to leave the European Union. This outcome is believed to be a result of fears relating to immigration and working class concerns over competition for employment and high housing costs, as well as a rise of nationalism and a general mistrust of politicians and past leaders. Similar sentiments are believed to have fuelled President Trump's rise to power in 2017 and the gains of right wing parties elsewhere. At the same time, global awareness has grown regarding social and environmental issues, including concerns about the quality of life and the happiness of individuals, and about the greater frequency of natural disasters, along with increased sensitivity to the impacts of globalisation, of which tourism is an example. While the tourism industry was historically viewed as a positive force, being a relatively clean industry compared others, wider recognition of the impacts of tourism has meant that the industry has now come under examination and criticism.

This chapter has discussed the enablers of the phenomenon known as overtourism. Fig. 2.5 shows some of the linkages between the factors that contribute to overtourism. Subsequent chapters provide specific examples of the issues arising from overtourism and describe some of the implications of overtourism for specific destinations and their environments, as well as discussing potential measures that can be taken to counter these problems.

References

ACI Europe (2016) *Airport Industry Connectivity Report*. https://www.aci-europe.org/component/downloads/downloads/4685.html (Accessed 20 November 2018.)

Airbnb (2012) Study finds that Airbnb hosts and guests have major positive effect on city economies, *Airbnb*, 9 November. http://www.marketwired.com/press-release/study-finds-that-airbnb-hosts-guests-have-major-positive-effect-on-city-economies-1723858.htm (Accessed 20 November 2018.)

Arlt, W. G. (2018) Editorial: Chinese outbound tourism data latest. China Outbound Tourism Research Institute (COTRI). https://china-outbound.com/editorial-chinese-outbound-tourism-latest/ (Accessed 20 November 2018.)

Bianchi, R.V. (2004) Tourism Restructuring and the Politics of Sustainability: A Critical View from the European Periphery (The Canary Islands), *Journal of Sustainable Tourism*, 12(6): 495–529.

Brendehaug, B., Aall, C. and Dodds, R. (2016) Environmental policy integration as a strategy for sustainable tourism planning: Issues in implementation, *Journal of Sustainable Tourism*, 25 (9): 1257–1274.

Butler, R. W. (2001) Seasonality in tourism: Issues and implications. In T. Baum and S. Lundtorp (Eds.), *Seasonality in Tourism*. Oxford: Elsevier, pp.5–22.

Christensen, C. M. and Raynor, M. E. (2003) The innovator's solution: Creating and sustaining successful growth. Boston, MA: Harvard Business School Press.

Cohen, E. (1988) Authenticity and commoditization in tourism, *Annals of Tourism Research*, 15 (3): 371–386.

Contiki (n.d.) Thailand beach holidays. https://www.contiki.com/eu/en/collections/beach-holidays/thailand (Accessed 27 November 2018.)

Christaller, W. (1963) Some considerations of tourism location in Europe: the peripheral regions – underdeveloped countries – recreation areas, *Regional Science Association Papers*, 12, Lund Congress: 95–105.

Cruise Line International Association (CLIA) (2017) 2018 Cruise Industry Outlook. https://cruising.org/docs/default-source/research/clia-2018-state-of-the-industry.pdf?sfvrsn=2 (Accessed July 2018.)

Dobruszkes, F. (2006) An analysis of European low-cost airlines and their networks. *Journal of Transport Geography*, 14 (4): 249–264.

Dodds, R (2007a) Sustainable tourism and policy implementation: Lessons from the case of Calviá, Spain, *Current Issues in Tourism*, 10 (1): 296–322.

Dodds, R. (2007b) Malta's Tourism Policy: Standing Still or Advancing Towards Sustainability? *Island Studies Journal*, 2 (1): 47–66.

Dodds, R. and Butler, R. W. (2009). Inaction more than action: Barriers to the implementation of sustainable tourism policies. In S. Gössling, C. M. Hall and D. Weaver (Eds.), *Sustainable tourism futures: Perspectives on systems, restructuring and innovations*. London: Routledge, pp. 63–77.

Dodds, R. and Butler, R. W. (2010) Barriers to implementing sustainable tourism policy in mass tourism destinations, *Tourismos*, 5 (1): 35–54.

Dodds, R., Graci, S. R. and Holmes, M. (2010). Does the tourist care? A comparison of tourists in Koh Phi Phi, Thailand and Gili Trawangan, Indonesia, *Journal of Sustainable Tourism*, 18 (2): 207–222.

Dredge, D. (2016) Are DMOs on a path to redundancy? *Tourism Recreation Research*, 41 (3): 348–353.

Ellis-Petersen, H. (2018) Thailand bay made famous by The Beach closed indefinitely, *The Guardian*, 3 October. https://www.theguardian.com/world/2018/oct/03/thailand-bay-made-famous-by-the-beach-closed-indefinitely (Accessed 27 November 2018.)

Eurostat (n.d.) 2015–2016 Growth in total passenger air transport by Member State. https://ec.europa.eu/eurostat/statistics-explained/index.php?title=File:2015-2016_growth_in_total_passenger_air_transport_by_Member_State.png (Accessed 5 September 2018.)

Garcia, M. (2017) What flights used to cost in the 'golden age' of air travel, Travel+Leisure, 13 August. https://www.travelandleisure.com/airlines-airports/history-of-flight-costs (Accessed 27 September 2018.)

Getz, D., and Timur, S. (2005) Stakeholder involvement in sustainable tourism: Balancing the voices. In W.F. Theobald (Ed.), *Global Tourism* (3rd edition). Burlington, MA: Elsevier, pp. 230–247.

Goldman Sachs (2015) The Asian Consumer: The Chinese tourist boom. 20 November. https://www.goldmansachs.com/insights/pages/macroeconomic-insights-folder/chinese-tourist-boom/report.pdf (Accessed July 2018.)

Government of Canada (2017) Canada's Tourism Vision. https://www.ic.gc.ca/eic/site/095.nsf/eng/00002.html (Accessed October 2018.)

Graci, S. R. and Dodds, R. (2010) Sustainable Tourism in Islands Destinations. London: Routledge.

Hall, C. M. and Veer, E. (2016) The DMO is dead. Long live the DMO (or, why DMO managers don't care about post-structuralism), *Tourism Recreation Research*, 41 (3): 354–357.

Hughes, G. (1995) Authenticity in tourism, *Annals of Tourism Research*, 22 (4): 781–803.

Ioannides, D. (2001) Sustainable development and the shifting attitudes of tourism stakeholders: toward a dynamic framework. In S. F. McCool and R. N. Moisey (Eds.), *Tourism, recreation and sustainability: Linking culture and the environment*, Wallingford, UK: CABI, pp. 55–76.

Kharas, H. (2017) The unprecedented expansion of the global middle class: An update. *Global Economy & Development Working Paper 100*. https://www.brookings.edu/wp-content/uploads/2017/02/global_20170228_global-middle-class.pdf (Accessed July 2018.)

Krippendorf, J. (1987) *The holiday makers: Understanding the impact of leisure and travel*. London: Heinemann.

Krutwaysho, O. and Bramwell, B. (2010) Tourism policy implementation and society, *Annals of Tourism Research*, 37 (3): 670–691.

Lalicic, L. and Weismayer, C. (2017) The role of authenticity in Airbnb experiences. In R. Schegg and B. Stangl (Eds.) *Information and Communication Technologies in Tourism 2017*. Proceedings of the International Conference in Rome, Italy, 24–26 January. Cham: Springer, pp. 781–794.

Lavery, B. (n.d.) Low-cost carriers: A force for globalization and growth. https://www0.gsb.columbia.edu/mygsb/faculty/research/pubfiles/2817/Low-Cost%20Carriers%20-%20A%20Force%20for%20Globalization%20and%20Growth.pdf (Accessed July 2018.)

Lawler, R. (2012) Airbnb: Our guests stay longer and spend more than hotel guests, contributing $56m to the San Francisco economy, TechCrunch, 9 November. http://techcrunch.com/2012/11/09/airbnb-research-data-dump/ (Accessed 20 November 2018.)

Neilson (2017) 2017 Outbound Chinese tourism and consumption trends. https://www.nielsen.com/content/dam/nielsenglobal/cn/docs/Outbound%20Chinese%20Tourism%20and%20Consumption%20Trends.pdf (Accessed September 2018.)

Papathanassis, A. (2017) Over-tourism and anti-tourist sentiment: An exploratory analysis and discussion, *Ovidius University Annals, Economic Sciences Series*, 17 (2): 288–293.

Presenza, A. and Cipollina, M. (2010) Analysing tourism stakeholders networks, *Tourism Review*, 65 (4): 17–30.

RDC Aviation (2016) Low cost airline penetration. 23 November. https://www.rdcaviation.com/News/Low-Cost-Airline-Penetration (Accessed July 2018.)

Saarinen, J. (2006) Traditions of sustainability in tourism studies, *Annals of Tourism Research*, 33 (4): 1121–1140.

Saarinen, J. (2013) Critical sustainability: Setting the limits to growth and responsibility in tourism, *Sustainability*, 6 (1): 1–17.

Sautter, E. T. and Leisen, B. (1999) Managing stakeholders. A tourism planning model, *Annals of Tourism Research*, 26 (2): 312–328.

Somerville, H. (2018) Stymied by regulators, Airbnb looks to luxury vacations, hotels for growth, *Reuters Business News*, 22 February. https://www.reuters.com/article/us-airbnb-expansion/stymied-by-regulators-airbnb-looks-to-luxury-vacations-hotels-for-growth-idUSKCN1G62BY (Accessed July 2018.)

Statista, (n.d.) Cruise industry and cruise ships – Statistics and facts. https://www.statista.com/topics/1004/cruise-industry/ (Accessed July 2018.)

Statista (2018a) Digital travel sales worldwide from 2014 to 2020 (in billion U.S. dollars). https://www.statista.com/statistics/499694/forecast-of-online-travel-sales-worldwide/ (Accessed 20 November 2018.)

Statista (2018b) Monthly number of active Facebook users worldwide as of 3rd quarter 2018. https://www.statista.com/statistics/264810/number-of-monthly-active-facebook-users-worldwide/ (Accessed September 2018.)

Statista (2018c) Leading countries based on number of Twitter users as of April 2018 (in millions). https://www.statista.com/statistics/242606/number-of-active-twitter-users-in-selected-countries/ (Accessed September 2018.)

Statista (2018d) Number of monthly active Instagram users from January 2013 to June 2018. https://www.statista.com/statistics/253577/number-of-monthly-active-instagram-users/ (Accessed 20 November 2018.)

Timur, S. and Getz, D. (2008) A network perspective on managing stakeholders for sustainable urban tourism, *International Journal of Contemporary Hospitality Management*, 20 (4): 445–461.

Thurm, M. C. (2014) The impact of travel blogging on the tourist experience: An e-ethnographic investigation. Tilberg University. https://arno.uvt.nl/show.cgi?fid=135452 (Accessed September 2018.)

Thompson, D. (2013) How airline ticket prices fell 50% in 30 years (and why nobody noticed), *The Atlantic*, 28 February. https://www.theatlantic.com/business/archive/2013/02/how-airline-ticket-prices-fell-50-in-30-years-and-why-nobody-noticed/273506/ (Accessed July 2018.)

Turner, L. and Ash, J. (1975) *The golden hordes: International tourism and the pleasure periphery*. London: Constable.

UNWTO (2017) *UNWTO Tourism Highlights*. Madrid: UNWTO. https://www.e-unwto.org/doi/pdf/10.18111/9789284419029 (Accessed 20 November 2018.)

Voellm, D. J. (2011) *The 21st century game-changer up close: China outbound tourism*. Hong Kong: HVS Global Hospitality Services. https://www.hvs.com/Content/3109.pdf (Accessed July 2018.)

Waligo, V. M., Clarke, J. and Hawkins, R. (2013) Implementing sustainable tourism: A multi-stakeholder involvement management framework, *Tourism management*, 36: 342–353.

Weidenfeld, A., Butler, R. and Williams, A.M. (2015) *Visitor Attractions and Events Locations and Linkages* London: Routledge.

Wheeller, B. (1994) Sustaining the ego, *Journal of Sustainable Tourism*, 1 (2), 121–129.

Whyte, P. (2017) The low cost, long haul carrier revolution in three charts, *Skift*, 19 June. https://skift.com/2017/06/19/the-low-cost-long-haul-carrier-revolution-in-3-charts/ (Accessed July 2018.)

World Travel & Tourism Council (WTTC) (2017) *Travel and Tourism Economic Impact 2017: World*. London: WTTC. https://www.wttc.org/-/media/files/reports/economic-impact-research/regions-2017/world2017.pdf (Accessed 27 November 2018.)

Part I: **Overtourism: theoretical positioning and implications**

This part of the volume places overtourism in a theoretical academic setting, examining the implications of the phenomenon in terms of the environment, cultural validity, the media and the Tourism Area Life Cycle (TALC) model of destination development. The chapters in this part set the scene for the individual case studies that follow, where the points made here are elaborated on through specific examples.

In the first chapter, Wall observes that destinations differ in terms of their capacity to withstand overtourism and he suggests viewing tourism as a form of urbanisation. He places overtourism in the context of resource management concepts such as "carrying capacity" and the relationship between visitor numbers, quality of experience and environmental impacts. Noting the decline in the application of carrying capacity, he discusses a more recent concept, the "limits of acceptable change", and how this may be more applicable in the context of tourist destinations experiencing or about to experience overtourism. Wall emphasises the complexity of determining causal relationships and problems of spatial discontinuity, as impacts in one location have effects in another location, and how the degree, nature and extent of impacts vary with the type of use and user behaviour. He notes that part of the complexity in resolving such issues is the relative lack of training and education in environmental sciences by those involved with tourism, and he suggests that more knowledge in this field is essential if the environmental impacts of tourism, are to be prevented or tackled effectively.

In a similar vein, Rickly examines the implications of overtourism from the perspective of the concept of authenticity. Authenticity is a well-established and important issue in tourism, and is evident in a range of contexts, from fake souvenirs and art work, to the decontextualisation of cultural performances and the loss of aspects of daily life and traditions. She notes that authenticity involves the perceptions of visitors, promoters, operators and residents, and can be weakened by the pressure of numbers and the desire to satisfy the demands of tourists. Often such demands are influenced by social media, as noted by Gretzel in the following chapter. Rickly notes that while tourists desire to be a part of local culture and life, one of the selling points of platforms such as AirBnB, such desires can cause dissatisfaction among locals, which results in tourists feeling they are not getting an authentic experience. Such conflicts and differences of perceptions and attitudes have major implications for the success or failure of tourism in communities, for the acceptance of tourism and tourists by locals, and for the differentiation of the authentic and inauthentic by tourists. Overtourism can threaten the perceived authenticity of destinations and thus the very appeal of the destination itself.

The role of the media in general, and of social media in particular, has not been explored properly in the context of overtourism. Gretzel discusses the profound implications of the development and expansion of the influence of the media, not only on the patterns of tourism but also on the behaviour of tourists. There can be no doubt that the rapid increase in the use of the media to promote, validate and evaluate tourist destinations and tourist behaviour has had a major influence on the development of tourism in many countries over the past two decades. This chapter examines the various roles of the media, including the dissemination of information, the framing of context and destinations, and persuasion (in the forms of praise and criticism), and as a social and political influence on tourists and potential tourists. Gretzel also notes the potential value of media in counteracting some of the negative aspects of overtourism through the use of information, demonstrating that the roles of media will continue to expand in the context of tourism development.

The final chapter in this part places overtourism in the context of the Tourism Area Life Cycle model developed by Butler (1980) several decades ago. While at the time the model was developed the terms "sustainability" and "overtourism" were not in use, some of the problems related to these concepts were anticipated in the basic hypothesis of the model, namely, that over-development of destinations could and probably would result in a loss of quality (of environment and appeal) and a resulting decline in visitation. This would provoke a downward spiral involving reduced visitor numbers, reduced expenditure and related income, less employment in tourism-related occupations, and reductions in investment in facilities, leading to even fewer visitors. The model notes the change in visitor characteristics as destinations develop and the general stages that most destinations pass through, culminating in continued development, stabilization (sustainable development) or decline. The final option tends to result from inappropriate planning and a lack of foresight in terms of scale and nature of development. This chapter describes the relevance of the model to overtourism and the process by which overtourism develops. Butler makes the point that busy destinations are not necessarily experiencing overtourism, and that mass tourism does not automatically result in overtourism, but that the phenomenon occurs when the level of visitation exceeds the capacity of the destination to withstand the undesirable impacts on the local fabric and residents. He argues that the presence of residents is partly what distinguishes overtourism from crowding or overuse (which occur in wilderness areas), along with the failure of infrastructure and facilities to handle excessive numbers of visitors.

Geoffrey Wall
3 Perspectives on the environment and overtourism

Introduction

Rigorous discussion of the environmental impacts of tourism has been ongoing for around 50 years, originating when evidence emerged that parks and protected areas were being over-used and that both the natural resources and the quality of the experiences in those places were being undermined. In 1982, along with a graduate student, this author published a book which, for the first time, provided a systematic statement regarding the economic, environmental and social impacts of tourism (Mathieson and Wall, 1982). The multiple impacts of tourism have been hotly debated ever since. Overtourism is therefore not a new topic, but it has become a more prominent concern in a greater variety of destination types as the number of tourists has increased.

Overtourism is a source of social tension, as seen in the case of Niagara-on-the-Lake, a town close to the Canada-USA border. This town was a key inspiration for Doxey (1976) to develop his "irridex", a framework that suggested that as the number of visitors increases, so does the risk of negative resident perspectives on tourism. In this case, the tension was essentially between outsider retirees and the local business community. The retirees had purchased properties in the town, thereby contributing to rising prices, and wanted fewer tourists so that the town's tranquil character could be retained. In contrast, the business community wanted more tourists, so as to increase the viability of their investments in a highly seasonal destination. Long-time residents found that their cost of living was rising and felt that their community had been hijacked by outsiders. Disagreements became overt in response to new initiatives, such as a proposal by the Canadian federal government to restore a historic fort on the edge of town as a heritage attraction, and acrimony abounded.

Context

Tourists elect to visit special places, whether natural, modified or built. Somewhat paradoxically, tourism is ubiquitous but also highly concentrated. Tourism is ubiquitous in that there are few parts of the world, perhaps only the ocean depths, that are not visited by tourists. At the same time, tourists are highly concentrated. This concentration occurs regardless of the scale of analysis: in regions such as the Alps, the Mediterranean and the Caribbean, by country, by destinations within countries and also within those destinations.

https://doi.org/10.1515/9783110607369-003

While there are many locations whose landscapes and economies are dominated by tourism, such that the impacts of tourism within them are pervasive and dominant, it is often forgotten that the major cities of the world are important recipients of tourists, both as destinations and access points, although the tourists may often be less conspicuous in the cosmopolitan atmosphere of such places, where the differences between tourists and locals may be less obvious. How many times have you been asked for direction by a visitor when you are on vacation? Probably more times than when you are at home!

It is helpful to view tourism as a form of urbanisation. Tourists need places to live, if only temporarily, and also need transportation, food, facilities and services; they are voracious consumers of water and electricity, and generators of waste. And with the increase in the scale of tourism (larger planes, hotels, resorts, stadia and related services), visitors are increasingly concentrated, making it more difficult to keep the components of supply in balance. Furthermore, tourists tend to be more demanding and consume more and different resources than when at home. This raises difficult questions for impact analysis as it is not clear, intuitively, which and how much of these impacts would have occurred anyway and are essentially relocated, and which are new and attributable to tourism. Regardless, the destination is responsible for meeting the needs and managing most of the waste. For this reason, issues of overtourism are primarily, but not exclusively, challenges for destinations.

Studies of the impacts of tourism have long concentrated on destination areas. However, this is changing as more recognition is given to the importance of the journey. Energy consumption in transportation and, hence, the production of much of the greenhouse gases occur en route but, unlike solid waste, the impacts of these are diffused. However, it is not difficult to find examples of overtourism in which public transportation systems are overwhelmed at peak periods, as occurs regularly, for example, during China's "Golden Week" holidays when millions leave the cities to reunite with their families in their places of origin and visit popular tourist attractions (Wu et al., 2012) (see Fig. 3.1).

The places that tourists visit differ substantially in their ability to withstand use and recover from damages once they have occurred. Antarctica (Splettstoesser and Folks, 1994) and Everest (Nepal, Kohler and Banzhaf, 2002) are examples of fragile destinations. The numbers of visitors to these places are not high compared to places such as Venice and Barcelona, but these numbers have risen substantially over the years, along with the environmental impacts, particularly those associated with waste disposal. Given that waste materials degrade extremely slowly in such cold climates, some claim that, while small, the numbers of visitors to these destinations are already excessive. Clearly, therefore, the nature of any attraction has implications for the impacts that will occur, as does the nature of the activity that is being undertaken. It is obvious that coral reefs, deserts and tropical forests differ in their make-up, and that swimming, off-road vehicles and wildlife viewing place different demands upon the respective environments.

Fig. 3.1: Great Wall of China (photo credit: Geoffrey Wall).

Useful generalisation requires a perspective that extends beyond the nature of the environment and the activities that are undertaken within it. The simple three-fold division of attraction attributes into points, areas and lines provides a useful way of looking at tourism resources from the perspective of the likelihood of them being subject to overtourism (Wall, 1997). Points are specific locations such as waterfalls, viewpoints, monuments and famous places such as Times Square or Trafalgar Square, where visitors must arrive at a very specific site to acquire the experience. At all such points, large numbers of visitors will be concentrated in a small area, with the danger that the resource is overwhelmed. The high concentration of people facilitates the making of money from tourism, which may also enable the introduction of overt management strategies to deal with the crowds.

At the other end of the spectrum, large natural areas, such as many national parks, tend to permit the wide dispersal of visitors. Many visitors to such areas wish to minimise their contact with others and, in consequence, are very demanding in terms of the desire to have a large amount of resources to themselves. Such visitors may also be difficult to manage because they are scattered over a very large area. For the same reason, it may not be easy to make much money from them. To make money from such visitors, it is necessary to concentrate them at access points and provide them with information and services in an efficient and cost-effective manner. Moreover, in national parks visitor numbers are a concern. While growing numbers are interpreted as increasing environmental threats, declining numbers have precipitated fears of insufficient funding to operate and maintain the parks.

Linear systems, such as coastlines, lakeshores, rivers and scenic routes, have an intermediate status. They concentrate users but spread them out along a particular route. Here, the challenge is to prevent development along the entire route so that the resource is not destroyed, but to also identify areas of concentration, like beads on a string, where support facilities can be provided and money can be made from the tourists. In Bali, Indonesia, early tourism plans identified scenic routes that visitors could drive along to get views of the magnificent rice terraces. However, entrepreneurs built restaurants and souvenir outlets along the routes to cater to the passing traffic, thereby interrupting the views that visitors were trying to see. As a result, the best views are no longer obtainable from the designated routes (Wall, 1995, 1998).

It is inevitable that the introduction of tourism will change the destination system, including the environment. This cannot be avoided. In China, for example, one of the most pleasing tourism offerings is the cruise on the Li River from near Guilin to Yangzhou. This cruise takes several hours through a magnificent rural karst landscape. However, as the route has become more popular with tourists, this peaceful experience has changed. The traffic on the river has increased enormously, resulting in congestion (see Fig. 3.2). Boat sirens pierce the air as overtaking occurs to get to berths, and the exhaust from the boats in the front pollute the air for those that follow. The karst peaks remain well worth seeing and the cruise is still not to be missed, but the context and experience are both different from what they were 20 years ago.

Fig. 3.2: Li River Boat Congestion (photo credit: Geoffrey Wall).

Recognising the inevitability of change means that it is necessary to identify the likely impacts of tourism, the means of managing them and the visitors that make them. Simplistic statements are not helpful. While the motto, "Leave only footprints, take only photographs" sounds very nice, it is the repeated pressure of thousands of feet that compresses soils and vegetation in natural areas and that damages the steps and floors of historic structures. Also, the taking of photographs can be extremely invasive for both people and wildlife; camera-toting tourists make it difficult for a predator to complete a hunt successfully, for example. Furthermore, the making of images conflicts with the religious beliefs of some groups, including my Mennonite neighbours. Thus, the management of overtourism in destinations requires a fundamental understanding of local environmental processes and specific aspects of human-environment interaction.

Measurement of impacts

There are essentially two main approaches to measuring the magnitude of impacts: physical and perceptual. The first attempts to measure impacts on the environment objectively using scientific methods, whereas the latter measures informants' assessments of environmental change and their significance. Both are important and legitimate approaches, although they may provide divergent results. Each will be considered in turn.

There is now a very large amount of literature on the environmental impacts of tourism. Most address changes in environmental components. For example, there are numerous studies that explore soil compaction and vegetation changes, particularly on paths and in campgrounds. There is also a substantial amount of literature on water quality and wildlife, and a smaller amount on noise and air pollution. This literature was first summarised in Wall and Wright (1977) and is updated in Wall and Mathieson (2006). One of the most detailed statements on the topic, which is seldom mentioned in the tourism literature, is that by Liddle (1997).

Researchers of these topics use scientific measures such as parts per cubic meter, species diversity, biochemical oxygen demand, decibels and parts per million. Some focus on the impacts on particular environments, such as coral reefs, whereas others concentrate on the impacts of specific recreational activities, such as skiing or diving. Unfortunately, since the methods are different for different elements, the studies are usually undertaken by people with different backgrounds, and there are few studies that provide a holistic perspective. Furthermore, as tourism education has become focused in business schools and scientific research methods are seldom taught as core tourism research methods, few tourism scholars are able to undertake such studies. Ultimately, the hope is that such measures can inform the development of environmental indicators, which has become a substantial research emphasis in recent years.

At the risk of overgeneralisation, some general comments can be made about these studies. First, while most studies in the past focused on destinations, particularly on relatively natural areas, in recent years the travel phase (the process of getting to and from the destination) has received more attention because this phase produces significant greenhouse gases. Second, many such studies are undertaken after the negative impacts have occurred, by which time it may be too late to measure the forces that caused the impacts (after-the-fact analysis) and to identify cause-effect relationships. Simultaneous monitoring of cause and effect is time-consuming and, therefore, expensive. Only a small number of studies use experimental methods to simulate environmental processes. However, it has been shown many times that relationships between cause and effect are not linear: substantial changes can occur with light levels of use, and the critical thresholds for each environment vary with the activity and may be difficult to determine in advance. Such observations raise questions concerning the efficacy of rotational strategies, which are designed to give areas time recover, as rates of impact may be much more rapid than rates of recovery. A shorthand way of viewing impacts is to consider them as being derived from feet and vehicles, with the latter being divided into mechanised and non-mechanised transportation. While, obviously, this does not cover all causes and impacts, it is a good starting point.

It is often said that perception is reality, in that people make decisions on the information that they have, which may be incomplete, and according to the values that they hold. A large amount of literature has examined perceptions of impacts and attitudes towards tourism (see, for example, Ap, 1992; Andereck et al., 2005). Often studies find that economic impacts are positive, environmental impacts are negative and socio-cultural impacts are mixed. These findings persist, even though it is frequently stated that tourists can provide resources that can be used to protect the environment – an outcome that is more easily wished for than implemented.

The findings of the perception and attitude studies vary greatly in terms of magnitude, especially when analyzed by socio-economic variables, causing some to suggest that they are contradictory. Rather, it may be better to regard them as contingent – varying with the circumstances. This means that it is particularly dangerous to generalise from perception studies, as they may produce results that are site-specific. This, in itself, is evidence for the need to encourage public input prior to making important management decisions, for it is risky to try to guess what others may think, or to assume that findings of perception studies are, or should be, ubiquitous and widely transferable.

Conceptualisation

The relationship between physical and perceptual studies is not simple; the scientists and the public use different criteria in making their assessments. For example, in the case of water quality, scientists may measure biochemical oxygen demand, pH value, turbidity and visibility. However, the public may be more interested in colour, smell and the presence or absence of algae or debris. Both types of study have value, are important and provide useful information for managers and other decision makers, but the differences in perspectives, and the impact of these on decision-making must be kept in mind. The differences can be illustrated with the example of acid rain, which was a prominent problem some years ago. The acidity made affected lakes clear, with visibility extending to great depths, which may have been appealing to the public. But the productivity of the lakes was low and they did not support desirable life, so the clarity of the water was not a valid criterion for scientists.

There are also differences in perspective when it comes to concepts such as density and crowding. While density is supposedly an objective measure of the number of users per unit area, figures can be manipulated by changing the boundaries of the study area. Crowding, on the other hand, is a subjective feeling resulting from the presence of other people. Researchers in parks and recreation working with these concepts, perhaps biased by their own preferences, assume that users prefer little contact with others and that as the number of users of parks increase, the likelihood of feeling crowded will also increase. This may not necessarily be the case, however, as discussed below.

Drawing in part on Hardin's (1968) *Tragedy of the Commons*, the concept of carrying capacity was proposed for application in the context of visitor numbers to parks (Wagar, 1964, 1974). Carrying capacity is the maximum number of people that can use a facility without an unacceptable decline in the quality of the environment (analogous to the physical impacts discussed above) or in the quality of the experience (the perceptual capacity). However, there are a number of problems with focusing solely on the numbers of visitors. These include:

- The quality of the experience does not always vary inversely with the number of visitors, especially in an urban setting where the presence of large numbers of other people may be a positive part of the experience.
- It is not only the number of visitors that it is important, but also how they behave.
- There are other types of capacity, for example, the willingness of local residents to accept tourists. Also, the capacity of ancillary facilities (such as the number of parking sites, hotel rooms or campsites) may limit use and be used as a management tool. While it is possible to calculate the capacity of a pipe of a certain diameter to transport water or sewage (and this can be extremely helpful), it is not possible to calculate relationships between level of use, environmental parameters and quality of experience in a straightforward manner. It is not helpful to suggest that when the pegs of the adjacent tent can be used as your own tent pegs, then the campsite is full!
- Capacity can be influenced by management (see below).

- At low levels of use, it may not be feasible to provide facilities (such as wash-rooms and regular garbage collection). But these could be justified by a larger number of visitors.

It is ironic that the concept of carrying capacity, while still widely used, moved into the tourism literature at a time when difficulties in applying the concept were widely acknowledged within the park and recreation fraternity; application of the concept in urban areas, which are complex, is fraught with difficulty. Faced with such challenges, the proponents of carrying capacity looked to other approaches, such as the "limits of acceptable change" (LAC) (Cole and McCool, 1997; Cole and Stankey, 1997).

Although seldom mentioned, the switch from carrying capacity to LAC implies changing from a technical to a participatory approach. Although most researchers no longer regard capacity as a magic number that can be approached with impunity and exceeded at peril, the search for such a number requires a technical approach and empowers "experts" to inform decision makers of how many is too many. The LAC approach, in contrast, requires determining what changes are acceptable, and this could potentially involve the inputs of multiple stakeholders, including local people. Such an approach acknowledges that land, although varying in resilience and recuperative power, does not have an inherent capacity. It may be more or less suitable for particular purposes, and appropriate levels of use can only be addressed once goals and objectives are known. The question is: "capacity for what?" Thus, in the absence of clear goals and objectives, it is not possible to address notions of appropriate use levels. The answer differs depending on the use of the place, whether a nature reserve, a golf course or a theme park.

Management

In some cases, managing a place, to protect the site and the values associated with it, involves "eliminating" tourists. For example, visitors are no longer permitted to visit the original Lascaux Cave in France, so as to protect the prehistoric paintings from damage caused by the changes in temperature and humidity that result from human breath and sweat. Instead, visitors are directed to a replica that has been built nearby (regardless of concerns tourists may have about the authenticity of their experience). In the case of Uluru (Ayers Rock) in central Australia, visitors are no longer permitted to climb the rock, in deference to aboriginal beliefs, and some rock art sites have been placed off limits, while other sites are actively managed to cater to and absorb the demand for such experiences. Such extreme management strategies are not common, however, because stakeholders in most destinations, including the visitors themselves, generally do not want to discourage tourism.

Two main approaches to management are common: managing the resource (site management) and managing the visitor, either directly or indirectly (Hendee, Stankey and Lucas, 1978). The former includes such techniques as hardening surfaces to resist erosion by feet and vehicles, watering and fertilizing vegetation to promote recovery following degradation, and building overpasses and underpasses to permit the safe passage of wildlife across highways. The "managing the visitor" approach focuses on manipulating the number, spatial distribution and behaviours of visitors, for example, by specifying permissible activities (direct) or providing interpretation (indirect). Some of the many possible visitor management interventions are listed in Tab. 3.1.

Tab. 3.1: Visitor management techniques (based on Wall and Mathieson, 2006 and Hall and McArthur, 1998).

Visitor management technique	Applications for rural and urban tourism development
Regulating access – By area	– All visitors are prohibited from visiting highly sensitive sites. – Different types and levels of use are regulated through zoning.
Regulating access – By transport	– Access is for pedestrians only. – Access is for pedestrians and cyclists only. – Public transport is the only allowable form of motorised transport. – "Car-free days" may be introduced in which alternative ways to enter and move about the site must be found.
Regulating visitation – Numbers and group size	– Regulations on total visitation per year, day or at any moment may be generated for a specific site. For example, group size restrictions have been implemented in some European cathedrals.
Regulating visitation – Type of visitor	– Some sites and attractions have a limit on visitation and the type of visitors. For example, some urban attractions target older high- and middle-income groups and actively discourage other segments using strict controls on all accommodation and services, keeping prices high and scrutinizing all marketing to maintain consistency.
Regulating behaviour	– Zoning in some cities and towns allocates different types of use to specified areas. – Restrictions on length of stay may be imposed. – Tour operators may be required to operate under a detailed set of guidelines of conduct for visitors. – Visitors must visit with a guide.

(continued)

Tab. 3.1 (continued)

Visitor management technique	Applications for rural and urban tourism development
Regulating equipment	– Vehicular access may be restricted. – Loudspeakers may be restricted because of noise disturbance.
Entry or user fees	– Most managers responsible for highly-visited heritage sites now charge fees to access the site and to use facilities at the site; influencing some visitors to choose either to visit or find an alternative destination. – Some heritage sites offer days during low season when residents are offered free entry. – Cities may require tourism operators to pay for a permit or licence to access the heritage site, and operators must also collect entrance fees from each of their clients. – A portion of the user fees collected is returned to local stakeholders as a means of demonstrating the value of tourism.
Modifying the site	– Some urban heritage sites may have specially designed walkways so as to reduce visitor impact. – The original uses of rooms in historic buildings may be changed to cater to the needs of tourists, e.g. conversions to cafes or souvenir outlets.
Market research	– A study of the domestic and international visitor market may be conducted in order to identify the market segments most likely to visit urban tourism attractions.
Visitor monitoring and research	– Visitors may be asked to complete special "day diary" forms to identify their motivations for visiting and the activities they undertook. – Visitors may be asked for their attitudes towards their experience and the performance of the respective heritage manager as a means of improving visitor management strategies. – Visitor impact monitoring and research is widely undertaken in sensitive urban heritage attractions.
Marketing – Promotional	– Visitation pressure may be relieved through the development, marketing and promotion of value-added alternative attractions. – Different urban organisations may undertake common promotional activities in order to reinforce the profile of the destination.

Tab. 3.1 (continued)

Visitor management technique	Applications for rural and urban tourism development
Marketing – Strategic information	– Tour guides can avoid sensitive areas by using a map and pictorial guide that identifies the best vantage points for attractions. – A walking "trail selector" (brochure and map) may be developed to provide information on lightly used walking trails in order to redistribute use away from heavily used areas.
Interpretation programmes and facilities	– Some urban tourism destinations may generate greater levels of visitor respect for the local culture through the provision of opportunities such as learning to cook with a local family or spending a night with a local family in a homestay. – Visitors may be taken on guided tours by local people who then convey their personal experiences and knowledge of the area to the visitor. This level of authenticity can greatly enhance the quality of the visitor experience.
Education programmes and facilities	– Theme trails may be created to educate visitors about specific aspects of local history and culture. – Many urban heritage attractions have interpretation and signage encouraging appropriate behaviour.
Modifying the presence of heritage management	– Most museums strategically position security staff in corners and corridors to create a high profile when visitors are moving between exhibits and a low profile when they are studying an individual exhibit.
Encouraging and assisting alternative providers - tourism industry	– Some urban destination management organisations encourage the development of small scale homestay accommodation and tours by local guides who are highly trained in heritage and interpretation, with tourism revenue thereby reinvested in the local community.
Encouraging and assisting alternative providers - volunteers	– Many urban heritage attractions, such as museums and historic sites, have volunteer and friends' associations which assist in various aspects of management as well as providing a source of financial support.
Concentrating on accredited organisations bringing visitors to a site	– National and regional accreditation may be used to check on the appropriateness of tourism operator practices and the quality of facilities, for example requiring accommodation providers to meet criteria and market cooperatively with others.

The conceptualisations discussed in the preceding section resulted in two main management thrusts: opportunity spectrums and visitor management models. Each will be discussed in turn.

Recognising that people do not all seek the same experiences and that one person can seek different experiences at different times, it was suggested that sites should be viewed in the context of the system of recreation opportunities of which they are a part. Thus, a recreation "opportunity spectrum" was proposed (Clark and Stankey, 1979), which led to the proposition of a tourism opportunity spectrum and even an ecotourism opportunity spectrum (Butler and Waldbrook, 1991; Boyd and Butler, 1996). The recreation opportunity spectrum (ROS) examines combinations of settings (sites and their accessibility), activities and experiences, and types of management strategies. Six classes of provision were proposed: primitive, semi-primitive non-motorised, semi-primitive motorised, roaded natural, rural and urban. Urban locations, for example, would be highly accessible by motorised transport, with the highest densities of use and highly visible management operations. Some park systems, such as that of the Province of Ontario, have classified their parks, as well as zones within parks, according to criteria that are somewhat similar to ROS to specify the nature of experiences (e.g., wilderness, recreation) and the intensity of management to be expected.

Another response was the proliferation of visitor management models for application, primarily, in parks and protected areas. These are essentially planning and management frameworks that are designed to keep visitor impacts within acceptable levels. Examples include Visitor Impact Management (VIM) (Graefe, Kuss and Loomis, 1985), the Tourism Optimisation Management Model (TOMM) (Kangaroo Island TOMM Management Committee, 2000), the Visitor Activity Management Process (VAMP) (Graham, Nilsen and Payne, 1987) and Visitor Experience Resource Protection (VERP) (Hof and Lime, 1997). Although they differ in detail, they essentially specify the steps that should be taken by decision makers concerning management of both the resources under their control and the visitors that use them. Descriptions, comparisons and evaluations of the differences between these approaches followed (see, for example, Newsome, Moore and Dowling, 2002) and much interest was generated. However, they did not travel well, and most achieved few actual applications beyond the specific park situations in which they were created.

Both opportunity spectrums and visitor management models are data intensive: They require a great deal of information, and therefore much time and resources, to be implemented effectively. While they attracted a great deal of attention among academics, they have not been widely implemented because they are complex, cumbersome and costly to work with.

Challenges

Although a great deal is known about tourism-environment relationships, as a result of academic research and practical tourism industry experiences, continued growth in the number of tourists and their concentration in particular places, have increased concerns. While much of the research has been conducted in relatively natural areas where there are usually few residents, such as parks and protected areas, the more strident voices now emanate from urban areas, where both density and crowding are high, and visitors and residents literally brush shoulders.

Four challenges will be introduced here that require acknowledgement if progress is to be made in addressing issues of overtourism. These are: the complexity of relationships that are involved, cultural differences, climate change and administrative structures.

Complexity

Relationships between the environment and humans are complex. "Beauty is in the eye of the beholder", but if it were possible to determine, analytically, the most beautiful place in the world in a way that would receive widespread acceptance, it would not resolve the management problem and might even exacerbate it. As the most beautiful place, questions would be raised such as: should it be placed off-limits to visitors who might otherwise overwhelm and destroy it, or should it be made accessible to all as part of their birthright even if this threatened its existence? Neither of these extreme perspectives is likely to be acceptable, but the appropriate point on the preservation-development continuum is not self-evident.

The author was raised and has lived most of his life in locations that were originally temperate forests. He is accustomed to being in a landscape with trees. It was therefore a surprise that in the Arctic, even after walking for over an hour, he could still see his point of departure, because the view was not foreshortened by the presence of trees. Thus, the exceptional nature of the Arctic landscape lies partly in the absence of trees and other items to block the view. Similarly, in the Inner Mongolia grasslands, the expansive views and wide open spaces are what make the destination so incomparable. Therefore, the presence of inappropriate buildings spoils the view and the illusion of solitude. Although they are vast, areas such as these are restricted in their ability to cater to large numbers of visitors because of, among other things, tourists' expectations. A joke is told concerning a resident of the Canadian Prairies who was visiting the Rocky Mountains. When asked if they liked the scenery, they replied that they could not see it because the mountains were in the way!

At the same time, it should be recognised that some precious landscapes are not purely natural or human-made but exist only because of the interaction of humans and nature. For example, the North and South Downs in southeast England would not be grasslands, but would revert to woodlands, if they were not grazed by sheep. Rice terraces, some of which have been designated as World Heritage by UNESCO, as in the Philippines and western China, must be farmed to be perpetuated. It is not possible to protect such landscapes by excluding people or solely by carefully managing the tourists. The land has to be worked to exist in its desired form, and tourism facilities and activities must be integrated into other uses.

Turning to a wildlife example, when the author first visited the small Tangkoko-Duasudara Nature Reserve in North Sulawesi, Indonesia, about 20 years ago, it took an hour or so to find one of the three groups of endangered black macaques that live in the reserve (Wall and Ross, 2001). On a return visit around 15 years later, there were more macaques and many were waiting at the entrance to the reserve, as they had become accustomed to interacting with tourists. The number of macaques seemed to have increased since my first visit but, unfortunately, they no longer behaved like wild macaques. One notorious macaque even took its own "selfie" with a photographer's camera and ownership of the copyright has been subsequently litigated in several American courts. A recent article claimed that the number of macaques has decreased (Holland, 2017). Perhaps the number of macaques has exceeded the ability of the small reserve to sustain them.

Situations such as these are difficult to manage. All require information, but management problems cannot be resolved merely by the provision of information, even accurate information. Many other factors come into play, such as funding, policies, precedents and power distributions, although environmental research can inform decisions if the decision makers are willing to engage with it and accept it.

Culture

In the environmental arena, one size does not fit all. Stakeholders differ in their opinions on the importance of tourism, and in their views on what should be protected and how this should be done. More broadly, cultures also differ in their engagements with their surroundings and with people. For example, Asian cultures exhibit a higher tolerance than Western cultures for the close presence of others, and therefore only perceive crowding at higher use densities. Also, Chinese tourists, at least at present, are more likely to travel in groups than Western travellers (Wu and Wall, 2016).

Fundamental differences exist between cultures in terms of perspectives on the human – environment relationship, such that the sharp dualism between humans and nature that is common in Western societies is more muted in the East (Sofield et al., 2017; Xu et al., 2014). In Europe, there are many old Christian churches and shrines on mountain peaks. This may not be the case in Canada or the USA, as the indigenous cultures may not have built such long-lasting structures. Similarly, many mountain peaks in China are graced with temples, but the presence of buildings in such places would be frowned on in some Western countries. Likewise, in China paths in natural areas are often concrete, and these paths often have side rails. As a result, people tend to adhere to the paths. In contrast, paths in Canada tend to be bare soil or covered in woodchips, which get messy in wet weather, so that walkers stray from them and take short cuts. Also, while interpretation in parks in China is more likely to rely on cultural matters, such as local stories and images that can be seen in the shapes of natural features (where believing is seeing, rather than the reverse!), in North American parks scientific interpretation is more common. Cultures also differ in terms of their expectations regarding interaction with wildlife (Cui et al., 2012).

Differences can also be found in terms of interpretations of authenticity in heritage contexts. In the West, original materials, restoration with such materials and use of original techniques are expected, but these things are sometimes considered less important in the East, provided that the place is the correct one and its value is confirmed by those in positions of authority.

It follows from the above observations that detailed scientific studies do not automatically lead to a suitable management outcome; rather, such studies are interpreted and acted upon according to local value systems.

Climate Change

Tourism both contributes to and is affected by climate change (Hall and Higham, 2005). Many of the places that are experiencing overtourism today are in coastal and lakeside locations, and are therefore subject to the challenges of sea level rise and declining lake water levels, as well as more extreme storms. More generally, because of rising temperatures and, therefore, higher evapotranspiration, competition for water is likely to increase worldwide, including in tourism destinations. The policies that may be introduced to address climate change may affect tourism even more than climate change itself, particularly if the cost of energy rises, which will increase transportation costs. In a context of massive environmental change, the past and present may not be a good guide to the future. While we cannot be certain, it is likely that climate change will change tourism opportunities and may even be a factor in increasing levels of overtourism, though to a smaller number of accessible attractions.

Global impacts and local administrative structures

While overtourism is usually a localised problem, the forces that impinge upon it are global. Tourists usually come from elsewhere and in places where the challenges of overtourism are particularly acute, the desires of regional, national and international markets are superimposed upon the needs of residents. Thus, while it is difficult to decide what to do, it may be even more difficult to get agreement on how to do it. This is partly because neither the tourism department nor the environmental department is among the most powerful of governmental agencies, and the issues relating to tourism span departmental responsibilities and jurisdictions. Furthermore, the issues must be addressed through administrative structures that vary from place to place. This is a highly significant challenge.

Conclusions

As the numbers of global tourists has increased, ideas that developed and evolved in relatively natural settings have sometimes been adopted and transposed to urban settings where the fit is not ideal. The carrying capacity concept is intuitively attractive as it addresses a vital question, "How many is too many?" But the answer that it provides falls short in addressing the full complexity of the issues that are involved. This is especially the case in urban areas where the overall numbers of people, including both residents and tourists, are large. Also, urban areas have attractions and other facilities that are shared by both residents and visitors.

Tourists have been accused of loving things to death. A relatively new concept, last-chance tourism, advises potential customers to "Come and see it before it's too late!" which can be interpreted as "Come and put the last nail in the coffin!" The word "overtourism" and much of the literature on the impacts of tourism, especially the environmental impacts, draws attention to the negative consequences of tourism for destinations and their residents. However, residents and visitors have more in common than is often recognised or acknowledged: they both like attractive and vibrant places, clean air and water, green spaces, efficient transportation and so on. Thus, it should be possible to specify goals and objectives that are compatible with the needs and desires of multiple stakeholders. Such analysis is vital. Without it, it is not possible to determine how many is too many.

On the other hand, it is difficult to identify the relative share of resources and determine appropriate payment for their use. This is made all the more complicated by spatial and temporal discontinuities in cause and effect. Environmentally, an event, such as erosion, may occur in one place, but may affect other places, e.g. soil deposition downstream. The tourists in Venice (Chapter 10) are concentrated in the city centre during the day, but do not spend much money there. Instead, most of their money is spent on (cheaper) accommodation in the suburbs at night (Van der Borg, 1998). The distribution of tourists varies on many temporal scales: diurnal, weekly and seasonally. If facilities are provided to meet peak demand, then they will be underutilised for much of the time, and this will reduce their economic efficiency. On the other hand, undersupply means that, at peak periods, facilities are overwhelmed, reducing both the quality of the environment and the experiences of visitors and residents. Thus, overtourism is a "wicked problem" of maintaining a balance between supply and demand, in a system that is continuing to grow and is made up of many moving parts.

Unfortunately, there is no easy resolution to the problems. Conferences on sustainable tourism often feature speakers who begin by providing tables of growth and upward trending graphs of visitor and expenditure statistics, symbolizing "success", but this narrow view of sustainability gives priority to economic growth, and neglects society and the environment. Tourists today, while subject to constraints of time, money, visas, health and so on, are able to exercise relatively free choice on where to go, what to do and where to do it. In the future, if the needs of residents and local environmental resources are taken into account, tourists' choices may be increasingly curtailed. However, the illusion of freedom of choice may be retained by the application of technologies, information and other means.

Progress will require the establishment of clear goals and objectives, to inform appropriate planning and management initiatives, and will require the administrative structures to implement them. But if the experience with climate change, another wicked but not independent problem, is a guide, such an approach may not be enough and positive outcomes are not assured.

References

Andereck, K. L., Valentine, K. M., Knopf, R. C. and Vogt, C. A. (2005) Residents' perceptions of community tourism impacts, *Annals of Tourism Research*, 32 (4): 1056–1076.

Ap, J. (1992) Residents' perceptions on tourism impacts, *Annals of Tourism Research*, 19 (4): 665–690.

Boyd and Butler (1996) Managing ecotourism: an opportunity spectrum approach, *Tourism Management*, 17 (8): 557–566

Butler, R. W. and Waldbrook, L. A. (1991) A new planning tool: the tourism opportunity spectrum. *Journal of Tourism Studies*, 2 (1): 2–14.

Cole, D. N. and McCool, S. F. (1997) The limits of acceptable change process: modifications and clarifications. In S. F. McCool, and D. N. Cole (Eds.), *Proceedings of a Workshop on Limits of Acceptable Change and Related Planning Processes: Progress and Future Directions*. General Technical Report INT-GTR-371.US Department of Agriculture Forest Service, Ogden, UT, pp. 61–68.

Cole, D. N. and Stankey, G. H. (1997) Historical developments of limits of acceptable change process: conceptual clarifications and possible extensions. In S. F. McCool, and D. N. Cole (Eds.), *Proceedings of a Workshop on Limits of Acceptable Change and Related Planning Processes: Progress and Future Directions*. General Technical Report INT-GTR-371. US Department of Agriculture Forest Service, Ogden, UT, pp. 5–9.

Cui, Q, Xu, H. and Wall, G (2012) A cultural perspective on wildlife tourism in China, *Tourism Recreation Research*, 37 (1): 27–36.

Doxey, G. V. (1976) When enough's enough: the natives are restless in Old Niagara, *Heritage Canada*, 2(2): 26–27.

Graefe, A. R., Kuss, F. R. and Loomis, L. (1985) Visitor impact management in wildland settings. In *Proceedings, National Wilderness Research Conference: Current Research*, US Department of Agriculture Forest Service, Ogden, UT. pp. 424–431.

Graham, R., Nilsen, P. W. and Payne, R. J. (1987) Visitor activity planning and management in Canadian national parks: Marketing within a context of integration. In M. L. Miller, R. P. Gale and P. J. Brown (Eds.), *Social Science in Natural Resource Management Systems*. Boulder: Westview, pp. 146–149.

Hall, C. M. and Higham, J. (2005) *Tourism, recreation and Climate Change*. Clevedon: Channel View Press.

Hall, C. M. and McArthur, S. (1998) *Integrated heritage management*. London: The Stationary Office.

Hardin, G. (1968) The tragedy of the commons, *Science*, 162: 1243–1248.

Hendee, J. C., Stankey, G. H. and Lucas, R. C. (1978) *Wilderness Management*. US Department of Agriculture Forest Service Miscellaneous Publication No 1365.

Hof, M. and Lime, D. W. (1997) Visitor experience and resource protection framework in the national park system: Rationale, current status and future direction. In R. N. Clark and D. N. Cole (Eds.), *Proceedings of a Workshop on Limits of Acceptable Change and Related Planning Processes: Progress and Future Directions*. General Technical Report INT-GTR-371. US Department of Agriculture Forest Service, Ogden, UT, pp. 29–36.

Holland, J. S. (2017) A fight to survive. *National Geographic*, 2311 (3): 86–103.

Kangaroo Island TOMM Management Committee (2000) *Tourism Optimisation Management Model TOMM*, Kangaroo Island, South Australia.

Liddle, M. J. (1997) *Recreation Ecology: The Ecological Impact of Outdoor Recreation and Ecotourism*. London: Chapman & Hall.

Mathieson, A. R. and Wall, G. (1982) *Tourism: Economic, Physical and Social Impacts*. Harlow, Essex: Longman.

McCool, S.F. and Stankey, G.H. (1979) *The recreation opportunity spectrum: A framework for planning, management and research*. General Technical Report PNW 98. Pacific Northwest Forest and Range Experiment Station, Portland, OR.

Nepal, S. K., Kohler, T. and Banzhaf, B. R. (2002) *Great Himalaya: Tourism and the Dynamics of Change in Nepal*. Zurich: Swiss Foundation for Alpine Research.

Newsome, D., Moore, S. A. and Dowling, R. K. (2002) *Natural Area Tourism: Ecology, Impacts and Management*. Clevedon, Channel View Publications.

Sofield, T. H. B., Li, F. M. S., Wong, G. H. Y. and Zhu, J. J. (2017) The heritage of Chinese cities as seen through the gaze of '*zhonghua wenhua*' 'Chinese common knowledge': Guilin as an exemplar. *Journal of Heritage Tourism*, 12 (3): 227–250.

Splettstoesser, J. and Folks, M.C. (1994) Environmental guidelines for tourism in Antarctica, *Annals of Tourism Research*, 21 (2): 231–244.

Van der Borg, J. (1998) Tourism management in Venice, or how to deal with success, in D. Tyler, Y. Guerrier, and M. Robertson (Eds.) *Managing Tourism in Cities: Policy, Process and Practice*. Chichester: John Wiley & Sons, pp. 125–137.

Wagar, J. A. (1964) The carrying capacity of wild lands for recreation, *Forest Science Monograph*, No. 7. Washington, DC: Society of American Foresters.

Wagar, J. A. (1974) Recreational carrying capacity reconsidered, *Journal of Forestry*, 72: 274–278.

Wall, G. (1995) "Forces for change: Tourism" and "Developing a strategy for tourism", in S. Martopo and B. Mitchell (Eds.), *Bali: Balancing Environment, Economy and Culture*, Department of Geography Publication Series 44, University of Waterloo, pp. 57–74 and pp. 335–350.

Wall, G. (1997) Tourist attractions: points, lines and areas, *Annals of Tourism Research*, 24 (1): 240–243.

Wall, G. (1998) Landscape resources, tourism and landscape change in Bali, Indonesia. In G. Ringer (Ed.), *Destinations: Cultural landscapes of tourism*, London: Routledge, pp. 51–62.

Wall, G. and Mathieson, A. (2006) *Tourism: Change, impacts and opportunities*. Harlow: Pearson.

Wall, G. and Ross, S. (2001) Wallace's line: implications for conservation and ecotourism in Indonesia. In D. Harrison (Ed.), *Tourism and the less developed world: Issues and case studies*, London and Wallingford: CAB International, pp. 223–233.

Wall, G. and Wright, C. (1977) *The environmental impact of outdoor recreation*, Publication Series No. 11. Department of Geography, University of Waterloo, Ontario.

Wu, B., Morrison, A. M. and Leung, X. Y. (2012) Frame analysis on golden week policy reform in China. *Annals of Tourism Research*, 39 (2): 842–862.

Wu, M-Y. and Wall, G. (2016) Chinese research on family tourism: review and research implications, *Journal of China Tourism Research*, 12 (3–4): 274–290.

Xu, H., Cui, Q., Sofield, T. and Li, F. M. S. (2014) Attaining harmony: Understanding the relationship between ecotourism and protected areas in China, *Journal of Sustainable Tourism*, 22 (8): 1131–1150.

Jillian M. Rickly
4 Overtourism and authenticity

Introduction

Authenticity is ubiquitous in tourism debates. From tourism marketing and place promotion claims of "originality", "exclusivity" and "genuine reproduction", to tourists' descriptions of experiences as "real" and "unique", authenticity functions as a relational and value-laden concept. It means different things to different people, sometimes concurrently (Rickly-Boyd, 2012a). This is arguably why it remains prevalent in both theoretical debates and the practical considerations of the tourism industry.

Authenticity was as a theme of a recent Sustainability Leaders Project (2017) expert panel on overtourism, which raised concerns from the two distinct perspectives of local community life and tourist experiences. While these experiences of authenticity are relational, they are also distinct as community perceptions of authenticity draw on some different parameters from tourists' perceptions. For residents, who carry out everyday activities and maintain long-term livelihoods within destinations, authenticity is associated more with parameters of agency, equity, sense of place and community well-being. For tourists, who are temporary visitors, authenticity is related to unique and iconic attractions, and therefore they are often unable to ascertain the subtle changes that occur in a place over time. The challenge is that these experiences – local and touristic – occur in shared spaces and the encounters between these groups certainly influence perceptions of one another and of the authenticity of experience (cf. Briedenhann and Ramchander, 2006). Thus, investigations of authenticity cannot be resolved by simply categorizing a destination or its attractions as authentic or inauthentic. Rather, we must attend to the social processes of authentication by considering who authenticates and how authentication is managed (Cohen and Cohen, 2012).

Approaches to authenticity

Tourism was once considered a pseudo-event by some academics, distinct from everyday life by its spectacle nature and general inauthenticity (Boorstin, 1961). It was argued that the "mass hordes" of tourists, later deemed *turistas vulgaris* by Lofgren (1999: 264), were driven by the inauthenticity of their everyday lives (Boorstin, 1961) and were therefore quite distinct from "travellers" (cf. McCabe, 2005). However,

https://doi.org/10.1515/9783110607369-004

MacCannell (1976, 1999) theorized that tourists are indeed in search of authenticity and that the popularity of leisure travel would continue to grow as a result of tourism's collective nature and ritual attitude. The research that followed aimed to understand the various types of authenticity sought by tourists (cf. Cohen, 1979; Redfoot, 1984). Authenticity has been viewed variously as a measure of originality, a symbolic association, an experience and a "state of Being", which Wang (1999) summarized through the approaches of: objectivism, constructivism, postmodernism and existentialism.

While "objectivism" assesses authenticity in terms of originality and genuineness (cf. Chhabra, 2008; Gable and Handler, 1996; Trilling, 1972), what many tourists seek is a "constructivist" authenticity that allows for pluralistic interpretations (Bruner, 1994; DeLyser, 1999; Rickly-Boyd, 2012b), individualized judgments (Moscardo and Pearce, 1986), contextuality (Salamone, 1997) and emergent processes (Cohen, 1988). However, in some tourism experiences, such as themed and fantasy-based destinations, it is not the symbolic but the *in*authentic that is crucial, as in such contexts tourists are seeking more stimulating, imaginative and immersive experiences (Buchmann et al., 2010; Bolz, 1998; Eco, 1986; Ritzer and Liska, 1997; Lovell, 2018).

More recent research has taken psychological and performative approaches, and has explored the relationality of authenticity in tourists' experiences. Existential authenticity has received considerable academic attention as a means to examine the interpersonal and intrapersonal dimensions of *Being* on holiday – the feelings, emotions, sensations, embodiment, relationships and the intersubjective (Belhassen et al., 2008; Brown, 2013; Buchmann et al., 2010; Kim and Jamal, 2007; Rickly-Boyd, 2012c, 2013a; Steiner and Reisinger, 2006; Wang, 1999). While Steiner and Reisinger assert, from Heidegger's theories of Being and *dasein* (existence), "the existential self is transient, not enduring, and not conforming to a type. It changes from moment to moment" (2006: 303), others suggest the very elusiveness of the experience of authenticity means it is a psychological fantasy (Knudsen et al., 2016) that will always be present in tourists' desire (cf. Oakes, 2006; MacCannell, 2011).

This research suggests the performativity of authenticity as something that tourists and practitioners *do* as well as *experience* (Knudsen and Waade, 2010; Shaffer, 2004; Send-Cook, 2012, Rickly and Vidon, 2017). Furthermore, authenticity is relational (Rickly-Boyd, 2012a). Researchers rarely use just one approach in investigating authenticity (cf. Andriotis, 2011; Belhassen et al., 2008; Buchmann et al., 2010; Chronis and Hampton, 2008; Cook, 2010; DeLyser, 1999; Gable and Handler, 1996; Kim and Jamal, 2007; Noy, 2004; Rickly-Boyd, 2013), as tourists take into consideration the various manifestations of authenticity in destinations. Performative approaches take particular notice of this relationality by recognizing authentication as a social process.

Authentication

Authentication is "the social process by which the authenticity of an attraction is confirmed" (Cohen and Cohen, 2012: 1296). Such processes can be "hot" (social/emic) or "cool" (scientific/etic), explain Cohen and Cohen (2012). "Cool" authentication is associated with objective notions of authenticity, such as certification and the act of assessing an object or site through a formal or official declaration, which is performed by experts with specialty knowledge and learned techniques that utilize evidence to support their claims. On the other hand, "hot" authentication relates to existential and constructive authenticities that attend to the traditions, beliefs, values and emotions that are reiteratively performed by individuals. The majority of tourism attractions represent a combination of cool and hot authentication processes.

Today, tourists themselves are increasingly significant in these authentication processes, particularly through social media and user-generated content (UGC) (Wise and Farzin, 2018). Not only do potential tourists place trust in social media (Munar and Jacobsen, 2013) and use it to establish expectations (Xiang and Gretzel, 2009), but they also contribute to place images by posting reviews, detailed descriptions and images of distinct attractions and place characteristics (Wise and Farzin, 2018). As a result, the authentication process is never complete.

Challenges of authenticity in the context of overtourism

Authenticity maintains an interesting relationship to the overtourism phenomenon, with media outlets focusing on crowding as a key issue and headlining "anti-tourism" protests. While the measureable impacts of large numbers of tourists and the exact threshold at which local communities feel overwhelmed by tourists are unique to each destination, news media and destination marketing organisations (DMOs) largely focus on the crowd itself as a mass that ruins both the destination and thereby any authenticity and potential for authentic experiences it might have held (The Place Brand Observer, 2017). The relationship between authenticity and touristic crowds is not so simple, however.

To examine this further, this chapter focuses on three aspects of overtourism and authenticity – crowds as consensus, touristification and inauthenticity, and efforts at reclaiming authenticity. In the "crowds as consensus" aspect, overtourism can actually function to confirm the significance of a destination, particularly as it is represented on social media. In this scenario, both real and virtual crowds authenticate tourism attractions. However, as these tourist crowds persist and touristification begins to take place, a destination's reputation can decline and become associated with *in*authenticity. While perceptions of inauthenticity due to crowding in some locations might inspire some tourists to choose different destinations, others attempt to reclaim authenticity in these "must see" places by using alternative approaches, such as choosing to rent accommodation in residential areas. Similarly, some destination marketing organisations are implementing new models, such as "localhood" campaigns, that aim to blur the lines between hosts and guests and involve diverse voices to co-innovate and reimagine tourism encounters.

Consensus as authentication

In his formative theories about tourist behaviour, MacCannell (1976, 1999) raises the question as to how tourist attractions are chosen from the innumerable possibilities in the world. To answer this, MacCannell suggests a "miracle of consensus" in which processes of "sight sacralization" and "ritual attitude" work in tandem to (re)produce tourism attractions.

The process of sacralization includes the stages of naming, framing and elevation, enshrinement, mechanical reproduction and social reproduction, and these work by identifying sites of significance, marking them and placing boundaries around (symbolically or physically), creating images (souvenirs, photographs, etc.) associated with them and fostering a reputation and collective knowledge about the attraction (MacCannell, 1976, 1999). Thus, local communities, individual tourists and tourism marketing organisations collectively operate in the choosing, disseminating and, thereby, the reproduction of tourism attractions. While historically destination marketing organisations held considerable power in shaping place images, contemporarily social media has shifted this power dynamic to afford individual tourists more agency to inspire, as well as dissuade, potential tourists. Indeed, social media and electronic word-of-mouth (eWOM) websites offer potential tourists a kind of consensus regarding the "best" or "top" attractions of a location, as well as an opportunity to learn about other tourists' experiences, and to then to report back on their own experiences (cf. Filieri, 2015; Fang et al., 2016).

The "miracle of consensus" (MacCannell, 1976, 1999) includes the sacralization processes that maintain or recreate tourism attractions, but it also requires the "ritual attitude" of sightseeing. Sightseeing "is a ritual performed to the differentiation of society", argues MacCannell (1999: 13), as tourism attractions are differentiations – sights marked as distinct from their surroundings and worthy of touristic attention. This ritual attitude is demonstrated in the collective behaviour of individual tourists who respond to the "must see" lists for each destination by, indeed, visiting some or all of these attractions. Once again, social media (Chapter 5) has evolved to vividly illustrate this process. Through Facebook, for example, tourists can "check in" to destinations as well as map their travels and post photographs for "friends" to see. On Instagram, photographs are accompanied by hashtags and geotags, which are searchable if one wishes to see the most attractive (and edited) images of a destination. On TripAdvisor individual reviews of attractions, restaurants and accommodation are collated to form a numerical rating. Furthermore, reviewers can include photographs to illustrate their descriptions and the companies being reviewed are able to respond to feedback.

These types of social media and eWOM platforms add a new dimension of authenticity, particularly as user-generated content informs potential tourists' expectations and the processes by which attractions are authenticated (Wise and Farzin, 2018). While the representations created and shared are not necessarily objective, as photographs are staged and edited, and reviews can be biased, it gives immediacy and subjectivity of experience to the never-ending "miracle of consensus". The descriptive reviews and accompanying photographs function as "eye witness" and "firsthand experience" accounts, cultivating a sense of authenticity and trustworthiness in a way that tourism promotions cannot. Potential tourists are able to imagine themselves in the same locations and use this to inform their travel decisions and expectations. The immediacy and accessibility of this information has the potential to influence tourism trends in the short term, causing steep fluctuations in tourist numbers at particular destinations and at specific attractions.

Two destinations in Norway aptly illustrate this phenomenon: Fjellstua and Trolltunga. Both viewpoints have become popular on social media because of the photo opportunities they provide, especially for selfies with breathtaking vistas as backdrops. Trolltunga is the more entrenched Instagram trend, with nearly 100,000 # trolltunga hashtags. The vast majority of the photographs are taken from a rock outcropping situated 1000 feet above Ringedalsvatnet Lake, creating an image of solitude and wilderness (Fig. 4.1). Indeed, it is a challenging hike to reach this spot, and the trek is advised only during the summer months. The site's popularity and the opportunity for an impressive photo, however, have resulted in a tremendous rise in the numbers of tourists trekking the 10 to 12 hour round trip to Trolltunga. Sometimes tourists trek in inappropriate attire and without the necessary equipment, to the effect that search and rescue teams have become more active in recent years (Evers, 2016). An increase from an estimated 800 hikers in 2010 to more than 80,000 in 2016 has created a continual flow of tourists along the trail, with queues at the cliff to capture the iconic image (Maclean, 2017). This surge in tourist numbers, resulting in overuse of the trail, has also had environmental impacts, including soil erosion (Evers, 2016). Despite the difficulty in reaching the viewpoint and the long wait times encountered once there, Trolltunga remains a "must see" destination with a 5 out of 5 star rating by TripAdvisor reviewers, who have ranked it "#1 of 20 things to do in Odda".

Fjellstua is a more recent hotspot, but its accessibility has resulted in serious crowding problems within a short period of time. Fjellstua is the viewpoint on Aksula Mountain overlooking Alesund (Fig. 4.2). The viewpoint gives visitors a unique perspective of the archipelago and an ideal photo opportunity. Alesund, as a fjord town,

Fig. 4.1: Queue for taking a photo at Trolltunga (source: https://commons.wikimedia.org/wiki/
File:Signs_warning_tourists_about_the_risk_associated_with_going_out_to_Trolltunga.jpg).

Fig. 4.2: Ålesund seen from Aksla Mountain – A popular backdrop for tourist selfies
(source: http://commons.wikimedia.org/wiki/File:Aalesund_from_Fjellstua.jpg).

is a stop on many cruise routes and Fjellstua is its most popular attraction. Accordingly, it is ranked "#1 of 74 things to do in Alesund" by TripAdvisor and as of 2018 had a rating of 4.5 out of 5 stars, with over 1300 reviews. The proximity of Fjellstua to the cruise port (only a 15-minute walk to reach the base of the 400+ steps to the viewpoint) makes it a convenient spot to visit and resulted in 12,000 visitors in a single day in July 2018 when four cruise ships docked in Alesund (The Local, 2018).

While this large number of visitors is unsustainable, the most immediate challenge for local authorities is managing the narrow roadway that leads up to the viewpoint, which becomes congested with buses and personal vehicles, thus requiring local police to direct traffic and restrict access both at peak times and on an ad hoc basis (Borgersen and Saetre, 2018). The rapid rise in the popularity of Fjellstua is a consequence of Norway's increased attention as a tourist destination, which came about as a result of its association with the animated Disney film, *Frozen* (2014), and of increased inclusion of the country in cruise ship itineraries (Metcalf et al., 2015). While the tourist influx was at first welcomed, with news headlines such as, "Disney's Frozen gives boost to Norwegian tourism" (Stampler, 2014), the large increase in numbers of tourists means that attractions in Norway are now uncertain of how to manage the crowds, with news headlines now communicating a different sentiment: "Norway slashes tourism adverts as it is overwhelmed thanks to 'Frozen effect'" (Orange, 2016).

The dramatic rise in the popularity of these destinations, resulting in queues of tourists and staging of photographs to capture the iconic views, raises questions as to the authenticity of the locations and the experiences. However, it is important to move beyond the categorization of authentic vs inauthentic and examine the social processes of authentication and the ways online platforms function to authenticate attractions while also contributing to overtourism. The sheer numbers of tourists contribute to the consensus that these sights are worth seeing, but perhaps more impactful is the user-generated content (Wise and Farzin, 2018). The ever growing numbers of virtual check-ins and geotags confirm to tourists influenced by social media that this *is* the place to be. Additionally, images shared on social media add real time experience and are accompanied by hashtags that demonstrate individual tourists participating in the collective behaviour of sightseeing. The consistency of these images is important, as this solidifies expectations and suggests the experience is accessible. Repeatedly finding the same image captured by a variety of tourists "hotly" authenticates the place, and when the uniformity of the images matches those produced by official tourism promotion organisations this adds a sense of "cool" authentication.

Although tourists have always captured photographs of their travels, and indeed many of these images replicate the similar iconic images used in place promotion (Jenkins, 2003), the immediacy of user-generated content and social media have the consequence that changes in tourism behaviour are more rapid. Tourists adjust travel plans and itineraries to experience the latest "hotspot" and tick off that "bucket list" experience, which can then be shared, further contributing to the user-generated content about the attraction. The ability of the tourist audience to respond so quickly to these trends can find some attractions that are less well equipped to manage a rapid increase in visitor numbers, such as the cases of Trolltunga and Fjellstua in Norway, with a rather immediate challenge of crowding, overtourism, and even liability regarding safety concerns. Thus, while the experiences of other tourists confirm tourism attractions and inspire potential tourists to visit particular places, thereby authenticating the practice of sightseeing, the presence of crowds can diminish and even ruin tourists' experience and degrade the destination's reputation.

Overcrowding, touristification and inauthenticity

While tourism is a collective activity that is performed individually, the very presence of other tourists can sometimes have the effect of diminishing the individual's experiences and, in the case of the presence of excessive numbers of tourists (overcrowding and overtourism), can damage the reputation of the destination. Indeed, Fyall and Garrod (1998) suggest that overcrowding is a significant detriment to visitor satisfaction and particularly to the authenticity of their experience in heritage tourism, specifically. Research on nature-based tourism (Chhetri et al., 2004) likewise suggests that in places where tourists expect small numbers of other visitors, overtourism can lead to perceptions of inauthenticity. This is also the case in urban destinations that experience high tourist densities on a daily basis.

Overtourism thus presents a real challenge for destination management, as the same attractions that are dependent on tourism and concerned about maintaining visitor satisfaction also worry about management practices that might too drastically reduce visitor numbers beyond financial viability (further explained in the other chapters of this book). Nevertheless, unmanaged tourist numbers have the potential to solve themselves, so to speak, as such attractions can come to be known as too "touristy", "commercial", and even "inauthentic" in the minds of potential tourists. Indeed, the "anti-tourism" protests in Athens, Barcelona, Venice (see Chapters 9 and 10) and elsewhere in the summer of 2017 exposed the extent of tourist crowding in some of Europe's most popular destination cities and drew global media attention to the notion of overtourism, bringing it into popular discourse. Overtourism was, however, already being studied by academia and the tourism industry, as the Sustainability Leaders Project hosted an expert panel on the topic in 2017. In this panel, authenticity surfaced as an important theme, particularly in relation to community well-being and sense of place, as well as with regard to genuine experiences for tourists. Importantly, while these aspects of authenticity are relational, they are also distinct, as community perceptions of authenticity draw on some different parameters from those that inform tourists' perceptions.

Community well-being and sense of place are related to residents' perceptions of agency and a feelings of balance related to insider-led versus outsider-led change, equity and the degree of relative deprivation, and the ability to practice cultural traditions and maintain belief systems (Andereck et al., 2007; Perdue et al., 1999). Thus, overtourism can certainly affect these perceptions and abilities, such that residents feel a loss of authenticity with regard to their ability to access and control their own public spaces, an imbalance in which outsiders hold more power than locals at particular times of the year, and even discomfort or an inability to continue their everyday practices and/or cultural traditions in the presence of tourists. Such changes to local communities have come to be known as "touristification", suggesting that tourists' wants are placed above locals' needs in terms of development of infrastructure and resources (Salazar, 2006; Burgold et al., 2013). While tourists may not be attuned to these changes in community well-being and the locals' sense of loss regarding authenticity of place, they may certainly encounter residents' responses to overtourism when those responses are in the forms of resentment, protest and fences (Boissevain, 1996; Dogan, 1989).

Encountering negative attitudes and *in*hospitality of locals is likely to reduce the perceived authenticity of the experience and also diminish enjoyment and visitor satisfaction. In particular, as Oakes (2006) observes, being treated as part of a mass of tourists, rather than a visiting "traveller" can cause individual tourists to rationalise that the destination is inauthentic, rather than inducing self-reflection and a change in their behaviour. Indeed, such research suggests that the fantasy of authenticity (ie. authenticity is always in the next town, on a future adventure or just over the horizon) is a central driver of tourism motivation and marketing (Knudsen et al., 2016).

Sharing economy, localhood and reclaiming authenticity

In the pursuit of authenticity, some tourists go off the beaten path while others approach well-trodden destinations from novel angles. While the crowding and congestion, along with resentment by locals, in destinations experiencing overtourism inspire some tourists to choose different holiday locations, others seek out alternative, or more "authentic", ways of experiencing these "must see" places (cf. Steylaerts and O'Dubhjhaill, 2012; Molz, 2013; Lalicic and Weismayer, 2017; Paulauskaite et al., 2017; Liang et al., 2018). Short-term rental of residential accommodation is a particularly popular option, as it is viewed as a way of experiencing a destination as a "local" (Molz, 2013; Steylaerts and O'Dubhghaill, 2012; Zuev, 2011). Online platforms, such as Airbnb, HomeAway, and Vacasa allow tourists to rent accommodation, which can include rooms in occupied houses or entire properties, in residential areas. Research suggests that tourists who rent this type of accommodation report more authentic experiences compared to when staying in conventional accommodation, such as hotels. Indeed, Paulauskaite et al (2017) found that the atmosphere of the accommodation, interaction with hosts and interaction with local culture were most cited by Airbnb users as contributing to an authentic tourism experience.

Other platforms, such as Couchsurfing, operate in the "gift economy" and offer site members the option to host visitors for free or to stay in destinations across the world free of charge. Molz (2013: 211) posits that Couchsurfing's specific moral agenda, which is expressed by the company's mission to "create a better world, one couch at a time" and create a world "in which people connect in more authentic and meaningful ways outside of the corporate grid of consumer society", also positions the company within the "moral economy". She contends that "Couchsurfing's moral affordances – connecting with strangers, sharing material resources, and engaging in caring relationships – are inseparable from the discourse of guilt, discipline, pleasure, authenticity, and virtue which shapes the moral terrain of alternative tourism more generally" (Molz, 2013: 226).

Such platforms offer the potential for tourists to have more intimate and more authentic experiences, and thereby overcome some of the *in*authenticating aspects of overtourism, while they also promise benefits to the resident communities of the destinations. However, such promises are not always delivered. Paulauskaite et al. (2017: 626) warn,

> services such as those offered by Airbnb may be contributing to a widening rift between tourists and host communities, particularly in mass tourism urban destinations. This was exemplified in recent times in Barcelona through the access that the sharing economy – and Airbnb in particular – has offered to tourists hitherto 'unspoilt' residential areas where locals could seek refuge from the crowds of visitors descending on their cities, particularly in the summer. The heavy concentration of tourists in some areas is negatively affecting neighbouring residents' quality of life (Aznar, Sayeras, Galiana, and Rocafort, 2016). This has also resulted in property rental prices increasingly beyond the reach of local communities who often contribute to local growth in less seasonal sectors of the economy and even cases of 'tourist phobia' in Barcelona.

Given the spread of tourists beyond conventional tourist spaces, residents are increasingly concerned that tourists are now infiltrating all spaces of destinations (Yang et al., 2013). Rather than restricting visitor numbers or establishing boundaries for touristic activities, some destination marketing organisations are turning to the new trend of "localhood". This further breaks down the barriers between hosts and guests and, in so doing, provides local residents more agency in crafting the destination brand. Most notable in the localhood trend is Wonderful Copenhagen (2017), which has explicitly shifted from being a destination "marketing" organisation to being a destination "management" organisation. This has required a new approach, one that draws local people into the core agenda of co-creating the destination through interactions among residents, travellers (no longer labelled tourists) and industry. Indeed, through localhood, Wonderful Copenhagen aims to create:

A future destination where human relations are the focal point, where the differentiation between destination and home of locals is one and the same. A destination, where locals and
visitors not only co-exist, but interact around shared experiences of localhood.

A destination where our global competitiveness is underpinned by our very own localhood: that which makes us stand out on an international scene of global brands and big
players, where we connect at scale by creating meaningful relationships with people – our
potential temporary locals. A future, where tourism growth is co-created responsibly across
industries with the destination's sustainable development and the locals' wellbeing at
heart. (2017: 10)

Localhood movements, such as that being implemented by Wonderful Copenhagen, demonstrate the desire for authenticity by both hosts and guests. They are
a response to the need of residents to reclaim their local communities and are
also a response to tourists' expectations of genuine hospitality and unique experiences. Such a strategy certainly bodes well for improving tourists' experiences
of authenticity, as it highlights hospitality, social encounters and local experiences, which resonate with the key attributes of alternative tourism. However,
research suggests that residents perceive any intrusion into their residential
spaces as "overtourism" (Yang et al., 2013; Kock et al., 2017). Therefore, while
they may produce more authentic experiences for tourists, localhood strategies
may not be able to recover the lost feelings of community well-being and
sense of place, and perceptions of authenticity for the residents of destinations
adopting this strategy.

Conclusion

In an increasingly connected world in which international tourist arrivals are growing each year, authenticity, far from losing its appeal, has remained a mainstay of
touristic motivation. However, this search for authenticity can contribute to overtourism, which threatens both residents and tourists and the reputations of
destinations.

With the rise of social media, individual tourists are more involved than ever
in the promotion of destinations and in the authentication processes that confirm attractions as worth visiting. Gone are the days when destination marketing
organisations crafted place brands with specific narratives and imagery that potential tourists could only read about in print brochures. Rather, today, DMOs
are just one of the ways potential tourists learn about tourism destinations. To
build their expectations of destinations, potential tourists increasingly turn to
online sources, particularly websites that provide user-generated content, usually in the form of reviews and ratings of attractions. Moreover, the images
shared on social media by one's "friends" or those whom one "follows" that portray destinations and travel experiences, have the potential to spark the

imagination or even inspire a new photo trend, such as in the cases of Trolltunga and Fjellstua. Thus, social media reveals that authentication is never complete. High levels of popularity on social media function to "hotly" authenticate attractions, while the replicability of "Instagrammable" photos promises the accessibility of the experience.

Of course, social media popularity can lead to overtourism, which can damage attractions, cause resentment among local residents and eventually lead to associations of *in*authenticity, thereby degrading the destination's reputation. As such, destination management that maintains both community well-being and tourists' perceptions of authenticity is crucial. While localhood movements aim to do this through greater involvement of residents in tourism encounters (cf. Wonderful Copenhagen, 2017), research suggests that removing boundaries between tourists and residents may further build resentment (Yang et al., 2013; Kock et al., 2017). In the case of less accessible, and potentially more vulnerable, attractions, some organisations are imploring tourists to practice ethical behaviour and "responsible Instagramming". Indeed, some environmental advocacy groups and outdoor recreation clubs are asking their members to use geotags with discretion when posting images of fragile ecosystems, for fear that once they are made popular on social media, relatively unknown sites will be overused (Cubbon, 2018). In this regard, Yellowstone National Park in the United States recently initiated the #YellowstonePledge campaign, which asks visitors to take a pledge to practice cautionary measures in the park and adhere to safe selfie practices. The campaign encourages visitors to use the #YellowstonePledge hashtag when posting photographs that follow the guidelines (Solomon, 2017). Such pledges do not dissuade tourists from taking selfies or sharing their experiences on social media, but focus on promoting "good" behaviour. Incorporating such campaigns into social media may function as both a self-policing mechanism and a way of bringing other park visitors into the process of monitoring for safety and reporting non-compliant and dangerous behaviour.

Rather than simply diminishing the authenticity of a destination, overtourism creates a more complex scenario for assessing authenticity and for understanding the social processes through which authentication takes place. Understanding authentication processes, however, requires an examination of power relations and addresses questions about who authenticates and how authentication is managed (Cohen and Cohen, 2012). Attention to overtourism has revealed serious inequities in some of the world's most popular destinations, and is raising concerns about the power dynamics and politics of these communities in relation to tourism. Authenticity and authentication processes are intimately interwoven with these power dynamics and extend beyond destinations to tourists the world over using social media to communicate their tourism experiences and to develop their expectations of potential destinations.

References

Andereck, K. L., Valentine, K. M., Vogt, C. A. and Knopf, R. C. (2007) A cross-cultural analysis of tourism and quality of life perceptions, *Journal of Sustainable Tourism*, 15 (5): 483–502.

Andriotis, K. (2011) Genres of heritage authenticity: Denotations from a pilgrimage landscape, *Annals of Tourism Research*, 38 (4): 1613–1633.

Aznar, J. P., Sayeras, J. M., Galiana, J. and Rocafort, A. (2016) Sustainability commitment, new competitors' presence, and hotel performance: The hotel industry in Barcelona, *Sustainability*, 8 (8): 755.

Boorstin, D. J. (1992 [1961]) *The image: A guide to pseudo-events in America*. New York: Vintage Books.

Belhassen, Y., Caton, K. and Stewart, W. P. (2008) The Search for authenticity in the pilgrim experience, *Annals of Tourism Research*, 35 (3): 668–689.

Bolz, N. (1998) The user-illusion of the world (1): On the meaning of design, *Mediamatic*, 9 (1). https://www.mediamatic.net/en/page/8677/the-user-illusion-of-the-world-1 (Accessed 25 July 2018.)

Boissevain, J. (1996) Introduction. In J. Boissevain (Ed.), *Coping with tourists: European reactions to mass tourism*. Oxford: Berghahn Books, pp. 1–26.

Borgersen, S. R. and Saetre, G. (2018) Turistikonene er sårbare nå, *NRK Møre og Romsdal*. https://www.nrk.no/mr/verdensarven-og-norges-omdomme-star-i-fare-pa-grunn-av-stor-turistvekst-1.14075209 and https://standbynordic.com/tourist-bus-chaos-at-viewpoint-in-norway/. (Accessed 25 July 2018.)

Briedenhann, J. and Ramchander, P. (2006) Township tourism: Blessing or blight? The case of Soweto in South Africa. In M. K. Smith and M. Robinson (Eds.), *Cultural tourism in a changing world: Politics, participation and (re)presentation*. Clevedon: Channel View, pp. 124–142.

Brown, L. (2013) Tourism: A catalyst for existential authenticity, *Annals of Tourism Research*, 40 (1): 176–190.

Bruner, E. M. (1994) Abraham Lincoln as authentic reproduction: A critique of postmodernism, *American Anthropologist*, 96 (2): 397–415.

Buchmann, A., Moore, K. and Fisher, D. (2010) Experiencing film tourism: Authenticity and fellowship, *Annals of Tourism Research*, 37 (1): 229–248.

Burgold, J., Frenzel, F. and Rolfes, M. (2013) Observations on slums and their touristification, DIE ERDE – *Journal of the Geographical Society of Berlin*, 144 (2): 99–104.

Chhabra, D. (2008) Positioning museums on an authenticity continuum, *Annals of Tourism Research*, 35 (2): 427–447.

Chhetri, P., Arrowsmith, C. and Jackson, M. (2004) Determining hiking experiences in nature-based tourist destinations, *Tourism Management*, 25 (1): 31–43.

Chronis, A. and Hampton, R. D. (2008) Consuming the authentic Gettysburg: How a tourist landscape becomes an authentic experience, *Journal of Consumer Behaviour*, 7 (2): 111–126.

Cohen, E. (1979) A phenomenology of tourist experience. In S. Williams (Ed.), *Tourism: Critical Concepts in the Social Sciences*, Vol. 2. London: Routledge, pp. 3–26.

Cohen, E. (1988) Authenticity and commoditization in tourism, *Annals of Tourism Research*, 15 (3): 371–386.

Cohen, E. and Cohen, S. A. (2012) Authentication: Hot and cool, *Annals of Tourism Research*, 39 (3): 1295–1314.

Cook, P. S. (2010) Constructions and experiences of authenticity in medical tourism: The performances of places, spaces, practices, objects and bodies, *Tourist Studies*, 10 (2): 135–153.

Cubbon, K. (2018) Social media-fueled overcrowding and your DMO's responsibility, *DestinationThink!* 9 July. https://destinationthink.com/social-media-fueled-overcrowding-dmo-responsibility/ (Accessed 28 July 2018.)

DeLyser, D. (1999) Authenticity on the ground: Engaging the past in a California ghost town, *Annals of the Association of American Geographers*, 89 (4): 602–632.

Eco, U. (1986) *Travels in Hyperreality* (W. Weaver, Trans.). London: Picador.

Dogan, H. Z. (1989) Forms of adjustment: Sociocultural impacts of tourism, *Annals of Tourism Research*, 16 (2): 216–236.

Evers, A. (2016) Transforming a Norwegian landscape into an iconic tourist attraction: The Trolltunga experience, Master's Thesis. University of Stavanger, Norway.

Fang, B., Ye, Q., Kucukusta, D. and Law, R. (2016) Analysis of the perceived value of online tourism reviews: Influence of readability and reviewer characteristics, *Tourism Management*, 52: 498–506. http://doi.org/10.1016/j.tourman.2015.07.018 (Accessed 28 July 2018.)

Filieri, R. (2015) Why do travelers trust TripAdvisor? Antecedents of trust towards consumer-generated media and its influence on recommendation adoption and word of mouth, *Tourism Management*, 51: 174–185.

Fyall, A. and Garrod, B. (1998) Heritage tourism: at what price? *Managing Leisure*, 3 (4): 213–228

Gable, E. and Handler, R. (1996) After authenticity at an American heritage site, *American Anthropologist*, 98 (3): 568–578.

Jenkins, O. H. (2003) Photography and travel brochures: the circle of representation, *Tourism Geographies*, 5 (3): 305–328.

Kim, H. and Jamal, T. (2007) Touristic quest for existential authenticity, *Annals of Tourism Research*, 34 (1): 181–201.

Knudsen, D. C., Rickly, J. M. and Vidon, E. S. (2016) The fantasy of authenticity: Touring with Lacan. *Annals of Tourism Research*, 58, 33–45.

Knudsen, B. T. and Waade, A. M. (2010) Performative authenticity in tourism and spatial experience: Rethinking the relations between travel, place and emotion. In B. T. Knudsen and A. M. Waade (Eds.), *Re-Investing authenticity: Tourism, place and emotions*, Bristol: Channel View Publications, pp. 1–21.

Kock, F., Zenker, S. and Josiassen, A. (2017) The dilemma of authentic tourist experiences and residential life in urban areas. 13th International Conference on Responsible Tourism in Destinations: Tackling overtourism – local responses.

Lalicic, L. and Weismayer, C. (2017) The role of authenticity in Airbnb experiences. In R. Schegg and B. Stangl (Eds.) *Information and Communication Technologies in Tourism 2017*. Proceedings of the International Conference in Rome, Italy, 24–26 January. Cham: Springer, pp. 781–794.

Liang, L. J., Choi, H. C. and Joppe, M. (2018) Understanding repurchase intention of Airbnb consumers: Perceived authenticity, electronic word-of-mouth, and price sensitivity, *Journal of Travel & Tourism Marketing*, 35 (1): 73–89.

Löfgren, O. (1999) *On holiday: A history of vacationing*. Berkeley: University of California Press.

Lovell, J. (2018) Hyperreal light simulacra: Performing heritage buildings. In J. M. Rickly, and E. S. Vidon, (Eds.) *Authenticity & Tourism: Materialities, Perceptions, Experiences*. Bingley, UK: Emerald Publishing.

MacCannell, D. (1976) *The tourist: A new theory of the leisure class*. New York: Schocken Books.

MacCannell, D. (1999) *The tourist: A new theory of the leisure class*. Berkeley: University of California Press.

MacCannell, D. (2011) *The ethics of sightseeing*. Berkeley: University of California Press.

Maclean, D. (2017) The depressing reality behind one of Instagram's most popular nature shots revealed, *The Independent*, 3 November. https://www.independent.co.uk/travel/norway-trolls-tongue-instagram-photo-reality-trolltunga-queues-how-to-a8036061.html (Accessed 20 July 2018.)

McCabe, S. (2005) "Who is a tourist?": A critical review, *Tourist Studies*, 5 (1): 85–106.

Metcalf, B. R., Linnes, C., Agrusa, J. F. and Lema, J. (2015) Do you want to build a snowman in Norway? The impact of Disney's Frozen movie on Norwegian tourism. Asia Pacific Tourism Association (APTA) 21st Annual Conference, Kuala Lumpur, Malaysia.

Molz, J. G. (2013) Social networking technologies and the moral economy of alternative tourism: The case of Couchsurfing.org, *Annals of Tourism Research*, 43: 210–230.

Moscardo, G. M. and Pearce, D. (1986) Historic theme parks: An Australian experience in authenticity, *Annals of Tourism Research*, 13 (3): 467–479.

Munar, A. M. and Jacobsen, J. K. R. (2013) Trust and involvement in tourism social media and web-based travelinformation sources, *Scandinavian Journal of Hospitality and Tourism*, 13 (1): 1–19.

Noy, C. (2004) Performing identity: Touristic narratives of self-change, *Text and Performance Quarterly*, 24 (2): 115–138.

Oakes, T. (2006) Get real! On being yourself and being a tourist. In C. Minca and T. Oakes (Eds.), *Travels in paradox: Remapping tourism* Lanham: Rowman & Littlefield Publishers, pp. 229–250.

Orange, R. (2016) Norway slashes tourism adverts as it is overwhelmed thanks to 'Frozen effect', *The Telegraph*, 16 September. https://www.telegraph.co.uk/news/2016/09/16/norway-stops-promoting-tourism-as-it-is-overwhelmed-thanks-to-fr/ (Accessed 25 July 2018.)

Paulauskaite, D., Powell, R., Coca-Stefaniak, J. A. and Morrison, A. M. (2017) Living like a local: Authentic tourism experiences and the sharing economy, *International Journal of Tourism Research*, 19 (6): 619–628.

Perdue, R. R., Long, P. T. and Kang, Y. S. (1999) Boomtown tourism and resident quality of life: The marketing of gaming to host community residents, *Journal of Business Research*, 44 (3): 165–177.

Redfoot, D. L. (1984) Touristic authenticity, touristic angst, and modern reality. *Qualitative Sociology*, 7 (4): 291–309.

Rickly, J. M. and Vidon, E. S. (2017) Contesting authentic practice and ethical authority in adventure tourism, *Journal of Sustainable Tourism*, 25 (10): 1418–1433.

Rickly-Boyd, J. M. (2012a) Authenticity & aura: A Benjaminian approach to tourism, *Annals of Tourism Research*, 39 (1), 269–289.

Rickly-Boyd, J. M. (2012b) 'Through the magic of authentic reproduction': tourists' perceptions of authenticity in a pioneer village, *Journal of Heritage Tourism*, 7 (2): 127–144.

Rickly-Boyd, J. M. (2012c) Lifestyle climbers: Towards existential authenticity, *Journal of Sport & Tourism*, 17 (2): 85–104.

Rickly-Boyd, J. M. (2013) Existential authenticity: Place matters, *Tourism Geographies*, 15 (4): 680–686.

Ritzer, G. and Liska, A. (1997) McDisneyization and post-tourism: Complementary perspectives on contemporary tourism. In C. Rojek and J. Urry (Eds.), *Touring culture* London: Routledge, pp. 96–109.

Salamone, F. A. (1997) Authenticity in tourism: The San Angel Inns, *Annals of Tourism Research*, 24 (2): 305–321.

Salazar, N. B. (2006) Touristifying Tanzania: Local guides, global discourse, *Annals of Tourism Research*, 33 (3): 833–852.

Senda-Cook, S. (2012) Rugged practices: Embodying authenticity in outdoor recreation, *Quarterly Journal of Speech*, 98 (2): 129–152.

Shaffer, T. S. (2004) Performing backpacking: Constructing 'authenticity' every step of the way, *Text and Performance Quarterly*, 24 (2): 139–160.

Stampler, L. (2014) *Frozen* has massively increased tourism to Norway, *Time*, 5 June. http://time.com/2827339/frozen-tourism-norway/ (Accessed 25 July 2018.)

Steiner, C. J. and Reisinger, Y. 2006 Understanding Existential Authenticity. Annals of Tourism Research, 33, 299–318.

Steylaerts, V. and Dubhghaill, S. O. (2012) CouchSurfing and authenticity: Notes towards an understanding of an emerging phenomenon, *Hospitality & Society*, 1 (3): 261–278.

Solomon, C. (2017) Is Instagram ruining the great outdoors? *Outside Magazine*, 29 March. https://www.outsideonline.com/2160416/instagram-ruining-great-outdoors (Accessed 28 July 2018.)

Sustainability Leaders Project (2017) Sustainable Tourism Expert Panel https://sustainability-leaders.com/panel/. (Accessed 25 July 2018.)

The Local (2018) Buses cause chaos at popular Norway tourist spot. *The Local*, 5 July. https://www.thelocal.no/20180705/buses-cause-chaos-at-popular-norway-tourist-spot (Accessed 20 July 2018.)

The Place Brand Observer (2017) How overtourism affects destination reputation and competitiveness: Issues, strategies and solutions. 17 October. https://placebrandobserver.com/overtourism-issues-strategies-solutions/ (Accessed 25 July 2018.)

Trilling, L. (1972) *Sincerity and authenticity*. London: Oxford University Press.

Wang, N. (1999) Rethinking authenticity in tourism experience, *Annals of Tourism Research*, 26 (2): 349–370.

Wise, N. and Farzin, F. (2018) "See you in Iran" on Facebook: Assessing user-generated authenticity. In J. M. Rickly and E. S. Vidon, (Eds.) *Authenticity & tourism: Materialities, perceptions, experiences*. Bingley, UK: Emerald Publishing.

Wonderful Copenhagen (2017) The end of tourism as we know it: Towards a new beginning of localhood: Strategy 2020. http://localhood.wonderfulcopenhagen.dk/ (Accessed 28 July 2018.)

Xiang, Z. and Gretzel, U. (2009) Role of social media in online travel information search, *Tourism Management*, 31 (2): 179–188.

Yang, J., Ryan, C., and Zhang, L. (2013) Social conflict in communities impacted by tourism. *Tourism Management*, 35 (1): 82–93.

Zuev, D. (2011) Couchsurfing as a spatial practice: Accessing and producingXenotopos, *Hospitality & Society*, 1 (3): 227–244.

Ulrike Gretzel

5 The role of social media in creating and addressing overtourism

Introduction

Overtourism is a real-life phenomenon experienced by destinations and one that has spurred a social movement that is increasingly featured and debated in the media (Milano, 2018). Dickinson (2018) notes the rapid growth of the search term "overtourism" on Google between mid-2017 and early 2018, suggesting that the concept has firmly entered public consciousness. In a recent tweet, PBS host Darius Arya highlighted the extent to which the term has saturated social media and traditional news outlets (Twitter, 2018). Brand24.com, a social media tracking tool, shows that #overtourism was mentioned 283 times on Twitter in the final week of August 2018 alone, reaching over one million social media users.

While a recently published news article blames technology, and specifically social media, for encouraging overtourism (Manjoo, 2018), the relationship between social media and tourism is not so direct or simple. This chapter seeks to disentangle this relationship by describing the various roles social media play in informing and connecting tourists and residents. In doing so, it uncovers the positive and negative influences of social media and also their potential to facilitate change.

Background

Overview of social media

The term "social media" describes a family of online platforms and mobile applications that take advantage of Web 2.0 technologies to facilitate the easy creation, curation and sharing of content by users without requiring technical skills (Gretzel, 2015). Social media allow users to affiliate with other users, with contents and with events, which explains why they are referred to as "social". These affiliations are usually visible to others, thus further emphasising the social dimension of their contents (Boyd and Ellison, 2007). Kietzmann et al. (2011) suggest that identity, conversations, sharing, presence, relationships, reputation and groups are the seven fundamental building blocks of social media. While social media were largely text-based in the beginning, they quickly evolved to include audio, visual and animated content. In recent years, there has been a noticeable shift towards

https://doi.org/10.1515/9783110607369-005

more visual and live content, with short video "stories" becoming popular across several platforms (Gretzel, 2017a; Huertas, 2018). In general, the social media landscape is highly dynamic, with new features and platforms/applications emerging on a regular basis and others disappearing.

Social media applications typically have a limited number of functions, e.g. content curation and affiliation through "following", in the case of Pinterest, while platforms like Facebook or WeChat combine various social networking, messaging, content dissemination and engagement features and often even support e-commerce. Gretzel (2018a) identifies ten dimensions across which social media typically differ, namely (1) the options for self-presentation; (2) the modes of content discovery; (3) the options for content visibility (e.g. public vs. private); (4) the editability of content after posting; (5) the persistence of content over time; (6) the level of control over where on the application the content appears; (7) the opportunities for engagement with contents and other users' activities; (8) the archivability of content; (9) the opportunities for establishing connections with individuals or groups of other users and with content; and (10) the message formats (length and modality) they support. Depending on their characteristics across these dimensions, social media afford different user behaviours and support different use goals. For instance, Facebook is suitable for mobilizing one's personal social network around a social cause while Twitter permits users to join in on global conversations via the use of hashtags.

The popularity of social media is grounded in their ability to serve a wide range of psychological, social, hedonic and functional needs that static, largely one-way communication media like traditional websites cannot fulfil (Tuten and Solomon, 2017). Social media use is a global phenomenon, although regional/national differences exist in terms of platform/application and feature availability as well as user characteristics and use behaviours (Gretzel, Kang and Lee, 2008). Social media are increasingly (and sometimes even exclusively) available via mobile technologies, which has further supported their penetration of global markets and their increased usage (Statista, n.d.).

Tourism has played and continues to play an important part in the emergence and development of social media (Minazzi, 2015), with a lot of social media content being travel-related and some platforms and applications being exclusively focused on tourism, e.g. TripAdvisor (Gretzel, 2018a). Due to their relevance for tourism, social media have been adopted extensively by travellers and such media influence tourists' expectations about destinations and their decision-making (Narangajavana et al., 2017; Zeng and Gerritsen, 2014; Yoo and Gretzel, 2008). As such, it is not surprising that social media have been linked to the phenomenon of overtourism in recent media reports. The following sections explore the specific roles social media play across various aspects of travel and tourism. It is against this theoretical backdrop that their contribution to overtourism and their potential for mitigation is then discussed.

Social media as information sources

Social media play an important role as sources of travel information. Travellers perceive their content as more relevant, up-to-date and credible than information available via other channels (Gretzel and Yoo, 2017). Social media also make travel planning more enjoyable for travellers (Chung and Koo, 2015). Even when not specifically looking for social media-related sources, travel planners will likely be exposed to social media-related content as part of their online travel searches (Xiang and Gretzel, 2010).

The use of social media for travel planning purposes and their impacts on travel decisions in the pre-trip stage has been a major focus in the literature on social media in tourism (Leung et al., 2013). With growing use of mobile devices in the context of travel (Wang et al., 2012), decisions are increasingly postponed, such that, with the help of social media, planning also occurs during the trip itself. Restaurant and attraction reviews, location-based social media, livestreaming and video sharing apps can feed travellers with context-relevant information and immediate feedback for their decision-making on the go. As such, social media inform not only where tourists go but also what they do at the destination, and often provide travellers with real-time and location-specific information when making en-route decisions (Fotis et al., 2011).

Social media as frames

Photography and tourism are intricately linked (Garrod, 2009) and social media provide new outlets for tourists to curate and share their travel photographs (Lo et al., 2011). Social media also change how tourists take photographs and videos, and how they frame their visuals (Dinhopl and Gretzel, 2016). What tourists depict in their photographs has been traditionally influenced by the iconic images they see in travel advertisements, travel guides and popular media. However, this so-called circle of representation (Jenkins, 2003) has changed because of social media, as tourists are now active participants in establishing what the iconic, must-see destinations are by sharing their photographs publicly on social media platforms (Månsson, 2011). Zhao, Zhu and Hao (2018) propose that such public sharing of travel photography on social media influences the image of a specific destination. Similarly, Balomenou and Garrod (2019) suggest that the changes in photo-taking and photo-sharing practices brought about by social media have important implications for the circle of representation, with the projected image of a destination now being constructed to a much greater extent by consumers, in addition to conventional media and marketers. This has repercussions for destination marketers, who are increasingly losing control over their brands (Gretzel, 2006). An interesting example in this context is the Quokka-selfie phenomenon on Rottnest Island in Western

Fig. 5.1: Quokka selfies on Rottnest Island, Australia (photo credit: Daria Müller and Jiayi Lee).

Australia, in which selfies posted on Instagram led to a steep increase in tourist visitation and a specific interest in interacting with the animals (see Fig. 5.1). This phenomenon was only recognised and exploited by the destination marketers after it had already become popular among travellers (Acott, 2018). Nowadays, visiting the island without taking a Quokka-selfie has become unimaginable to many tourists.

Social media not only frame destination images, they also influence the relative importance of the destination in the visuals and the visit experience. While travel photographs have always featured the self as a proof that one was actually there, selfies taken for the purpose of social media sharing are usually taken by oneself with a smartphone, firmly directing the gaze to the screen and away from the surroundings. Dinhopl and Gretzel (2016) posit that social media foster a self-directed tourist gaze that moves the self into the foreground and the destination into the background. This means that it is not enough to get a picture of oneself with the Mona Lisa; instead, the self must be featured in the visual in interesting ways to make it shareworthy. The focus on the self requires closeness to the object and elaborate posing (Kozinets et al., 2017). As a result, the consumption of and interaction with the attraction or destination has changed. Also noteworthy is the extensive and sophisticated editing of visuals that social media encourage and facilitate (Dinhopl and Gretzel, 2015). Consequently, visuals on social media are carefully framed and significantly altered to fit the aesthetics of the platform and to encourage engagement from others. The need to frame the experience for social media purposes has also inspired the use of tripods, selfie sticks and wearable cameras, which add possibilities for the tourists but bring about additional management challenges for attractions. Overall, not only the picture is framed but also the experience. Even the mundane needs to look extraordinary.

Gretzel (2017b) argues that social media spur creativity in tourists in their quest to impress. The desire to capture the best shot from the best angle to achieve social media fame can also encourage reckless behaviour and unsustainable practices (Pearce and Moscardo, 2015). Concerns include potential crowd stampedes at festivals because of bottlenecks created by selfie-takers, serious damage to heritage monuments as a result of tourists climbing them to capture unique selfies, and, in some instances, the deaths of selfie-takers who take risks and fall from cliffs and bridges, and the deaths of locals who try to save the selfie-taking tourists.

Social media as panoptic forces

Travellers who present themselves and their travel experiences on social media are subject to the gaze of social media audiences (Magasic, 2016). These audiences not only praise but are also quick to shame and punish. Their disciplinary surveillance is often extended to traditional media, which are eager to report on trending social media phenomena (Hess and Waller, 2014). Lo and McKercher (2015) as well as Balomenou and Garrod (2019) propose that travelling with these social media audiences in mind influences photographic practices and social media sharing, as impressions have to be carefully managed. This means that, although social media are assumed to encourage spontaneity and portrayals of experiences in real-time, posts are typically scrutinized to avoid being shamed or, perhaps worse, ignored. User-generated content on social media thus represent ideal selves and experiences that are socially acceptable, unless the goal is to create engagement by shocking one's social media audience. Dinhopl and Gretzel (2018) describe this networked gaze as being omnipresent and powerful as a disciplinary force, shaping both social media-related behaviours and real-life experiences because tourists seek out experiences that will particularly look good on social media or they rehearse these experiences to later receive the approval of others. It is important to social media users that posts add to their individual and social identity projects in positive ways, because their reputations are at stake. Dinhopl and Gretzel (2018) explain that some social media users might not post at all, so as not to jeopardize their ability to belong to an online tribe; however, what they see posted on social media platforms still critically influences how they behave and structure their experiences.

Social media as persuasive technologies

Because of the business models underlying most social media platforms and applications (Gretzel, 2018a), such media are designed as persuasive technologies

(Fogg, 2002). This means they integrate techniques of persuasion to encourage particular behaviours, mostly to ensure that users feel the need to check their social media feeds and post regularly. For instance, TripAdvisor awards travel reviewers with so-called "badges" to psychologically reward them and to motivate them to produce more reviews, while Facebook uses notifications to condition users to stay engaged. Indeed, social media use can be so rewarding that it can become addictive. The fear-of-missing-out (FOMO) spurred by social media further fuels their addictive potential (Blackwell et al., 2017). Tourism marketers are aware of the power of social media and have been known to amplify the persuasiveness of social media by "gamifying" content and encouraging playful interaction with social media, such as through travel personality quizzes or social media supported treasure hunts at destinations (Xu et al., 2014).

Social media as social forums

Social media support various types of sociality in general, including in relation to tourism (Munar et al., 2013). This sociality goes beyond known and unknown consumers and can extend to destinations and tourism companies. As indicated above, connections are also possible with specific events, contents or conversation threads through "following", "tagging" or "hashtagging". Overall, social media represent a complex, networked conversation space, which supports diverse types of affiliations and exchanges, and enables feelings of belonging and community. A critical aspect for travel and tourism is that social media facilitate sociality across time and space, e.g. allowing patrons of a hotel to share their experiences with potential guests, connecting locals and tourists in travel forums, and permitting the sharing of experiences with those who stay at home, as described by White and White (2007).

Social status in the world of social media is gained via two routes: (1) through affiliation and engagement; and (2) through reputation. The first route gave rise to the 'influencer' phenomenon, with influencers on social media referring to accounts that either have a very large following or a highly-engaged audience (Gretzel, 2018b). Starting with travel bloggers and now including YouTube vloggers and Instagram influencers, travel influencers have become an important stakeholder in the tourism information ecosystem. Social status can also be achieved through high engagement on social media, e.g. reaching status through frequent check-ins on Foursquare or earning a Destination Expert designation on TripAdvisor. The second route is mostly based on the reputation attained via ratings and reviews. While this kind of reputation was once reserved for businesses, attractions and destinations, it is now also applied to individuals. Everyone and everything is rated and reviewed, spurring a so-called "reputation economy" in which a positive reputation can be monetized. The reviewing technologies and rating culture introduced by social media constitute a critical element of peer-to-peer and sharing economy applications.

Social media as political means

Literature on social media is increasingly recognising not only their social, psychological and economic significance, but also their political power. Miller (2017: 251) explains that social media "help foster social change by creating a conversational environment based on limited forms of expressive solidarity as opposed to an engaged, content-driven, dialogic public sphere". Importantly, social media have been identified as tools that support activism because they allow for more fluid membership and asynchronous participation in movements (Cammaerts, 2015). In a nutshell, social media make activism more accessible. Furthermore, the archival function of social media platforms and persistence of social media content allow activism to be sustained over time. The network ties visible in social media and the ability to identy and target like-minded others help activism spread more quickly, beyond individuals and beyond local communities. The literature also identifies unique constraints to social media activism, such as government or company control over social media platforms and the need to reach beyond like-minded others to realize change.

Vegh (2003) categorizes social media activism efforts into the following three types: (1) awareness/advocacy; (2) organization/mobilization; and (3) action/reaction. Awareness/advocacy focuses on distributing information via social media, while organization/mobilization involves using social media to recruit supporters and to coordinate online and offline events, and can also include crowdfunding campaigns. Action/reaction involves using social media to encourage particular actions, ranging from requests for likes and reposts to encouragement of so-called hacktivism, e.g. the spamming or hacking of a company's social media platform. Social media activism is sometimes referred to as "clicktivism" or "slacktivism" (Karpf, 2010), suggesting that it might not translate into real commitment and offline actions, and emphasizing the ease with which support can be rallied via social media.

Social media enable forms of activism that were previously difficult in tourism contexts because of the myriad of stakeholders involved in tourism and the often substantial geographic distances between them. A wide variety of social media activism types apply to tourism, ranging from individual actions against companies to large-scale consumer boycotts and social movements like #antitourism (Gretzel, 2017c). Examples of such activism include the use of YouTube videos to highlight overtourism problems in Barcelona, which have been significant in fuelling the residents' anti-tourism movement (Karyotakis, 2018) and the sharing of photos of trophy-hunters on social media as part of the anti-trophy-hunting movement. The current overtourism sentiment is largely sustained via discussions and calls for action on social media.

Challenges

Just as answering the question "Do guns or people kill people?" requires a comprehensive understanding of the underlying socio-technical forces, answering the question of "Do social media cause overtourism?" requires a discussion beyond simple deterministic or technology neutral arguments.

Social media as catalysts of overtourism

Justin Francis, the chief executive of Responsible Travel, has been quoted extensively for blaming social media for at least part of the problem of overtourism. He reportedly said that,

> [s]eventy-five years ago, tourism was about experience seeking. Now it's about using photography and social media to build a personal brand. In a sense, for a lot of people, the photos you take on a trip become more important than the experience. (Manjoo, 2018)

The above discussion on social media affordances and impacts supports this argument in critical ways: First, the persuasive power of social media technologies encourages users to post, and travel experiences lend themselves perfectly to the purpose of producing and posting lots of shareworthy content, especially on visual platforms like Instagram and location-based applications like Foursquare and Snapchat. In essence, social media are networks of desire that fuel the creation and consumption of content (Kozinets et al., 2016), and travel-related content is particularly attractive.

Second, travel is indeed an important element of the personal and social media-based identity of many individuals and the travel lifestyles modelled by travel influencers can motivate social media users to pursue travel, so as to at least get a glimpse of what such a life might be like and be able to impress others. In addition, seeing one's friends post about their vacations creates so-called Facebook envy. Social-media induced FOMO and "you only live once" (YOLO) sentiments further contribute to the desire to travel and can give rise to travel trends such as "last chance tourism".

Third, social media not only present up-to-date rich experiential information that supports decision-making processes, they also present ratings and reviews and often use this information to create lists of top destinations and attractions. Such lists provide information seekers with a convenient decision heuristic and exert social influence. Many of the lists are automatically generated based on ratings (for instance, the TripAdvisor "Top Things to do") or are curated and disseminated by influencers. Checking places off these lists then becomes an important pursuit for some social media users, as it allows them to build reputation, feel closely connected to the influencers and their audience, and obtain approval from their own social network. The travel blogger Nomadic Matt writes that this is comparable to effects that other media, such as films and travel guidebooks, have had but he argues that "social media has an amplifying effect that didn't exist in the past. It makes it easier for everyone to find – and then overrun a destination" (Nomadic Matt, 2018).

Social media not only heighten motivations to travel, they also foster travel to specific destinations and influence behaviours at destinations. For example, city tourism provides the diverse experiences and the connectivity needed by travellers to satisfy their social media posting needs much more than rural tourism does (Magasic and Gretzel, 2017). In addition, the social media lists of "top places to visit" further concentrate tourism demand in certain areas. Huertas (2018) specifically looks at live videos and stories and claims that they change both the perceptions of a place and social media users' vacation behaviours at the destination. This can be seen on Pinterest and Instagram, which are full of posts that advertise the most instagrammable spots at various destinations.

A recent ABC News article (Fisher and Bullock, 2018) asked: "Are we killing tourist destinations for an Instagram photo?" This is a valid question as many instagrammable spots are small places, such as bookstores or cafes, which are usually not managed as tourist attractions and are unable to cope with sudden increases in demand. But such spots also include traditional attractions. While the Dinhopl and Gretzel (2016) analysis of the quest for the extraordinary in the context of travel photography would suggest that tourists seek out unique places away from the crowds, Gretzel (2017b) finds that, rather than depicting unusual destinations, social media tourists find ways to display the extraordinary in front of iconic attractions, for instance by framing the site or the self differently or engaging with the attraction in ironic ways.

Some commentators on tourism have argued that this is nothing new. For example, Manavis, in a recent blog post (2018) claimed that "the idea that, before social media, we weren't 'endlessly queuing behind backpacks of hundreds of other tourists', as the NYT article puts it, at places like the Louvre, taking pictures of historic landmarks, and doing embarrassing poses next to graffitied walls and statues, is simply untrue". While it is indeed true that there is nothing new about mass tourism and travel photography, social media-induced travel photography and videography is a qualitatively different kind of practice. Smartphone cameras redirect gazes, and social media audiences provide immediate feedback. "Do it for the 'gram" has become a common dare, and this phrase is now officially listed in online dictionaries.

Thus, while social media use is not the only, and likely not the most important, reason for overtourism, it certainly encourages behaviours that lead to crowding and it perpetuates images that influence others to travel to certain places and, once there, behave in certain ways.

Social media as tools to combat overtourism

As persuasive technologies and panoptic forces, social media not only encourage overtourism but can also play an important role in promoting sustainable tourism behaviour (Murphy et al., 2018; Gössling, 2017; Negruşa et al., 2015). Indeed, the need of social media users to portray themselves in their best light to support their identity construction projects (Lo and McKercher, 2015) can be used to the advantage of destinations when behaviours that worsen overtourism are openly shamed and those that address it are encouraged. Alternatively, gamification through social media can be used to nudge tourists into desirable directions, e.g. by making information about overtourism playful and by rewarding destination stewardship behaviours in social media applications. Similarly, behaviour change can be encouraged through using the power of social media influencers. Zygmont (2018) explains how Switzerland Tourism actively works with influencers to target very specific tourists for lesser known destinations.

Dispersion of tourists away from the main pressure points appears to be especially critical. Almeida-Santana and Moreno-Gil (2017) suggest that social media use can indeed spur interest in multiple destinations. The World Travel and Tourism Council (2018) proposes that technologies can help combat overcrowding in various ways, including through augmented reality applications, which provide compelling experiences without the need to be close to an attraction or a particular vantage point, and through recommender systems that disperse tourists by providing suggestions not simply based on what other tourists like but on the basis of highly-personalized solutions or by specifically using lack of crowdedness as a selection criterion.

It is also important to acknowledge the indispensable role social media play in educating stakeholders and the public about the causes and consequences of overtourism. The visuals posted by tourists on social media can serve as a rich data source to identify overtourism and, if subjected to big data analytics, could be used as an early-warning system to trigger crowd management. Furthermore, social media's role in helping residents organize and initiate virtual and real-life protests is significant in creating and sustaining #overtourism and #antitourism as social movements that reach far beyond the boundaries of individual destinations. Translating online support into real-life action remains a challenge, however.

Conclusion

A recent article shared widely on social media claims that "The next trend in travel is [. . .] don't" (Smith, 2018), but the above discussion indicates that it is possible to reduce the negative effects of tourism if technologies like social media are used strategically to encourage certain behaviours over others and to put strong social norms in place, which are then policed by social media audiences and subsequently integrated into the self-disciplinary gazes of social media-using tourists. Indeed, preventing and combating overtourism is a responsibility that is shared by all tourism stakeholders (Milano et al., 2018) and social media can provide a forum in which stakeholders can organize, exchange ideas and feedback, and work towards potential solutions. What is clear is that a discussion of overtourism, whether relating to its causes or to potential solutions, requires the consideration of social media because of how intricately linked these media have become with the business of tourism, the planning of travel and the tourism experience. Yet, it must be noted that not every tourist is on social media and that social media behaviours are not the only drivers of overtourism. Social-media based solutions will only be effective in combating overtourism when used in conjunction with other measures.

References

Acott, K. (2018) Rottnest Island quokka-selfie as popular as ever thanks to celeb snaps. News.com. au, 22 September. https://www.news.com.au/national/western-australia/rottnest-island-quokkaselfie-as-popular-as-ever-thanks-to-celeb-snaps/news-story/1efd4c127e38a544b0eca d80a102316a (Accessed 22 September 2018.)

Almeida-Santana, A. and Moreno-Gil, S. (2017) New trends in information search and their influence on destination loyalty: Digital destinations and relationship marketing. *Journal of Destination Marketing & Management*, 6 (2): 150–161.

Balomenou, N. and Garrod, B. (2019) Photographs in tourism research: Prejudice, power, performance and participant-generated images. *Tourism Management*, 70: 201–217.

Blackwell, D., Leaman, C. Tramposch, R. Osborne, C. and Liss, M. (2017) Extraversion, neuroticism, attachment style and fear of missing out as predictors of social media use and addiction. *Personality and Individual Differences*, 116: 69–72.

Boyd, D. M., and Ellison, N. B. (2007) Social network sites: Definition, history, and scholarship. *Journal of Computer-Mediated Communication*, 13 (1): 210–230.

Cammaerts, B. (2015) Social media and activism. In R. Mansell and P. Hwa (Eds.), *The International Encyclopedia of Digital Communication and Society*. Oxford: Wiley-Blackwell, pp. 1027–1034.

Chung, N. and Koo, C. (2015) The use of social media in travel information search. *Telematics and Informatics*, 32 (2): 215–229.

Dickinson, G. (2018) Dear dictionaries, this is why 'overtourism' should be your 2018 word of the year, *The Telegraph*, 20 April. https://www.telegraph.co.uk/travel/comment/overtourism-word-of-the-year/ (Accessed 25 August 2018.)

Dinhopl, A. and Gretzel, U. (2015) Changing practices/new technologies: Photos and videos on vacation. In I. Tussyadiah and A. Inversini (Eds.), *Information and Communication Technologies in Tourism 2015*, Proceedings of the International Conference, Lugano, Switzerland, 3–6 February. Cham: Springer, pp. 777–788.

Dinhopl, A. and Gretzel, U. (2016) Selfie-taking as touristic looking, *Annals of Tourism Research*, 57: 126–139.

Dinhopl, A. and Gretzel, U. (2018) The networked neo-tribal gaze. In A. Bennett, A. Hardy and B. Robards (Eds.), *Neo-Tribes: Consumption, Leisure and Tourism*. Cham: Springer.

Fisher, A. and Bullock, C. (2018) Are we killing tourist destinations for an Instagram photo? *ABC News*, 5 September. http://www.abc.net.au/news/2018-09-06/mass-tourism-proving-disas trous-is-instagram-to-blame/10198828 (Accessed 7 September 2018.)

Fogg, B. J. (2002) Persuasive technology: using computers to change what we think and do. *Ubiquity*, December.

Fotis, J., Buhalis, D. and Rossides, N. (2011) Social media impact on holiday travel planning: The case of the Russian and the FSU markets. *International Journal of Online Marketing*, 1 (4): 1–19.

Garrod, B. (2009) Understanding the relationship between tourism destination imagery and tourist photography. *Journal of Travel Research*, 47 (3): 346–358.

Gössling, S. (2017) Tourism, information technologies and sustainability: an exploratory review. *Journal of Sustainable Tourism*, 25 (7): 1024–1041.

Gretzel, U. (2006) Consumer generated content–trends and implications for branding. *E-review of Tourism Research*, 4 (3): 9–11.

Gretzel, U. (2015) Web 2.0 and 3.0. In L. Cantoni and J. A. Danowski (Eds.), *Communication and Technology*, Handbooks of Communication Science Series, Vol. 5. Berlin: De Gruyter Mouton, pp. 181–192.

Gretzel, U. (2017a) The Visual Turn in Social Media Marketing. *Tourismo*, 12 (3): 1–18.

Gretzel, U. (2017b) # travelselfie: a netnographic study of travel identity communicated via Instagram. In S. Carson and M. Pennings (Eds.), *Performing Cultural Tourism*. New York: Routledge, pp. 129–142.

Gretzel, U. (2017c) Social Media Activism in Tourism. *Journal of Hospitality and Tourism*, 15 (2): 1–14.

Gretzel, U. (2018a) Tourism and social media. In C. Cooper, W. Gartner, N. Scott and S. Volo, (Eds.), *The Sage Handbook of Tourism Management*. Thousand Oaks: Sage.

Gretzel, U. (2018b) Influencer marketing in travel and tourism. In M. Sigala and U. Gretzel, (Eds.), *Advances in Social Media for Travel, Tourism and Hospitality: New Perspectives, Practice and Cases*. New York: Routledge, pp. 147–156.

Gretzel, U., Kang, M. and Lee, W. (2008) Differences in consumer-generated media adoption and use: A cross-national perspective. *Journal of Hospitality & Leisure Marketing*, 17 (1–2): 99–120.

Gretzel, U. and Yoo, K-H. (2017) Social Media in Hospitality and Tourism. In S. Dixit (Ed.), *Routledge Handbook of Consumer Behaviour in Hospitality and Tourism*, New York: Routledge, pp. 339–346.

Hess, K. and Waller, L. (2014) The digital pillory: media shaming of 'ordinary' people for minor crimes. *Continuum*, 28 (1): 101–111.

Huertas, A. (2018) How live videos and stories in social media influence tourist opinions and behaviour. *Information Technology & Tourism*, 19 (1): 1–28.

Jenkins, O. (2003) Photography and travel brochures: The circle of representation. *Tourism Geographies*, 5 (3): 305–328.

Karpf, D. (2010) Online political mobilization from the advocacy group's perspective: Looking beyond clicktivism, *Policy & Internet*, 2 (4): 7–41.

Karyotakis, M.-A. (2018) Tourist go home: Communication and propaganda on YouTube. PhD dissertation, Aristotle University of Thessaloniki, Greece.

Kietzmann, J. H., Hermkens, K., McCarthy, I. P. and Silvestre, B. S. (2011) Social media? Get serious! Understanding the functional building blocks of social media, *Business Horizons*, 54 (3): 241–251.

Kozinets, R., Gretzel, U. and Dinhopl, A. (2017) Self in art/self as art: Museum selfies as identity work. *Frontiers in Psychology*, 8: 731.

Kozinets, R., Patterson, A. and Ashman, R. (2016) Networks of desire: How technology increases our passion to consume, *Journal of Consumer Research*, 43 (5): 659–682.

Leung, D., Law, R., Van Hoof, H. and Buhalis, D. (2013) Social media in tourism and hospitality: A literature review, *Journal of Travel & Tourism Marketing*, 30 (1–2): 3–22.

Lo, I. S. and McKercher, B. (2015) Ideal image in process: Online tourist photography and impression management. *Annals of Tourism Research*, 52: 104–116.

Lo, I. S., McKercher, B., Lo, A., Cheung, C. and Law, R. (2011) Tourism and online photography, *Tourism Management*, 32 (4): 725–731.

Magasic, M. (2016) The 'selfie gaze' and 'social media pilgrimage': Two frames for conceptualising the experience of social media using tourists. In *Information and Communication Technologies in Tourism 2016*. Cham: Springer, pp. 173–182.

Magasic, M. and Gretzel, U. (2017) Three modes of internet connectivity during travel: Remote, transit and residential. *e-Review of Tourism Research*, 8.

Manavis, S. (2018) Overtourism is a problem – but social media is not to blame. *New Statesman*, 30 August. https://www.newstatesman.com/science-tech/social-media/2018/08/overtour ism-problem-social-media-not-blame-instagram (Accessed 1 September 2018.)

Manjoo, F. (2018) 'Overtourism' worries Europe. How much did technology help get us there? *New York Times*, 29 August. https://www.nytimes.com/2018/08/29/technology/technology-over tourism-europe.html (Accessed 30 August 2018.)

Månsson, M. (2011) Mediatized tourism, *Annals of Tourism Research*, 38 (4): 1634–1652.

Milano, C. (2018) Overtourism, social unrest and tourismphobia: A controversial debate. *PASOS: Revista de Turismo y Patrimonio Cultural*, 16 (3): 551–564.

Milano, C., Cheer, J. M. and Novelli, M. (2018) Overtourism is becoming a major issue for cities across the globe. *World Economic Forum*, 20 July. https://www.weforum.org/agenda/2018/07/ overtourism-a-growing-global-problem (Accessed 28 August 2018.)

Miller, V. (2017) Phatic culture and the status quo: Reconsidering the purpose of social media activism. *Convergence*, 23 (3): 251–269.

Minazzi, R. (2015) *Social media marketing in tourism and hospitality*. New York: Springer.

Mkono, M. (2018) The age of digital activism in tourism: Evaluating the legacy and limitations of the Cecil anti-trophy hunting movement, *Journal of Sustainable Tourism*, 1–17.

Munar, A. M., Gyimóthy, S. and Cai, L. (Eds.) (2013) *Tourism social media: Transformations in identity, community and culture*. Bingley, UK: Emerald Publishing.

Murphy, J., Gretzel, U., Pesonen, J., Elorinne, A-L. and Silvennoinen. K. (2018) Household Food Waste, Tourism and Social Media: A Research Agenda. (2018) In *Information and Communication Technologies in Tourism 2018*. Cham: Springer, pp. 228–239.

Narangajavana, Y., Callarisa Fiol, L. J., Moliner M. A., Rodríguez-Artola, R. M. and Sánchez-Garcia, J. (2017) The influence of social media in creating expectations. An empirical study for a tourist destination. *Annals of Tourism Research*, 65: 60–70.

Negruşa, A. L., Toader, V., Sofică, A., Tutunea, M. F. and Rus, R. V. (2015) Exploring gamification techniques and applications for sustainable tourism, *Sustainability*, 7 (8): 11160–11189.

Nomadic Matt (2018) Overtourism: How you can help solve this worldwide problem. 6 September. https://www.nomadicmatt.com/travel-blogs/overtourism-solutions/ (Accessed 7 September 2018.)

Pearce, J. and Moscardo, G. (2015) Social representations of tourist selfies: New challenges for sustainable tourism. In *Conference Proceedings of BEST EN Think Tank XV: The Environment-People Nexus in Sustainable Tourism: Finding the Balance*, 17–21 June, Kruger National Park, South Africa, pp. 59–73.

Smith, A. J. (2018) The next trend in travel is … don't, *Bright Magazine*, 7 June. https://brightthe mag.com/the-next-trend-in-travel-is-dont-226d4aba17f6 (Accessed 30 October 2018.)

Statista (n.d.) Mobile social media – Statistics & Facts. https://www.statista.com/topics/2478/mo bile-social-networks/ (Accessed 20 August 2018.)

Tuten, T. L. and Solomon, M. R. (2017) *Social media marketing*. Thousand Oaks: Sage.

Twitter (2018) @DariusAryaDigs, 2 September. https://twitter.com/DariusAryaDigs/statuses/
    1036363733088579584 (Accessed 3 September 2018.)
Vegh, S. (2003) Classifying forms of online activism. In M. D. Ayers and M. McCaughey (Eds),
    Cyberactivism: Online activism in theory and practice, New York: Routledge, pp. 71–95.
Wang, D., Park, S. and Fesenmaier, D. R. (2012) The role of smartphones in mediating the touristic
    experience. Journal of Travel Research, 51 (4): 371–387.
White, N. R. and White, P. B. (2007) Home and away: Tourists in a connected world, Annals of
    Tourism Research, 34 (1): 88–104.
World Travel and Tourism Council (2018) How can new technologies help deal with overcrowding?
    31 August. https://medium.com/@WTTC/how-can-new-technologies-help-deal-with-over
    crowding-dda554fb164b (Accessed 31 August 2018.)
Xiang, Z., and Gretzel, U. (2010) Role of social media in online travel information search, Tourism
    Management, 31 (2): 179–188.
Xu, F., Weber, J. and Buhalis, D. (2014) Gamification in tourism. In Information and Communication
    Technologies in Tourism 2014. Cham: Springer, pp. 525–537.
Yoo, K. H. and Gretzel, U. (2008) Use and impact of online travel reviews. In P. O'Connor,
    W. Höpken and U. Gretzel (Eds.), Information and Communication Technologies in Tourism
    2008. Vienna: Springer, pp. 35–46.
Zeng, B. and Gerritsen, R. (2014) What do we know about social media in tourism? A review,
    Tourism Management Perspectives, 10: 27–36.
Zhao, Z., Zhu, M. and Hao, X. (2018) Share the Gaze: Representation of destination image on the
    Chinese social platform WeChat Moments, Journal of Travel & Tourism Marketing, 35 (6):
    726–739.
Zygmont, N. (2018) So erklärt ein irakischer Influencer die Schweiz, 20 minuten, 31 August.
    https://www.20min.ch/schweiz/news/story/Arabischer-Influencer-versinkt-in-der-Kaese
    grotte-10021078 (Accessed 7 September 2018.)

Richard W. Butler
6 Overtourism and the Tourism Area Life Cycle

Introduction

As discussed elsewhere in this volume, overtourism is a relatively recent phenomenon in terms of what is perceived as too many tourist visitors and too much tourist-related development in specific destinations. While complaints about tourists, both by local residents and other tourists, have been recorded for over two centuries (Butler, 2006a), the frequency of such complaints, in the current media in particular, suggest that tourism development in an increasing number of destinations is approaching or has exceeded what is felt, particularly by residents of those destinations, to be an appropriate level. This state of affairs in terms of individual destinations and resorts has been discussed in papers dating back to at least the 1930s (Ogilvie, 1933; Christaller, 1963, Young, 1973; Krippendorf, 1987).

The idea that overdevelopment and over-visitation would result in the emergence of negative attitudes towards tourists and tourism was summarised by Doxey (1975) in an "irridex" (irritation index), which posited that as tourist numbers grow, resident attitudes move through certain stages, changing from being positive towards tourists to a feeling of apathy, then moving through irritation towards antagonism, and perhaps finally to action to prevent further development (Doxey, 1975). Meanwhile, Plog (1973) proposed a model involving the changing characteristics of tourists, rather than of destinations. He suggested that the types of tourists change as destinations alter in character and move from underdevelopment to development (and overdevelopment). Some of the classic early resorts such as Coney Island and Atlantic City in the United States were suggested by Plog as having gone through this process, and in the case of Coney Island, became a suburb of greater New York. Similar processes occurred at older resorts such as Blackpool and Brighton in the United Kingdom, and at second home (cottage) resorts north of Toronto in Canada.

The theory of there being a common pattern of development of tourist destinations was encapsulated by Stansfield (1978) who was the first to use the term "cycle" in his paper on Atlantic City and its rejuvenation through the legalisation of gambling. These early models were brought together and their ideas incorporated into what has become known as the Tourism Area Life Cycle (Butler, 1980). The model presented by Butler is now the most frequently-cited model relating to destination development and one of the most cited of all tourism articles (Wang et al., 2016).

The Tourism Area Life Cycle (TALC) model proposes that most tourist resorts progress through a development process similar to the conventional business product cycle, beginning with a slow start with few visitors and little if any tourism development, through a period of growth of both numbers of visitors and facilities to cater for them, to a period of rapid growth, followed by a period of

https://doi.org/10.1515/9783110607369-006

limited growth and a cessation of the rate of growth of visitor numbers and developments. These stages were named Exploration, Involvement, Development, Consolidation, Stagnation, followed by a number of options including Rejuvenation and Decline. (see Fig. 6.1). As a destination moves through the cycle it may continue to grow at a reduced rate, may go through a period of no growth or may enter into a decline, illustrated by a drop in visitor numbers and a disappearance of some facilities, with few or no new facilities being created (Butler, 1980).

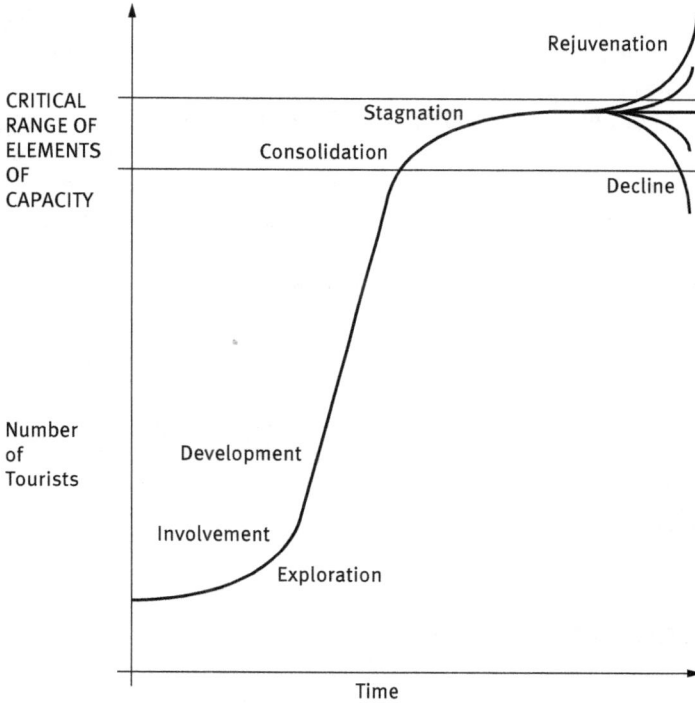

Fig. 6.1: Tourism Area Life Cycle (source: Richard W. Butler, 1980).

The original article by Butler (1980) postulated that most, if not all, tourist destinations go through this, or a similar cycle of development, although the time scale involved and the absolute numbers of visitors vary with the characteristics of the specific destinations. The article argued that without appropriate management and control of the resources on which tourism was based, and was therefore dependent, the majority of destinations would experience a decline phase, which could prove the beginning of a long term negative feedback loop, potentially resulting in continuing decline and even a possible departure from tourism. It further argued that management of the key resources on which tourism at any destination is based is essential if growth is to be proportional and appropriate, and if the quality of the destination (environmentally and socially) is to be maintained for both visitors and residents. Without such control, excessive development and loss of some or most of the basic attributes and attractions of these destinations would take place (Butler, 1980). Such a result is close to what is now known as overtourism.

While the TALC model (Fig. 6.1) has received a great deal of use and is frequently cited in current literature (Wang et al., 2016) some four decades after it was first presented (Butler and Brougham, 1972) and published (Butler, 1980), the proposition that there is a common pattern to the development process of tourist destinations has been subject to various criticisms. One objection is that it does not fit reality at certain scales (Choy, 1992); another is that a uni-directional focus, as with Doxey's irridex, is not necessarily appropriate (E. Cohen, personal correspondence), and another is whether the model could in fact be made operational (Haywood, 1986). Other researchers, such as Agarwal (1994, 2002), have argued that there should be additional or alternative stages of development in the model, while Weaver (1988), for example, postulated that the initial entry of a destination into tourism may be different in what he categorised as "plantation economies". Many of the suggested modifications and rejections of certain aspects of the model have been discussed elsewhere (Butler, 2006a, 2006b, 2015) and it is not proposed to review the extensive literature on the TALC model here. In this chapter, the discussion will focus on the relevance of the TALC model to the issue of overtourism and what lessons might be learned from it for destinations currently experiencing excessive visitation and development, which are widely held to cause loss of appeal and damage to existing and potential tourist markets.

Overtourism and overdevelopment

It is important in the context of the relationship between overtourism and the TALC to note that there needs to be a distinction made between overtourism and overdevelopment. Although in many respects there are many similarities, equally there are important differences. Overtourism, as noted earlier, is primarily a situation experienced by a destination receiving what many residents, and perhaps visitors, perceive as too many tourists. This may or may not be related to the level of development, as noted two decades ago by Wanhill (1997), long before the term "overtourism" had been conceived. It may be that excessive (over) development of tourism attractions, services and facilities leads to a destination receiving what is regarded as an excessive number of tourists, i.e. the rate and extent of development results in what are perceived to be too large a number of visitors. One can argue, however, that if the level and rate of development have kept pace with the growth in numbers of visitors, then while a destination may be busy and have a large number of tourists, this may not be over-tourism in the generally accepted view of the term. A good example of such a situation would be Las Vegas, which has shown continual development and expansion for over half a century, with little criticism of such development, although some dissatisfaction with aspects of the attractions offered there. To visitors, such a situation is even less likely to be viewed as overtourism, for while a destination may be busy, it may not be congested or crowded as long as the capacity of the infrastructure is not being over-taxed. Where development has not kept pace with visitor numbers however, overtour-ism may be experienced even when tourist numbers may be small in an absolute sense. In such contexts, visitor numbers may be excessive relative to the capacity of the destination and the tolerance of the residents (Fig. 6.2). This issue is discussed in more detail in the context of overtourism in rural areas in Chapter 14.

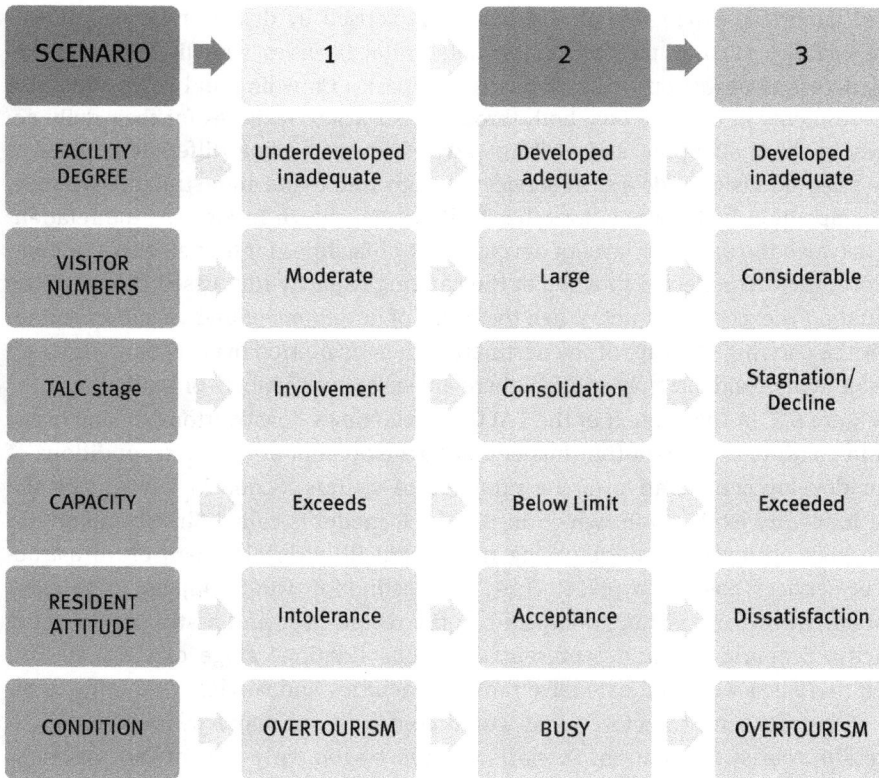

SCENARIO	1	2	3
FACILITY DEGREE	Underdeveloped inadequate	Developed adequate	Developed inadequate
VISITOR NUMBERS	Moderate	Large	Considerable
TALC stage	Involvement	Consolidation	Stagnation/ Decline
CAPACITY	Exceeds	Below Limit	Exceeded
RESIDENT ATTITUDE	Intolerance	Acceptance	Dissatisfaction
CONDITION	OVERTOURISM	BUSY	OVERTOURISM

Fig. 6.2: Destination characteristics and carrying capacity.

In some respects, the balance between development and excessive tourism (or over-development of tourism) is related to the idea of a tipping point, beyond which de-velopment causes irreversible change, with resulting costs and problems for local residents and some visitors alike. This aspect was discussed by Russell (2006: 176) in the context of applying Chaos Theory to the TALC model, where she argued that development might not always follow a linear model but might approach a point representing a "phase shift" in the life cycle process, resulting in an unanticipated change in direction and nature of development. Such a change could have multiple repercussions, including opposition to further development, a radical change in the nature of development and even a decline in development and visitor numbers.

Thus, there are a number of relationships involved. An over-riding factor in the TALC model is that of carrying capacity (Wall, 1982). As long as the carrying capacity (potentially defined in the context of a range of variables) of the destination is not exceeded, it is hard to use the term overtourism correctly, for "busy" and "overtourism" are not synonymous. "Congestion" and "overcrowded" are much more relevant and appropriate terms by which to describe overtourism and these terms imply a loss of quality of experience for visitors, characterised by delays in service, inadequate facilities such as parking, inadequate rental facilities, and limited or inadequate access to attractions such as beaches or parks. Crowding and congestion also affect residents of destinations, both through insufficient facilities for their daily activities, such as shopping and visiting services, even if using different services to those used by visitors, delays in service through traffic and infrastructure overuse, and competition with tourists for other facilities. As shown in Fig. 6.2, the relationship between the extent or level of development of facilities for tourists and the numbers of tourists is reflected in whether the carrying capacity (discussed below) of the destination is exceeded or not. When the levels of development and visitation remain under the carrying capacity of the destination there is no true overtourism, although some or many residents may still feel there are excessive numbers of tourists.

Figure 6.2, in the context of the TALC model, shows how overtourism can occur both in conditions of great (but inadequate) development and also in conditions of minor development relative to the numbers of visitors. Scenario 1 would be the stage following exploration, which in the TALC model is called "involvement", in which visitor numbers are increasing rapidly but little development of infrastructure or services has taken place. Thus, the destination would appear to be over-crowded, with many visitors compared to the recent past and a still low carrying capacity. Scenario 2 would represent the "consolidation" stage of the TALC, in which there is a wide and extensive range of facilities and services and large numbers of visitors, and therefore what would constitute, in many peoples' minds, a successful tourist destination. Scenario 3 could be the early part of the "development" stage of the TALC, in which numbers of tourists are rising rapidly and outstripping the development and supply of facilities. It could also represent a point between the "stagnation" and "decline" stages, at which there has been a lack of new development but numbers of visitors have not started to decline appreciably.

Overtourism can also be experienced at other stages of the TALC depending on the individual and specific characteristics of the destination. Resident attitudes appear to be a major factor in a destination being described as experiencing overtourism, but resident attitudes are dynamic and do not remain constant in any destination as Butler (1975); Doxey (1975) and Gill and Williams (2018) have argued. Clearly, overtourism, despite its name, involves more than either simple numbers or development. This point is developed further in later chapters; this chapter focuses on the more conceptual links between the term and conceptual models such as the TALC and carrying capacity.

Carrying capacity

The concept of carrying capacity is critical to discussion of the issue of overtourism. Since the 1960s and 1970s carrying capacity in tourism research has declined in terms of being a topic of relevance in tourism and recreation (Butler, 1997). Leading researchers, such as Lucas (1964), Wagar (1964) and Lime and Stankey (1971), produced highly relevant and important studies applying the concept of carrying capacity to the field of outdoor recreation. These studies showed clear links between visitors' perceptions of the level of use of an area and the quality of their experience. What visitors felt to be crowding (overuse) of destinations was strongly related to a decline in the perceived enjoyment of the visitors. The direct implication of this research to tourism destinations was weakened, however, by the fact that most such studies were conducted with surveys of visitors in wilderness or rural areas that had few or no residents. As well, most of the users interviewed were similar in terms of their activities, demographics and preferences, unlike the far more varied population of tourists at most tourist destinations.

Thus, carrying capacity has had less of an influence on tourism development and planning than in the recreation context, although a few studies (e.g. An Foras Forbatha, 1966) have explored the relevance of the concept to tourist destinations. However, with the rise in interest in sustainable development and sustainable tourism, especially in relation to the background and origin of that concept (e.g. Meadows et al., 1972) with the implication of the need to live within the capacity of the environment, both at a local and a global scale, the ongoing relevance of carrying capacity to tourist destinations is clear.

While the TALC model argued that development beyond the carrying capacity of a destination would result in a decline in the quality of the visitor experience, it also implied a potential decline in the quality of life for residents of such a destination, although this was not discussed explicitly in detail in the original article (Butler, 1980). What was discussed, in line with the arguments of Plog (1973) and Doxey (1975), was that as the character of a destination changed, the attitudes of residents and visitors was also likely to change, and rarely in a universally positive manner towards tourism. The early models of destination development, such as those mentioned above, have been criticised for being overly simplistic and there is clearly some validity in that criticism. Not all residents or visitors find crowding problematic at a tourist destination, indeed, an absence of other visitors might well be off-putting and unattractive if one is seeking company and interaction with other visitors, e.g. as in Las Vegas. This implies that both the relative level of visitor numbers compared to facilities and services and the perceptions of visitors and residents are crucial to determining if overtourism is present at any stage of the TALC, and indeed, if it is related at all to the model.

It is also necessary to consider that residents may have differing views on tourism and tourists (Brougham and Butler, 1981). In remote and thinly-populated areas (see Chapter 14) residents may view the appearance of tourists as desirable, providing opportunities for social interaction, as found in New Zealand with the Local Host programme of the 1980s. This was a programme developed in rural parts of the South Island, New Zealand, whereby local farmers, in particular, were encouraged to take in paying guests (generally bed and breakfast tourism) to provide social interaction for remote households and provide supplementary income for the farms. According to responses from participants, it proved popular with farmers' wives, who were often without company for much the day (Simmons, 1986).

In situations where tourist numbers are greater than desired, residents are clearly able to distinguish between tourism, which they often accept, albeit grudgingly in some cases, as being necessary for employment and income generation, and tourists. Residents can be less accepting of tourists themselves, sometimes seeing them as intrusive, generating litter and generally being a nuisance through disturbance and traffic congestion. Residents may perceive positive economic benefits of tourism for their communities, even if they do not perceive any direct benefits for themselves, but residents may have to make behavioural adjustments for tourists and may be directly inconvenienced by tourists, without any direct personal benefits. The level and scale at which such disruptions occur are in part related to the level of development; there are normally more tourists in a destination in the middle and later stages of the TALC than in the initial stages of development, but this must be seen in the context of the morphology, size and above all, the carrying capacity of the destination.

In the context of development and overtourism, the physical development of tourism facilities and services tends to be tolerated more readily than the visitors these facilities and services attract, in some cases because the facilities and services can be used by residents as well, thus providing personal benefits as well the more general economic ones. Improvements in access to destinations, for example, are often supported by residents, even when such improvements are designed primarily for tourists, although there may be resentment expressed if such services close during the non-tourist season (Brougham and Butler, 1981).

Discussion

The basic premise of the TALC was that destination development is essentially evolutionary. That is, development is based on the attractions that are already in a destination (such as beaches, climate, cultural heritage) and that the original attributes of the destination remain attractive to subsequent generations of tourists as the resort is developed. If development changes or degrades those inherent attributes, then the appeal and attraction of a destination may be threatened and, with that, the viability of future development. Inevitably, however, the tastes and preferences of different generations of tourists change over time, and what may have been attractive and inviting to the first visitors to a destination may not be appealing to subsequent generations of visitors. Thus, the TALC should not be seen as a call for no change in a destination, for any development will cause change, from increasing the numbers of visitors to increasing the choice and range of facilities and services, both for visitors and locals. As Plog (1973) pointed out, as resorts change, so do their visitors, and almost any changes in a destination are likely to deter some of the very earliest visitors who presumably had been attracted to a destination as it was when they first visited that location. As opportunities increase and broaden in range, an increasing number of potential visitors are likely to find the altered destination attractive and become actual visitors. This is what is meant by an evolutionary process in this context, namely that changes in visitors both bring about and respond to changes in facilities, services, access, design and morphology of tourist destinations.

The morphology of destinations has been illustrated and analysed by Stansfield and Rickert (1970) and despite the many improvements and changes in size, quality and nature of tourist services, the basic design of the vast majority of tourist destinations, even in the 21st century, follows many of the forms discussed in the recreational business district model, and often illustrate an evolutionary process of development. Examples exist in many countries including Manly in Australia (Butler and McDonnell, 2011); Playa del Carmen and Puerto Vallarta in Mexico; Port Stanley and Wasaga Beach in Canada (Wolfe 1952); and Nice and Biarritz in France. The recreational business district model argues that resorts, particularly those on a coast, have a common morphology or layout. Land adjoining the seafront is the most valuable and it is here that major features such as hotels, amusement facilities, piers, and casinos are located, with lower level facilities and services further back from the seafront. Such resorts are also characterised by an absence of many of the features found in conventional business districts, such as banks, insurance and government services, large department stores and high-end retailers such as furniture stores. The pattern of activity, including opening hours, is different in resorts compared to other urban centres, reflecting the fact that visitors use the facilities in the evenings and are looking for entertainment and food and beverage operations. This is particularly noticeable in resorts focused on casinos. The seafront, particularly the beach and the main access road to it, represents the Peak Value Intersection (often coinciding with a pier), where land values are highest, reflected in the nature and cost of development. It has to be acknowledged, however, that this traditional morphology can prove to be limiting in terms of visitor appeal and can also present problems for extensive replacement and rejuvenation, both psychologically and physically.

A difficulty with the evolutionary process is that there is an implication of a certain inevitability about the way that development will take place. In general, it suggests more of the same, with relatively minor modifications and diversions from the common pattern. One major diversion can be seen perhaps, in casino dominated resorts, such as Las Vegas, Macao and perhaps most of all, Atlantic City, where casinos have been added to, or in the latter case, imposed on, the morphology of an established conventional seaside resort. Such a diversion, catering to and attracting a very different market with very different patterns of behaviour to the traditional seaside visitors, means that, almost inevitably, the new form becomes predominant and perhaps permanently changes the whole fabric and image of the destination. Such has been the scale of development of casino destinations that such transformations appear to be universal and irreversible, although their permanent success is not guaranteed, as has been shown at Atlantic City over the past decade, with a number of major casinos closing as market share has fallen. Recent changes in legislation in the United States may see a rebirth yet again of the tourist fortunes of Atlantic City, however. Destinations where casinos are better integrated with other attractions, and are not so overwhelmingly dominant, seem to have withstood changes in market tastes somewhat more successfully.

One may consider the major casino destinations, (major in terms of income generation and numbers of casinos) Las Vegas, Macao and Atlantic City, as providing some evidence of overdevelopment and overtourism in the sense that other forms of tourism and other tourists have to some degree disappeared from those destinations. They have therefore become single-form tourism (gambling) destinations, sometimes to the frustration of local residents. What has characterised the development in such destinations has been the dominance of a few very powerful enterprises and, in some cases, individuals, such as Stanley Ho in the case of Macao (McCartney, 2010), most of which were external to the destination and which made large investments and major infrastructure developments. In many respects these were often too large to be denied, particularly by local governments that were desperate, or at least desirous, for investment and employment, particularly from a branch of an industry (tourism) with which they were familiar. The ease with which powerful enterprises and individuals came to dominate some destinations may also reflect political considerations at several levels of government.

The argument in the original TALC article was that as development took place in a destination, numbers of visitors would increase, and vice versa (which is the chicken and which is the egg in that situation has not been resolved), and if such development was not adequately and appropriately managed, the likely result would be a loss of quality and attractiveness of the destination and a resulting decline in visitation and future investment and development. The concept of overtourism was not expressed as such, hardly surprising as the term had not come into vogue at that time, but there was discussion of the implications that exceeding the carrying capacity of the destination might bring about. As noted earlier, the concept of carrying capacity was significant in the early tourism literature and a number of destinations and agencies had begun to examine the concept and consider how to handle excessive numbers. The difficulties in implementing controlling strategies, however, and the emergence of related but less restrictive theories, such as the limits of acceptable change (LAC) (Stankey et al., 1985) meant that carrying capacity declined in consideration and in research priorities (Butler, 2010).

The LAC model incorporates managerial perspectives and sometimes visitors' perceptions and the degrees of acceptance of change brought about by tourism and/ or recreational use of an area. While in many ways this is an advance on determining a fixed level of use, mostly derived from the perceptions and preferences of a generally homogenous set of users, it is also vulnerable to favouring ever-increasing levels of use. As users and managers experience heavier use of an area, the characteristics of users, at least, may change, in that users who find heavier use levels unacceptable may cease to visit the area and will be replaced by those with higher tolerance of heavier use. This in turn may persuade managers that increased use is acceptable and that the resulting changes in the experience and to the environment are also acceptable. Such a situation can result in ever-increasing use until none of the original users of the area visit. In a commercial tourism destination this may not be a major problem if alternative markets are found and maintained, but in natural areas the new user populations may require and demand increased and, in some cases, inappropriate services and facilities. Those in control of tourist destinations are never as concerned about the issue of excessive numbers as are managers of natural and sensitive environments, where overuse (a commonly used phrase) is of growing concern and its effects on the natural environment are much more quickly observed and problematic (See Chapter 3).

In the often heavily human-created environment of most tourist resorts, crowding, overuse and congestion can sometimes be mitigated by additional development and enlargement of facilities, and if overall expenditure and employment increase at the expense of a minor loss of quality of experience, this is often felt a price necessary to pay. The situation may be different in destinations that were not initially focused on tourism but have become tourist destinations either by accident or in the absence of viable economic alternatives, as residents in these destinations perhaps have less positive attitudes towards tourism than residents of places created specifically for tourism.

There may well be different attitudes towards overtourism and excessive development between, on the one hand, residents in destinations relying on one or more unique threatened features, particularly natural environmental ones that are irreplaceable and, on the other hand, residents in destinations relying on created attractions that can be renewed or expanded if demand becomes excessive. Few, if any, destinations want to experience a decline in visitor numbers that might harm their image and reputation; this might be taken to represent the image of a destination out of favour with current potential visitors and the market in general, and a destination that is therefore entering the stagnation or decline stages of the TALC.

Thus, until matters became critical, Destination Management Organisations (DMOs) had little incentive to plan for limiting tourist numbers or halting development (Hall and Veer, 2016). In many cases, there were no effective or even nominal managers for most destinations. DMOs have traditionally been, and mostly still are, promotion-focused bodies charged with at least maintaining, if not increasing, visitor numbers (Dredge, 2016). In the past, if the destination was crowded at peak times, that was generally perceived by DMOs as desirable. It was thought that no-one would to want to visit a half-empty resort, unless they paid far less than the normal cost. Discounted prices are used to attract visitors at times when a resort is not full, normally early and late summer, before and after school holiday periods, in order to maintain a market large enough to justify keeping facilities open and staff employed.

Conclusion

While the original TALC model did not deal directly with overuse or overtourism, it did discuss overdevelopment of tourism and of tourism facilities and services, and the problems such developments might cause in the absence of effective and appropriate management. Such management has not been present in many destinations, and even in those destinations in which efforts have been made to contain development to appropriate forms and levels (see Chapter 9), success has not been permanent. Thus, many tourist destinations continue on a path of overdevelopment, often contrary to stated goals of sustainable development because of the ineffectiveness of attempted policies and interventions, as discussed elsewhere in the cases of Malta and Calvia (Dodds, 2007a, 2007b).

As a destination reaches the "stagnation" stage of its development, residential and formerly-commercial tourist properties are often sold to private individuals or companies and developed as second home properties. In the case of successful time-share operations, visitor numbers often exceed the numbers experienced when the property was a hotel, as property owners are more likely to come to their property outside of peak times. Time-share owners are highly likely to visit their property for their specific time period, at least some of which will be outside of the peak period, or rent that property to others, so occupancy rates can be significantly higher than for conventional accommodation properties. Much of this visitation is difficult, if not impossible, to record and to limit, however. As property owners, such individuals often have the right to vote in local elections and thus could prevent local legislation aimed at reducing the use of properties or curtailing visitor numbers. Thus, many deliberate actions and a considerable number of inactions (Dodds and Butler, 2009) combine to forestall steps that might mitigate or prevent overdevelopment and overtourism.

As noted above, overtourism can occur at a number of points in the TALC model of a destination's cycle of growth and potential decline, not simply at the final stage of growth. Thus, preparing for the spectre of overtourism and the problems warned of by Doxey (1975), Plog (1973) and Young (1973) is something that should be done at the earliest stages of the life cycle of any destination that values its long term viability as a place attractive to both tourists and residents alike. Perhaps understandably, many destinations in their initial stages of tourism development focus primarily, if not exclusively, on developing and growing a market, often with scant regard to the nature of the destination or its tourism in later years, but a lack of anticipatory planning and the setting of goals, also known as "path creation" (Gill and Williams, 2018), can leave many destinations facing an undesirable future in the later stages of their development. The call in the original TALC article (Butler, 1980) for the management of resources would appear to be well founded in the light of the appearance of overtourism.

References

Agarwal, S. (1994) The resort cycle revisited: Implications for resorts. In C. R. Cooper and A. Lockwood (Eds.), *Progress in Tourism Recreation and Hospitality Management*, Vol. 5. Chichester: Wiley, pp. 194–208.

Agarwal, S. (2002) Restructuring seaside tourism. The resort life-cycle, *Annals of Tourism Research*, 29 (1): 25–55.

An Foras Forbatha (1966) *Planning for amenity and tourism*. Dublin: Bord Failte.

Brougham J. E. and Butler, R. W. (1981) A segmentation analysis of resident attitudes to the social impact of tourism, *Annals of Tourism Research*, 8 (4): 569–590.

Butler R. W. (1975) Tourism as an agent of social change. In *Tourism as a Factor in National and Regional Development Occasional Paper 4*, Department of Geography. Peterborough, Canada: Trent University, pp. 85–90.

Butler, R. W. (1980) The concept of a tourist area cycle of evolution: Implications for management of resources, *The Canadian Geographer*, 24 (1): 5–12.

Butler, R. W. (1997) The concept of carrying capacity for tourism destinations: Dead or merely buried? In C. Cooper and S. Wanhill *Tourism Development environmental and Community Issues*. Chichester: Wiley, pp.11–22.

Butler, R. W. (2006a) *The Tourism Area Life Cycle Volume 1: Applications and Modifications*. Clevedon: Channelview Publications.

Butler, R. W. (2006b) *The Tourism Area Life Cycle Volume 2: Conceptual and Theoretical Issues*. Clevedon: Channelview Publications.

Butler, R. W. (2010) Carrying capacity in tourism: paradox or hypocrisy? In D. G. Pearce and R.W. Butler (Eds.), *Tourism research: A 20-20 vision*. Oxford: Goodfellow, pp. 53–64.

Butler, R. W. (2015) Tourism area life cycle. In C. Cooper (Ed.) *Contemporary Tourism Reviews*, Volume 1.: Woodeaton: Goodfellow Publishers, pp. 183–226.

Butler, R. W. and Brougham, J.E. (1972) The applicability of the asymptotic curve to the forecasting of tourism development. Paper presented to the Research Workshop, Travel Research Association 4th Annual Conference, Quebec City.

Butler, R. W. and Brougham, J. E. (1977) *The social and cultural impact of tourism: A case study of Sleat, Isle of Skye*. Edinburgh: Scottish Tourist Board.

Butler, R. W. and Hinch, T. (1989) The rejuvenation of a tourism centre: Port Stanley, Ontario, *Ontario Geography*, 32: 29–52.

Butler, R. W. and McDonnell, I. G. (2011) One man and his boat (and hotel and pier. . .)Henry Gilbert Smith and the establishment of Manly, Australia, *Tourism Geographies*,13 (3): 343–359.

Choy, D. (1992) Life cycle models for Pacific island destinations, *Journal of Travel Research*, 30 (3): 6–31.

Christaller, W. (1963) Some considerations of tourism location in Europe: the peripheral regions – underdeveloped countries – recreation areas, *Regional Science Association Papers*, 12, Lund Congress: 95–105.

Dodds, R. (2007a) Malta's tourism policy – Standing still or advancing towards sustainability? *Island Studies Journal*, 2 (1): 44–66.

Dodds, R. (2007b) Sustainable tourism and policy implementation: Lessons from the case of Calviá, Spain, *Current Issues in Tourism*, 10 (4): 296–322.

Dodds, R. and Butler, R. W. (2009) Inaction more than action: Barriers to the implementation of sustainable tourism policies. In S. Gossling, M. C. Hall and D. B. Weaver (Eds.), *Sustainable Tourism Futures*. London: Routledge, pp. 43–57.

Dodds, R. and Butler, R. W. (2010) Barriers to implementing sustainable tourism policy in mass tourism destinations, *Tourismos*, 5 (1): 35–53.

Doxey, G. V. (1975) A causation theory of visitor-resident irritants: Methodology and research inferences. *Conference proceedings of the 6th Annual Travel Research Association*. San Diego: Travel Research Association, pp. 195–198.

Dredge, D. (2016) Are DMOs on a path to redundancy? *Tourism Recreation Research*, 41 (3): 348–353.

Gill, A. and Williams, P. (2018) Transitioning towards sustainability in the mountain resort community of Whistler, British Columbia, *Tourism Recreation Research*, 43 (4): 528–539.

Hall, C. M., and Veer, E. (2016) The DMO is dead. Long live the DMO (or, why DMO managers don't care about post-structuralism), *Tourism Recreation Research*, 41 (3): 354–357.

Haywood, K. M. (1986) Can the tourist area life-cycle be made operational? *Tourism Management*, 7 (3): 154–167.

Krippendorf, J. (1987) *The holiday makers: Understanding the impact of leisure and travel*. London: Heinemann.

Lime, D. and Stankey, G. (1971) Carrying capacity: Maintaining outdoor recreation quality. In *Proceedings Forest Recreation Symposium*. Syracuse, NY: New York College of Forestry, pp. 171–184.

Lucas, R. C. (1964) The recreational carrying capacity of the Quetico-Superior area, *Forest Service Research Paper* LS-15. St. Paul: USDA.

McCartney, G. (2010) Stanley Ho Hung-sun: The 'King of Gambling'. In R.W. Butler and R.A. Russell (Eds.), *Giants of Tourism*. Wallingford: CABI, pp.170–181.

Meadows, D. H., Meadows, D. L., Randers, J. and Behrens, W.W. (1972) *The limits to growth*. New York: Universal Books.

Ogilvie, F. W. (1933) *The Tourism Movement*. London: Staples Press.

Plog, S. C. (1973) Why destination areas rise and fall in popularity. *Cornell Hotel and Restaurant Association Quarterly* 13: 6–13.

Russell, R. (2006) Chaos theory and its application to the TALC model. In R. W. Butler (Ed.), *The Tourism Area Life Cycle Volume 2 Conceptual and Theoretical Issues*. Clevedon: Channelview Publications, pp. 164–180.

Simmons, D. (1986) The socio-cultural impacts of tourism, *NZTP Social Research Series*. Wellington, NZ. Accessed November 2018 from https://core.ac.uk/download/pdf/92972993.pdf.

Stankey, G. H., Cole, D. N., Lucas, R. C., Peterson, M. E. and Frissell, S. S. (1985) The limits of acceptable change (LAC) systems for wilderness planning, *USDA Forest Service General Technical Report* INT-176. Ogden, UT: Intermountain Forest Experiment Station.

Stansfield, C. A. (1978) Atlantic City and the resort cycle: Background to the legalization of gambling, *Annals of Tourism Research*, 5 (2): 238–251.

Stansfield, C. A. and Rickert, J. E. (1970) The recreational business district, *Journal of Leisure Research*, 2 (4): 213–225.

Wagar, J. A. (1964) The carrying capacity of wild lands for recreation, *Forest Science*, Mongraph 7. Washington, DC: Society of American Foresters.

Wall, G. (1982) Cycles and capacity: Incipient growth or theory? *Annals of Tourism Research* 9 (2) 52–56.

Wang, X., Weaver, D. B., Li, X. and Zhang, Y. (2016) In Butler (1980) we trust? Typology of citer motivations, *Annals of Tourism Research*, 61: 216–218.

Wanhill, S. (1997) Introduction: Tourism development and sustainability. In C. Cooper and S. Wanhill (Eds.) *Tourism development: Environmental and community issues*. Chichester: Wiley, pp. xi–xvii.

Weaver, D. B. (1988) The evolution of a 'plantation' tourism landscape on the Caribbean island of Antigua, *Tijdschrift voor economische en sociale geografie [Journal of Economic and Social Geography]*, 79 (5): 319–331.

Wolfe, R. I. (1952) Wasaga Beach: The divorce from the geographic environment, *The Canadian Geographer*, 2: 57–66.

Young, G. (1973) *Tourism Blessing or Blight?* Harmondsworth: Penguin.

Part II: **Case studies**

The following part of the book comprises eight examples of overtourism, illustrating the widespread nature of the phenomenon, its characteristics and its causes. Two of the case studies, Thailand and the Philippines (Chapters 7 and 8), show the problems that emerge when a lack of control over development results in overdevelopment, which is accompanied by severe environmental problems. In such cases, the situation is made worse by extensive media promotion. In these cases, the solution to the issues was in the form of the closure of highly popular tourist areas.

Three examples are cities of considerable size (Barcelona, Venice and Prague, Chapters 9, 10 and 11), where one might expect tourist numbers to be relatively inconspicuous among residents, but this is clearly not the case. In Barcelona and a further chapter Prague (Chapter 11), the rental of residential accommodation by tourists has become a major problem in recent years despite efforts to counter this trend. While Venice has been exposed to tourism for centuries and negative opinions upon their presence noted over a century ago (Ruskin, 1980), the issues of crowding and problems of behaviour have been exacerbated by an increasing influx of cruise ship passengers and day visitors staying in hotels outside the city limits. In Prague and Barcelona, the presence of tourists staying in rental accommodation has been a major problem that has grown rapidly in recent years despite efforts to counter this trend. All these examples illustrate the problems faced when key enablers of tourism growth lie outside municipal control, cruise ports and hotels in the cases of Venice and Barcelona, and low cost airlines in the case of Prague. When looking at a smaller city such as Lucerne (Chapter 12), the issue is more specific. This case relates to the overly successful promotion of the town to a specific market, the Chinese, and the subsequent impacts on the town centre through coach traffic and pedestrian behaviour.

In the case of the Hajj (Chapter 13), a very different scenario is described, both in terms of the scale of the tourist numbers, millions of visitors in a very short period of time, and in terms of the obligatory and religious nature of the visits. In this case, it is not possible to close the site or to alter significantly the behaviour or the concentration of the visitors, nor the time at which the visitors come, which means that there are limited solutions to mitigate the problems. The key approach taken to reducing overtourism has been massive investments in infrastructure and facilities, which are implemented with religious and political sensitivities in mind.

The final case study (Chapter 14) examines overtourism in rural areas and reveals that although the scale, in terms of numbers of tourists and residents involved in such areas is very different to that in cities, many of the causes of overtourism are similar. In particular, a key factor enabling overtourism in all cases is the emphasis given to economic growth by national, regional and local authorities. Moreover, the lack of foresight is a common feature in many of the case studies. The case of the Isle of Skye illustrates what can happen when municipalities ignore or fail to anticipate tourist needs in terms of local facilities (public toilets, parking, etc.). Such capacity problems often goes hand-in-hand with an all-too-common tendency to ignore the concerns and opinions of local residents. The general failure of authorities at all levels to listen and respond to local concerns is a feature of many of the case studies.

The lack of foresight is a common feature in many of these examples. Cruise ships have long been seen as a potential problem because they create the problem of a large number of visitors being placed in a specific location over a very short time for a limited period. In addition, the visitors have limited mobility, in many cases limited knowledge of the destination and often spend relatively little in the centres they visit.

The popular news media carry accounts of overtourism on a regular basis, although not every example recently cited in media was portrayed in this book, as there are too many but the issues are similar and the examples in these chapters are neither unique nor overstated. The general failure of authorities at a number of levels to listen and respond to local concerns is a common feature. While some cities, such as Barcelona, have acknowledged the problem of overtourism and have taken action, the problem persists. While Barcelona started to formulate policies at the local level over a decade ago, the past two years have seen a marked increase in local complaints and demonstrations against tourism, suggesting that the problem is far from solved there. Other cities, such as Venice seem perpetually tied into local problems of disagreement, ineffectual actions and lack of clear goals as to how to resolve the problems faced.

Unfortunately there is little confidence to be drawn from these examples to conclude that governments and agencies at any level have found satisfactory solutions to mitigating or preventing overtourism. While the specific causes and symptoms of overtourism may vary from case to case, the overall effects and lack of progress on resolution remain depressingly common.

Reference

Ruskin, J. (1980) *The Stones of Venice*. Volume 2., J. Wiley & Sons. Chicago.

Reil G. Cruz and Giovanni Francis A. Legaspi

7 Boracay beach closure: the role of the government and the private sector

Introduction

In February 2018, Philippines President Rodrigo Duterte declared Boracay to be a "cesspool" that smelled of "human waste", and he soon afterwards placed the country's top tourist destination under a "state of calamity". The island was closed to tourist traffic from 26 April to 25 October 2018 in an effort to rectify problems accrued over decades of unbridled tourism growth and rampant violations of environmental and physical development guidelines. The shutdown drew mixed reactions from the island's stakeholders: residents, workers and investors, and incited lively debates about the implications for the tourism industry at the local and national levels.

This chapter will discuss the causes and effects of overtourism in Boracay, and the immediate antecedents that led to the island's temporary closure. In addition, this chapter will examine the issues brought about by the closure, and the efforts exerted by the government and the private sector during the closure, along with planned interventions to prevent previous problems from reappearing. Finally, the authors offer suggestions for avoiding the problems induced by overtourism in the future.

Background

Boracay is an island off the north-western tip of Aklan Province in the municipality of Malay in the Philippines. The island is situated 315 kilometres south of Manila and has an area of 10.32 square kilometres. Three of Malay's 17 *barangay* (villages, the smallest political unit) are located on the island. These are Balabag, Manocmanoc and Yapak. The island has 13 beaches, only three of which are well-known: White Beach, Bolabog Beach and Puka Beach (Boracay Go). In 2015 Boracay had a population of 32,267 (Philippine Statistics Authority, 2016a).

Boracay was catapulted to fame after German national Jens Peter wrote about it in the 1979 travel guide book, *Philippinen: Paradies für Globetrotter,* which was translated into English in 1981 for Lonely Planet Publications as *Philippines: A Travel Survival Kit.* As a result, tourism became established in Boracay and increased by nearly 25 times between 1995 and 2017, rising from just 81,197 visitors in 1995 to 2,001,974 visitors in 2017 (Department of Tourism; Aklan Provincial Tourism Office). Apart from a dip in arrivals in 1997 and 1998, following reports of a coliform contamination of the island's waters, tourist arrivals have grown steadily. The average annual growth rate between 1995 and 2017 was 17.24% (see Fig. 7.1).

https://doi.org/10.1515/9783110607369-007

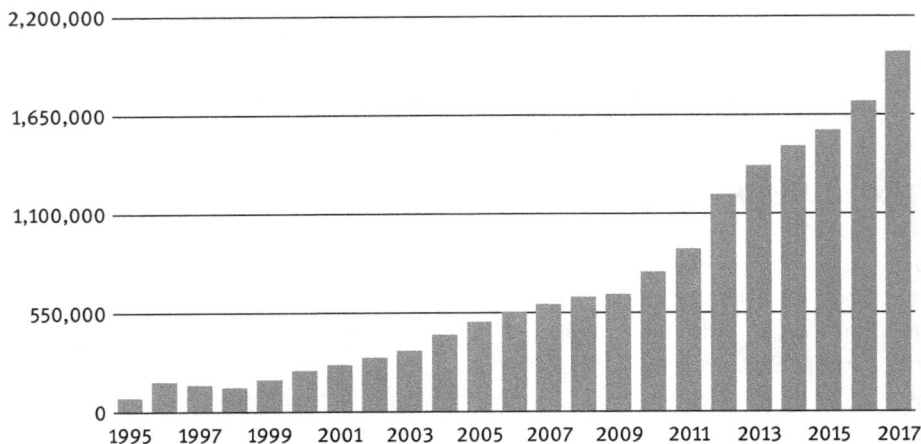

Fig. 7.1: Boracay tourist arrivals, 1995–2017 (source: Department of Tourism, and Aklan Provincial Tourism Office).

Over the years, both the government and the private tourism sector have featured Boracay heavily in tourism promotion campaigns, which successfully drew tourists to the island. The construction of an airport in Caticlan, Malay, and the opening of new areas for development under the Comprehensive Land Use Plan of Boracay also helped to increase tourism volume. Boracay was named Travel + Leisure Magazine's "Best Island" in 2012, and was ranked the top island in the world in the 2016 Condé Nast Traveler Readers' Choice Awards (Presidential Communications, 2018a).

Tourism has drawn both investors and people seeking employment to the island. In 2017, Boracay generated 17,737 direct tourism jobs or 66% of employment in the Western Visayas region (Burgos, 2018). In 2018 the National Disaster Risk Reduction and Management Council estimated that there were 17,328 registered local and foreign workers, and 19,289 unregistered workers in Boracay (Arboleda, 2018). And as of April 2018 there were around 2,600 tourism establishments in Boracay (Webb, 2018a). Tourism revenue was worth P56 billion (more than a billion US dollars) in 2017 (Aklan Provincial Tourism Office, 2018 personal communication).

Issues caused by overtourism

Overtourism in Boracay is evident from the sheer number of tourists and the densely packed structures lining the four-kilometre stretch of White Beach (see Fig. 7.2). At 6,859 persons per square kilometre, Boracay's population density is higher than that of Angeles City, the third highest of the highly urbanized cities outside Metro Manila (PSA, 2016b).

Fig. 7.2: Boracay Crowds (photo credit: Jungkyu Lee).

According to a Department of Environment and Natural Resources (DENR) study of the island's carrying capacity, the island can only accommodate 6,405 tourist arrivals per day (Arboleda, 2018), but during the peak month of April in 2017 the average number of daily arrivals was 7,774 persons (Tab. 7.1). Indeed, the island's carrying capacity was exceeded almost every month. Likewise, the number of hotels and resorts in Boracay (430) exceeded the carrying capacity, by 72.69% (Arboleda, 2018).

Tab. 7.1: Tourism numbers, by month in 2017 (source: Department of Tourism (DOT) Region VI, 2018).

January	169,843
February	174,183
March	167,445
April	233,233
May	202,755
June	159,708
July	153,791
August	144,065
September	124,872
October	139,856
November	158,332
December	173,891
	2,001,974

The primary reason the government closed Boracay down for six months in 2018 was that the excessive numbers of visitors had led to a host of health and environmental problems. Numerous independent studies (e.g. Takano, 2006; University of San Carlos (USC), 2006; Department of Environmental and Natural Resources Environmental Management Bureau (DENR-EMB), 2015; Japan International Cooperation Agency (JICA), 2016) had found the island waters to be contaminated with coliform. The DENR reported back in 1997 that Boracay's swimming area was contaminated with Escherichia coli. This bacteria, found in human faeces, can cause various diseases, including amoebiasis, typhoid fever, hepatitis A, gastroenteritis and ear infection.

According to the DENR, of the 2,600 establishments in Boracay, 32% (834) were discharging wastewater into the sea, but only 4% (118) had wastewater discharge permits (Pulido, 2018). Using radars, several underground pipes were discovered to be illegally discharging wastewater into the sand (Webb, 2018b). In 2016 the DENR reported that bacteria levels on Bolabog Beach close to a drainage pipe reached 47,460 MPN per 100 millilitres, which was 47 times the standard for recreational water safety: 1,000 MPN/100 ml (Dones, 2015). That same year, JICA found that untreated sewage was one of the key factors to blame for the decline in Boracay's coral cover, which shrank by 70.5% between 1988 and 2011 (Taruc, 2016).

Excessive groundwater extraction was another key issue. During the peak tourist season it would reach 2,300 cubic metres, which is far beyond the island's daily maximum capacity of 1,500 cubic metres (Senate, 2006). Not only was too much groundwater being extracted, but the groundwater was polluted. A study by the USC found that Boracay's groundwater was contaminated with bacteria and with seawater, due to over-extraction. Water pollution was being exacerbated by residents tapping into rainwater drainage pipes to evacuate their households' untreated sewage (Pulido, 2018; Failon, 2015).

Overtourism not only polluted seawater and groundwater, it also damaged the island's land, plants and animals. Of the nine original wetlands on the island, five have disappeared. The remaining four wetlands are occupied by business establishments (shops, resorts and boarding houses) and illegal settlers (De Guzman, 2018). Construction around the wetlands involves draining the wetlands and changing their hydrology: blocking outlets and preventing water from flowing in and out. Furthermore, the construction of hotels and other buildings leads to pollution of the wetlands with building materials. When wetlands are destroyed, the local population loses the benefits wetlands once provided, including protecting shores from wave action and preventing flooding (Scientific American, n.d.; De Guzman, 2018).

In 1997, Trousdale sounded the alarm that Boracay had already exceeded three of the six indicators of physical carrying capacity (ground water quality, ground water quantity, marine water quality, land, sewage and solid waste), while two more were unsustainable. In response to this warning, in the late 1990s the Department of Tourism (DOT) established the Boracay Task Force to address carrying capacity limitations. The Boracay Task Force was an ad-hoc committee spearheaded by the Secretary of Tourism and composed of national, regional and local bureaucrats and politicians, private sector, the Boracay Foundation and *barangay* captains (elected village heads) (Trousdale, 1999). The task force developed infrastructure for water, sewage and solid waste, as well as airports and jetties. But the island was already densely populated (Trousdale, 1999; Rey, 2018). The task force's actions may have had some benefits but in 2008 the DENR's Ecosystems Research and Development Bureau announced that Boracay would likely exceed its carrying capacity by 2010 or 2011 (Fernandez, 2008).

Factors contributing to overtourism

Overtourism in Boracay was a result of uncontrolled tourism development, which can be attributed to six main factors: lack of clarity regarding zoning, the government's failure to carry out its planning and regulatory functions, lack of law enforcement, the devolution of regulatory powers from the central to local government units, the governments' tendency to be reactive instead of proactive, and land use plans that encourage overdevelopment.

A key issue was the lack of clarity regarding the zoning classification of Boracay. This issue first arose in 1978 when a presidential decree declared Boracay as a tourist zone and maritime zone, and therefore government property (Presidential Communications, 2018a). Unfortunately, tourist zone and marine reserves were not recognized as land classifications by the Philippine Constitution as only four classifications of land existed: agricultural, forest or timber, mineral land, and national park (Presidential Communications, 2018a). Therefore, the land was classified as forest by default, which meant that any private individual could not own it. Private landowners on the island, however, countered this and in 1999 the appeals court ruled in favour of the landowners. Following further debate and appeals, in 2008 the Supreme Court affirmed Proclamation 1064 (Case Digests, 2010), which had been signed by the president in 2006 and which classified 40% (377.68 hectares) of Boracay as forest land (protected), and 60% (628.96 hectares) as agricultural land (alienable and disposable) (Government of the Philippines, 2006). The Boracay Comprehensive Land Use Plan, which was made possible due to the decision to affirm the validity of Proclamation No. 1064, could have rationalized the development of the island, but by then massive development had already taken place on the island. Much of the island had become residential and commercial areas, and more than 800 structures, including large hotels, had been built on Boracay's forest and agricultural land (The World Tonight, 2018).

While it was intended to protect Boracay, Proclamation 1064 opened the island to even further tourism development. Then DOT Secretary Joseph Ace Durano observed that the Supreme Court ruling facilitated "further classification of forest land into multi-use and no-use zones and the agricultural land into alienable and disposable" (ABS-CBN News, 2008). That is, by designating 60% of the island as agricultural land, the proclamation made most of the island alienable and disposable.

Related to the zoning issue was the second factor: the government's failure to carry out land surveys and implement a zoning plan. This has led to overtourism because even a decade after Proclamation 1064 was affirmed, no actual ground survey and zoning has been carried out (Presidential Communications, 2018). In the absence of zoning and land titles, tourism development has been difficult to regulate and the government could not uphold environmental laws.

Even when laws could be upheld, however, the government was not doing so. Indeed, the third factor contributing to overtourism in Boracay was the weak or non-existent enforcement of laws and regulations (Trousdale, 1999) and the failure on the part of the government to strictly follow procedures. For example, despite its planned location in a no-build zone (NBZ) a resort was allowed to go ahead by then DENR Secretary Joselito Atienza, allegedly upon the intercession of Senator Manny Pacquiao (Chanco, 2018). The resort in question has been operating since 2013, but as of 2018 still had no permit (Failon, 2018). Furthermore, although hefty fines of between USD 185 and USD 3,704 per day per infraction existed, violations continued unabated. For example, the DENR Boracay Office reported a total of 181 notices of violations involving 161 establishments in November 2018 (Failon, 2018). Additional issues are also a result of this. For example, between 90–115 tons of solid wastes were produced daily in Boracay but only 30 tons of waste could be hauled away (Presidential Communications, 2018).

A fourth factor in the rise of overtourism in Boracay was that the government had a tendency to be reactive instead of being proactive in terms of environmental safeguards. For example, a resort built on public land was only demolished because it was exposed on national television (Failon, 2018). The government also had a tendency to deny instead of confront problems. After tourist arrivals fell in the aftermath of the 1997 coliform report, DOT Secretary Mina Gabor attempted to allay public fears by swimming in the contaminated waters herself (Clemente, 2018). Similarly, in 2015 then Tourism Secretary Ramon Jimenez Jr. maintained that the overcrowding was exaggerated because "Filipinos feel that if you're within 10 feet [...] it's a crowded beach" (Burgos, 2015b).

A deeper reason for the uncontrolled development of tourism on Boracay was the devolution of the functions for regulating the tourism industry to the local government units as mandated by Republic Act 7160, otherwise known as Local Government Code of 1991. This handover of functions resulted in local government units (LGUs) taking on roles and tasks that were beyond their capacity, such as environmental management. Trousdale (1999) noted several challenges confronting the local government, including the failure to recognize the negative consequences of rapid tourism growth on the island, conflict between local groups, and inefficient *barangay* and municipal politicians who lacked accountability. Furthermore, the transfer of regulatory functions to the LGUs resulted in the Malay municipal government not fully implementing the DOT Boracay Tourism Master Plan, which had prescribed setback and building height guidelines. According to Maguigad (2013), the decentralization of tourism regulation to the local government units caught them unprepared in planning land uses that included tourism as a sector.

This lack of capacity was seen in the implementation of the National Tourism Development Plan of 2011–2016 (DOT, 2011). While the plan specified a "visitor management plan" as a sustainability indicator, in practice the DOT only collected statistics such as tourist arrivals and tourist receipts. This type of data created both pressures and incentives for the government and the private sector to prioritize mass tourism (which increases the figures for tourist receipts) over environmental concerns.

Closure of Boracay

Recognizing the seriousness of the health and environmental issues, in February 2018 DOT Secretary Wanda Teo backed the closure of non-compliant establishments on the island (Basa, 2018). On 4 April 2018, President Rodrigo Duterte went even further. In a surprise to the tourism industry, he signed Proclamation 475, which declared "a state of calamity" in Boracay and closed the island temporarily as a tourist destination (Government of the Philippines, 2018a). The closure was to cover the period 26 April to 25 October 2018. The signing followed pronouncements by the president that the island had turned into a "cesspool" (Ranada, 2018). President Duterte also created the Boracay inter-agency task force (ITF), which was given "the authority to reverse the degradation of the island" over a period of two years (Government of the Philippines, 2018b). The ITF is composed of the heads of the agencies listed in Tab. 7.2.

Tab. 7.2: The inter-agency task force.

Chair	Department of Environment and Natural Resources
Vice-Chairs	Department of the Interior and Local Government
	Department of Tourism
Members	Department of Justice
	Department of Public Works and Highways
	Department of Social Welfare and Development
	Department of Trade and Industry
	Tourism Infrastructure and Enterprise Zone Authority
	Philippine National Police
	Aklan Provincial Government
	Malay Municipal Government

With the closure of the island to tourism, non-residents, including tourists, were no longer allowed to access the island. Only residents who could show valid identification cards were allowed access. The three main objectives of the six-month hiatus were to rehabilitate Boracay's waste management systems, remove illegal structures and widen the roads. The government earmarked P4.2 billion (USD 77.8 million) for these tasks. Construction work was to include extension of utilities and sewerage facilities and the creation of walking paths and bike lanes. The DOT, through the Tourism Infrastructure and Enterprise Zone Authority (TIEZA), was given P1.1 billion (USD 20.4 million) to repair discharge pipes and sewerage lines (ABS-CBN News, 2018). The Department of Public Works and Highways (DPWH) brought in heavy equipment and personnel to demolish structures and widen the roads to provide pedestrian paths and bike lanes (Presidential Communications, 2018b).

Displaced workers, totalling 5,000, were to be given minimum wage assistance by the Department of Labor and Employment (DOLE), and the DOLE would implement livelihood programmes and provide assistance through the Tulong Panghanabuhay sa Ating [Disadvantaged and Displaced] (Tupad) Workers programme (Livelihood Assistance to Our Displaced Workers) (Ranada, 2018). In May, the Department of Social Welfare and Development (DSWD) requested P524 million (USD 9.7 million) for the implementation of its Cash-for-Work and Sustainable Livelihood programmes. The children of displaced workers were assisted by the Department of Education to transfer to other public schools. The DSWD also paid out a total of P7.1 million (USD 132 thousand) in transportation subsidies to displaced workers and residents of Boracay who decided to leave the island (Adel, 2018). In addition, the DOT was authorised to provide training modules worth P10 million (USD 185.2 thousand), which could be used by displaced workers and students who returned to their provinces (ABS-CBN News, 2018).

According to the Department of Interior and Local Government (DILG) Region 6 Office, P400 million (USD 7.4 million) was allotted for the Boracay Employment Adjustment Measures. At the same time, the Department of Trade and Industry (DTI) was authorised to extend small business loans to environmentally compliant businesses to enable them to pay off the loans they had taken out from loan sharks (ABS-CBN News, 2018).

The responses to the closure

Most responses to the closure by the private sector were negative. In a press briefing, Christine Ibarreta, President of the Hospitality, Sales and Marketing Association, said that the Boracay closure would have a severe and long-lasting impact on the Philippine economy because Boracay, the centrepiece of the nation's tourism industry, contributed 20% of all tourist revenues. Furthermore, she complained that the closure would affect 103,143 persons as well as their families and dependents (Leagogo, 2018). Ibarreta warned that it would take years for Boracay to recover after the closure. Jojo Clemente, the President of the Tourism Congress of the Philippines aired concerns for the small workers who would be deprived of their USD 5–10 daily income. He also lamented that even the "good Boracay" (environmentally compliant establishments) would not be spared. He remarked that,

> [i]t took years to have Boracay included in the tour programme of foreign travel agents and tour operators for 2018–2019, but with the closure the Philippines will lose out to other destinations. (Webb, 2018a)

Anabella Wiesnewski, the President of the Raintree Hospitality Group, which manages Coast Boracay Resort, expressed outrage at the closure, remarking that staff would not have an income but would still have a lot of expenses, and asked where staff would go to look for employment. She said that the root causes of the problems in Boracay were incompetence and corruption, and asked:

> Why did they allow this to happen? [Government officials] saw an opportunity to stuff their pockets so they allowed everyone to come in. They didn't enforce the laws. What happened to the environmental fees the tourists have been paying every year? Where did that go? [...] Why are we, the island stakeholders, paying for the government's own mistakes? (Arnaldo, 2018b)

The timing of the closure was difficult for many to accept. A sales and marketing director at a resort in Boracay remarked that the month of May is a particularly bad time to close because it is when La Boracay, the island's most popular event, is held. The closure resulted in many cancellations and created problems for those who already booked tickets. Functions like weddings, which in some cases had been booked more than a year in advance, were particularly problematic. Closure so close to the event also meant a multi-million peso revenue loss to tourism establishments on the island. In addition, the closure affected the incomes of tourism workers, tour guides, drivers and musicians. Some found odd jobs under the government's cash for work programme during the closure period, however (Adel, 2018).

The Boracay Foundation, which has over 150 members, including resorts, hotels, restaurants, water sports operators, airlines, banks, island organizations, residents and expatriates, released an official statement on their Facebook page expressing alarm about the President's decision to close Boracay. The Foundation said that the President had been misinformed by unverified data. The group maintained that most of the island's establishments had been complying with ordinances and regulations and they therefore saw the closure as unjust (Boracay Foundation, 2018).

Many residents, tourists and environmental groups complained about the lack of stakeholder consultation, and that they were not given time to comply with the new laws (Arab News, 2018). Some residents and tourists even asked the Supreme Court to issue a temporary restraining order against the closure, arguing that the closure was illegal in the absence of a law or order calling for the closure of the island and it violated the right to travel (Dipasupil, 2018).

Punongbayan (2018), a PhD candidate and teaching fellow at the University of the Philippines School of Economics examined water quality data and observed that Boracay's water was actually safer in 2017 than it was in 2012, as shown in Tab. 7.3, and felt that the island's poor water quality was therefore not a valid reason for the closure.

Tab. 7.3: Coliform levels, 2012–2017 (source: Punongbayan, 2018).

Year	Coliform level
2012	101.2 MPN/100ml
2017	8 MPN/100ml

Punongbayan suggested that the closure was a pretext to prepare the island for the entry of big hotels and casinos owned by Chinese and Chinese Filipinos, and asked why the government agreed to allow the construction of a 1,001 room beachfront hotel and mega-casino on a 23-hectare property. The Leisure and Resort World Group (a local partner of Galaxy) is rumoured to have been given a provisional license by the Philippine Amusement and Gaming Corporation and will open in three years (Punongbayan, 2018).

Not everyone was negative about the closure, however. The owner of Boracay West Cove was in favour of some aspects of the closure, remarking that "Everyone who has occupied wetland, timberland and easement will be discovered and should be held accountable" (Failon, 2018). A Canadian who had been a resident of Boracay for 30 years remarked that, "It's time to leave. Boracay has lost its soul, even if restored" (Arab News, 2018). He demolished his 10-year-old resort before leaving the island for good. Similarly, a hotel owner said that everyone should cooperate because the demolition could not be stopped anyway (Presidential Communications, 2018b). Another resort owner was hopeful that the closure would fix the problems on the island (Arab News, 2018). Some entrepreneurs responded to the closure by using it as an opportunity to refurbish their properties, and some of the bigger resorts retained their employees during the closure period. Other resorts established pop-up operations elsewhere, including in Metro Manila (Cabuag, 2018). A driver commented that he approved of the closure, and that he just needed to weather the situation (Presidential Communications, 2018b).

The way forward

On 26 October 2018, it was reported that the government had been able to meet its rehabilitation objectives and had reopened Boracay. DENR Secretary Cimatu told a news conference, "We have already done the first phase, this is the rehabilitation. There is no more cesspool" (The Straits Times, 2018).

Coastal water quality had improved and had passed a coliform test by the DENR EMB earlier in the year (Presidential Communications, 2018b). With new regulations in place, there would be zoning for the souvenir shops and for water sports, all public vehicles would be electric to minimise air and noise pollution and the main roads would be pedestrianized. Furthermore, non-tourism related businesses such as hardware stores would be relocated to the mainland, and fire dancers would be required to use light emitting diodes (LEDs) instead of kerosene (Webb, 2018b). There have also been a number of rules posted for visitors. The new rules include travelers needing to have booked with a DOT-accredited accommodation, and no more partying on the beach (McKirdy, 2018).

Prior to the reopening, Cimatu introduced the government's plan to establish a critical habitat zone in the north of the island (Webb, 2018b). As this is the location of several high-end resorts, these resorts therefore face the risk of demolition. Cimatu announced that giant companies: San Miguel Corporation (SMC), Aboitiz, Lopez Development Group, Lucio Tan Group and Cebu Pacific had volunteered to rehabilitate Wetlands 1, 2, 3, 4 and 6 (not in any particular order) (Webb, 2018b).

Cimatu also announced plans to relocate about 15,000 informal settlers from the wetlands to the Malay mainland (Arboleda, 2018). To this end, SMC is pushing the government to construct a bridge to link Boracay to Caticlan so that workers and tourists do not have to stay on the island overnight (Cabuag, 2018). However, Aklan Governor Florencio Miraflores has suggested building an all-weather port with a reliable and affordable ferry system to encourage workers to go back to the mainland every evening. In this regard, developers will be required to provide housing units for their workers on the mainland. Moreover, a master plan submitted by Palafox Associates (a design and architectural firm), to the Malay LGU in November 2017 may be implemented. The plan features modern infrastructure, such as glass-walled transportation terminals, electric vehicles and trams (Arab News, 2018).

In August Cimatu commented that his task force had a remaining lifespan of 1.5 years, and he hoped that an agency would take over the responsibilities of the task force at the end of its lifespan in order to sustain the improvements in Boracay (The Webb, 2018b).

Likewise, others have recommended creating a strong tourism authority to manage Boracay. In this case TIEZA could take over the Malay LGU's role of managing Boracay, as the LGU has proven to be incompetent. Suggested environmental measures include having a daily cap on visitors, like that being implemented at the Puerto Princesa Underground River in Palawan province. According to then Tourism Secretary Wanda Teo, tourists would have to wait at the Caticlan Port on mainland Malay in order not to overcrowd the island (Esmaquel, 2018).

Conclusions and recommendations

It can be concluded that overtourism in Boracay was a result of unchecked market forces along with government incapacity, and the exploitation of legal loopholes by tourism establishments. Furthermore, a paradigm based on volume rather than quality had framed the island's development and pushed the island towards overtourism. The closure proved that the government could impose its will for the common good. In order to stop further decline of the island, the national government may consider taking control over the entire island, so as to recover public lands from illegal structures and settlers, and maintain essential facilities, including for water treatment, water supply and solid waste management.

Moving forward, new areas should only be opened up when essential infrastructure is already in place. Boracay could remain a haven for the right kind of tourism (no party events and no casinos as per DOT Secretary Bernadette Romulo-Puyat) by focusing on quality visitors, rather than mass tourism. Development measures must focus not on expanding the capacity for tourism but rather on remaining within the island's ecological and social capacities. This should be reflected in the use of sustainable development indicators, instead of econometric measures of arrivals and receipts.

It is recommended that the government evict repeat violators and only allow establishments with a track record for sustainable development. The national government should primarily carry on the task of developing Boracay along sustainable principles, while developing the LGU's capacity to govern the island through technical assistance. Given that the private sector and ordinary citizens tend to abide by the rules when they are strictly enforced, enforcement is essential. Furthermore, environmental protection should not stop with the collection of fees from tourists. Tourists should be educated to behave responsibly.

Another recommendation is to repeat the closure in future. If Boracay were shut down on a regular basis, such as during the off-season each year, it would allow the island's ecosystems to regenerate. Such measures would be an effective way of protecting Boracay for future generations and are recommended in other small and sensitive tourist destinations in the country.

References

ABS-CBN News (2008) SC ruling paves way for new Boracay land use plan–DOT chief. *ABS-CBN News*, 13 October. https://news.abs-cbn.com/nation/regions/10/13/08/sc-ruling-paves-way-new-boracay-land-use-plan (Accessed 25 October 2018.)

ABS-CBN News (2018) Officials give updates on first day of Boracay closure, *ABS-CBN News*, 26 April. https://www.youtube.com/watch?v=_A6cRVtrxzg (Accessed 25 October 2018.)

Adel, R. (2018) Changing roles: How some residents are coping with Boracay closure, *Philstar Global*, 5 July. https://www.philstar.com/headlines/2018/07/05/1830941/changing-roles-how-some-residents-are-coping-boracay-closure (Accessed 25 October 2018.)

Aklan Provincial Tourism Office (2018) Boracay tourist arrivals and receipts, 2006–2017. 20 July, personal communication.

Arab News (2018) Philippines' tourist island Boracay shuts down for rehabilitation, *Arab News*, 25 April. http://www.arabnews.com/node/1291091/travel (Accessed 25 October 2018.)

Arboleda, V. (2018) Bilang ng mga hotels at resorts sa Boracay, mas higit sa naiulat na carrying capacity [Number of hotels and resorts in Boracay higher than reported carrying capacity], *UNTV News and Rescue*, 28 September. https://www.youtube.com/watch?v=OaGysZ6bR2I (Accessed 25 October 2018.)

Arnaldo, M. S. F. (2018a) Government addresses major problems in Boracay. *Business Mirror*, 1 February. https://businessmirror.com.ph/government-addresses-major-problems-in-boracay-3/ (Accessed 25 October 2018.)

Arnaldo, M. S. F. (2018b) Groups cry foul over planned closure of Boracay, *Business Mirror*, 17 March. https://businessmirror.com.ph/groups-cry-foul-over-planned-closure-of-boracay/ (Accessed 25 October 2018.)

Basa, M. (2018) Wanda Teo: 'High time' to shut down 200 erring establishments in Boracay, *Rappler*, 16 February, https://www.rappler.com/nation/196216-time-shut-down-erring-estab lishments-boracay-tourism-department-chief (Accessed 25 October 2018.)

Boracay Foundation (2018) Official statement of the Boracay Foundation Incorporated on President Duterte's statement on the closure of Boracay. https://www.facebook.com/BoracayFounda tion/posts/official-statement-of-the-boracay-foundation-incorporated-on-president-dutertes-/1235063939960386/ (Accessed 25 October 2018.)

Boracay Go (2018) 13 Boracay Beaches, *Boracay Go*, 30 September. http://www.boracaygo.com/boracay/beaches/ (Accessed 25 October 2018.)

Burgos, N. P. Jr. (2015a) Boracay coliform level prompts DENR warning, *Inquirer.net*, 10 February. https://newsinfo.inquirer.net/674082/boracay-coliform-level-prompts-denr-warning (Accessed 25 October 2018.)

Burgos, N. P. Jr. (2015b) Boracay not yet full, says DOT secretary, *Inquirer.net*, 23 June. http://news info.inquirer.net/700150/boracay-not-yet-full-says-dot-secretary (Accessed 5 April 2018.)

Burgos, N. P. Jr. (2018) The economic cost of Boracay, *Manila Standard*, 23 March. http://manilas tandard.net/mobile/article/261657 (Accessed 5 April 2018.)

Cabuag, V. G. (2018) Firms grin and bear it as 'Bora' closure marks one month. How about the workers? *Business Mirror*, 26 May. https://businessmirror.com.ph/firms-grin-and-bear-it-as-bora-closure-marks-one-month-how-about-the-workers/ (Accessed 25 October 2018.)

Case Digests (2010) DENR et al. vs. Yap et al., 11 November. https://vbdiaz.wordpress.com/2010/11/11/denr-et-al-vs-yap-et-al/ (Accessed 25 October 2018.)

Chanco, B. (2018) The Boracay test, *Philstar Global*, 19 March. https://www.philstar.com/busi ness/2018/03/19/1798027/boracay-test (Accessed 25 October 2018.)

Clemente, J. (2018) What to do with Boracay? *The Manila Times*, 17 February. https://www.manila times.net/what-to-do-with-boracay/380720/ (Accessed 25 October 2018.)

Davila, K. (2018) Interview with DOT Secretary Wanda Teo, Headstart, *ANC*, 11 April.

De Guzman, C. (2018) DENR: 5 of 9 Boracay wetlands damaged; 4 to be reclaimed, *CNN Philippines*, 4 March. http://cnnphilippines.com/news/2018/03/03/DENR-5-of-9-Boracay-wetlands-dam aged-4-to-be-reclaimed.html (Accessed 25 October 2018.)

Department of Tourism (DOT) (2011) The National Tourism Development Plan: Strengthening the Philippines Strategic Planning Process. 6th UNWTO Executive Training Program, 25–28 June 2011, Bhutan. http://asiapacific.unwto.org/sites/all/files/pdf/philippines_5.pdf (Accessed 25 October 2018.)

Dipasupil, W. (2018) SC asked to stop Boracay closure, *Philippine Star*, 26 April. https://www.phil star.com/headlines/2018/04/26/1809476/sc-asked-stop-boracay-shutdown (Accessed 25 October 2018.)

Dones, P. (2015) High levels of bacteria found in Boracay water – DENR, *Kicker Daily News*, 25 February. https://kickerdaily.com/posts/2015/02/high-levels-of-bacteria-found-in-boracay-water-denr/ (Accessed 25 October 2018.)

Esmaquel, P. II (2018) Philippines eyes limiting Boracay tourists after 6-month closure. *Rappler*, 11 April. https://www.rappler.com/nation/200002-philippines-plan-limit-boracay-tourists-clo sure (Accessed 25 October 2018.)

Failon, T. (2015) Failon Ngayon: Isla Bora, *ABS-CBN News*, 28 March. https://www.youtube.com/ watch?v=2BkQ5aSn8dI (Accessed 25 October 2018.)

Failon, T. (2018) Failon Ngayon: Burak-ay, *ABS-CBN News*, 10 March. https://www.youtube.com/ watch?v=IOGLL3X62F0 (Accessed 25 October 2018.)

Fernandez, R. A. (2008) Boracay nears carrying capacity. *Philstar Global*, 18 October. https://www. philstar.com/nation/2008/10/18/407984/boracay-nears-carrying-capacity (Accessed 25 October 2018.)

GMA News (2018) Interview with Jojo Clemente, President of the Tourism Congress of the Philippines. 4 April.

GMA News Online (2018). Boracay businesses dread lack of income during 6-month closure. *GMA News Online*, 5 April. http://www.gmanetwork.com/news/news/nation/649041/boracay-busi nesses-dread-lack-of-income-during-6-month-closure/story/ (Accessed 5 April 2018.)

Government of the Philippines (1975) Presidential Decree No. 705: Revising Presidential Decree No. 389, otherwise known as the Forestry Reform Code of the Philippines. *Official Gazette*. https://www.officialgazette.gov.ph/1975/05/19/presidential-decree-no-705-s-1975/ (Accessed 26 October 2018.)

Government of the Philippines (1978) Proclamation No. 1801: Declaring Certain Islands, Coves and Peninsulas in the Philippines as Tourist Zones and Marine Reserve under the Administration and Control of the Philippine Tourism Authority. *Official Gazette*. http://www.officialgazette. gov.ph/1978/11/10/proclamation-no-1801-s-1978/

Government of the Philippines (1991) Republic Act No. 7160, *Official Gazette*. https://www.official gazette.gov.ph/1991/10/10/republic-act-no-7160/ (Accessed 25 October 2018.)

Government of the Philippines (2006) Proclamation 1064: Classifying Boracay Island Situated in the Municipality of Malay, Province of Aklan into Forestland (Protection Purposed) and into Agricultural Land (Alienable and Disposable) Pursuant to Presidential Decree No. 705 (Revised Forestry Reform Code of the Philippines). *Official Gazette*. http://www.officialgazette.gov.ph/ downloads/2006/05may/20060522-PROC-1064-GMA.pdf (Accessed 26 October 2018.)

Government of the Philippines (2018a). Proclamation 475: Declaring A State of Calamity in the Barangays of Balabag, Manoc-Manoc and Yapak (Island of Boracay) in the Municipality of Malay, Aklan, and Temporary Closure of the Island as a Tourist Destination. *Official Gazette*. https://www.officialgazette.gov.ph/2018/04/26/proclamation-no-475-s-2018/ (Accessed 26 October 2018.)

Government of the Philippines (2018b) Executive Order No. 53: Creating a Boracay inter-agency task force, providing for its powers and functions and those of the member-agencies thereof, and other measures to reverse the degradation of Boracay Island. *Official Gazette*. http://www.officialgazette.gov.ph/2018/05/08/executive-order-no-53-s-2018/ (Accessed 26 October 2018.)

Leagogo, R. (2018) Boracay closure has 'massive, long-standing' implications, groups warn, *Inquirer.net*, 22 March. https://www.youtube.com/watch?v=YSuQ7Wqeqi0 (Accessed 26 October 2018.)

Lujan, N. C. (2003) Boracay's road to ruin, *Malaya News*, 20 January. http://web.archive.org/web/20030523190147//www.malaya.com.ph/jan20/news6.htm (Accessed 26 October 2018.)

Maguigad, V. M. (2013) Tourism planning in archipelagic Philippines: A case review,*Tourism Management Perspectives*, 7: 25–33.

McKirdy, E. (2018) Boracay reopens to tourism but its party days are over, *CNN Travel*, 26 October. https://www.cnn.com/travel/article/boracay-reopening-restrictions-intl/index.html (Accessed 13 November 2018.)

Philippine Daily Inquirer (2018) In the know: Facts about Boracay, *Philippine Daily Inquirer*, 3 April. http://newsinfo.inquirer.net/979688/in-the-know-facts-about-boracay#ixzz5OEaMoiRv (Accessed 25 October 2018.)

Philippine Statistics Authority (2016a) Population of Region VI – Western Visayas. https://psa.gov.ph/content/population-region-vi-western-visayas-based-2015-census-population (Accessed 25 October 2018.)

Philippine Statistics Authority (2016b) Philippine Population Density (Based on the 2015 Census of Population). http://www.psa.gov.ph/content/philippine-population-density-based-2015-census-population (Accessed 25 October 2018.)

Presidential Communications (2018a) Boracay, Naghihingalong Paraiso [Boracay, Paradise on the Throes of Death]. A Presidential Communications video. RTVM. 13 June. https://www.youtube.com/watch?v=C6laRC-Uqr0 (Accessed 25 October 2018.)

Presidential Communications (2018b) Changes in Boracay since President Duterte placed the island under a state of Calamity, 8 July. https://www.youtube.com/watch?v=7hN4XkoaxsM (Accessed 25 October 2018.)

Pulido, M. (2018) Isla ng Boracay: Unti-unti na nga bang namamatay? [Boracay Island: Slowly dying?] *GMA Public Affairs*, 22 February. https://www.youtube.com/watch?reload=9&v=Sz5B-RDAeOA (Accessed 25 October 2018.)

Punongbayan, J. C. (2018). The glaring double standard in Duterte's Boracay shutdown, *Rappler*, 22 March. https://www.rappler.com/thought-leaders/198704-double-standard-duterte-order-boracay-closure (Accessed 25 October 2018.)

Quintos, P. (2017) Time to limit the number of tourists in Boracay: experts, *ABS-CBN News*, 18 May. https://news.abs-cbn.com/focus/05/18/17/time-to-limit-number-of-tourists-in-boracay-experts (Accessed 25 October 2018.)

Ranada, P. (2018) Cheat Sheet: What to expect from the Boracay closure, *Rappler*, 5 April, https://www.rappler.com/nation/199623-cheat-sheet-what-expect-boracay-closure (Accessed 25 October 2018.)

Rey, A. (2018) Is the government prepared for Boracay's closure? *Rappler*, 8 April. https://www.rappler.com/nation/199746-government-preparation-boracay-closure (Accessed 25 October 2018.)

Rey, A. (2018). Boracay Water completes sewerage system connecting 2 treatment plants, *Rappler*, 10 May. https://www.rappler.com/nation/202200-boracay-water-sewerage-completed (Accessed 25 October 2018.)

Scientific American (n.d.) Why Are Wetlands So Important to Preserve? *Scientific American*. https://www.scientificamerican.com/article/why-are-wetlands-so-important-to-preserve/ (Accessed 25 October 2018.)

Senate Economic Planning Office (2006) Tourism as a Development Strategy, *Policy Insights*, PI-01–06. https://www.senate.gov.ph/publications/PI%202006-01%20-%20Tourism%20as%20a%20Development%20Strategy.pdf (Accessed 25 October 2018.)

Supreme Court (2008) *Decision: General Register No. 167707*. http://sc.judiciary.gov.ph/jurisprudence/2008/october2008/167707.htm (Accessed 25 October 2018.)

Takano, M. (2006) *Boracay Environmental Infrastructure Project*. Tokyo: Nomura Research Institute. https://www.jica.go.jp/english/our_work/evaluation/oda_loan/post/2006/pdf/project16_full.pdf (Accessed 27 May 2008)

Taruc, P. (2016) Bye-bye Boracay? Island 'highly endangered' – JICA, *CNN Philippines*, 5 January. http://cnnphilippines.com/regional/2015/06/04/boracay-highly-endangered-jica-2015.html (Accessed 25 October 2018.)

The Editorial Team (2017) A systemic analysis of overtourism and tourismophobia: And what destinations can do about it, *The Place Brand Observer*, 17 November. https://placebrandobserver.com/overtourism-tourismophobia-causes-solutions/

The Straits Times (2018) Cleaner, leaner Boracay welcomes tourists back after makeover, *The Straits Times*, 26 October. https://www.straitstimes.com/asia/se-asia/philippines-spruced-up-boracay-re-opens-with-new-rules (Accessed 26 October 2018.)

The World Tonight (2018) What Cimatu found in Boracay wetlands, *ABS-CBN News*, 9 March. https://news.abs-cbn.com/video/news/03/09/18/what-cimatu-found-in-boracay-wetlands (Accessed 26 October 2018.)

Trousdale, W. J. (1997) Carrying capacity considerations: The need for managing change in a unique tourism destination (Boracay Island Philippines). Vancouver: EcoPlan International. http://epiconsulting.ca/Downloads/carrying_capacityboracay.pdf (Accessed 25 October 2018.)

Trousdale, W. J. (1999) Governance in context: Boracay Island, Philippines. *Annals of Tourism Research*, 26(4),840–867. https://dirp4.pids.gov.ph/popn_pub/governance_boracay.pdf (Accessed 25 October 2018.)

Villanueva, R. (2018) Bike lanes, walkways to be built in Boracay, *Philstar Global*, 12 May. https://www.philstar.com/headlines/2018/05/12/1814474/bike-lanes-walkways-be-built-boracay#oOuI8DXPJxChMBAx.99 (Accessed 25 October 2018.)

Webb, P. (2018a) Interview with Jojo Clemente, *CNN Philippines*. 6 April. https://www.youtube.com/watch?v=JDtjbE8hyZo (Accessed 25 October 2018.)

Webb, P. (2018b) Interview with Roy Cimatu, *CNN Philippines*, 12 August. https://www.youtube.com/watch?v=kk4a6uucR9w (Accessed 25 October 2018.)

Janto S. Hess
8 Thailand: too popular for its own good

Introduction

The Kingdom of Thailand is one of the most popular destinations in Southeast Asia. The "Land of Smiles" attracts visitors with its diverse landscape of mountains and islands, beaches, excellent food, a year-round favourable climate and a welcoming society. These attractions, in combination with easy accessibility through relaxed visa regulations and its strategic marketing campaigns, have led to sustained tourism growth in recent decades, resulting in Thailand becoming known as a low-cost mass tourism destination. In 2017 Thailand, a country with a population of 68.9 million people, received more than 35 million visitors (Jing Travel, 2018).

While the growth in tourism was economically benefitting and triggering infrastructure developments (including roads, health facilities and service sectors), the large numbers of visitors and the concentration of tourism at certain hotspots led to environmental damage and social conflict. The various issues from the general lack of regulation of tourism have led to debates over the carrying capacities of certain destinations within Thailand and the desired future development pathway for the tourism sector.

"Overtourism" is an increasingly common theme in newspaper articles, which describe overcrowded beaches (e.g. Phi Phi Island and the Similan Islands), widely unregulated development and record-breaking group tours (e.g. between 2,000 and 3,000 Chinese travelling together in Pattaya). While most stories are negative, some articles highlight proactive action by the government to preserve natural resources through closures (seasonal or permanent) of attractions, islands and national parks, and attempts to diversify visitor flows. These actions have, however, been criticised for not being sufficiently comprehensive.

This chapter discusses the recent pattern of tourism development in Thailand, how the continuous growth in visitor numbers has tested carrying capacities at some sites, and what kind of approaches are being taken to mitigate the negative impacts of overtourism.

Tourism development in Thailand

Thailand is located in Southeast Asia and shares land borders with Cambodia, Laos, Malaysia and Myanmar. The country has several distinct geographical areas, with mountainous highlands in the northwest, the Khorat Plateau in the north-east, the predominantly flat area around the Chao Phraya river, and a long stretch of land in

https://doi.org/10.1515/9783110607369-008

the south that is bordered by two seas: the Gulf of Thailand and the Andaman Sea (Indian Ocean). This southern area, along with the 936 islands within Thailand's territory, contributes to the nation's extensive coastline of 3,219 kilometres (Nations Encyclopedia, 2018). The islands and coastline are a key tourist attraction.

The country has a total population of 68.9 million (2016); around 15 million of which live in the Bangkok metropolitan region (National Statistical Office, 2016). Between 1985 and the Asian financial crisis in 1997, Thailand experienced a period of high economic growth – averaging around 12% per year. Since 2010, growth has fluctuated between 0.8% and 7.5% per annum, with some striking correlations appearing between political turmoil and economic growth (World Bank, 2018). In 2017, with a gross domestic product (GDP) of 455,221 billion USD (World Bank, 2018), Thailand was the second-largest economy in Southeast Asia. It is categorised as an upper middle-income country (or an "emerging economy"). In 2017, tourism contributed 21.2% (or USD 95 billion) of Thailand's GDP and provided 15.5% (5,834,000 jobs) of total employment opportunities, making it the most important service sector in the country (World Travel and Tourism Council, 2018). This total contribution comprises direct, indirect, and induced income generated through the tourism sector. Thus, the local economy depends heavily on tourism, particularly in coastal regions.

Tourism started to become an important economic sector during the Vietnam War, when Thailand became a rest and recreation destination for United States military forces (Nimmonratana, 2000; Suntikul 2013). The significant revenue from tourism in subsequent years led to recognition by the Thai government of the sector's potential. In 1960, the government established the Tourism Authority of Thailand (TAT) as an official organisation to promote the sector (McDowall and Wang, 2009). Eleven years later, tourism was recognised as an integral part of Thailand's (fourth) National Economic and Social Development Plan 1972–1981 (Ministry of Tourism and Sports, 1991). This laid the foundation for the promotion of tourism and influenced policy-making processes with all subsequent development plans including tourism.

In its early days, tourist arrivals increased steadily, rising from 3.4 million in 1980 to 4.8 million in 1989 (Chon et al., 1993) and additional boosts in growth were achieved through successful marketing campaigns. In 1991 and 1992 factors such as high airfares and room prices, and an oversupply of hotel rooms, led to a drop in Thailand's tourism competitiveness compared to alternative destinations, with package tours from Europe being approximately 20 percent more expensive in Thailand than in other destinations in Southeast Asia (Chon et al., 1993). In addition, negative media coverage about regional political unrest, Thailand's sex industry, the AIDS epidemic and environmental destruction damaged the country's reputation and many visitors chose alternative destinations (McDowall and Wang, 2009; Li and Zhang, 1997). Thailand has since struggled to free itself from this negative image and many continue to associate Thailand with the sex industry (Nuttavuthisit, 2007; Rittichainuwat, 2006; Tapachai and Waryszak, 2000). Henkel et al. (2006) confirmed these findings when they surveyed tourists and locals about their image of Thailand and discovered that "friendly people", "Thai culture" and "food" led to strong associations with Thailand from both tourists and locals, but tourists also strongly associated Thailand with "nightlife and entertainment".

Throughout the 1990s and early 2000s, Thailand's tourism industry experienced continuous growth triggered by increasing foreign investment in tourism infrastructure. In the two decades between 1997 and 2017 international tourist arrivals saw an increase of approximately 485% (Fig. 8.1).

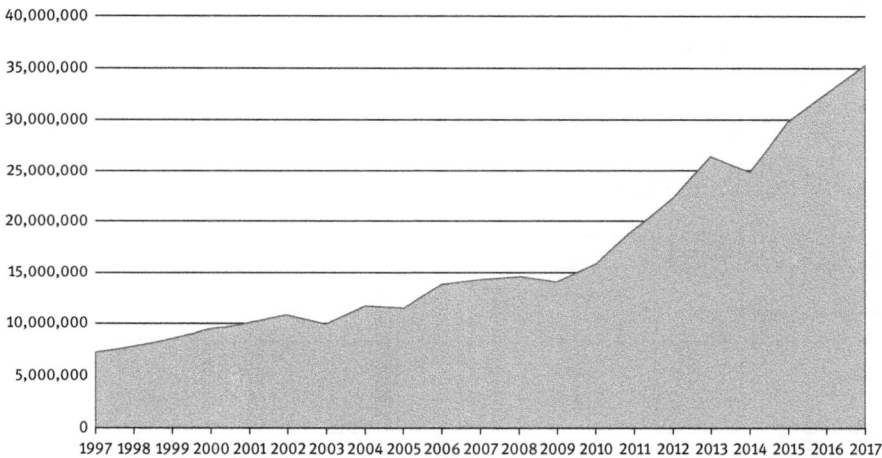

Fig. 8.1: International tourist arrivals in Thailand, 1997–2017 (source: Ministry of Tourism and Sports, 2018).

With the negative consequences of growth in tourism becoming increasingly visible, in 1995 the Thai government began commissioning reports on environmentally and socially compatible tourism (e.g. ecotourism). While the intention and direction of these reports and work was appreciated, they were criticised for being vague, weak and meaningless (Kontogeorgopoulos, 1999).

In 2004, the Andaman sea coast of Thailand, along with its extensive tourism infrastructure, was hit by a tsunami (McDowall and Wang, 2009) killing 5,395 people, nearly half of which were foreigners (Rittichainuwat, 2006). Visitor numbers consequently dropped in 2005, but recovered in the following year.

In 2012, the Government of Thailand released its first National Tourism Development Plan 2012–2016 (Royal Thai Embassy Singapore, n.d.). The plan supported the establishment of eight tourism clusters and sought a growth rate of more than

15% (Ministry of Tourism and Sports, 2017). This plan suffered a setback in 2013 and 2014 due to a military coup, resulting in a drop of around 6.6 percent in visitor numbers (Ministry of Tourism and Sports, 2017). In response, the TAT launched the "Discover Thainess" campaign in the same year and tourism numbers rebounded. Since 2015, visitor numbers have experienced continuous growth and have broken all previous records.

In 2018, the country attracted more international visitors than all similar destinations in Southeast Asia and arrivals were projected to reach 40 million visitors that year (see Fig. 8.2).

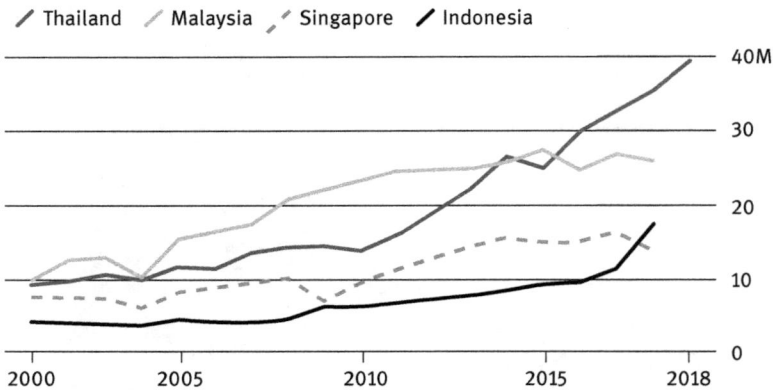

Fig. 8.2: International arrivals for selected countries, 2000–2018 (source: Jagtiani and Chuwiruch, 2018).

Tourism is not evenly spread across Thailand. In 2015 the majority of tourists (77% of total arrivals) visited the southern region, while only 1.4 million (5%) visited the northern region (Ministry of Tourism and Sports, 2017). This shows the preference of visitors for the beach and sun, and highlights the extent to which tourists are concentrated at certain "hotspots". With ever-increasing visitor numbers, this concentration of tourism will inevitably test the carrying capacities and the local infrastructure of some destinations and will lead to negative cultural and environmental impacts. Thailand's tourism minister Weersak acknowledged the destructive potential of an expanding tourism sector saying, "Tourism can create, and at the same time, tourism can disrupt". While he supports further increases in visitor numbers, he believes this must be in combination with improved management as well as diversification of visitor flows, and has referred to some European countries as examples of best-practice (Jagtiani and Chuwiruch, 2018).

Factors contributing to overtourism

This section discusses three of the main factors that have led to overtourism in Thailand. One factor is that Thailand has featured in many popular international films, including "The Man With The Golden Gun" (1974), "Tomorrow Never Dies" (1997), "The Beach" (2000), "Lost in Thailand" (2012) and "The Hangover 2" (2011) (Nam, 2018). Several of these movies feature Thailand's islands and beaches (Law et al., 2007), while others were filmed in Bangkok. The promotional effect of such movies has been considerable, and the films have attracted visitors to the specific places featured in the films, including Phang Na Bay, Koh Phi Phi and the rooftop bar at Lebua State Tower in Bangkok, which is nowadays widely-known as the "Hangover Sky Bar" because it was featured in "The Hangover 2". Likewise, the Chinese movie "Lost in Thailand", filmed in Chiang Mai, led to a massive surge in Chinese visitors to that city, with the result that each year up to 200,000 Chinese tourists visit sites in Chiang Mai where the movie was filmed. Indeed, one of the sites, Chiang Mai University, has become a "must-see destination" and attracts up to 500 Chinese visitors a day, many of whom rent or buy student uniforms to pose for pictures in (Cohen, 2017). The transformation of the university into a tourist attraction has disrupted classes and led to extensive littering on campus.

A second factor leading to overtourism is the easing of visa regulations. Thailand was one of the first countries in the region to ease visa regulations for Chinese citizens. As a result, the number of Chinese visitors increased by 1,032% over 11 years, rising from approximately 950,000 arrivals in 2006 to 9.8 million in 2017 (Jing Travel, 2018; Cohen, 2017). This has resulted in the overuse of infrastructure. For example, the two international airports of Bangkok: Don Mueang and Suvarnabhumi, are run at 40% over their designed capacity (Chuwiruch, 2017).

A third factor is the concentration of tourists in certain areas. Most visitors in Thailand visit the same regions, national parks and islands, putting significant pressure on the local host communities and ecosystems. Overcrowded tourism "hotspots" include the Similan Islands and some islands of the Phang Nga Bay archipelago. An estimated 10,000 guests visit the Phi Phi Islands each day during the high season (GoKohPhiPhi, 2007). The famous 'Maya Bay' (on Koh Phi Phi Leh) with its roughly 200 metre long beach, became a tourist hotspot after it served as a set for "The Beach". In 2016 visitor numbers to that beach reached 5,000 tourists per day, with many tourists commuting from nearby destinations such as Phuket, Krabi and Koh Phi Phi (Fig. 8.3). Given the overcrowding, many tour operators have begun offering "early bird tours" and opportunities to sleep on a boat close to the bay, so as to give their guests the chance to enjoy the beach in the mornings for a few moments before being surrounded by hundreds of other tourists.

Fig. 8.3: Maya Bay beach (photo credit: Janto Hess).

Issues related to overtourism

The continuous growth of tourism has been a driver of development and although it had led to some improvements in infrastructure and job creation, tourism is also being rejected by many communities due to the negative impacts (McDowall and Choi, 2010). For example, a study in Chiang Mai and Chiang Rai (in northern Thailand) found that, overall, local communities had negative attitudes towards tourism. Among other reasons, this is because of tourism's damaging impact on the environment, its contribution to increasing crime rates and communal conflict, and because the industry only provides low-paid jobs for local residents (Untong, 2007).

A key issue related to overtourism is the intrusive and inappropriate behaviour of many of the visitors. Most visitors come from cultural backgrounds that differ greatly from that in Thailand and have different behavioural norms, and when such visitors arrive in large numbers these differences often lead to discomfort among the local population.

A particular problem of this kind is the recent phenomenon of travellers begging for money, selling small items and busking on the streets of Thailand's larger cities. This "beg-packers" behaviour led to a massive outcry in Thai society and international criticism of privileged foreigners asking the Thai population to finance their holidays (Spinks, 2018; Coffey, 2017). This heightened the already negative attitude towards backpackers in Thailand, who have long been criticised for their low level of spending and anti-social behaviour. Backpackers tend to spend little while leaving the same amount of trash as higher-spending tourists and also tend to be more disruptive in terms of noise and drunken behaviour in host communities.

The behaviour of Chinese and Russian visitors has also been highly criticized by local residents and the Thai media (Pack Thailand, 2018; Bohwongprasert, 2015). While many nationalities break Thai taboos, the Thai public's reaction to these tourists has been particularly harsh. Chinese travellers, in particular, have been censured for spitting on the street and disrespecting religious sites and symbols, and for their messy dining habits (Eade, 2015; Parameswaran, 2015). The harsh reaction to Chinese visitors is perhaps due to the especially rapid influx of Chinese tourists over a very short period of time. In an attempt to address this issue, the TAT published an etiquette manual in Mandarin targeting Chinese visitors and set up large billboards in Bangkok reminding all visitors that Buddha images and religious symbols should be treated with respect, e.g. should not be used as tattoos (Eade, 2015).

Another problem associated with Chinese tourists is that they have so far tended to travel on organised group tours, with the result that large numbers of tourists are concentrated together (Bangkok Post, 2011a). Some group sizes have reached record-breaking proportions. For example, in 2015 one Chinese company invited all of its staff and regular customers on a trip to Bangkok and Pattaya. They travelled in groups of between 2,000 and 3,000 people, using 400 coaches to accommodate them and held a banquet for 3,935 people at a leading hotel in Pattaya (Cohen, 2017).

A particular problem with Chinese group tours is that such tours generally bring in very little revenue for Thailand as operators tend to take such groups to restaurants, accommodation and shopping malls that are co-owned by Chinese, with the result that profits do not remain in the country. These tours have therefore been labelled "zero-dollar tours". Furthermore, operators only take the tourists to designated shops that pay the guides sales commissions (Bangkok Post, 2011b). Indeed, it is not uncommon for Chinese visitors to be forced to go shopping and to become the targets of scams (Cohen, 2017). Operators of zero-dollar tours are also targeting other nationalities (e.g. Russians and Koreans). Recognizing the lack of financial benefits for Thailand and the negative impacts of these mass group tours, the Thai authorities have attempted to crack down on them, but have so far been unsuccessful as these tours operate in a legal "grey area" and the identification of such tours is challenging (Jing Travel, 2018). In recent years, however, more Chinese visitors have begun travelling independently, which has brought some economic benefits to Thai tourism operators. The Tourism Authority of Thailand has welcomed this trend and intends to promote it, as independent travellers tend to spend more than package tour visitors (Bangkok Post, 2011a).

Another key issue related to overtourism is the congestion it causes. Bangkok is an over-crowded city and is made even more so by excessive numbers of tourists. In 2017 it was ranked the second-most congested city in terms of traffic globally (TomTom Traffic Index, 2017). Over-crowding is increasingly frustrating locals and it is likely that rising visitor numbers will heighten tensions. Recognizing this, a Thai Travel Agents Association spokesperson, Thongyoo Suphavittayakorn, pointed to the need to consider local carrying capacities and remarked that "the problem with the Thai government is they want to increase the number of visitors, but they don't stop to check first if we're able to accommodate them" (The Straits Times, 2017).

Congestion is not only a problem in Bangkok, it is a feature of all tourism hotspots in Thailand, including those in national parks. Maya Bay on Koh Phi Phi Leh, for example, is part of the Had Nopparat Thara-Mu Ko Phi Phi National Park. The park was established in 1983 and covers a marine area of 325 square kilometres (Christiernsson, 2003). Its status as a national park has not protected it from the impacts of tourism, however. The national parks in Thailand are officially administered by the Department of National Park, Wildlife and Plant Conversation (DNP), whereas on Koh Phi Phi Don and some other islands private property rights exist due to historic claims, which are widely accepted by public authorities. Koh Phi Phi Don has a total area of 12.25 km^2 and is another tourism hotspot that has experienced overtourism. Its topography is unusual as the island is split in two parts that are connected by a narrow flat sandy strip. This topography led to the development of nearly the entire infrastructure (village, accommodations, restaurants, etc.) of the island on the sandy strip that connects the two hilly limestone islands, as well as gives access to the beaches of Ton Sai Bay and Loh Dalum Bay. The island's population in 2013 was 2,500 people, whereas it can be assumed that the actual population figure is higher when considering seasonal workers and those who were considered gypsies. Increasing numbers of tourists and unregulated tourism development on Koh Phi Phi Leh and other islands have led to many environmental issues (Dodds, 2010), including severe pollution, and have disturbed and damaged the marine ecosystems (Wongthong and Harvey, 2014; Yeemin et al., 2006; Wonga, 1998).

Studies of reef ecosystems in other areas of Thailand (e.g. Hoeksema et al., 2013; Chavanich et al., 2012; Tanzil et al., 2009) have shown that the increasing numbers of divers and snorkelers are putting significant pressure on reef ecosystems as these visitors inevitably disturb and destroy marine animals and plants (e.g. Wongthong and Harvey, 2014; Flumerfelt, 2000; Yeemin et al., 2006). Particularly damaging to marine biodiversity are boats with outboard motors, especially when reckless drivers accelerate above coral reefs in shallow water. According to observers, as many as 100 boats, including traditional longtail boats, can be found in Maya Bay by 11am, even in low season (Heaver, 2018).

Thailand has also seen massive land-based environmental impacts as a result of tourism development. Due to the relatively smaller space, islands are particularly vulnerable to impacts related to extensive infrastructure developments and high visitor numbers. The waste water and solid waste created by tourists is a particular issue in such closed ecosystems. Some islands already ship solid waste generated by tourists to the mainland (e.g. Thepgumpanat and Tanakasempipat, 2016; Nara et al., 2014; Weterings, 2011; Kontogeorgopoulos, 2004). This is a difficult issue for small destinations, such as Koh Phi Phi Don, which attracts a large numbers of low-cost visitors (backpackers) and day tourists. If eight visitors are squeezed into one room (dormitory), instead of only two guests elsewhere, it is apparent that they generate four times as much waste and waste water per room.

Response strategies to overtourism and changing development aspirations for Thailand's tourism industry

The rapid growth of Thailand's tourism industry, without adequate measures to mitigate associated risks, jeopardises not only the local environment but also potential future economic benefits. According to marine expert Thon Tamrongnawasawat, about 77% of coral reefs in Thailand have been damaged by overtourism (Bangkok Post, 2018). The Thai government and tourism stakeholders have recognised the negative social and environmental impacts of overtourism and have begun to address them.

One recent measure was the media-effective closure of Maya Bay to tourists in recognition of the limits of the bay's carrying capacity (Coldwell, 2018). After an initial closure of three months, Thailand's government announced in October 2018 that the Bay continues to be prohibited for tourists until the ecosystem 'fully recovers to a normal situation' (Ellis-Petersen, 2018). While the Maya Bay closure made international headlines, the seasonal closure of attractions for environmental protection is not rare in Thailand. In 2018, the Department of National Parks, Wildlife and Plant Conservation (DNP) closed sites in 66 out of Thailand's 147 national parks either for the season or permanently (The Nation, 2018). These sites include 24 entire islands (five of which were permanently closed), 53 waterfalls, 17 caves, 11 trails and 43 other sites (e.g. temples, summits and Rafflesia kerrii flower sighting areas). Most attractions are closed during the entire rainy season (for between four and five months) so as to give their ecosystems time to recover. Tunya Netithammakul, the Director General of the Department of National Parks, Wildlife and Plants Conservation, remarked that such closures are needed in order to "allow the rehabilitation of the environment both on the island and in the sea ... before the damage is beyond repair" (Holmes, 2016).

Such measures have, however, highlighted tensions between environmental, social, and economic considerations. Often, economic considerations are ranked more highly. For example, a spokesperson of Thailand's government noted in 2015 that due to the economic importance of tourism, Thailand had to tolerate the bad behaviour of tourists (Lefevre, 2015). However, a change of thinking may now be underway. Thon Tamrongnawasawat, who became famous as the driving force behind the closure of Maya Bay indicated such a change when he observed the following:

> In the past, we made some mistake because we think that the money is very important. But now we are trying to change our idea. [. . . Overseas visitors are] very important to our country, but the most important thing is our national resource. (Vejpongsa, 2018)

The effectiveness of measures to temporarily close sites is questionable, however, if visitors are allowed to flood the sites once again after restrictions are lifted. Accordingly, it is necessary to either keep them closed or keep tourist numbers down. Professor Bob McKercher, an expert in regional tourism development, has proposed three measures to keep visitor numbers down and minimize pressure on popular sites: (i) the introduction of higher entrance fees; (ii) stricter policing of behaviour and enforcement of fee payment; and (iii) quotas to limit the total number of visitors per day (Heaver, 2018). All of these measures are expected to be implemented in Maya Bay in case it will reopen to tourists. It was discussed that a reopening of the bay will be accompanied by a likely increase of national park entry fees, a restriction of boats to enter the bay and a mandatory anchoring at a floating platform on the other side of the island, as well as a limitation of visitor numbers to 2,000 visitors per day (The Phuket News, 2018).

Another measure being implemented to address overtourism is to geographically diversify visitor flows through community based tourism and similar means. As Jiraporn Prommaha, the Director of the International Affairs Division at the Thai Ministry of Tourism and Sports, remarked, "we are trying to push for [community based tourism] to disperse tourists away from popular sites beyond Bangkok, Chiang Mai or the beaches to promote the 'unseen Thailand" (Jing Travel, 2018). Under this strategy, new tourist destinations are evolving, such as Chiang Khan, a city on the Mekong River in the north of Thailand that has a night market and trekking opportunities.

At the same time, however, the government is planning a Japanese-backed 15 billion USD project to extend the existing railway system by constructing a double-rail link from Bangkok to Chiang Mai, and is also planning to construct new airports and to upgrade existing major ones, thereby doubling the capacity of Thailand's airports (Chuwiruch, 2017). These plans are seen as counterproductive as new airports and railways in these locations are likely to attract more visitors to these hotspots, compounding the pressures of overtourism.

To address overtourism in the future, the Thai government plans to focus less on attracting large numbers of low-spending tourists and instead seeks to attracting high-end visitors (Ministry of Tourism and Sports, 2017) who will presumably generate more revenue compared to low-end tour group guests and backpackers (Jing Travel, 2018). As Suvit Maesincee, a former minister attached to the Prime Minister's office, observed "I think in the near future we need to change from volume to value" (Chuwiruch, 2017). There is, however, no defined strategy on how the low-end tourism segments are to be phased out. Furthermore, Thailand will be competing with almost every country in the world in targeting high-yield conscious consumers. The regional competition includes countries such as Indonesia, Malaysia, Philippines, the Maldives and Sri Lanka. Some of these countries have well-managed pristine coral reefs and beach destinations in the higher price segment that are not flooded with tourists, so the competition will be fierce. In order to succeed in this approach, Thailand must improve its performance in managing tourism development.

Conclusion

Thailand is one of the most popular tourist destinations in Southeast Asia but increasing discontent among the host communities in tourism hotspots in response to culturally-inappropriate behaviour among tourists, over-crowding and environmental degradation caused by unchecked tourism development have revealed that the country has exceeded its carrying capacity for tourism. In response, the Thai government has closed down attractions in national parks during the low-season to allow the ecosystems to recover and intends to diversify the tourist flow. The government also wants to shift away from mass tourism. However, the factors contributing to overtourism in Thailand are difficult to manage. Loopholes prevent the government from clamping down on zero-dollar tours and the government faces opposition to increase fees for national attractions. While greater overall awareness by central government entities of the impacts of overtourism and the carrying capacities of local destinations raises hopes, finding the right approaches and ensuring responsible tourism development will be a difficult journey that will demand proactive public regulations.

References

Bangkok Post (2011a) TAT woos wealthy Chinese tourists. Bangkok Post, 20 May.
Bangkok Post (2011b) Rising tide of Chinese tourists lifts Asia-Pacific fortunes. Bangkok Post, 3 October.
Bangkok Post (2018) Ecologist rates Thai coral reef decay rate as alarming, Bangkok Post, 29 January. https://www.bangkokpost.com/news/general/1403638/ecologist-rates-thai-coral-reef-decay-rate-as-alarming (Accessed 30 October 2018.)
Bohwongprasert, Y. (2015) Sending up red flags. Bangkok Post, 15 April. https://www.bangkokpost.com/news/topstories/528995/sending-up-red-flags (Accessed 4 September 2018).
Calgaro, E., Naruchaikusol, S. and Pongponrat, K. (2009) Comparative Destination Vulnerability Assessment for Kao Lak, Patong Beach and Phi Phi Don (Project Report). Bangkok: Stockholm Environment Institute.
Chavanich, S., Viyakarn, V., Adams, P. and Klammer, J. (2012) Reef Communities after the 2010 mass coral bleaching at Racha Yai Island in the Andaman sea and Koh Tao in the Gulf of Thailand, Phuket Marine Biological Center Research Bulletin, 71: 103–110.
Chon, K-S., Singh, A. and Mikula, J. R. (1993) Thailand's Tourism and Hotel industry, Cornell Hotel and Restaurant Administration Quarterly, 34 (3): 43–49.
Christiernsson, A. (2003) An Economic Valuation of the coral reefs at Phi Phi Island: A travel cost approach. Master's thesis, Lulea University of Technology.

Coffey, H. (2017) Thailand tourist visa: Country cracks down on begpackers as visitors asked to show 20,000 baht before entering country, The Independent, 18 July. https://www.indepen dent.co.uk/travel/news-and-advice/thailand-tourist-visa-begpackers-crack-down-show-20000-baht-before-entering-country-immigration-a7846906.html (Accessed 30 August 2018.)

Cohen, E. (2017) Mass Tourism in Thailand: The Chinese and Russians. In D. Harrison and R. Sharpley (Eds.), Mass Tourism in a Small World. Wallingford, UK: Centre for Agriculture and Biosciences International, pp. 159–166.

Coldwell, W. (2018) Thailand's Maya Bay, location for The Beach, to close to tourists. The Guardian, 14 February.

Dodds, R. (2010) Koh Phi Phi: Moving Towards or Away from Sustainability? Asia Pacific Journal of Tourism Research, 15: 251–265. https://doi.org/10.1080/10941665.2010.503615 (Accessed 30 August 2018.)

Eade, C. (2015) Thailand releases behaviour guide for Chinese tourists, Daily Mail Online, 18 February. http://www.dailymail.co.uk/travel/travel_news/article-2958432/Don-t-defecate-public-places-don-t-touch-paintings-Thailand-releases-behaviour-guide-Chinese-tourists.html (Accessed 4 September 2018.)

Ellis-Petersen, H., 2018. Thailand bay made famous by The Beach closed indefinitely. The Guardian.

Flumerfelt, S. L. (2000) Dive tourism on Koh Tao, Thailand: Community heterogeneity and environmental responsibility. Thesis, University of Guelph, Ontario.

GoKohPhiPhi (2007) Phi Phi fun facts and cool things to know. http://www.gokohphiphi.com/phi-phi.html (Accessed 4 September 2018).

Heaver, S. (2018) Chinese tourism boom blamed as Thai beach from Leonardo DiCaprio film closes, South China Morning Post, 1 June. http://www.scmp.com/magazines/post-magazine/long-reads/article/2148751/thailand-tourist-beach-maya-bay-closes-combat (Accessed 22 August 2018.)

Henkel, R., Henkel, P., Agrusa, W., Agrusa, J. and Tanner, J. (2006) Thailand as a tourist destination: Perceptions of international visitors and Thai residents, Asia Pacific Journal of Tourism Research, 11: 269–287. https://doi.org/10.1080/10941660600753299 (Accessed 22 August 2018.)

Hoeksema, B. W., Scott, C. and True, J. D. (2013) Dietary shift in corallivorous snails following a major bleaching event at Koh Tao, Gulf of Thailand, Coral Reefs, 32: 423–428. https://doi.org/10.1007/s00338-012-1005-x (Accessed 22 August 2018.)

Holmes, O. (2016) Thailand to close 'overcrowded' Koh Tachai island to tourists, The Guardian, 17 May https://www.theguardian.com/world/2016/may/17/thailand-closes-koh-tachai-andaman-sea-island-to-tourists-coral-reefs. (Accessed 22 August, 2018.)

Jagtiani, S. and Chuwiruch, N. (2018) An onslaught of tourists is stressing out Thailand. Bloomberg, 12 July.

Jing Travel (2018) Thailand doubles down on tourism hotspots with new airports despite overtourism woes, Jing Travel, 7 June. https://jingtravel.com/thailand-doubles-down-on-tour ism-hotspots-with-new-airports-despite-overtourism-woes/ (Accessed 22 August 2018.)

Kontogeorgopoulos, N. (2004) Ecotourism and mass tourism in Southern Thailand: Spatial interdependence, structural connections, and staged authenticity. GeoJournal, 61: 1–11. https://doi.org/10.1007/s10708-005-8631-6 (Accessed 22 August 2018.)

Kontogeorgopoulos, N. (1999) Sustainable tourism or sustainable development? Financial crisis, ecotourism, and the "Amazing Thailand" campaign. Current Issues in Tourism, 2: 316–332. https://doi.org/10.1080/13683509908667859 (Accessed 22 August 2018.)

Law, L., Bunnell, T. and Ong, C-E. (2007) The Beach, the gaze and film tourism. Tourist Studies, 7: 141–164. https://doi.org/10.1177/1468797607083499 (Accessed 22 August 2018.)

Lefevre, A. S., 2015. Thais smile through gritted teeth for China's tourists, Reuters, 26 March. https://www.reuters.com/article/us-thailand-china-tourism-idUSKBN0MM0FK20150326 (Accessed 4 September 2018.)

Li, L. and Zhang, W. (1997) Thailand: The dynamic growth of Thai tourism. In F. M. Go and C. L. Jenkins (Eds.), Tourism and Economic Development in Asia and Australia, London: Cassell, pp. 286–303.

Maps.com (n.d.) Thailand's physical regions. http://jotisthailand.weebly.com/geography-and-envi ronment.html (Accessed 23 March 2018.)

McDowall, S. and Choi, Y. (2010) A comparative analysis of Thailand residents' perception of tourism's impacts, Journal of Quality Assurance in Hospitality & Tourism, 11: 36–55. https://doi.org/10.1080/15280080903520576 (Accessed 22 August 2018.)

McDowall, S. and Wang, Y. (2009) An Analysis of International Tourism Development in Thailand: 1994–2007, Asia Pacific Journal of Tourism Research, 14, 351–370. https://doi.org/10.1080/10941660903023952 (Accessed 4 September 2018.)

Ministry of Tourism and Sports (2018) Tourism Statistics. http://www.mots.go.th/main.php?file name=index (Accessed 21 March 2018.)

Ministry of Tourism and Sports (2017) The Second National Tourism Development Plan (2017–2021), Bangkok: Ministry of Tourism and Sports.

Ministry of Tourism and Sports (1991) Annual Report Tourism in Thailand 1991. Bangkok: Ministry of Tourism and Sports.

Mueanhawong, K. (2017) Koh Phi Phi – Thailand's most profitable national park. The Thaiger, 10 October. https://thethaiger.com/news/koh-phi-phi-thailands-profitable-national-park (Accessed 4 September 2018.)

Nam, S. (2018) Movies filmed in Thailand, TripSavvy, 29 May. https://www.tripsavvy.com/on-loca tion-in-thailand-1658297 (Accessed 4 September 2018.)

Nara, P., Mao, G-G. and Yen, T-B. (2014) Applying environmental management policy for sustainable development of coastal tourism in Thailand. International Journal of Environmental Protection and Policy, 2(1): 19–23. https://doi.org/10.11648/j.ijepp.20140201.13 (Accessed 4 September 2018.)

National Statistical Office (2016) Thailand National Statistical Office. http://web.nso.go.th/index1. htm (accessed 14 March 2018.)

Nations Encyclopedia (2018) Thailand http://www.nationsencyclopedia.com/geography/Slovenia-to-Zimbabwe-Cumulative-Index/Thailand.html (Accessed 23 March 2018.)

Chuwiruch, N. (2017) Chinese tourists could cause years of misery for Thai airports. Bloomberg, 20 December. https://www.bloomberg.com/news/articles/2017-12-20/thai-airport-misery-may-last-years-as-chinese-overwhelm-upgrades (Accessed 4 September 2018.)

Nimmonratana, T. (2000) Impacts of tourism on a local community: A case study of Chiang Mai. In K. S. Chon (Ed.), Tourism in Southeast Asia: A New Direction. New York: Haworth Hospitality Press, pp. 65–86.

Nuttavuthisit, K. (2007) Branding Thailand: Correcting the negative image of sex tourism. Place Branding and Public Diplomacy, 3(1): 21–30. https://doi.org/10.1057/palgrave.pb.6000045 (Accessed 4 September 2018.)

Pack Thailand (2018) Rude Chinese tourists: How to improve their behaviour? Pack Thailand. http://packthailand.com/rude-chinese-tourists-behaviour/ (Accessed 4 September 2018.)

Parameswaran, P. (2015) Thailand tells Chinese tourists how to behave. The Diplomat, 19 February. https://thediplomat.com/2015/02/thailand-tells-chinese-tourists-how-to-behave/ (Accessed 4 September 2018.)

Rittichainuwat, B. N. (2006) Tsunami recovery: A case study of Thailand's tourism, Cornell Hospitality Quarterly, 47 (4): 390–404. https://doi.org/10.1177/0010880406289994 (Accessed 4 September 2018.)

Royal Thai Embassy Singapore (n.d.) Thailand's National Tourism Development Plan | https://www. thaiembassy.sg/press_media/news-highlights/thailand%E2%80%99s-national-tourism-devel opment-plan (Accessed 22 March 2018.)

South China Morning Post (2016) Love it to death: One of Thailand's most beautiful islands is closing because tourists are destroying it, South China Morning Post, 18 May. https://www.scmp.com/news/asia/southeast-asia/article/1946678/love-it-death-one-thailands-most-beau tiful-islands-closing (Accessed 22 August 2018.)

Spinks, R. (2018) The 'begpacker' phenomenon shows how fake poverty has become a status symbol, Quartzy, 30 January. https://qz.com/quartzy/1192690/begpackers-the-trend-of-west erners-traveling-without-money/ (Accessed 30 August 2018.)

Suntikul, W. (2013) Thai tourism and the legacy of the Vietnam War. In R. W. Butlerand W. Suntikul, Tourism and War, London: Routledge, pp 92–105.

Tanzil, J. T. I., Brown, B. E., Tudhope, A. W. and Dunne, R. P. (2009) Decline in skeletal growth of the coral Porites lutea from the Andaman Sea, South Thailand between 1984 and 2005. Coral Reefs, 28 (2): 519–528. https://doi.org/10.1007/s00338-008-0457-5 (Accessed 30 August 2018.)

Tapachai, N. and Waryszak, R. (2000) An examination of the role of beneficial image in tourist destination selection. Journal of Travel Research, 39 (1): 37–44. https://doi.org/10.1177/004728750003900105 (Accessed 30 August 2018.)

The Nation (2018) Thailand's national park system starts annual seasonal closure of attractions. The Nation, 20 April. http://www.nationmultimedia.com/detail/Travel_log/30343568 (Accessed 3 September 2018.)

The Phuket News (2018) Maya Bay to get extra protection, The Phuket News, 16 May. https://www.thephuketnews.com/maya-bay-to-get-extra-protection-67138.php#3yFowK2hCkBBXfd1.97 (Accessed 4 September 2018.)

The Straits Times (2017) Thailand struggles to cope with deluge of tourists, The Straits Times, 22 December. https://www.straitstimes.com/asia/se-asia/thailand-struggles-to-cope-with-del uge-of-tourists (Accessed 27 September 2018.)

Thepgumpanat, P. and Tanakasempipat, P. (2016) Thailand facing worst water shortage in two decades – government, Reuters, 9 March.

TomTom Traffic Index (2017) Full ranking, TomTom Traffic Index. https://www.tomtom.com/en_gb/trafficindex/list?citySize=LARGE&continent=ALL&country=ALL (Accessed27 September 2018.)

Untong, A. (2007) Local residents' attitudes towards tourism: A case study in Chiang Mai and Chiang Rai, Thailand. In M. Kaosaard (Ed.), Mekong Tourism: Blessings for All? Chiang Mai: Social Research Institute, pp. 125–136.

Vejpongsa, T. (2018) Ailing Thai beach made famous by film gets tourist timeout, Business Insider, 31 May. https://www.businessinsider.com/ap-ailing-thai-beach-made-famous-by-film-gets-tourist-timeout-2018-5?IR=T (Accessed 4 September 2018.)

Weterings, R. (2011) A GIS-based assessment of threats to the natural environment on Koh Tao, Thailand, Kasetsart Journal of Natural Sciences, 45: 743–755.

Wonga, P. P. (1998) Coastal tourism development in Southeast Asia: Relevance and lessons for coastal zone management, Ocean & Coastal Management, 38 (2): 89–109. https://doi.org/10.1016/S0964-5691(97)00066-5 (Accessed 4 September 2018.)

Wongthong, P. and Harvey, N. (2014) Integrated coastal management and sustainable tourism: A case study of the reef-based SCUBA dive industry from Thailand, Ocean & Coastal Management, 95: 138–146. https://doi.org/10.1016/j.ocecoaman.2014.04.004 (Accessed 4 September 2018.)

World Bank (2018) Country Profile: Thailand. https://data.worldbank.org/country/thailand (Accessed 14 March 2018.)

World Travel and Tourism Council (WTTC) (2018) Travel & Tourism Economic Impact 2017: Thailand. London: World Travel and Tourism Council.

Yeemin, T., Sutthacheep, M. and Pettongma, R. (2006) Coral reef restoration projects in Thailand, Ocean & Coastal Management, 49: 562–575. https://doi.org/10.1016/j.ocecoaman.2006.06.002 (Accessed 4 September 2018.)

Harold Goodwin

9 Barcelona – crowding out the locals: a model for tourism management?

Introduction

Barcelona as a tourist destination has experienced very rapid growth since the 1992 Olympics. While it attracted under two million day tourists in 1990 (Ajuntament de Barcelona and Barcelona Activa, 2014a), in 2017 Barcelona had close to nine million day tourists and over 18 million overnight tourists, who spent 48 million bednights in the destination (Barcelona Tourist Activity Report, 2017). Around half of those staying in hotels are repeat visitors and more than a quarter are visiting for a third time or more. Not all hotel guests are on holiday, however, with only around 50% visiting Barcelona for that reason (Ajuntament de Barcelona and Barcelona Activa, 2014a). Data on the economic value of tourism to Barcelona from the University of Girona indicates that the aggregate turnover for tourism in 2013 lay between 8 and 9.7 billion euros, representing between 10% and 12% of the city's GNP (Ajuntment de Barcelona, 2017a: 29). In 2013 tourism generated between 96,000 and 120,000 jobs; approximately 14% of total employment in the city (Ajuntment de Barcelona, 2017a: 29).

As tourism has become more intense in Barcelona, and given the rapidity of the increase, it is not surprising that it was the first city in which the issue of overtourism gained prominence. Overtourism was identified as an issue in Barcelona in 2004; the City of Barcelona began formally addressing it in 2008, long before overtourism resulted in public demonstrations in 2015.

Tourism policy-making processes of Barcelona involve a greater degree of public participation than in most democracies. For example, residents are encouraged to actively engage in discussions about tourism policy, informed by a wealth of published data. This approach to policy making and implementation has resulted in the building of consensus, which secures a high degree of positive engagement by stakeholders and consequently continuity of management of tourism by the city. Barcelona has successfully evolved a whole-of-government approach to tourism management and a rich variety of management strategies and tools, each worthy of study.

This chapter will provide a background of tourism development in Barcelona, followed by a discussion of the overtourism issues in the city. It will then discuss governance and how the city has addressed the issues. For anyone interested in researching or teaching about tourism in a city or about the issue of overtourism, Barcelona is remarkably open in its governance, with proceedings and data publicly available. Barcelona also publishes district-level data on residents' opinions about the impact of tourism on their neighbourhood and the city as a whole. This makes Barcelona an excellent laboratory and learning resource.

https://doi.org/10.1515/9783110607369-009

Background

Barcelona is located in Catalunya (Catalonia) Province, in the northeast of Spain. Tourism began developing on the coast in the 1960s. In the 1980s, Barcelona, a tired, provincial, heavily-industrialized port city was transformed through a major urban renewal programme that tore down the old docks and dredged sand to create beaches that stretch from Barceloneta to the Port Olimpic. It emerged as a cosmopolitan city *oberta a la mar* (open to the sea), ready to host the Olympic Games in 1992. This, combined with the iconic Gaudi architecture and the vistas of the city, launched Barcelona as a major European destination (Degen and Cabeza, 2012).

Barcelona is today ranked sixth among European cities attracting international tourists, behind London, Paris and Rome (Euromonitor, 2017). While tourism has grown in all of these cities, Barcelona's growth has been the most spectacular. London tourism grew by 16% between 2005 and 2013, while Barcelona grew by more than 54% in that time (Ajuntament de Barcelona and Barcelona Activa, 2014b). It was the pace of growth as much as the volume of tourists that created issues. And these issues were exacerbated by the small size of the city, with a population of only 1.6 million (see Figs. 9.1 and 9.2).

Fig. 9.1: Crowds on Barcelona's Las Ramblas (photo credit: Radu Bercan).

Tourism is valued in Barcelona and city leaders and cultural figures articulate a vision of Barcelona that is on the sea, open and pluricultural (Ramoneda, 2011).

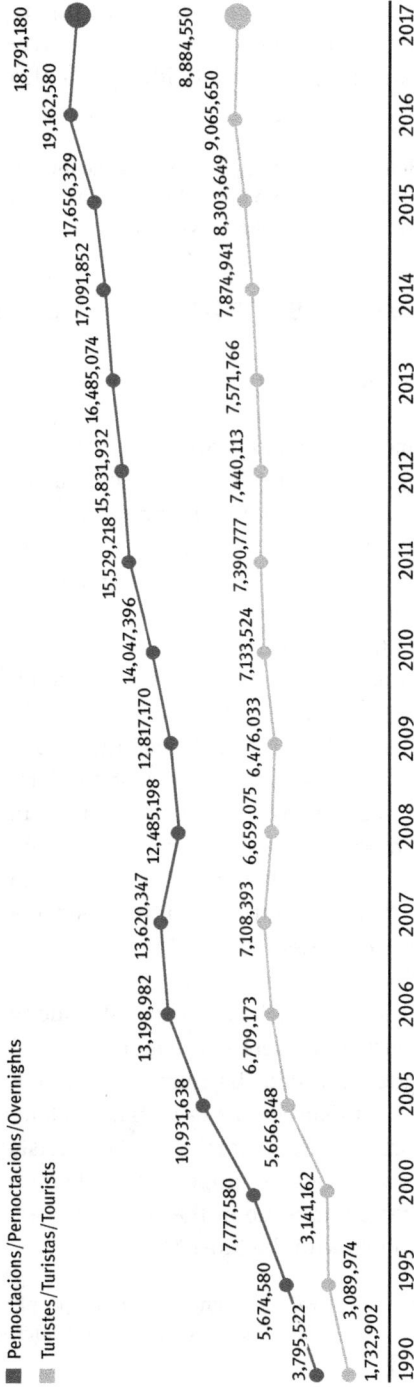

Fig. 9.2: Overnight vs day visitors to Barcelona 1990–2017 (source: Barcelona Tourist Activity Report, 2017).

Legend:
- Pernoctacions/Pernoctacions/Overnights
- Turistes/Turistas/Tourists

Data values (Overnights): 3,795,522; 5,674,580; 7,777,580; 10,931,638; 13,198,982; 13,620,347; 12,485,198; 12,817,170; 14,047,396; 15,529,218; 15,831,932; 16,485,074; 17,091,852; 17,656,329; 19,162,580; 18,791,180

Data values (Tourists): 1,732,902; 3,089,974; 3,141,162; 5,656,848; 6,709,173; 7,108,393; 6,659,075; 6,476,033; 7,133,524; 7,390,777; 7,440,113; 7,571,766; 7,874,941; 8,303,649; 9,065,650; 8,884,550

Years: 1990 1995 2000 2005 2006 2007 2008 2009 2010 2011 2012 2013 2014 2015 2016 2017

Tourism is one of the city council's priorities because of the economic value it generates, the employment it creates and the contribution it makes to building Barcelona's international image (see Smith, 2005). Barcelona's open city identity is also used to attract mobile highly-skilled labour:

> Barcelona is one of the world's most dynamic, cosmopolitan cities, figuring among the top European cities in quality of life rankings. It is a modern, tolerant and open city, offering a wide range of cultural and tourist attractions. (Institute for Research in Biomedicine, n.d.)

History of overtourism issues and its management

Critical comment about tourism and sustainability in Barcelona was seen as early as 2004, during the Forum of Cultures (Agència Catalana de Turisme et al., 2013). In 2009, negative reports about the tourist experience of Barcelona and the experience of residents increased in frequency (Goodwin, 2017). By that year, adverse comments were being voiced regularly in mainstream and social media about stag parties and drug dealing. Furthermore, "drunken tourists, desperate prostitutes and petty crooks" were reported to have rendered the main pedestrian walkway, Las Ramblas, "charmless, tawdry and dangerous" (Tremlett, 2009). In December 2009, residents and traders in neighboring Raval, sent over 500 Christmas cards to city officials with candid photographs of prostitutes, drug dealers and tourists using the street as a toilet or having sex in public. Banners appeared on balconies with a single phrase in Catalan: "Volem un barri digne!" ("We want a dignified district!") (Rainsford, 2009).

In August 2014, a series of protests about the negative impacts of tourism, dubbed the "Barceloneta Crisis", took place in the city. The demonstrations were not so much anti-tourist as demanding a new model of tourism, one that did not involve tourists staying in residential apartments. Residents demanded "un barrio para los vecinos y no un turismo de 'low cost'" ("a neighbourhood for the residents not 'low-cost' tourism") (La Vanguardia, 2014). Protesters sought out owners of tourism rentals in Barconeleta urging them to close their businesses.

Barcelona's mayor promised an inspection and crackdown on illegal holiday apartments in La Barceloneta and 24 holiday apartments were subsequently closed (O'Sullivan, 2014). The city authorities had under-recorded the number of tourist flats, however. While there were only 72 licensed tourism rentals in La Barconeleta, "a quick search of online rental portals like Airbnb show[ed] more than 600 tourists lets available in the area" (Kassam, 2014). Residents were not appeased by the major's response and tourism consequently emerged as an issue in the 2015 city elections. Ada Colau, a mayoral candidate drew parallels with the fate of Venice:

> Any city that sacrifices itself on the altar of mass tourism will be abandoned by its people when they can no longer afford the cost of housing, food, and basic everyday necessities. (Colau, 2014)

Colau argued that the scale of visitor numbers was affecting not only residents' quality of life, but also their ability to live in the city. This was demonstrated by the number of complaints about noise, nudity, public drunkenness and littering (Kassam, 2014; Gillman, 2014; Sinkeviciute, 2014; Mount, 2015; Becker, 2015).

After Ada Colau was elected mayor in June 2015, she halted further licensing and development of accommodation while a new plan was discussed and developed. Bloomberg carried an article in September that reflected the tone of much international media coverage of the new mayor, the city council and its policies: "Barcelona's new mayor wants to send tourists packing" (Faris, 2015). This was a misrepresentation of the mayor's approach,but the administration was indeed seeking to take control.

While it was perhaps not apparent to local residents, the municipality had begun addressing the challenge of overtourism long before it had been so named and protests spilled on to the streets. In 2008, the city council had approved a municipal action plan that committed the city to develop a strategic tourism plan. This strategic plan was developed with Turisme de Barcelona between 2008 and 2010 and was intended to promote a tourism model that would "strengthen the balance between local residents and tourists while preserving the identity values of the city" (Ajuntament de Barcelona and Barcelona Turisme, 2010: 5). This involved planning the city's capacity for hosting tourists; guaranteeing quality and the sustainability of the tourism sector; promoting cultural tourism based on the role of Barcelona as the Catalan capital, and using an inclusive rather than exclusive model.

In June 2009, a Tourism and City Technical Committee was established, chaired by the municipal manager and coordinated by the Economic Promotion Department. Its members included representatives from the municipal departments: Municipal Management; Economic Promotion, Environment; Prevention, Mobility and Safety; General Services and Territorial Coordination; Urban Planning and Infrastructures; Education, Culture and Welfare; and the Ciutat Vella District Council (Ajuntament de Barcelona and Barcelona Turisme, 2010). It is rare for a municipal government to create a tourism committee that brings together so many departments to co-ordinate action to manage tourism.

In 2010, the authorities recognised that tourism was having both positive and negative impacts on the city. They explicitly recognised that some of the negative effects of tourism were creating an anti-tourism discourse.

> The inconvenience experienced by some local residents, which creates a feeling of unease and anti-tourist sentiments, ends up converging on and having feedback in certain discourses and public (and/or published) opinions by journalists, intellectuals and professionals who can make their opinions heard, thereby constructing a social discourse which is sceptical about or against tourism. (Ajuntament de Barcelona and Barcelona Turisme, 2010: 4)

The 2010–2015 Strategic Tourism Plan acknowledged that "the massification and standardisation" of the tourism offer, and the negative impacts associated with it, could "become a contributing factor to the deterioration of Barcelona", negatively impacting on the "quality of life the local community and spoiling the visitors' experience" (Ajuntament de Barcelona and Barcelona Turisme, 2010: 23). The strategy also asserted that tourism "must be everyone's concern" because the whole population of the city receives both the positive and negative impacts; therefore tourism had to become "a shared, not-sectorial, project" requiring a new approach to urban tourism "with the greatest possible involvement of the community and institutions (Ajuntament de Barcelona and Barcelona Turisme, 2010: 23).

There was a marked rebalancing in the tourism plan, with a shift from promotion and marketing to placing considerably more emphasis on managing tourism. In this regard, working commissions were established to "create a dialogue and shared analysis about the way tourism fits in with the needs of the city" (Ajuntamant de Barcelona and Barcelona Turisme, 2010: 7).

The tourism plan identified four key challenges, which remain at the core of the city's current strategy:
- Territorial deconcentration; moving from promotion to governance using data to generate shared knowledge to facilitate management.
- Moving from managing tourists to managing visitors.
- Generating synergies to integrate tourism "naturally" into the city "fostering hospitality, extending a warm welcome to visitors, coexistence and reciprocal exchanges".
- "Reinforcing Barcelona's role as the Catalan capital and raising the profile of Catalonia" (Ajuntamant de Barcelona and Barcelona Turisme, 2010)

While recognising the negative aspects, since 2010 both the City of Barcelona and the destination marketing organisation (DMO) avoided negative and divisive language when discussing the impact of tourism and tourist behaviour in the city. They have instead emphasized "identity and coexistence as the imperative" to better manage tourism and have referred to tourists as "temporary residents" (Ajuntament de Barcelona and Barcelona Turisme, 2010: 13).

In the past decade, Barcelona's tourism strategy has consistently followed the "responsible tourism" principle that tourism is about making better places for people to live and for people to visit – in that order (Responsible Tourism Partnership, n.d.). Accordingly, the people of Barcelona are seen as active participants and creators of the city and of tourism, expressed as, "The health of the city's tourist activity stems from the well-being of its population, which must be cause and effect of the successful development of Barcelona as a tourist destination" (Ajuntament de Barcelona and Barcelona Turisme, 2010: 9).

In 2017, the City of Barcelona published a new tourism strategic plan, "Barcelona Tourism for 2020: A collective strategy for sustainable tourism" (Ajuntament de Barcelona, 2017a). This strategy runs to 139 pages with sections on the diagnosis and challenges, and ten action programmes. It is an ambitious programme with 30 lines of action and close to 100 measures (Ajuntament de Barcelona, 2017a).

The 2020 plan acknowledges the two main goals of the 2010–2015 plan: helping to improve tourist activities in Barcelona and ensuring tourism fitted in better with the city, and observes that these goals were based on "criteria that were extremely innovative in their time and have proved to be essential today" (Ajuntament de Barcelona, 2017a: 12). The new plan recognises that "many of the 150 aspects, trends and dynamics noted in 2009, after considerable analytical work, are just as valid today and can be completely integrated into the current diagnosis" (Ajuntament de Barcelona, 2017a: 12) and reaffirms many of the conclusions of the previous work, including the conceptual shift from tourist to visitors, reflecting and respecting the diversity of travel motivations and activities in the destination, the need for comprehensive management, and the inseparable pairing between sustainability and competitiveness. Five criteria for establishing desirable action frameworks for public tourism policies are outlined in the new plan: sustainability, responsibility, redistribution, cohesion and innovation, and the plan asserts that:

> To ensure a destination's success, maintain its uniqueness, add value to the whole value chain, guarantee and promote new experiences, and turn tourism into an innovative activity with added value, the commitments to sustainability and responsibility signed by the city need to be ratified and, most important of all, conveyed through bold, specific proposals for action. (Ajuntament de Barcelona, 2017a: 19)

Governance

Barcelona's evidence-based approach to tourism management is unusual, even rare, in three respects: there has been a remarkable degree of continuity across administrations; tourism marketing has been separated from management; and there has been a notable degree of democratic engagement and transparency underpinning a determination to manage tourism to enable it to develop synergistically with the city.

Barcelona has divided the destination management functions. The management of tourism in the city is the responsibility of the Ajuntament de Barcelona and Barcelona Activa, and marketing is undertaken by Turisme de Barcelona. In 2010, the city created a Directorate for Tourism and Events, which had responsibility for managing tourism in the city, seeking to maintain the economic importance of tourism while improving the quality of life of citizens. In the same year, the Barcelona City Council established the Technical Council for Tourism and the City, which sought to coordinate the management of tourism across the various functions of the council and which answered to the Chief Executive Officer. In 2013, the local tourism authorities in the city recognised that the "common goal of making tourism in Catalonia a tool to achieve the social, economic and environmental aspirations through responsible tourism requires coordination, communication and the co-ordinated work of the various administrations and sectors involved" (Agència Catalana de Turisme et al., 2013).

The groups and individuals with responsibility for implementing the strategic plan are in the public domain. The government established a municipal Council for Tourism and the City, which recognises the need for a long term vision that is supported by both the public and private sectors. The council includes representatives from the general public and local residents, the tourist business sector, the commerce sector, the restaurant and catering sector, sports and culture, trade unions, environmental associations, social groups and every district, as well as expert professionals, technical managers and representatives from each municipal political group. It is a participatory body that debates the planning and management of tourism in the city. It serves as a formal platform for exchanging ideas, assessing the impact of actions that have been taken and generating proposals that might serve as a guide to future tourism policies, although these are not binding (Ajuntament de Barcelona and Barcelona Activa, 2014b: 8–10).

Difficulties in addressing overtourism

The management of tourism and overtourism is always the responsibility of local government. Various departments in the local authority are responsible for traffic, parking, litter, noise, public transport, and all parts of the city government have some potential to manage and plan tourism within the city, although not beyond it. However, a number of elements that are beyond local control have contributed to excessive tourist numbers in Barcelona and to the issues associated with overtourism.

The first is Barcelona's El Prat airport. It is Spain's second largest airport and was ranked 10th in passenger traffic among European airports in 2015 (El Prat Airport, n.d.). The Barcelona city government has little or no influence over the growth of the airport and the numbers arriving there as the airport is run by a pubic company that is responsible for all Spanish airports.

The second element is that the airport and the Barcelona Trade Fair are both located in Hospitalet de Llobregat (generally shortened to "Hospitalet"), the most densely populated city in Europe, which is situated immediately to the southwest of Barcelona. Hospitalet's local government plans and manages its tourism accommodation separately from the city of Barcelona.This situation is very similar to the relationship between Mestre and Venice. Thus, while the attraction is Barcelona, the "attraction" cannot manage the accommodation in L'Hospitalet. The city of Barcelona also cannot control the numbers of people holidaying in nearby Girona or along the Costa Brava who visit Barcelona on day excursions.

The third element is the cruise lines. In 2000, 572,000 cruise passengers arrived in Barcelona; in 2015 this rose five fold to 2.54 million, and in 2017 the number rose to 2.7 million (Statista, 2018). In 2014, over half (57.5%) of cruise passengers were day excursionists in Barcelona and only about a quarter (23.9%) spent a night or more ashore in the city (many passengers only transited to the airport or remained on the ships) (Port de Barcelona and Barcelona Turisme, 2014). The port is answerable only to the central government. So, as in the case of Venice (Chapter 10), the city authorities of Barcelona have virtually no means of limiting the number of tourists and day excursion arrivals by air, rail, road and sea.

Addressing the issues

Overtourism, whether experienced by hosts or guests or both, is a problem with a range of symptoms and multiple causes. In Barcelona, a specific range of issues – the symptoms – have been identified and they are being addressed individually.

In a city like Barcelona where the public realm is at the heart of the experience, the strategies available to the local authorities are limited to dealing with the impacts of tourists and day excursionists in the city. The authorities can reduce marketing and can implement policies that affect the supply of accommodation but, as discussed earlier, they have little or no influence over the numbers of tourists arriving. Barcelona instead issues warnings and crowd forecasts about when the city is likely to be particularly congested, enabling residents to avoid tourist areas on the peak days.

The city's vision remains, however, to address the major issues of overtourism. The 2020 strategy includes the following key elements:

- **Governance**: Focusing on strengthening the management of tourism and cooperating across government sectors.
- **Knowledge:** This is recognised as being essential for effective decision making and management.
- **Destination Barcelona**: Building a destination that spreads tourism beyond the city boundaries, that is committed to economic, social and environmental sustainability and that focuses on the quality of life of its citizens and balanced territorial development. Since 2013, district tourism plans have been developed to disperse tourism across the city, so as to spread the benefits and reduce overcrowding and overtourism in the "honeypot" areas. Marketing has also been turned into a central management tool and focuses on events as well as non-residential spaces. Visitor attractions and tourist products now have to meet sustainability criteria.
- **Mobility**: The city is using smart technology to understand tourism flows and crowding issues and to intervene where possible, for example changing bus routes and stops, and metro entrances and exits.
- **Accommodation**: Focusing on issues arising from the overdevelopment of tourism in some districts and addressing issues around unlicensed accommodation.

This strategy is unique for five reasons. First, it manages spaces and opts to reduce pressure on the most congested areas to ensure a balance between residents and tourists. Second, it focuses on social returns on tourist activities to ensure the redistribution of wealth. Third, it makes an effort to communicate with and involve the resident population and visitors. By fostering such communication, it seeks to meet visitors' expectations while also providing a balance for residents living and working in the city. Fourth, it introduces new taxation measures and seeks to design an investment and funding plan. Finally, it involves revision of regulation and planning, which will include changes in municipal by-laws, planning tools and the monitoring and inspecting of tourist activities to "enable a greater level of control and effective sanctioning power over all irregular activities that lead to unfair competition and strong externalities, regardless of their nature" (Ajuntament de Barcelona, 2017a: 129, 130).

Addressing issues relating to rental accommodation

Accommodation is one of the major areas of conflict. Displacement may be experienced as dispossession, which fuels protest. Protest has been organised through the Sindicat de Logaters, the Tenant's Union and the Neighbourhood Assembly for Sustainable Tourism (ABTS) established in November 2015. These groups demand fair rents, decent housing and an end to evictions.

The use of private residential units by tourists is a common complaint by residents for a number of reasons, including disturbance and rental price increases. Rising rents change the socio-demographics of residents, as low-income residents are displaced, changing the identity or the area, and this may reduce social cohesion and commodify what was public space. While increases in rental costs in Barcelona are not only due to overtourism, it is a major contributor. Other reasons for the increase in rents include, "household debt, urban entrepreneurialism and the marketing of the city, evictions, investment by speculative capital, [and] changes in tenancy" (Blanco-Romero et al., 2018: 5). Blanco-Romero et al report that in addition to causing rent rises, short-term rentals for tourism have been associated with deteriorating labour conditions, falling profits in the hotel sector and real estate speculation facilitated by neoliberal urban policies. Furthermore, changes in the form and intensity of housing have impacted sustainability, affecting the consumption of water, energy and materials and the production of waste (Blanco-Romero et al., 2018: 5).

The regional and city governments have implemented various policies designed to address issues associated with tourist accommodation. In 2012, the regional government of Catalonia introduced a tax on stays at tourist establishments. Barcelona receives 34% of this, of which half goes to promotion through Turisme de Barcelona and half is used by the city for management. In October 2014, the Barcelona City Council ceased issuing new licenses for tourist apartments. This moratorium was imposed to enable the administration to develop the capacity to inspect, license and manage tourist accommodation, and was extended by the new administration in 2015. To avoid residential evictions, the Barcelona City Council purchased five buildings in 2017, undertook a census of empty housing properties (some 4% of all homes in the city) and encouraged the owners to rent them out by providing facilities for renovation and guarantees on rent payment.

To address public concern about the growth of tourism and tourist accommodation in particular, and achieve a better balance between residential life, tourism and other economic activities, in January 2017 the government introduced the Special Urban Plan for Tourist Accommodation (PEUAT). It is an urban planning instrument designed to regulate tourism accommodation using the urban planning law of Catalunya (Legislative Decree 1) of 2010. The introduction of the PEUAT, as part of the 2020 Strategic Tourism Plan, brought to an end the moratorium on new licenses for tourist apartments. The PEUAT regulates the development of new tourism accommodation, including youth hostels and Habitatge d'Ús Turístic (HUT) licences. Zero growth in HUTs has since been established and new (licensed) ones can only be opened as others close. For the purposes of the PEUAT, the city was divided into four zones with regulations on: ratios of residents to tourist accommodation, the presence of tourist attractions and the use of public space. Some "hot spots", as "areas of specific treatment", are subject to more detailed planning regulation.

The issue of illegal tourist accommodation is now addressed by teams of inspectors working closely with the tax authorities. In addition, residents and tourists alike can check online whether or not an apartment or house is licensed as tourist accommodation and if not licensed they can report it online or by phone (Ajuntament de Barcelona, n.d.a; Fair Tourism, n.d.). In 2017, the Census of Tourist Accommodation Establishments in Barcelona identified 149,058 tourist units of which only 58,951 (39%) were licensed. Data analysed by Inside Airbnb identified 15,369 units, and of these fewer than half were in an inhabited unit (genuinely part of the shared economy). Thus, over 50% were units fully devoted to tourist use and therefore subject to tax (Blanco-Romero et al, 2018).

In December 2017, one third of current home purchases in Barcelona were investments for tourist rental and Barcelona ranked fourth behind New York, Berlin and London in attracting such investments in whole buildings (Blanco-Romero et al., 2018). Thus, the problem had yet to be fully resolved. Recognising that housing remains an issue in Barcelona, in February 2018 the city council supported the building of additional public rental housing (Blanco-Romero et al, 2018). In addition, in May 2018, in a further crack-down on short-term rentals, the council secured access to all data from Airbnb adverts (Ajuntament de Barcelona, n.d.b). This assisted in identifying apartments that were illegally operating as short-term rentals for tourists. Between July 2016 and July 2018, 2,355 tourism appartments were closed, and as of July 2018 a further 1,800 were in the process of being closed. As of October 2018, a team of over 100 spotters and inspectors continued to check that tourist rentals that had been closed had not re-opened, to detect new cases and to go after organised networks operating more than one property (Ajuntament de Barcelona, n.d.c).

Conclusion

Barcelona has an ambitious programme for addressing overtourism and one that will take much coordinated effort and a number of years to achieve. Because Barcelona is a tourist city, it is a brand with a culture and lifestyle that is created and shared by citizens and tourists, and it has had to learn to manage tourism effectively. The strength of Barcelona's approach has been in developing broad policies and micromanagement interventions over, for example, coach parking (Zonabus, n.d.), limiting the opening of new outlets for the sale of souvenirs in hot spots (Ajuntament de Barcelona, n.d.d), agreements with guides about the guiding of groups in public spaces (Barcelona Ciutat Refugi, 2017), and regulating vehicles like Segways (Ajuntament de Barceona, 2017b). Effective management requires a whole of government approach in the destination and careful planning. As a result of this management approach, Barcelona is today a leading example of how tourism can be used to make a city a better place to live and a better place to visit.

References

Agència Catalana de Turisme, Turisme de Barcelona, Ajuntament de Barcelona and Diputació de Barcelona (2013) Catalunya 2020 Vision for Responsible Tourism: TheBarcelona Declaration. https://ajuntament.barcelona.cat/turisme/sites/default/files/documents/the_catalunya_2020_vision_for_responsible_tourism_-_the_barcelona_declaration_eng.pdf (Accessed August 2018.)

Ajuntament de Barcelona (n.d.a) Cercador de pisos [Accommodation search engine]. http://meet.barcelona.cat/habitatgesturistics/ (Accessed 30 October 2018.)

Ajuntament de Barcelona (n.d.b) Municipal inspections to get access to all data from Airbnb adverts. https://ajuntament.barcelona.cat/turisme/en/noticia/municipal-inspections-to-get-access-to-all-data-from-airbnb-adverts_668222 (Accessed September 2018.)

Ajuntament de Barcelona (n.d.c) Over 2,300 illegal tourist lets closed down in two years. https://ajuntament.barcelona.cat/turisme/en/noticia/over-2300-illegal-tourist-lets-closed-down-in-two-years_686807 (Accessed September 2018.)

Ajuntament de Barcelona (n.d.d) Barcelona is not a souvenir. https://ajuntament.barcelona.cat/turisme/en/noticia/barcelona-is-not-a-souvenir_619163 (Accessed 30 October 2018.)

Ajuntament de Barcelona (2017a) *Barcelona Tourism for 2020: A collective strategy for sustainable tourism*. Barcelona: Ajuntament de Barcelona. https://ajuntament.barcelona.cat/turisme/sites/default/files/barcelona_tourism_for_2020.pdf (Accessed 30 October 2018.)

Ajuntament de Barcelona (2017b) Limited routes for Segways for commercial use in Ciutat Vella, El plan de los barrios de Barcelona, 9 August 2017. http://pladebarris.barcelona/en/noticia/limited-routes-for-segway-tours-in-ciutat-vella_542406 (Accessed 30 October 2018.)

Ajuntament de Barcelona and Barcelona Activa (2014a) The Tourism Sector in Barcelona. https://ajuntament.barcelona.cat/turisme/sites/default/files/documents/150514_the_tourism_sector_eng_0.pdf (Accessed August 2018.)

Ajuntament de Barcelona and Barcelona Activa (2014b) Barcelona's tourism activity development and management. https://ajuntament.barcelona.cat/turisme/sites/default/files/documents/141204_barcelonas_tourism_activity_0.pdf (Accessed September 2018.)

Ajuntament de Barcelona and Barcelona Turisme (2010) *Pla Estratègic de Turisme de la ciutat de Barcelona [City of Barcelona Tourism Strategic Plan]*. Barcelona: Ajuntament de Barcelona. http://cbab.bcn.cat/uhtbin/cgisirsi/x/0/0/57/520/6413?user_id=CATALA (Accessed 30 October 2018.)

Barcelona Ciutat Refugi (2017) Good practice to reduce inconvenience caused by tourist groups. Barcelona City Refuge, 15 September 2017. http://ciutatrefugi.barcelona/en/noticia/good-practice-to-reduce-inconvenience-caused-by-tourist-groups_551237 (Accessed 30 October 2018.)

Becker, E. (2015) The revolt against tourism, *The New York Times*, 17 July. http://www.nytimes.com/2015/07/19/opinion/sunday/the-revolt-against-tourism.html?_r=0 (Accessed September 2018.)

Blanco-Romero, A., Blázquez-Salom, M. and Cànoves, G. (2018) Barcelona, housing rent bubble in a tourist city: Social responses and local policies. *Sustainability*, 10(6): 1–18.

Colau, A. (2014), Mass tourism can kill a city – just ask Barcelona's residents, *The Guardian*, 2 September. https://www.theguardian.com/commentisfree/2014/sep/02/mass-tourism-kill-city-barcelona (Accessed 30 October 2018.)

Degen, M. and Garcia Cabeza, M. (2012) The transformation of the 'Barcelona Model': An analysis of culture, urban regeneration and governance. *International Journal of Urban and Regional Research*, 36 (5): 1022–1038.

El Prat Airport (n.d.) Barcelona Airport. https://www.aeropuertobarcelona-elprat.com/ingl/index.html (Accessed August 2018.)

Euromonitor International (2017) WTM London 2017 Edition. Top 100 City Destinations Ranking. https://www.euromonitor.com/top-100-city-destinations-ranking-wtm-london-2017-edition/report (Accessed 25 August 2017.)

Fair Toursim (n.d.) We've closed down more than 2,000 illegal tourist beds. http://www.fairtourism.barcelona/

Faris, S. (2015) Barcelona's new mayor wants to send tourists packing. *Bloomberg Businessweek*, 23 September. https://www.bloomberg.com/news/features/2015-09-23/barcelona-s-new-mayor-wants-to-send-tourists-packing (Accessed September 2018.)

Gillman, O. (2014) Brits out! Fury in Barcelona at boozy tourists: Locals in revolt over revellers from UK, *Mail Online*, 22 August. http://www.dailymail.co.uk/news/article-2732041/Picture-Italian-men-running-naked-Barcelona-supermarket-lunchtime-sparks-mass-anti-drunken-tourists-protests-city.html (Accessed September 2018.)

Goodwin, H. (2016) Managing Tourism in Barcelona, *Responsible Tourism Partnership Working Paper 1*. http://haroldgoodwin.info/RTPWP/01%20Managing%20Tourism%20in%20Barcelona.pdf (Accessed September 2018.)

Goodwin, H. (2017) The Challenge of Overtourism, *Responsible Tourism Partnership Working Paper 4*. http://haroldgoodwin.info/pubs/RTP'WP4Overtourism01'2017.pdf (Accessed August 2018.)

Institute for Research in Biomedicine (n.d). Living in Barcelona. https://www.irbbarcelona.org/en/phd-and-postdocs/irb-barcelona-international-postdoctoral-programme/living-barcelona (Accessed August 2018.)

Kassam, A. (2014). Naked Italians spark protests against antics of drunken tourists in Barcelona, *The Guardian*, 21 August. https://www.theguardian.com/world/2014/aug/21/naked-italians-protests-drunken-tourists-barcelona (Accessed September 2018.)

La Vanguardia (2014) Segunda noche de protestas en la Barceloneta contra el turismo de borrachera, *La Vanguardia*, 21 August. www.lavanguardia.com/local/barcelona/20140821/54413250547/segunda-noche-protestas-barceloneta-turismo-borrachera.html (Accessed September 2018.)

Mount, I. (2015) Barcelona: A victim of its own tourism success? *Fortune*, 30 March. http://fortune.com/2015/03/30/barcelona-tourism/ (Accessed September 2018.)

Observatori del Turisme a Barcelona (2017) Barcelona tourism activity report. https://ajuntament.barcelona.cat/turisme/sites/default/files/1_turisme_estadistiques_2017_caps1_1.pdf (Accessed August 2018.)

O'Sullivan, F. (2014) Barcelona organizes against 'binge tourism' – and eyes a street protester for mayor, *CityLab*, 27 August. https://www.citylab.com/equity/2014/08/barcelona-organizes-against-binge-tourismand-eyes-a-street-protester-for-mayor/379239/ (Accessed September 2018.)

Port de Barcelona and Barcelona Turisme (2014) Cruise activity in Barcelona: Impact on the Catalan economy and socioeconomic proile of cruise passengers. https://professional.barcelonaturisme.com/imgfiles/estad/Informe_ACPBCN_2014_ENG_web.pdf (Accessed September 2018.)

Rainsford, S. (2009) Shock tactics to fight Barcelona crime, *BBC News*, 24 December. http://news.bbc.co.uk/1/hi/world/europe/8427888.stm (Accessed September 2009.)

Ramoneda, J. (2011) Barcelona, open city. *Journal of Contemporary Culture*, 6: 6–13.

Responsible Tourism Partnership (n.d.) What is Responsible Tourism? http://responsibletourismpartnership.org/what-is-responsible-tourism/ (Accessed 28 October 2018.)

Sinkeviciute, N. (2014) Tourism boom in Barcelona: Strengthening the economy or troubling local residents? *Catalan News*, 7 October. http://www.catalannewsagency.com/life-style/item/tourism-boom-in-barcelona-strengthening-the-economy-or-troubling-local-residents (Accessed September 2018.)

Smith, A. (2005) Conceptualizing city image change: The 're-imaging' of Barcelona, *Tourism Geographies*, 7 (4): 398–423.

Statista (2018) Number of cruise passengers in in the Port of Barcelona from 1990 to 2017. https://www.statista.com/statistics/457624/cruise-passengers-in-barcelona-spain/ (Accessed August 2018.)

Tremlett, G. (2009) Barcelona split over campaign to banish sleaze from Ramblas, *The Guardian*, 24 May. https://www.theguardian.com/world/2009/may/24/barcelona-crime-las-ramblas (Accessed September 2018.)

Zonabus (n.d.) Parking for tourist coaches. https://www.zonabus.cat/en/home/ (Accessed 30 October 2018.)

Emma Nolan and Hugues Séraphin
10 Venice: capacity and tourism

Introduction

In many countries, particularly in Europe, residents of tourism destinations are forming and joining anti-tourism movements. These movements are particularly vigorous in Spain, Italy, United Kingdom and Croatia. The motives behind these movements are mainly related to the negative impact of too much tourism on: the heritage of the destination, the quality of life of residents and the state of the local environment, and are also sometimes related to the economic impacts of tourism for some local businesses (Buckley, 2017a; Coldwell, 2017; Leadbeater, 2017; Paris, 2017; Routledge, 2001; Séraphin, Sheeran and Pilato, 2018; Tapper, 2017). The rise of anti-tourism movements demonstrates that some destinations are not managing their tourism industries sustainably. Equally important, anti-tourism movements are evidence of the fact that residents are prioritising their quality of life over income that may be generated locally by tourism (Croes et al., 2017; Séraphin, Sheeran and Pilato, 2018).

In this chapter, the focus is on Venice, perhaps the most famous destination in the world (Russo, 2002). The city appeals to a variety of tourists, but most come to visit its unique canal system and rich array of heritage buildings. Many tourists arrive by train or road (Russo, 2002) but Venice is also a busy port city and attracts a high number of cruise liners, so many day visitors arrive by boat. The number of overnight visitors per year rose from 7.5 million to well over 10 million between 2005 and 2015. Even more significantly, in 2017 the number of day-trippers reached just under 35 million (Milano, 2017). This ever-growing swell of visitors has begun to considerably erode the condition of some of Venice's key attractions and reduce the quality of life of the city residents (Ganzaroli et al., 2017; Modak, 2017; WCED, 1987). Today, many Venetians feel that the local authorities prioritise the economic value of tourism over their wellbeing and, as such, the tension between visitors, the dwindling number of residents and policy makers has reached boiling point.

Venice is now clearly struggling to cope with the vast number of tourists that it receives. The city appears to have exceeded its "carrying capacity" for tourism; in other words, exceeded the maximum limit of tourism development (Borg et al., 1996). Government officials, residents and business owners have put forward a number of proposals for managing tourism, but as yet they have all proved unworkable. In terms of destination management, Venice can be considered to be a "falling destination" (Séraphin Sheeran and Pilato, 2018: 374) due to the strain of too much tourism in the city. The destination's stakeholders must therefore introduce measures to sustainably manage this beautiful lagoon city, to ensure its future prosperity.

https://doi.org/10.1515/9783110607369-010

This chapter will explore the development of this unique tourist destination and, in particular, the impact of the rising number of visitors and of cruise tourism on Venice. The chapter will also review the challenges of destination management that are relevant to Venice and demonstrate how the lack of a coordinated approach to destination management is hampering efforts to control visitor numbers and ameliorate the negative impacts of mass tourism on the city.

Background

Venice was established in the 5th century and was initially designed to provide a haven from invasion. The city later emerged as a destination known for its architecture and culture, largely thanks to the wealth generated by international trade merchants (Deheyna and Shaffer, 2007). Indeed, Venice became a prestigious city, recognised throughout the world (Brown, 1997) for its palaces and churches, including the Palazzo Moncenigo, Palazzo Ca d'Oro, Cathedral of San Marco and San Geremia, which greatly contributed to Venice's reputation as the golden city of the West (Fisher, 1996). The city's image eroded somewhat, however, with the introduction of new trade routes and the ports that were developed in the modern age (Jay, 2000).

The 20th century saw Venice rise again in triumph, this time as one of the most popular tourist destinations in the world, with tourists drawn to its beauty, heritage and unique landscape. Between 1949 and 1977 the number of overnight visitors to the city rose from 400,000 to over 1 million (Massiani and Santoro, 2012). At the end of the 1970s, changes in the Italian economy led to a new interest in urban planning to embrace tourism and develop Venice accordingly (Russo, 2002). Then in 1987, UNESCO recognised Venice and its lagoon as a World Heritage site (WCED, 1987), which generated even greater interest in the city as a destination and contributes to this day to its enduring attraction.

The city has felt the strain of the large numbers of tourists since the 1980s, however. In 1991, the first quantitative study to measure the carrying capacity for Venice was published, which posited a maximum number of 25,000 visitors per day, a figure that was already being surpassed (Massiani and Santoro, 2012). Despite this and other clear warnings to Venetian policy makers about overtourism, not only did the local authorities ignore the advice (Ganzaroli et al., 2017), they began to put in place further infrastructure to support the developing cruise industry. With its ease of access to the Adriatic Sea, Venice became the fourth-busiest cruise port in Europe and an immensely popular cruise destination, and as of 2018 had nearly 1 million cruise passengers visiting each year (Séraphin, Sheeran and Pilato, 2018). The cruise industry is lucrative, with Venice obtaining an economic input of around half a billion Euros per year from cruise passengers alone (Pesce et al., 2018). At the same time, the emergence of budget transport (discount airlines and coaches) and budget accommodation have made Venice more affordable for tourists (Séraphin,

Sheeran and Pilato, 2018). This, in addition to cruise ship tourism, has seen the overall number of tourist arrivals rise alarmingly and in 2017 visitor numbers averaged 60,000 per day (Modak, 2017) (see Fig. 10.1). As a result, the destination is losing its alluring reputation, and was recently described as being in danger of becoming 'Disneyland on the Sea' (Horowitz, 2017).

Fig. 10.1: Venice crowds (photo credit: Kefca-shutterstock).

The impacts of overtourism

Overtourism has been particularly evident in Venice, and has led to the expression "the Venice Syndrome", which refers to "the phenomena of tourism saturation and the exodus of local residents to the surrounding urban centres" (Milano, 2017: 9). The figures below (Figs. 10.2 and 10.3) present the rise in the number of overnight stays and the concurrent decrease in Venice's population, illustrating the severity of the Venice Syndrome.

The impacts of overtourism in Venice can be seen in terms of damage to built heritage and local lagoon ecosystems, increasing housing prices and rising crime. Furthermore, overtourism has led to a decrease in the quality of visitor experiences. The vast number of tourists poses a threat to the heritage of Venice because the city is built on wooden piles, which makes it fragile. Heritage structures are therefore damaged by the high footfall generated by the tourism industry. The cruise industry

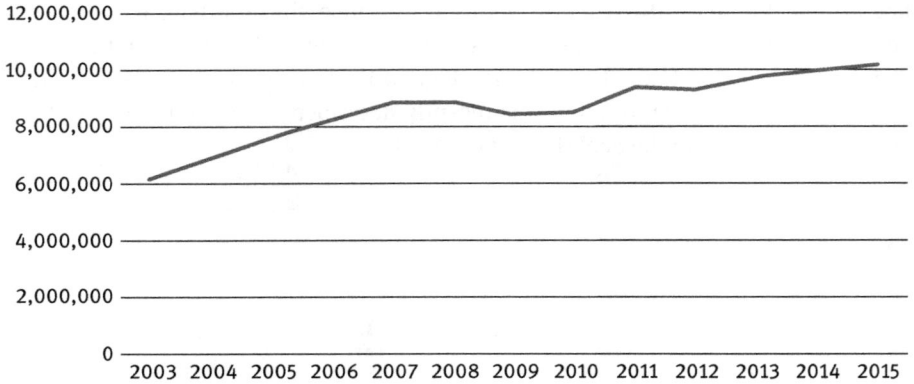

Fig. 10.2: The number of overnight stays in Venice, 2000–2015 (source: Milano, 2017: 9).

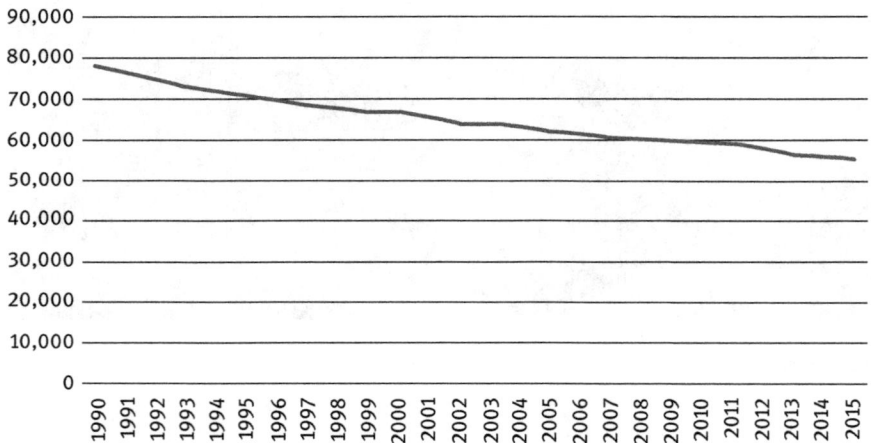

Fig. 10.3: The Decrease in Venice's Population (source: Milano, 2017: 10).

poses a particular threat, and the damage it causes could place Venice at risk of joining the UNESCO list of World Heritage in Danger (Pesce, 2015). Cruise ships not only bring in large numbers of tourists, adding to the footfall and the associated damage to local heritage, but in addition the ships churn up the silt from the bed of the lagoon, which, along with the waves and vibrations created by the massive ships, undermines the foundations of the city (DW, 2017). Furthermore, the current cruise routes into Venice are through environmentally sensitive waters, and the pollution they create harms local ecosystems.

Venice is also facing a major threat that is not helped by overtourism. It is sinking. Since the beginning of the 20th century, Venice has sunk by 23 centimetres due to the combination of rising sea level and a drop in land level (Ministry of

Infrastructure and Transport and Venice Water Authority, 2009). This has resulted in floods becoming more frequent and intense, causing further damage to the city's built heritage and to the lagoon ecosystem. St Mark's Square (Piazza San Marco), for example, the principal public square of Venice, gets flooded regularly (Camuffo, et al., 2017). In December 2008 and again in October 2018, the water level in Venice rose to 156 cm, the fourth-highest level ever recorded, and with the impact of Climate Change ever-rising tides are predicted, with flooding set to become an even more serious issue (The Guardian, 2018).

With the increase in tourists, demand has increased for accommodation and recently many people have taken advantage of new online means of renting short-term accommodation, such as Airbnb. A 2017 study found that the number of Airbnb properties in Venice was 6,027, with 74% of these rentals including use of the entire house or apartment (Milano, 2017). This has led to a rise in housing prices and a shortage of rental apartments for residents. Indeed, Venice has become the most expensive city on the Italian Peninsula. Consequently, many locals are being squeezed out (Russo, 2002).

A related issue is the resident to visitor ratio (see Tab. 10.1 and Fig. 10.4). In the central area around St Mark's Square, approximately 34% of the users are tourists and 49% are residents (the balance of 17% is attributable to commuters and students) on average during the year, but in peak season (July to October) tourists account for 67% of users (Russo, 2002).

Tab. 10.1: Comparison of overnight tourists and residents in Venice (source: Milano, 2017).

Year	Overnight stay tourists	Population of Venice	Ratio of overnight stay tourists to population
2003	6,212,412	63,947	1.03%
2004	6,930,073	63,353	0.91%
2005	7,670,433	62,296	0.81%
2006	8,245,154	61,611	0.75%
2007	8,842,874	60,755	0.69%
2008	8,847,539	60,311	0.68%
2009	8,445,911	59,942	0.71%
2010	8,521,247	59,621	0.70%
2011	9,417,872	58,991	0.63%
2012	9,310,132	58,215	0.63%
2013	9,778,225	56,683	0.58%
2014	9,983,416	56,311	0.56%
2015	10,182,829	55,583	0.55%

With tourists outnumbering residents to such an extent, residents feel that their city is being taken over and is being changed in ways they dislike (DW, 2017). Resident satisfaction and attitudes towards visitor arrivals fluctuate with the seasonality of tourism

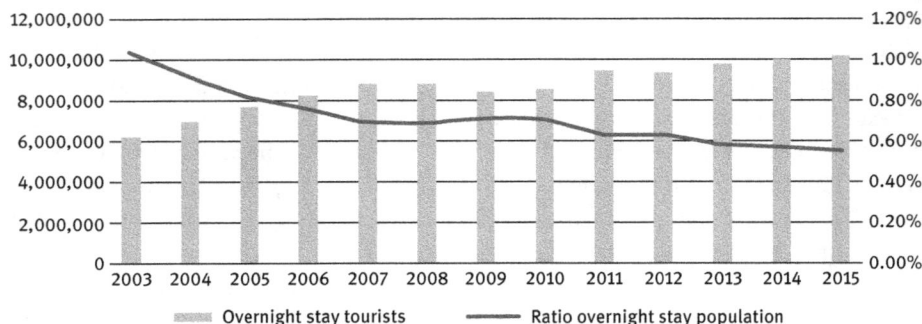

Fig. 10.4: Comparison of overnight tourists and residents in Venice (source: Milano, 2017).

(Bimonte and Faralla, 2016, Kim et al., 2013), and in the summer months, the city has been likened to a warzone (Buckley, 2017b). Another key issue for residents is that the majority of tourists are day-trippers, so their economic contribution to Venice per person is relatively small. This has provoked anger among some business owners and residents who feel that these visitors take from the destination and give nothing in return (Al Jazeera, 2014). Such anger is fuelled by anti-social behaviour by tourists, such as paddling in the fountains and drinking on the street (Coldwell, 2017).

As a consequence of these factors, tension between residents and visitors, and between business owners and visitors has grown extremely high and this has led to a rise in crime levels and protests by residents (Yazdi and Khanalizadeh, 2017). For example, anti-tourist protests were held in spring 2018, with protesters chanting "free Venice" (Smith, 2018). Reports of flagrant overcharging of tourists may be another symptom of the growing resentment towards visitors (Kington, 2017).

The large numbers of cruise ships and passengers in Venice and the damage caused by these ships and tourists sparked a "no big ships campaign", and the accompanying protests by residents had the result that only half of the cruise terminals are now in regular use (DW, 2017). This has increased tension between residents and the Venice Port Authority, which claims that cruise liners are a scapegoat and are not to blame for Venice's problems (CBS, 2016). In response to demands by residents, in November 2017 the city government announced a ban on the largest cruise ships. The ban will come into effect in 2021 (Buckley, 2017b).

Overtourism has not only had negative impacts on the city of Venice and its residents, but it has also diluted the visitor experience. This is because crowding contributes to a decrease in tourists' level of satisfaction with the destination (Ganzaroli et al., 2017). This dissatisfaction can lead to poor visitor behaviour (Zehrer and Raich, 2016). Anti-social behaviour by tourists then, in turn, further antagonises residents, as noted above. This resentment has in turn led to a negative image of the destination among visitors and there has been much negative media coverage of the situation in Venice. Thus, overtourism promotes and sustains resentment, anger and intolerance among visitors and residents alike.

Governance and marketing of Venice: responses to overtourism

While the governors of Venice recognise the issues, overall there has been very little progress in developing a system of governance that both supports tourism and protects the city and its residents (Ganzaroli et al., 2017). Furthermore, Venice lacks a coordinated approach to combating the effects of overtourism. The absence of a strategy is another factor fuelling anger and resentment among residents. Residents do not think that enough is being done to protect the fragile heritage structures of Venice and retain the local population. They believe that the municipality is more interested in growth and profits than in the well-being of locals (DW, 2017).

The urban areas of Venice are governed by the municipality, a body comprising an elected mayor and town councillors, and major decisions regarding tourism in Venice are taken by the mayor (currently Luigi Brugnaro) and the council. Among the latest measures taken are fines for tourists who sit in undesignated areas and the installation of barriers to separate locals and tourists (Coffey, 2018). Earlier measures included the introduction of the 'Venice Card' in 2004. The scheme was designed to give pre-booked visitors priority access to attractions; it sought to manage the flow of tourists to key sites and to encourage visitors to pre-plan their itineraries. The various public and private owners of attractions did not cooperate, however, as they differed in their views on how to manage tourists and had different priorities, which led to the failure of this initiative (Massiani and Santoro, 2012). Other strategies tried by the municipality have included introducing new taxes, developing advance booking systems, creating alternative access routes, providing virtual access to the city, limiting the number of hotel beds and restricting access to the main piazza. To deal with the flow of tourists generated by the cruise sector, the Venetian authorities suggested a redirection of passenger traffic. This suggestion was not supported by local merchants, however, who were keen to ensure the direct flow of tourists to the centre of the city (Séraphin et al., 2018).

To ensure better management of the cruise industry, with the aim of making it sustainable, the government established a committee, the Comitatone, led by the Italian minister for transport. However, as of 2018 the committee had not produced an official plan and the situation remained stagnant (Pesce et al., 2018). The Comitatone was tasked with finding a way to minimise the impact of cruise liners by the year 2021 (Buckley, 2017b) and has proposed changes, but the largely-privatised Venice Port Authority has considerable influence over the management of the destination and is resisting some of these changes (Pesce et al., 2018). An added issue is that the local authorities want to see a return on their investment in the city's modern port facilities and cruise terminals. The authorities are therefore unlikely to give in to all of the residents' demands regarding the cruise ships.

In managing tourism in the future, the municipality is faced with a dilemma. On one hand, around 28% of the Venetian population are heavily dependent on tourism, and a further 17% derive a regular income from the industry (Quinn, 2007). On the other hand, it has become evident that the growth of tourism must be restricted to ensure the long-term survival of the city.

Challenges and discussion

A key issue is the high number of day visitors to the destination, with excursionists visiting from other hotspots such as Lake Garda, Cortina and Rimini (Buckley, 2017b) and a vast number of cruise passengers passing through. Day visitors tend to stay around eight hours in the city but spend very little money (Massiani and Santoro, 2012). The lack of preplanning by these visitors, combined with poor marketing of the destination's lesser-known attractions, means that the most famous attractions and locations become congested quickly while the city's other attractions struggle to attract visitors (Russo, 2002).

Another key issue is poor management of access routes to the city, and of the waterways in particular (Massiani and Santoro, 2012). The poor management of Venice as a tourist destination has been attributed to political instability (Massiani and Santoro, 2012) and the lack of a coherent tourism strategy or the support of key stakeholders (Russo, 2002).

To date, the strategies to address overtourism, such as establishing rules and checkpoints for visitors (Peltier, 2018), have proven to be ineffective (Russo, 2002). A suggested strategy is to segregate tourists from locals to minimise antagonistic contact (Lam, 2018). This approach, labelled Trexit (tourist exit) by Séraphin et al. (2018), is not an economically sustainable solution, however, and could damage the image of the destination. Successful approaches to reducing the negative impacts of mass tourism elsewhere in Europe include: the education of tourists, the provision of an authentic experience focused on gastronomy, diversion to other destinations, and the use of a "respect" campaign (e.g. Amsterdam) (Séraphin et al., 2018).

In the case of Venice, there are two key barriers to progress. First, Venice lacks an inclusive and effective decision-making platform and second, key stakeholders (residents, businesses and port authorities) have divergent views on what is in Venice's best interest (Pesce et al., 2018). Thus, a major challenge is to find solutions that will not only address the issue of overtourism but, equally important, will also be supported by all of the destination's stakeholders.

To operate efficiently, the destination must be managed by a clearly identifiable destination marketing organisation (DMO) that works towards achievable goals, within a flexible but robust strategic plan (Ritchie and Crouch, 2003). Part of the role of the DMO is to ensure the competitiveness of the destination, including through managing the image of the destination (Séraphin et al., 2016) and maintaining the quality of life of the local residents (Croes et al., 2018; Ivlevs, 2017). Furthermore, a DMO can influence the perception of the destination by potential visitors through careful marketing (Gómez et al., 2018).

Venice does not have an official DMO, however, and the elected politicians tasked with managing the destination are struggling to meet the conflicting demands of residents (who oppose tourism) and the business owners and cruise industry that welcome them, and are also seeking the cooperation of an array of government departments and authorities. Such cooperation is difficult to achieve due to the large number of stakeholders. For example, managing cruise tourism requires the involvement and cooperation of the municipality, the Harbour Master's Office, the Port Authority, the Venice Waters Superintendent's Office, the Prime Minister's Office, the Ministry of Transportation, the Ministry of Culture and Environment, the Minister of Education, the Governor's Office and the local community (Butowski, 2018).

The lack of a definable DMO means that there is no overarching marketing strategy for the destination and no coherent or effective marketing campaign in place. As such, efforts to manage the flow of tourists have been ineffective. Séraphin, Sheeran and Pilato (2018) suggest that Venice must move towards an "ambidextrous" approach to managing tourism. This approach consists of using existing strategies to mitigate the negative impacts of tourism (exploitation) and developing a new strategy tailored to meet the needs of the destination (exploration).

An important part of the solution is to develop a marketing campaign for the city (Russo, 2002) that enables the destination to attract the desired type and number of visitors (Séraphin, Yallop, Capatina and Gowreesunkar, 2018). A coordinated marketing campaign can also control the key messages, such as drawing attention to some of the lesser-known attractions and promote appropriate behaviour among tourists. Additionally, it has been suggested that soft interventions (providing information, incentives, etc.) will be more effective in Venice than hard interventions (Russo, 2002), as the latter are not well-received by visitors; for example, restricting access to attractions (Ganzaroli et al., 2017).

The sustainability of a tourism destination is achieved through the retention and protection of its resources and the ability to compete within the marketplace (Ritchie and Crouch (2003) and this must be underpinned by a long-term strategy for the destination (Falk and Hagsten, 2018, and Grzinic and Saftic, 2012). For plans to be effective in counteracting the effects of overtourism, they must be supported by the destination's principal stakeholders; namely residents, attraction owners, transport operators and local businesses. As such, it is now imperative that the municipality creates, funds and supports a discernible destination management plan (DMP) for the city, with the power and resources to draw together the city's stakeholders, who must agree upon and implement a strategy for the destination. Until the management of the destination is in control, the impacts of overtourism and the "Venice Syndrome" will continue to be felt and further deterioration of the city will be inevitable, which will inevitably impact all of the city's stakeholders.[1]

Conclusion

The combined number of overnight tourists, day-trippers and cruise passengers visiting Venice has reached an all-time high and the city is now unable to cope with them. Visitors outnumber residents to an enormous degree, and tourism is negatively affecting residents. As well as causing damage to the city's built heritage, the large numbers of visitors, and sometimes their behaviour, has antagonised locals. As a result, tourismphobia and the anti-tourism movement are growing.

In spite of this, few measures have been implemented to reduce the flow of tourists to the city. Most efforts to combat overtourism in Venice have been hard interventions and have so far proved largely ineffective. This failure is attributable to the lack of cooperation between the destination's stakeholders and the absence of clear direction and strategy from the city's policy makers.

Overtourism has been apparent in Venice for more than 20 years; yet the problem persists. And, so the question remains, how much longer can Venice survive under the strain of too much tourism?

References

Al Jazeera (2014) Venice considers fees on daytime tourists, Al Jazeera, 3 September. https://www.youtube.com/watch?v=cY4vuGGgj1s (Accessed 20 July 2018.)

Bimonte, S. and Faralla, V. (2016) Does residents' perceived life satisfaction vary with tourist season? A two-step survey in a Mediterranean destination, *Tourism Management*, 55: 199–208

Borg, J. V. D., Costa, P. and Gotti, G. (1996) Tourism in European heritage cities. *Annals of Tourism Research*, 23(2): 306–321.

Brown, P. F. (1997) *The Renaissance of Venice*, London: Weidenfeld and Nicolson.

Buckley, J. (2017a) Florence launches campaign telling tourists how to behave. http://www.cntraveler.com/story/florence-launches-campagin-tellingtourists-how-to-behave (Accessed 9 July 2018.)

---

[1] Editors' note: In January, 2019, the recently approved Italian budget announced a provision for an "entrance tax" on day visitors to be introduced in Venice. The precise amount and method of collection is to be determined by the city council, but is expected to be in the region of 10 euros. Those staying visitors paying the current bednight tax will not pay the new tax. Crowd management, policing, waste and garbage disposal are intended purposes for the additional funds raised.

Buckley, J. (2017b) Italy bans huge cruise ships from Venice city centre, *The Independent*, 8
    November. https://www.independent.co.uk/travel/news-and-advice/venice-cruise-ship-ban-
    55-tonnes-marghera-port-where-is-it-italy-a8044026.html (Accessed 21 July 2018.)
Butowski, L. (Ed.) (2018) *Mobilities, Tourism and Travel Behavior*, London: IntechOpen.
Camuffo, D., Bertolin, C. and Schenal, P. (2017) A novel proxy and the sea level rise in Venice, Italy,
    from 1350 to 2014, *Climatic Change*, 143 (1): 73–86.
CBS (2016) Famed Italian city suffering from too much of a good thing, *CBS*, 9 December. https://
    www.cbsnews.com/news/venice-italy-threatened-mass-tourism-unesco-world-heritage-site-
    in-danger/ (Accessed 20 July 2018.)
Chacko, H. E. and Marcell, M. H. (2008) Repositioning a tourism destination: The case of New
    Orleans after Hurricane Katrina, *Journal of Travel & Tourism Marketing*, 23 (2–4): 223–235.
Cisneros-Martinez, J. D. and Fernandez-Morales, A. (2015) Cultural tourism as tourist segment for
    reducing seasonality in a coastal area: The case study of Andalusia, *Current Issues in Tourism*,
    18 (8): 765–784.
Coffey, H. (2018) Venice tourists could be fined £500 for sitting down, *The Independent*, 20
    September. https://www.independent.co.uk/travel/news-and-advice/venice-sitting-ban-fine-
    tourists-overtourism-sit-mayor-luigi-brugnaro-a8547086.html (Accessed 25 September 2018.)
Coldwell, W. (2017) First Venice and Barcelona: Now anti-tourism marches spread across Europe,
    The Guardian, 10 August. https://www.theguardian.com/travel/2017/aug/10/anti-tourism-
    marches-spread-across-europe-venice-barcelona (Accessed 9 July 2018.)
Colomb, C. and Novy, J. (Eds.) (2016) *Protest and resistance in the tourist city*. New York: Routledge.
Croes, R., Rivera, M. A., Semrad, K. and Khalizadeh, J. (2017) *Happiness and tourism: Evidence from
    Aruba*, Orlando: The Dick Pope Sr. Institute for Tourism Studies.
Croes, R., Ridderstaat, J., and van Niekerk, M. (2018) Connecting quality of life, tourism
    specialization, and economic growth in small island destinations: The case of Malta. *Tourism
    Management*, 65: 212–223.
Deheyna, D. D. and Shaffer, L. R. (2007) 'Saving Venice: Engineering and ecology in the Venice
    lagoon', *Technology in Society*, 29: 205–213.
Dholah, D., Haw Fan Lun, N., Labonne, C., Lebon, S. and Munboth Lekh, A. (2015) *Carrying Capacity
    in Barbados*, BSc dissertation, Mauritius: University of Mauritius.
Dion, D. and Mazzalovo, G. (2016). Reviving sleeping beauty brands by rearticulating brand
    heritage, *Journal of Business Research*, 69 (12): 5894–5900.
DW (2017) Venice's battle against cruise ships, *DW English*, 16 November. https://www.youtube.
    com/watch?v=n7-rSbUWOvA (Accessed 20 July 2018.)
Falk, M. (2018) The art of attracting international conferences to European cities, *Tourism
    Economics*, 24 (3): 337–351.
Fischer, D. H. (1996) *The great wave: Price revolutions and the rhythm of history*, Oxford: Oxford
    University Press.
Ganzaroli, A., De Noni, I. and Van Baalen, P. (2017) Vicious advice: Analysing the impact of
    TripAdvisor on the quality of restaurants as part of the cultural heritage of Venice. *Tourism
    Management*, 61: 501–510.
Garay, L. and Canoves, G. (2011) Life cycles, stages and tourism history: The Catalonia (Spain)
    experience, *Annals of Tourism Research*, 38 (2): 651–671.
Gómez, M., Fernández, A. C. Molina, A. and Aranda, E. (2018) City branding in European capitals:
    An analysis from the visitor perspective, *Journal of Destination Marketing & Management*,
    7: 190–201.
Gowreesunkar, V. G., Séraphin, H. and Morrison, A. (2018) Destination Marketing Organisations:
    Roles and Challenges. In D. Gursoy, and C. G. Chi, (Eds.), *Routledge Handbook of Destination
    Marketing*, Abingdon, OX and New York: Routledge, pp. 16–34.

Gržinić, J. and Saftić D. (2012) Approach to the development of destination management in Croatian tourism, *Journal of Contemporary Management Issues*, 17 (1): 59–74.

Hano, K. (2012) Tourism and the creative destruction in Krasiczyn, Poland, *Journal of Hospitality and Tourism*, 10 (1): 113–128.

Horowitz, J. (2017). Venice, invaded by tourists, risks becoming 'Disneyland on the Sea', *The New York Times*, 2 August. https://www.nytimes.com/2017/08/02/world/europe/venice-italy-tourist-invasion.html (Accessed25 September 2018.)

Ivlevs, A. (2017) Happy hosts? International tourist arrivals and residents' subjective well-being in Europe, *Journal of Travel Research*, 56 (5): 599–612.

Jay, P. (2000) *Road to Riches or The Wealth of Man*, London: Phoenix.

Kim, K., Uysal, M. and Sirgy, M. J. (2013) How does tourism in a community impact the quality of life of community residents? *Tourism Management*, 36: 527–540.

Kington, T. (2017) Venice mayor mocks tourists who were ripped off by waiters, *The Times*, 10 November. https://www.thetimes.co.uk/article/venice-mayor-mocks-tourists-who-were-ripped-off-by-waiters-rn5z7pzkx (Accessed 21 July 2018.)

Kirillova, K., Fu, X., Lehto, X. and Cai, L. (2014) What makes a destination beautiful? Dimensions of tourist aesthetic judgement, *Tourism Management*, 42: 282–293.

Lam, S. (2018) Overtourism in Venice: City will segregate tourists and locals this summer, *iNews*, 26 April. https://inews.co.uk/inews-lifestyle/travel/overtourism-in-venice-city-will-segregate-tourists-and-locals-this-summer/ (Accessed 9 July 2018.)

Leadbeater, C. (2017) Anti-tourism protesters in Barcelona slash tyres on sightseeing buses and rental bikes, *The Telegraph*, 2 August. https://www.telegraph.co.uk/travel/news/bus-attack-in-barcelona-adds-to-fears-as-tourism-protests-grow/ (Accessed 9 July 2018.)

Massiani, J. and Santoro, G. (2012) The Relevance of the Concept of Capacity for the Management of a Tourist Destination: Theory and Application to Tourism Management in Venice, *Rivista Italiana di Economia Demografia e Statistica*, 66 (2): 141–156.

Milano, C. (2017) *Overtourism and Tourismphobia; Global trends and local context*, Barcelona: Ostelea School of Tourism & Hospitality.

Miller, K. M. and McTavish, D. (2013) *Making and managing public policy*, London: Routledge.

Ministry of Infrastructure and Transport and Venice Water Authority (2009) Venice 02 – Mose System. https://www.youtube.com/watch?v=7HMVT8OMPA4 (Accessed 25 September 2018.)

Modak, S. (2017) Venice looks to limit tourist numbers with new measures, *Conde Nast Traveler*, 28 April. https://www.cntraveler.com/story/venice-looks-to-limit-tourist-numbers-with-new-measures (Accessed on 9 July 2018.)

Paris, N. (2017) Tourists have turned Oxford into 'hell', locals claim, *The Telegraph*, 8 August. https://www.telegraph.co.uk/travel/news/oxford-tourist-hell-overcrowding-residents-locals-complain/ (Accessed 9 July 2018.)

PBS (2017) Irresistible to tourists, has Venice become unwelcoming to its inhabitants? *PBS News Hour*, 29 August. https://www.youtube.com/watch?v=P-TQf9NS5Yw (Accessed 20 July 2018.)

Peltier, D. (2018) Venice tourism checkpoints are a sign of Europe's fractured approach to overtourism, *Skift*, 2 May. https://skift.com/2018/05/02/venice-tourism-checkpoints-are-a-sign-of-europes-fractured-approach-to-overtourism (Accessed 9 July 2018.)

Pesce, M., Terzi, S., Al-Jawasreh, R. I. M., Bommarito, C., Calgaro, L., Fogarin, S., Russo, E., Marcomini, A. and Linkov, I. (2018) Selecting sustainable alternatives for cruise ships in Venice using multi-criteria decision analysis, *Science of the Total Environment*, 642: 668–678.

Pike, S. and Mason, R. (2011) Destination competitiveness through the lens of brand positioning: The case of Australia's Sunshine Coast, *Current Issues in Tourism*, 14 (2): 169–182.

Quinn, B. (2007) Performing tourism in Venice: Local residents in focus, *Annals of Tourism Research*, 34 (2): 458–476.

Rigby, S. (2017) Venice's cruise ship ban is hiding its tourism problem, not fixing it, *Quartz*, 10 November. https://qz.com/1125137/venices-cruise-ship-ban-is-hiding-its-tourism-problem-not-fixing-it/ (Accessed 9 July 2018.)

Richardson, D. (2017) WTM 2017: Europe suffering the strain of tourism, *TTG*. https://www.ttgmedia.com/wtm/wtm-news/wtm-2017-europe-suffering-the-strain-of-tourism-12206 (Accessed 9 July 2018.)

Ritchie, J. R. B. and Crouch, G. I. (2003) The *Competitive Destination: A Sustainable Tourism Perspective*, Wallingford: CABI.

Routledge, P. (2001) 'Selling the rain', resisting the sale: Resistant identities and the conflict over tourism in Goa. *Social & Cultural Geography*, 2 (2): 221–240.

Russo, A. P. (2002) The 'vicious circle' of tourism development in heritage cities, *Annals of Tourism Research*, 29 (1): 165–182.

Séraphin, H., Ambaye, M., Gowreesunkar, V. and Bonnardel, V. (2016) A marketing research tool for destination marketing organizations' logo design, *Journal of Business Research*, 69 (11): 5022–5027.

Séraphin, H., Yallop, A., Capatina, A. and Gowreesunkar, V. (2018) Heritage in tourism organisations' branding strategy: The case of a post-colonial, post-conflict and post-disaster destination, *International Journal of Culture, Tourism and Hospitality Research*, 12 (1).

Séraphin, H., Smith, S., Scott, P. and Stoakes, P. (2018) Destination management through organisational ambidexterity: A study of Haitian enclaves, *Journal of Destination Marketing & Management*, 9: 389–392.

Séraphin, H., Sheeran, P. and Pilato, M. (2018) Over-tourism and the fall of Venice as a destination, *Journal of Destination Marketing & Management*, 9: 374–376.

Séraphin, H., Gowreesunkar, V., Roselé-Chim, P., Duplan, Y. J. and Korstanje, M. (2018) Tourism planning and innovation: The Caribbean under the spotlight, *Journal of Destination Marketing & Management*, 9: 384–388.

Smith, O. (2018) Anti-tourist protests erupt: Chaos on streets of Venice as locals tear down barriers, *Express*, 30 April. https://www.express.co.uk/news/world/952796/Tourism-tourists-Venice-travel-segegration-checkpoints-protest (Accessed 28 September 2018.)

Tapper, J. (2017) As touting for punt trips becomes a crime, is tourism overwhelming Britain's cities? *The Guardian*, 30 July. https://www.theguardian.com/uk-news/2017/jul/29/cambridge-tourist-boom-ruins-city (Accessed 30 October 2018.)

The Guardian (2018) Three-quarters of Venice flooded by exceptional high tide, *The Guardian*, 29 October. https://www.theguardian.com/world/2018/oct/29/venice-experiences-worst-flooding-since-2008 (Accessed 30 October 2018.)

World Commission on Environment and Development (WCED) (1987) *Our common future*, Oxford: Oxford University Press.

Yazdi, S. K. and Khanalizadeh, B. (2017) Tourism demand: A panel data approach. *Current Issues in Tourism*, 20 (8): 787–800.

Zehrer, A. and Raich, F. (2016) The impact of perceived crowding on customer satisfaction, *Journal of Hospitality and Tourism Management*, 29: 88–98.

Miroslav Rončák

11 Prague and the impact of low-cost airlines

Introduction

Prague, the capital of the Czech Republic, has experienced a tourist boom in recent decades (Prague City Tourism, 2017). This boom has brought economic benefits, but has also had numerous negative impacts. Johnson (1995) already saw the signs of high tourist concentration in the historical centre of Prague in 1995. Since then, the historic centre of Prague, and the Royal Way in particular, have evolved into a "tourist ghetto" (Dumbrovska, 2017). Although most local residents do not have a negative attitude towards tourists, tourism development has begun to constrain their everyday movement and quality of life (Dumbrovska, 2017). As tourism has grown and changed, new problems have arisen. For example, the rapid growth of Airbnb in Prague has led to increased night-time disturbances and has increased the cost of real estate, pricing many residents out of central Prague; while the uptake by tourists of Uber and other taxi alternatives has adversely affected Prague taxi drivers, who have protested the lack of regulation and unfair competition (Idnes.cz, 2018c).

This chapter will briefly discuss the reasons for the tourist boom in Prague, and will outline the problems that have arisen in connection with that boom along with the countermeasures that the city has adopted.

Background

The Czech Republic is located in Central Europe and shares borders with Germany, Austria, Slovakia and Poland. It has an area of 78,866 km^2, making it one of the smallest countries in Europe. The country has a population of approximately 10 million people (Czech Tourism, 2018). The country was formerly part of Czechoslovakia, which was a member of the "Soviet Bloc" from 1948 to 1989. Following the so-called "Velvet Revolution" of 1989 in which students demonstrated against the Communist one-party state, Czechoslovakia peacefully separated into two states (Czech Republic and Slovakia) in 1993 (Dumbrovska, 2013).

The capital city of the Czech Republic, Prague, is located in the northwest part of the country on the River Vltava. The city has an area of 496 km^2 and a population of 1.3 million. Dating back to the Romanesque period, Prague features a mix of architectural styles. The city was not seriously damaged during the world wars of the 20th century and today boasts rich cultural heritage. In 1992, the historic centre of Prague was inscribed as UNESCO World Heritage (UNESCO World Heritage Centre, n.d.). In 2000, the European Union designated Prague as a "European Capital of Culture", in recognition of the city's built heritage and rich culture (European Commission, n.d.).

https://doi.org/10.1515/9783110607369-011

Tourism development in Prague

Czechoslovakia's membership of the Soviet Bloc meant that the initial sources of tourists after World War II were communist countries. It was a highly closed destination in the 1950s and was one of the most expensive destinations in central Europe. In the 1960s, visitors from the Soviet Bloc accounted for around 90% of incoming tourists (Palatkova, 2014). After the revolution of 1989, the quality of accommodation facilities and services improved and tourism diversified. Prague was initially attractive to tourists as a developing "former Eastern Bloc" destination, but the city's charm later made it one of the most popular city destinations in the world. According to a Euromonitor study, in 2017 Prague was the fifth most visited city in Europe, following London, Paris, Rome and Istanbul (see Tab. 11.1).

Tab. 11.1: Arrivals of tourists and overnight stays – Top 10 European Cities (source: Euromonitor International, 2017).

Cities	Arrivals		Growth	Rank Change	Forecasted arrivals	
	2016	2017			2020	2025
London	19,190.3	19,842.8	3.4%	0	22,335.0	25,804.3
Paris	14,392.0	14,263.0	−0.9%	0	15,249.2	17,557.2
Rome	9,396.4	9,565.5	1.8%	▼2	10,404.4	11,951.9
Istanbul	9,174.4	8,642.3	−5.8%	▼4	9,541.2	11,622.3
Prague	8,182.5	8,550.7	4.5%	▼2	9,552.4	11,362.5
Barcelona	7,037.8	7,624.1	8.3%	0	8,024.4	8,899.4
Milan	6,695.1	6,882.5	2.8%	▲1	7,434.3	8,488.6
Amsterdam	6,345.1	6,570.4	3.6%	▼2	6,815.6	7,529.0
Antalya	6,173.4	6,457.4	4.6%	▼2	7,056.9	8,605.2
Vienna	5,867.6	6,043.7	3.0%	▼5	6,533.2	7,429.2

As illustrated in Fig. 11.1, tourist numbers increased from 1.6 million in 1989 to 2.6 million in 2000, and then to 7.6 million in 2017 (Prague City Tourism, 2017). The number of overnight stays likewise increased, rising from only 4.4 million in 1989 to 7.3 million in 2000, and then to 18.06 million in 2017 (Prague City Tourism, 2017). Experts predict further tourist growth in the coming years (Tab. 11.1).

Following the split of Czechoslovakia into the Czech Republic and Slovakia in 1993, the Czech Tourist Authority (Czech Tourism) was founded (Palatkova, 2014). Its activities focus on the promotion of the Czech Republic as an attractive tourist destination both domestically and abroad. The tourist boom was caused not only by the active marketing policy of Czech Tourist Authority and Prague, but also especially by global influences as noted in Chapter 2.

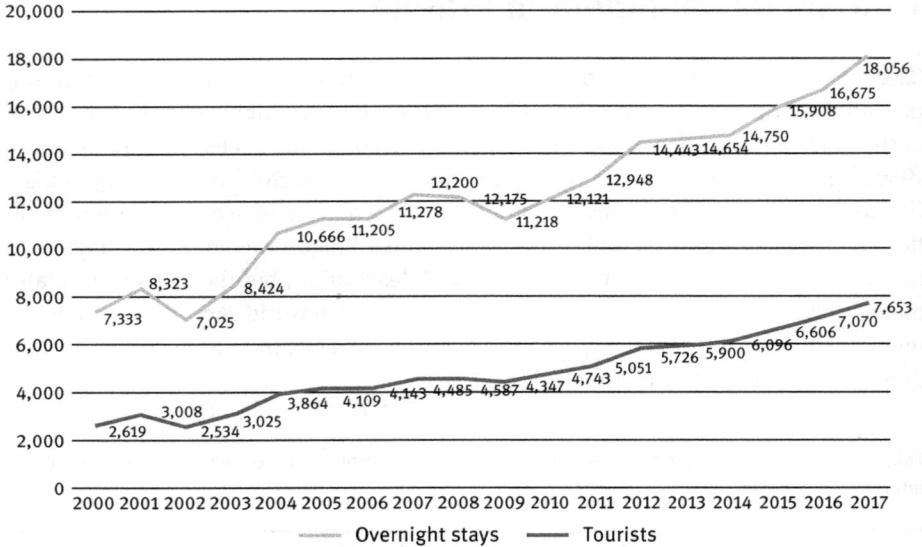

Fig. 11.1: Arrivals of tourists and overnight stays in collective tourist accommodation facilities in Prague 2000–2017 (source: Prague City Tourism, 2017).

The Czech Republic joined the European Union (EU) in 2004 and became a member of the Schengen area in 2007. These memberships had a major impact in terms of facilitating and accelerating visitor arrivals from the EU and Schengen member countries.

Marketing of Prague

On 1 January 1958, Prague City Tourism, the body that deals with the marketing and promotion of Prague, was established as the Prague Information Service. In 2016, Prague City Hall approved the use of "Prague City Tourism" as the official name for the marketing organisation. The change of the name had a positive impact on international recognition of the organisation and coincided with a change in the entire identity and philosophy of the organization. Prague City Tourism was established as a true destination marketing organization and as of 2018 was focused on spreading the reputation of Prague as a top tourist destination (Prague City Tourism, 2018). On 1 July 2018, Prague City Tourism made the transition from a public sector organisation sponsored by Prague City Hall to a joint stock company (COT Newsletter, 2018e).

Restitution and investment in restoration

In the 1990s, a number of initiatives led to changes in the ownership of buildings in Prague's historic centre. The most important mechanisms at the urban level were restitution and privatization (mostly the so-called "small privatization") (Dumbrovska, 2017). At this time, 70% of the entire housing stock in the historic core was restituted to the original owners or their heirs (Kadar, 2018). In Prague 1 district, which covers the Old Town, the Jewish Quarter, the Little Quarter, Hradcany, the New Town and tiny parts of Holesovice a Vinohrady (Municipal District Prague 1, 2018), 1178 houses were claimed for restitution in 1991 and 1992. Between 1992 and 1993 approximately 2500 apartment buildings were put up for sale, mostly in the historic inner city (Sykora and Simonickova, 1994).

In the early 1990s, tourism was one of the few prosperous sectors in the urban economy, and to keep up with demand from tourists it was necessary to invest in tourist infrastructure and to renovate the historic centre. Recognising the tourism potential, foreign investors with capital relocated tenants to other properties, renovated historic buildings and used them as rental flats for foreigners or converted them into hotels and office spaces. Indeed 76.2% of the hotels in the historical centre were formerly residential buildings (Kadar, 2018). Cooper and Morpeth (1998) calculated that 20,000 apartments were lost every year in the Czech Republic in the 1990s as a result of this process. This process helped with physical conservation, but it led to over-commercialization of the centre of Prague (Hammersley and Westlake, 1996). The number of collective accommodation establishments rose from 111 units in 1989 to 385 in 1996, and by 1996 the number of beds in collective accommodation had increased by more than 300% (Dumbrovska, 2017).

Meanwhile, the "small privatization" of 1991 and 1992 had a profound impact on retail outlets and services in Prague's historic centre. According to Sykora, "nearly 2,500 shops, restaurants and smaller enterprises found new owners or tenants in the small privatization auctions" (Sykora, 1994: 1156). Over time, facilities for residents such as cinemas, cafeterias, bookstores and essential stores (e.g. grocers, butchers, bakers, ironmongers, etc.) disappeared and were replaced by facilities that served tourist demand. In 2015, there were 168 retail outlets, 121 restaurants and 44 accommodation establishments on Prague's Royal Way. More than 90% of these facilities were tourist oriented (judging by the types of goods and services they provided and their prices). The retail outlets included souvenir shops, jewellery shops (mostly Czech garnet) and crystal shops (mostly labelled as Czech crystal) (Dumbrovska, 2017).

In August 2002, Prague was hit by destructive floods, which had a significant impact on tourist numbers that year. However, the floods also had a positive impact on the city of Prague because in response to the damage there was an immediate and extensive wave of reconstruction and many hotels, residences and historical monuments were refurbished (Prague City Tourism, 2018). This renovation work, along with the active marketing policy of Prague City Tourism, contributed to rapid tourism growth in the city.

The impact of low-cost airlines on Prague's tourism growth

Until 1989, air travel in Czech territory was heavily regulated. The state monopoly on air travel was abolished in March 1990, enabling companies to enter the Czech market. The first low-cost airline entered the Czech market at a time when the Czech Republic was not yet a member of the European Union. Low-cost airlines allowed cheap connections between Prague and other countries (Toman, 2008).

The entry of low-cost companies into the Czech market, connected Prague to a significantly larger number of cities throughout the world, and the numbers of flights to Prague per year grew rapidly, especially in the years 2004 to 2008. Figure 11.2 shows the growth in the number of flights.

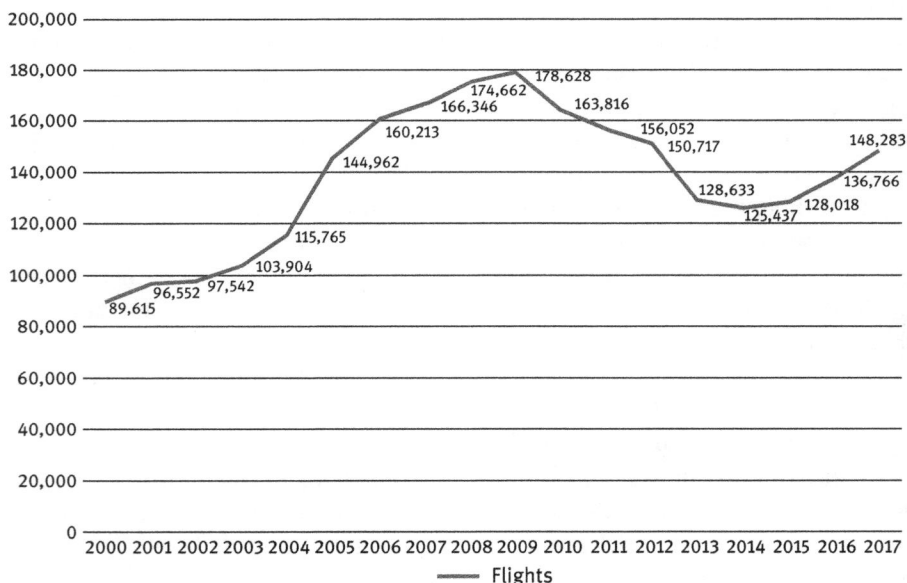

Fig. 11.2: Total number of flights at Prague Airport in 2000–2017 (source: based on Prague City Tourism, 2017).

Thanks to the low-cost airlines and Prague's relatively low prices, British and Irish visitors selected the city as a destination for "stag and hen trips" (Telegraph, 2004). Unfortunately, these weekend outings had negative impacts, including night-time disturbances caused by drunken youth and hooligans, and these visitors made certain areas of Prague off-limits to locals (Hoffman and Musil, 1999).

In spite of the negative impacts of tourism, marketing efforts continued and tourist numbers continued to grow. Figure 11.3 shows the immense growth of arrivals. While the numbers of arrivals by plane dropped in the years following the world economic crisis of 2008, in 2014 arrivals began to pick up again.

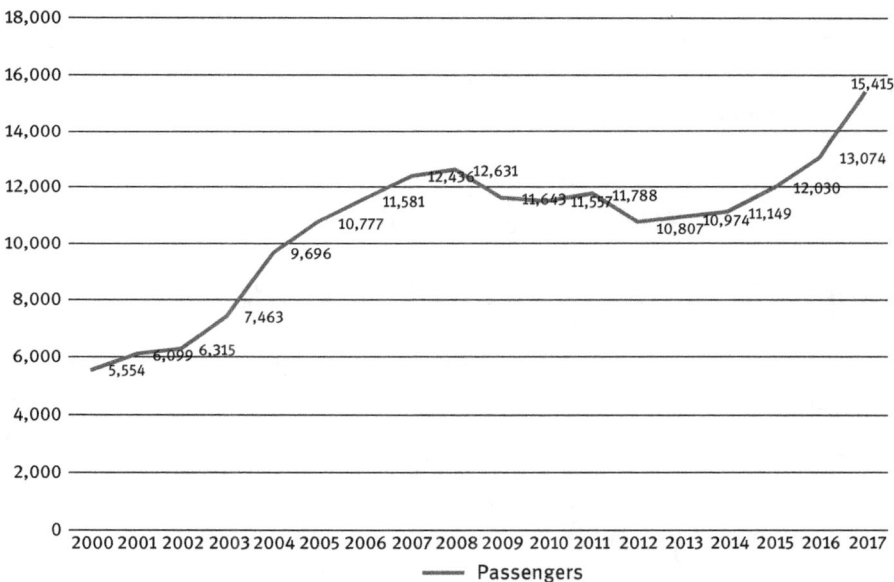

Fig. 11.3: Total number of passengers at Prague Airport in 2000–2017 (source: based on Prague City Tourism, 2017).

Tourist arrivals and overnight stays in collective tourist accommodation facilities rose steadily between 2009 and 2017 (Tab. 11.2).

As of 2016 almost 70 airlines were operating in the Czech market, with more than ten being low-cost. Nearly a quarter of the low-cost market was served by the British company EasyJet (Muchova, 2016). In 2017, the number of passengers of low-cost companies in the Czech market increased by 19.6% (Prague Airport, 2018b).

Tab. 11.2: Arrivals of tourists and overnight stays in collective tourist accommodation facilities in Prague in 2009–2017 (thousands) (source: Czech Statistical Office, 2018).

Year	2009	2010	2011	2012	2013	2014	2015	2016	2017
Tourist arrivals	4,347	4,743	5,051	5,726	5,900	6,096	6,606	7,070	7,653
Overnight stays	11,218	12,121	12,948	14,443	14,654	14,750	15,908	16,675	18,056

The low-cost share of the market has risen over the years and it is predicted to rise further (Muchova, 2016). Low-cost companies accounted for 22% of the market in 2010 and the share grew to 34% in 2016 (see Tab. 11.3).

Tab. 11.3: Airline seat and LCC share in the Czech Republic (source: OAG, 2016).

February 2010		February 2016	
Seats	**LCC share**	**Seats**	**LCC share**
529,012	22%	475,895	34%

Changes in tourism as a result of AirBNB and Uber

In recent years, tourist accommodation preferences have changed in line with technology, with more visitors choosing to stay in private accommodation, booked via Airbnb. In 2017, 1.02 million tourists to the Czech Republic booked their accommodation via Airbnb, which was far more than in the neighbouring countries of Hungary, Poland or Slovakia (Idnes.cz, 2018b). According to Airbnb, guests spent 324 million euros in the Czech Republic in 2017 (Idnes.cz, 2018b), and Airbnb lessors in Prague earned 2.1 billion Czech crowns ($94 million USD) annually.

Airbnb's share of the number of overnight stays in Prague increased by 4.7 percentage points to 14.7% between 2016 and 2017. This share is greater than in London (6.9%), Amsterdam (11.8%), Berlin (6.5%) or Madrid (10.1%) (COT Newsletter, 2018b). Prague's Airbnb occupancy rates are also higher than other cities. A study by Coyle and Yu-Cheong Yeung (2016) found that the average occupancy rate in Airbnb rentals, calculated as the ratio of the bookings to the total number of days when the property is available for lease, in the reference period in Prague reached 50.21%, well above the average of 13 other European cities. Furthermore, while only 1.56% of users in the 14 EU cities simultaneously offered five or more accommodation units (Coyle and Yu-Cheong Yeung, 2016,) more than 7.4% of the users in Prague rented that number of units. A European comparison of the number Airbnb listings per user is presented in Tab. 11.4.

Tab. 11.4: European comparison of the number of Airbnb listings per user (Coyle and Yu-Cheong Yeung, 2016; Klucnikov et al., 2018).

City	1 listing	2 listing	3 listing	4 listing	5 listing
Paris	90.97%	6.73%	1.16%	0.36%	0.77%
Nantes	89.03%	8.61%	1.60%	0.35%	0.42%
Cologne	88.55%	8.33%	1.46%	0.66%	0.99%
Amsterdam	88.53%	7.92%	1.85%	0.69%	1.01%
Strasbourg	88.53%	9.01%	1.27%	0.47%	0.72%
Toulouse	87.55%	9.30%	1.53%	0.37%	1.15%
Munich	87.30%	9.47%	1.81%	0.79%	0.63%
Berlin	86.18%	9.73%	2.19%	0.72%	1.07%
Frankfurt	86.18%	10.34%	1.88%	0.86%	0.74%
Glasgow	83.50%	11.97%	2.45%	1.09%	1.00%
London	80.89%	12.03%	3.12%	1.27%	2.69%
Manchester	78.61%	13.18%	3.72%	1.62%	2.87%
Edinburg	77.88%	14.03%	4.11%	1.66%	2.31%
Prague	**70.63%**	**13.94%**	**5.28%**	**2.75%**	**7.40%**
Barcelona	69.37%	16.57%	6.11%	2.65%	5.30%

Challenges brought about by overtourism

Overtourism has had various negative impacts on Prague in recent decades, including overcrowding (Simpson, 1999), loss of quality of life for residents, environmental damage (Deichmann, 2002) and commercialization (Hoffman and Musil, 1999; Sykora, 1999).

Overcrowding

Prague is one of the smallest of the leading tourist destinations in Europe and the historical part of Prague is made up of very narrow streets. In terms of tourist penetration, the density of tourists per square kilometre and the level of tourist intensity, Prague markedly exceeds the Vienna and Berlin and is double that of Budapest (Dumbrovska, 2013). Because of overtourism, certain parts of the city have become overcrowded, in particular, the Royal Way (see Fig. 11.5). This route is 2.4 kilometres long and connects the major sights in Prague on both sides of the river Vltava, including Charles Bridge (Dumbrovska, 2017). The situation is particularly problematic in the summer and Easter holidays (see Fig. 11.4).

In 1995, the most important factor contributing to overcrowding in the historical centre was guided tours, which had the effect of keeping large numbers of slow-moving people together (see Fig. 11.5). This was seen as "overcrowding" by 60% of local residents (only 24% of visitors classified the streets as "overcrowded") (Simpson, 1999).

Fig. 11.4: Overcrowding at Charles Bridge (photo credit: Miroslav Roncak).

Fig. 11.5: Slow-moving group of tourists on Royal Way (photo credit: Miroslav Roncak).

By 2016, the situation had become much worse and touristification was seen as a problem by many local residents, especially women (Dumbrovska, 2017). Respondents to a survey conducted on the Royal Way complained that goods offered for sale were kitschy or fake. Despite this, the majority of respondents (88%) expressed either neutral or positive attitudes to tourists. Prague residents tended to perceive the negative impacts of tourism as a consequence of mismanagement by the local authorities rather than the fault of visitors (Dumbrovska, 2017).

Prague Airport has also struggled with overcrowding. In 2017, a record of 15.4 million passengers was recorded, and an additional 1.5 million passengers were predicted for 2018. The airport has taken a number of steps to increase capacity, including a new security site, constructed at a cost of 8 million Euros (9.2 million USD), which should increase the hourly check-in capacity of Terminal 2 by almost 40% (COT Newsletter, 2018c). The airport plans a massive expansion, which is expected to cost 1.1 billion Euros ($1.25 billion USD). The plan is to build a new parallel runway and substantially expand Terminal 2 by 2026. Upon completion of the expansion, the airport should have a capacity of around 21 million passengers per year (COT Newsletter, 2018b). While this will reduce overcrowding at Prague Airport, it will allow more tourists to enter and will therefore amplify overtourism issues in Prague.

Transformation of central Prague into a commercialised "tourism ghetto"

According to Dumbrovska (2017), the entire Old City, including the Royal Way, is losing its original use and value as a residential area and is being transformed into a "tourism ghetto". This has created a division of territory that Hoffman and Musil call "tourist Prague and Prague for locals" (2009: 14–15). The creation of a tourist ghetto implies the separation of Prague's tourism from local culture, which has led to erosion of the sense of place and the identity of the historic core (Simpson, 1999).

Loss of tax and fee income

In 2018, 80% of the real estate units offered through the Airbnb platform were normal entrepreneurial activity, not the "sharing economy", so should have been subject to taxes (Kljucnikov et al., 2018). But many Airbnb lessors do not declare their income. When Airbnb hosts do not voluntarily include their earnings in their tax returns, the state does not gain anything from such tourist accommodation. According to governmental analysis, the state loses 460 million Czech crowns (approximately 20 million USD) annually in taxes related to these concealed rents in the capital. Furthermore, Prague City Hall loses about 50 million Czech crowns ($2 million USD) on unpaid accommodation fees (Hospodarske noviny, 2018).

Rising rents and loss of residents' quality of life

The problem is not just about lost taxes and fees, however. The use of Airbnb by tourists is changing the nature of the Old City and is reducing the quality of life of residents. The use of residential buildings for short-term tourist accommodation disrupts neighbourly relations and creates excessive noise, as many visitors do not respect quiet hours in the night. In the first three months of 2018 the City Hall of Prague 1 registered 250 complaints concerning rentals of flats via Airbnb (COT Newsletter, 2018d). Some residents are so badly affected that they are moving away from the centre of the city (Idnes.cz, 2017).

The rise of Airbnb has increased demand for apartments, which has driven real estate prices up and also increased the rents for "normal" housing (Lidovky.cz, 2017). Since 2015, the prices of new apartments in Prague have risen by about three-fifths (Novinky.cz, 2018). Developers believe that the short-term rental market has led to one third of apartment purchases being for investment purposes rather than housing (Lidovky.cz, 2017). Prague hoteliers, like residents, have also been adversely affected by tourist use of Airbnb, as this has led to a decrease in hotel occupancy rates (COT Newsletter, 2018b).

Increased competition and lower incomes

The increasing use by tourists of alternative transport services, such as Uber, Taxify and Liftago, is another issue that has arisen in recent years (Idnes.cz, 2018c). Before such services began operating in Prague in 2014, more than 7000 taxi drivers were working in the metropolis, but with the launch of Uber and other services, around 3000 additional drivers joined the field, increasing competition. The market was already saturated, so this has made the situation worse, and taxi drivers' earnings have declined steeply. The first protest by taxi drivers was held in February 2016. Taxi drivers argue that many Uber and Taxify drivers do not comply with the applicable laws as they do not use taximeters, and they are not obliged to pass tests of about the topography of the city. Furthermore, in the Czech Republic (and in Poland, Slovakia and Ukraine) Uber drivers do not need to have a valid taxi licence, which is in blatant contravention of the law (Idnes.cz, 2018c).

Discussion: addressing the issues of overtourism

With careful planning, the financial resources of the tourism sector could have contributed to an even growth and gradual upgrade of the city, but this has largely not happened (Kadar, 2018). In recent years, therefore, the municipal government has been under increasing pressure from the civil society to address the challenges of tourism-related development in the historical centre of Prague through regulations and strategic planning (Pixova and Sladek, 2016).

The City of Prague and Prague City Tourism recognise the overcrowding issues in the city centre and are striving to address them. According to a representative, the City of Prague, does not want the city to be a mass tourism destination. Today, the aim is not to increase the number of tourists, but rather to focus on more affluent and sophisticated target groups, and to encourage this group to extend the lengths of their stays and make repeat visits. To achieve this, the City of Prague will aim to offer ever better services and to improve the personal experiences of visitors to Prague (COT Newsletter, 2018f). As part of these efforts, at the beginning of 2018 Prague City Tourism renovated the visitor centre in the arrivals hall of Terminal 2 at Prague Airport and extended the daily opening hours until 10 pm.

One strategy Prague City Tourism is following to combat overcrowding in the historical centre has been to promote lesser-known pedestrian trails, so as to redirect visitors to other neighbourhoods and away from the overcrowded Royal Way. The walk campaign, with the slogan "Prague is yours, too", encourages visitors to explore the less well-known parts of Prague on foot (Prague City Tourism, 2017). Prague City Tourism expects this will motivate tourists to visit different parts of Prague on repeat visits (Prague City Tourism, 2018), which is expected to disperse visitors and gradually relieve pressure on the overcrowded Old Town. To this end, Prague City Tourism has published information in its quarterly newsletters and two guidebooks (Fig. 11.6), and it plans to follow up in 2019 with smaller leaflets dedicated to particular neighbourhoods.

Another strategy being pursued by Prague City Tourism to address overtourism is the "attractive tourism" approach, which is one of the six key areas of the approved Strategic Plan of the Prague City Smart Concept 2030 (Deloitte Ceska Republika, 2014). This strategy uses new technology, including 3D technology and augmented reality, as a tool to promote locations less frequented by tourists (Prague City Tourism, 2017). In this regard, in April 2019 ICT Operator will launch a new "Prague Card" in the form of a mobile application (Smart Prague, 2018a). The purchase of a Prague Card currently gives visitors free entry to the 50 top attractions in the city and many discounts. The new card will help monitor the movement of tourists, which will improve the accuracy of predictions about overcrowding in the city centre during the summer months.

Another new initiative is a mobile app that will offer topical tourist information and a variety of additional features to visitors to Prague, e.g. sights and interesting places, including information about them, routes for various target groups, discounts, navigation to points of interest and information about cultural, sports, social and other events. To help deal with visitor flows, timetables will be adjusted according to numbers of passengers (Smart Prague, 2018d). Prague City Tourism envisages intensive cooperation on strategic projects in the field of digital technologies within the framework of the Smart Cities concept (Prague City Tourism, 2017).

Fig. 11.6: Brochures: Five Prague Walks, 1 and 2 (source: Prague City Tourism, 2018).

At the same time, Prague City Tourism is trying to convey to residents the positive aspects of tourism. For example, Prague City Tourism participates in the "Hotel Night" initiative. Organised by Czech Association of Hotels and Restaurants and their partners, the Hotel Night was held for the second time in 2018 and some 71 hotels participated. Under this initiative, local residents get a chance to experience hotels in their neighbourhoods at reduced prices. This is viewed as a way of thanking Prague residents for putting up with the occasionally less-than-pleasant conditions in a massively popular tourist destination (Prague City Tourism, 2017). The Hotel Night initiative is very popular among residents, as indicated by the booking of all the rooms within just a few minutes. The hotels are continuously adding more and more rooms. This year, 750 rooms were offered in three categories:

777 Czech crowns (30 Euro), 999 Czech crowns (40 Euro) and 1111 Czech crowns (45 Euro) (The Czech Association of Hotels and Restaurants, 2018).

Residents were not forgotten by the Prague City Smart Concept 2030 either. Through the "I Have an Idea" campaign, local inhabitants have the opportunity to suggest new things that will help improve the quality of life in their city (Smart Prague, 2018a). One of the projects is mobile application which enable parents to follow the movement of their children in real-time, connect their children with a group, and learn that they have arrived safely to school (Smart Prague, 2018c).

To address the issues related to short-term rentals, the City of Prague is planning to regulate Airbnb. They have approached the Ministry for Regional Development of the Czech Republic to prepare an amendment to the law that would limit the use of shared accommodation facilities to between 90 and 120 days a year (COT Newsletter, 2018f). On 12 September 2018 the government also approved a draft amendment to the law that will make accommodation fees, which are payable to municipalities, also apply to private accommodation. From 2020, the maximum limit will reach 21 CZK (0,9 USD). One year later, the fee will increase to 50 CZK (2,2 USD). This amendment will prevent the people running a business through the Airbnb platform from enjoying an unfair advantage over other suppliers of tourist accommodation. The new fees will apply to the provision of paid accommodation regardless of whether the accommodation is approved as an accommodation facility or not (Idnes.cz, 2018a).

The government also plans to register all Airbnb hosts and ensure the payment of applicable taxes (Hospodarske noviny, 2018). Prague authorities will use this information to collect accommodation fees, which are to be paid by all short-term rental providers, as well as hotels and guesthouses. The General Financial Directorate and the City of Prague intend to check whether tenants pay the taxes (COT Newsletter, 2018a).

Recognising the impact of its services on Prague residents, Airbnb has prepared a host guide especially for Prague hosts, which includes tips for the peaceful cohabitation of accommodated tourists with neighbours. All Prague hosts operating on the platform will receive a handbook (Idnes.cz, 2018b).

In recognition of the problems drivers are facing, the Ministry of Transport is preparing an amendment to the law that will require all Uber and Taxify drivers to obtain the necessary licences (Idnes.cz, 2018c). Furthermore, Uber now has the obligation to provide data on the drivers who make money through it (Hospodarske noviny, 2018).

Conclusion

Prague transformed in a relatively short time from a developing destination of the former Soviet Bloc into one of the most visited cities in the world. This came about through marketing of Prague, its renovated buildings and its greater accessibility and affordability after the Czech Republic joined the Shengen area and allowed entry into the market of low cost airlines. Due to a lack of proper planning and foresight by local authorities, however, the city was not prepared for the transformation to its historical centre that mass tourism brought or the changes in tourist accommodation and transport preferences brought about by new technology, which have led to numerous issues. Furthermore, until recently the government was unwilling to interfere with the market and to risk losing tourism revenue.

The city authorities are aware of many of the problems and have begun to take measures to address the negative effects of overtourism. The City of Prague recognises the limits of Prague's carrying capacity and is therefore no longer focusing on increasing the numbers of tourists but is instead seeking to improve the quality of the services offered and to provide an optimal and unique experience for its visitors. Prague has implemented actions through six key areas of the approved Strategic Plan of the Prague City Smart Concept 2030 (Deloitte Ceska Republika, 2014).

There are still issues to address however. The airport is still planning to increase capacity and the services of Airbnb and Uber are not yet regulated, so residents still complain, real estate prices continue to rise and taxi drivers still organize protests. Nevertheless, although the problems cannot be solved immediately, the first signs of progress are apparent.

The numbers of incoming tourists are expected to keep rising in the future. Prague therefore needs a clear vision for tourism development and must implement clear regulations. Inactivity is likely to result in the devaluation of Prague's historical and culture treasures and a continued decline in residents' quality of life.

References

COT Newsletter. (2018a) Vedeni Prahy bude požadovat změnu zákona na regulaci Airbnb.
COT Newsletter. (2018b) Obsazenost prazskych hotelu v lete klesla, vini Airbnb.
COT Newsletter. (2018c) Letiste Praha chysta expanzi a investice za 27 mld. korun.
COT Newsletter. (2018d) MPO: Regulace sdileneho ubytovani je dostatecna.
COT Newsletter. (2018e) Prague City Tourism bude od 1.cervence akciovou spolecnosti.
COT Newsletter. (2018f) Jan Wolf: Praha se nesmi stat lacinou destinaci.
Czech Statistical Office. (2018) Casova rada – dlouhodoby vyvoj kraje ve vybranych ukazatelich. https://www.czso.cz/csu/xa/casova-rada-dlouhodoby-vyvoj-kraje-ve-vybranych-ukazatelich (Accessed 25 October 2018.)
Cooper, C. and Morpeth, N. (1998) The impact of tourism on residential experience in central-eastern Europe: The development of a new legitimation crisis in the Czech Republic. *Urban Studies*, 35 (12): 2253–2275.
Coyle, D. and Yu-Cheong Yeung, T. (2016) Understanding Airbnb in fourteen European cities. *The Jean-Jacques Laffont Digital Chair Working Papers.*
CzechTourism. (2018) Destinations. http://www.czechtourism.com/destinations/
Deichmann, J. I. (2002). International tourism and the sensitivities of central Prague's residents. *Journal of Tourism Studies*, 13(2): 41–52.
Deloitte Ceska Republika (2014) Koncepce Smart Prague do roku 2030. https://www.smartprague.eu/files/koncepce_smartprague.pdf (Accessed 25 August 2017.)

Dumbrovska, V. (2013) Vyvoj postaveni Prahy – destinace cestovniho ruchu ve stredoevropskem prostoru. Unpublished bachelor's thesis. Faculty of Natural Sciences, Charles University in Prague.

Dumbrovska, V. and Fialova, D. (2014) Tourist intensity in capital cities in central Europe: Comparative analysis of tourism in Prague, Vienna and Budapest. *Czech Journal of Tourism*, 3(1): 5–26.

Dumbrovska, V. (2017) Urban tourism development in Prague: From tourist mecca to tourist ghetto. In N. Bellini and C. Pasquinelli (Eds.), *Tourism in the city: Towards an integrative agenda on urban tourism*, Cham: Springer International Publishing, pp. 275–283.

European Commission (n.d.) European Capitals of Culture. https://ec.europa.eu/programmes/crea tive-europe/actions/capitals-culture_en (Accessed 30 October 2018.)

Hammersley, R. and Westlake, T. (1996) Planning in the Prague region: Past, present and future. *Cities*, 13 (4): 247–256.

Hoffman, L. M. and Musil, J. (1999) Culture meets commerce: tourism in postcommunist Prague. In D. Judd and S. Fainstein (Eds.), *The tourist city*, New Haven, CT: Yale University Press, pp. 179–197.

Euromonitor International (2017) WTM London 2017 Edition. Top 100 City Destinations Ranking. https://www.euromonitor.com/top-100-city-destinations-ranking-wtm-london-2017-edition/re port (Accessed 25 August 2017.)

Hospodarske noviny (2018) Zacal velky zatah proti sdilene ekonomice, financni sprava pujde po danich z pronajmu bytu pres Airbnb. https://archiv.ihned.cz/c1-66205190-zacal-velky-zatah-proti-sdilene-ekonomice (Accessed 27 July 2018.)

Idnes.cz (2018a) Sluzby jako Airbnb budou hradit poplatek az 50 korun, schvalila vlada. https:// ekonomika.idnes.cz/airbnb-ubytovani-poplatek-dc5-/ekonomika.aspx?c=A180912_082509_ ekonomika_fih (Accessed 12 September 2018.)

Idnes.cz (2018b) Jen za lonsky rok je diky nam Cesko o 10 miliard bohatsi, tvrdi Airbnb. https:// zpravy.idnes.cz/airbnb-2017-studie-byty-nedostatek-praha-cesko-deset-miliard-milion-hostu-1n5-/domaci.aspx?c=A180606_153435_domaci_hell (Accessed 9 June 2018.)

Idnes.cz (2018c) Analyza: Proc Prahu ceka nejvetsi taxikarsky protest v dejinach? https://zpravy. idnes.cz/protest-taxikari-uber-liftago-taxify-strahov-nejvetsi-protest-analyza-1az-/domaci. aspx?c=A180207_112305_domaci_hell (Accessed 7 February 2018.)

Idnes.cz (2017) Praha 1 chce bojovat s Airbnb. Centrum jinak rychle vymre, boji se. https://praha. idnes.cz/praha-1-boj-proti-airbnb-odchod-rezidentu-fdy-/praha-zpravy.aspx?c=A171018_ 161924_praha-zpravy_mav (Accessed 21 October 2017.)

Johnson, M. (1995) Czech and Slovak tourism patterns – Problems and Prospects. *Tourism Management*, 16 (1): 21–28.

Kadar, B. (2018) Hotel development through centralized to liberalized planning procedures: Prague lost in transition. *Tourism Geographies*, 20 (3): 461–480.

Kljucnikov, A., Krajcik, V. andVincurova, Z. (2018) International sharing economy: The case of Airbnb in the Czech Republic. *Economics & Sociology*, 11 (2): 126–137.

Lidovky.cz. (2017) Airbnb a spol. sponuji ceny bytu i najmu. Bydleni v Praze je cim dal drazsi. https:// byznys.lidovky.cz/airbnb-a-spol-sponuji-ceny-bytu-i-najmu-bydleni-v-praze-je-cim-dal-drazsi-1nj-/ moje-penize.aspx?c=A170809_145645_moje-penize_pave (Accessed 10 August 2017.)

Muchova, A. (2016) Nizkonakladove letecke spolecnosti na ceskem trhu. Unpublished bachelor's thesis, Department of Philosophy, Palacky University Olomouc.

Municipal District Prague 1 (2018) Informace o uzemi. https://www.praha1.cz/mestska-cast/o-mestske-casti/informace-o-uzemi/ (Accessed 25 October 2018.)

Novinky.cz. (2018) Raketovy rust cen novych bytu v Praze nebere konce. https://www.novinky.cz/ ekonomika/469570-raketovy-rust-cen-novych-bytu-v-praze-nebere-konce.html (Accessed 18 April 2018.)

OAG, Eastern Europe (2016) Eastern Europe – low cost and loving it. http://www.oag.com/eastern-europe-0 (Accessed 30 March 2016.)

Olipra, L. (2012) The impact of low-cost carriers on tourism development in less famous destinations. *Cittaslow.*

Palatkova, M. and Zichova, J. (2014) *Ekonomika turismu: turismus Ceske republiky.* Grada: Prague.

Pixova, M. and Sladek, J. (2016) Touristification and awakening civil society in post-socialist Prague. In J. Novy and C. Colomb (Eds.), *Protest and Resistance in the tourist city, contemporary geographies of leisure, tourism and mobility,* London: Routledge, pp. 73–89.

Prague Airport (2018a) Vaclav Havel Airport Prague summer schedule features six new destinations and 157 direct connections worldwide. https://www.prg.aero/en/vaclav-havel-airport-pragues-summer-schedule-features-six-new-destinations-and-157-direct-0 (Accessed 22 March 2018.)

Prague Airport (2018b) Vaclav Havel Airport Prague is the fifth fastest growing airport in Europe in the category of 10 to 25 million passengers. https://www.prg.aero/en/vaclav-havel-airport-prague-fifth-fastest-growing-airport-europe-category-10–25-million-passengers (Accessed 6 February 2018.)

Prague City Tourism (2018). Press release. (Accessed 14 September 2018 from www.prague.eu)

Prague City Tourism (2017) *Annual Report 2017.* https://www.praguecitytourism.cz/file/edee/en/annual-reports/a4-vyrocni-zprava-2018_2-verze_en_web.pdf (Accessed 22 September 2018.)

Prague City Tourism (2016) *Annual Report 2016.* https://www.praguecitytourism.cz/file/edee/en/annual-reports/vz_pis_cz_en-2017_online.pdf (Accessed 22 September 2018.)

Prague City Tourism. (2015) Vyrocni zprava 2015. Available online: https://www.praguecitytourism.cz/file/edee/en/annual-reports/pct_annual_report.pdf (Accessed 22 September 2018.)

Simpson, F. (1999) Tourist impact in the historic centre of Prague: Resident and visitor perceptions of the historic built environment. *The Geographical Journal,* 165 (2): 173–183.

Smart Prague (2018a) Nova prazska turisticka karta zacne platit v dubnu 2019. https://www.smartprague.eu/aktuality/nova-prazska-turisticka-karta-zacne-platit-v-dubnu-2019 (Accessed 27 August 2018.)

Smart Prague (2018b) Attractive tourism. https://www.smartprague.eu/about-smart-prague/attractive-tourism (Accessed 27 August 2018.)

Smart Prague (2018c) Projects. https://www.smartprague.eu/projects (Accessed 27 August 2018.)

Smart Prague (2018d) Tourist application. https://www.smartprague.eu/projects/tourist-application (Accessed 27 August 2018.)

Sykora, L. (1999) Changes in the internal spatial structure of post-communist Prague. *GeoJournal,* 49 (1): 79–89.

Sykora, L. (1994) Local urban restructuring as a mirror of globalisation processes: Prague in the 1990s. *Urban Studies,* 31 (7): 1149–1166.

Sykora, L. and Simonickova, I. (1994) From totalitarian urban managerialism to a liberalized real estate market: Prague's transformations in the early 1990s. In M. Barlow, P. Dostal and M. Hampl (Eds.), *Development and administration of Prague,* Amsterdam: University of Amsterdam, pp. 47–72.

The Czech Association of Hotels and Restaurants. (2018). Press release. (Accessed 18 September 2018 from www.ahrcr.cz)

The Telegraph (2004). Is the party over for Prague? https://www.telegraph.co.uk/travel/destinations/europe/czechrepublic/731377/Is-the-party-over-for-Prague.html (Accessed 4 October 2004.)

Toman, M. (2008) Prostorova analyza nizkonakladove letecke dopravy v Evrope. Unpublished diplomova prace. Ekonomicko-spravni fakulta. Brno: Masarykova Univerzita.

UNESCO World Heritage Centre (n.d.) Historic Centre of Prague. https://whc.unesco.org/en/list/616 (Accessed 18 September 2018.)

Fabian Weber, Florian Eggli, Timo Ohnmacht and Jürg Stettler

12 Lucerne and the impact of Asian group tours

Introduction

Lucerne is one of the most visited cities in Switzerland, delighting guests from all around the world with its historic old town and charming sights. This city of around 80,000 inhabitants is located on the shores of Lake Lucerne and is surrounded by picturesque mountain scenery, providing an exemplary Swiss holiday experience.

Tourism to the city began as early as the 1830s, leading to the cityscape being characterised by monumental hotel buildings from the Belle Époque. Today, tourism still plays an important role in Lucerne's economy. A study found that, at over a billion Swiss francs, tourism provided approximately 5% of the region's gross added value in 2014, an increase of 19% since 2005 (Hanser und Partner AG, 2015). The same study found that tourism is responsible for 11,000 full-time jobs or 6% of all employment. In Switzerland overnight stays are growing (up 14% since 2005), but in the Lucerne region they have boomed, showing a growth rate of 25% in the same period (Hanser Consulting AG, 2018).

While tourism remains a dominant industry, Lucerne's source market has seen a remarkable shift, with the numbers of European overnight guests declining (−7.3%) and the numbers of Asian overnight visitors swelling (+42%) (Federal Statistical Office of Switzerland, 2018). At the same time, the Lucerne region now receives an estimated 450,000 day-visits per year from Asian guests; visits that do not figure in the overnight statistics (Hanser und Partner AG, 2015). Most visitors travel in large groups, by tour coaches. While such groups contribute to most of the turnover of watch and jewellery stores, this group spends little on food and accommodation.

This significant growth in tourism in recent years and the change in the type of tourists dominate the current local discourse in Lucerne. The large numbers of tour buses disrupt local traffic and the predominance of group travellers has changed the composition of shops in the old town, affecting the quality of life of the city's residents and leading to resentment. Local attitudes towards mass tourism are becoming increasingly hostile, and city officials have been asked to address the problem. In particular, the city government has been commissioned by the local parliament to revise its tourism strategy and to develop a new forward-looking vision for the future of tourism in the city that takes into account the needs and ideas of local residents. Until now, most of the measures have dealt with the traffic problems. Only recently have suggestions been raised to better manage group visitor flows or even restrict them. One approach suggested is to target other tourism segments, those that have less potential for conflict.

https://doi.org/10.1515/9783110607369-012

This chapter will examine Lucerne's tourism history and the rise of group tours, which have brought the phenomenon of "overtourism" to Lucerne. This chapter will also discuss the various ways Lucerne is addressing overtourism and the potential future direction of tourism in Lucerne.

History of tourism in Lucerne

When the road over the Saint Gotthard Pass was paved in 1830, travel between northern and southern Europe was boosted significantly, and traders and travellers became able to reduce the risk and time involved in crossing the Alps. This was the start of a long and successful era of tourism in central Switzerland, which in Lucerne focused on the stunning scenery of the mountains, the lake and the historic city centre (Bürgi, 2016).

In 1837, the first steamboat began offering a service on Lake Lucerne carrying both goods and passengers (SGV, 2018). Early guests, mainly from Britain, were amazed by the spectacular mountains and started visiting them for reasons of pleasure (Towner, 1985). This constituted quite a revolutionary interpretation of the Alps, which until then were perceived rather as being evil and were disregarded by the local population of Lucerne. Many of the Swiss did not at first understand why their guests wanted to expose themselves voluntarily to such risks and dangers, only later recognising the sensations that mountaineering evokes. In 1871, Europe's first mountain railway was inaugurated, on Rigi Mountain, followed in 1889 by the world's steepest cogwheel railway up Pilatus Mountain; both mountain peaks being within sight of Lucerne (Rigi, 2018; Pilatus, 2018).

Source markets

As of 2018, the Asian market generated 33% of overnight stays in Lucerne. This represents an increase of 42% since 2012. China is one of the main drivers of tourism growth, with an increase of 31.2% since 2012 (Federal Statistical Office of Switzerland, 2018). These figures are in line with the worldwide development of the Asian travel market, which is expected to continue to grow significantly in the future (UNWTO, 2017).

As shown in Tab. 12.1, another strong source market with high growth rates is the United States of America (USA). The USA is the second-largest country of origin and is responsible for 16% of overnight stays, a figure that grew by 48.7% between 2012 and 2017.

In contrast, the numbers of visitors from the home market of Switzerland and neighbouring European countries have declined. The Swiss remain an important source market, with 22% of total share, but growth was negative (−4.8%) between

Tab. 12.1: City of Lucerne – selected markets of origin, 2012 and 2017 (source: Federal Statistical Office of Switzerland, 2018).

Country	Indicator	2012	2017	Growth (%) 2012 – 2017
Switzerland	Overnight stays	311	296	-4.8
	Growth	-1.4	-3.2	
	Market share	27.3	22.1	
Germany	Overnight stays	100	91	-9.0
	Growth	2.8	2.6	
	Market share	8.8	6.8	
Europe	Overnight stays	291	285	-7.3
	Growth	-5.5	2.8	
	Market share	25.5	21.2	
USA	Overnight stays	146	217	48.7
	Growth	6.3	7.0	
	Market share	12.8	16.2	
China	Overnight stays	95	125	31.2
	Growth	17.0	2.9	
	Market share	8.4	9.3	
India	Overnight stays	42	71	67.0
	Growth	-4.3	22.0	
	Market share	3.7	5.3	
Total	Overnight stays	1,140	1,343	17.7
	Growth	1.1	5.8	

2012 and 2017. Likewise, Europe has declined as a source market, losing 7.3% over the five years between 2012 and 2017 (Federal Statistical Office of Switzerland, 2018).

Lucerne Tourism Ltd. is responsible for the marketing of central Switzerland, including the city of Lucerne. At the national level, the tourism organisation is called Switzerland Tourism. For both levels, China is one of the priority markets (Luzern Tourismus, 2018). Indeed, a special representative has the mandate to promote Lucerne in China and to bring Chinese groups to the city. This agency has existed for 15 years. It is co-financed by "Lucerne Lake Region", a group that includes the major watch companies and some transport companies (SRF, 2013). Such promotional efforts are one of the reasons for the popularity of Lucerne in the Chinese market and the strong growth of tourists from Asia in recent years.

Although the decline in European tourists can mainly be attributed to the strong Swiss franc, these statistics could also be read as first signs of the "crowding-out" phenomenon, in which, by gaining market share, new visitors change the destination in ways that make it unappealing to traditional tourists

(Chou et al., 2014). Guests from traditional source markets such as Germany, Britain or Switzerland may no longer feel at ease in Lucerne, and they might therefore choose other destinations. This theory has been raised in media debates (cf. Aschwanden, 2018; Blumer, 2017). Although there is no empirical evidence to support this. assumption, political and cultural debates in the media reflect this perception of the development of tourism in Lucerne (cf. Aschwanden 2018; Blumer 2017).

The rise of group travellers

Little data is available regarding numbers of day-visitors, but a study by Hanser und Partner AG (2015) suggests that the canton of Lucerne receives up to 10 million day-visitors a year. Of these, the largest proportion is from Switzerland itself, but an estimated 750,000 are foreigners. It can be assumed that almost all of the foreign day-tourists in the region visit the city of Lucerne. Day-visitors only pass through; they do not stay overnight in the city or in the wider Lucerne region. For them, Lucerne is merely a brief stop on the classic route through Europe, which typically goes from Paris to Venice or from Salzburg to Rome. Most of these day-visitors are group tourists travelling in tour coaches. Some of these buses are rather small in size: minibuses with six to twelve passengers, while others are large coaches with up to 45 passengers (see Fig. 12.1).

Fig. 12.1: Tour coaches with tourist groups at Schwanenplatz, Lucerne (photo credit: Team Projekt Metro-Luzern).

Typically, these coaches travel on a given route with a fixed itinerary. Due to their intense travel programme, usually covering several European countries within a short space of time, visits to each destination are consequently very concentrated. Lucerne is no exception, where most of the sights and activities are located within short distances from one another.

The main reason for visits by tour groups to Lucerne is the attractive shopping opportunities. Lucerne offers many typical Swiss watch and jewellery stores, which are mainly located around a central square called Schwanenplatz. This medium-sized square of approximately 1,000 square metres is located between the lakefront and the entry to the historic city centre. The stores at the Schwanenplatz offer the most popular Swiss luxury brands, and acquiring an original watch or clock in this typical Swiss environment is viewed as something special. Product authenticity and proof against forgery are guaranteed by the high reputations of the retailers. International duty-free refunds and other tax advantages, like exemptions from the luxury tax for exported goods to China, are also factors in boosting sales (Li, 2016).

Tour groups are accompanied by a guide who is responsible for managing all activities, including shopping, excursions and transfers, as well as room and board. The salaries of most tour guides are based on commissions and other payments from local service partners, so their remuneration depends on the amounts spent by the tourists (cf. Acklin et al., 2013; Hug, 2013).

A study by Price Waterhouse Coopers (PWC, 2014) recorded, between 2009 and 2013, an average of 55 coach movements daily on the Schwanenplatz (over 20,000 movements a year). In 2017, the city registered more than 50,000 vehicles making brief stops at this central location to drop off and pick up travellers (Hanser Consulting AG, 2018). With an average of 30 to 35 passengers per coach (Hanser Consulting AG, 2018), this amounts to an estimated 1.5 million group travellers in this specific area in 2017.

In response to growing tourist numbers, more and more souvenir shops have opened in the historic old town. These sell typical Swiss products, such as army knives and small cowbells, targeting international visitors. The growing numbers of confectionery stores selling Swiss chocolate, and restaurants serving typical Swiss food, also manifest the tendency towards the touristification of the area.

A study commissioned by local businesses calculated that, collectively, the retail stores in Schwanenplatz had a turnover of 224 million Swiss Francs in 2017. The watch and jewellery stores generated most of this total, at 196 million Swiss Francs (87.5%), making the Schwanenplatz one of the top five locations worldwide in this sector. The study also revealed that the retail watch and jewellery business is dominated by group travellers (making up 90% of the customers). Likewise, souvenir shops indicated that 90% of their turnover was generated by group travellers. Confectionery stores reported group travellers having a share of 30%, which is roughly the same for tobacco stores and the shoes and leather goods sector. On the other hand, group travellers only accounted for 10% of the turnover of the gastronomy sector in the Schwanenplatz area (Hanser Consulting AG, 2018) (see Tab. 12.2).

Tab. 12.2: Importance of group tourism for different sectors at the Schwanenplatz 2017 (assumptions) (source: Hanser Consulting AG, 2018).

Sector	Share of group tourism in total turnover (%)
Retail sale of watches and jewellery in specialised stores	90
Other retail sale of new goods in specialised stores (especially souvenirs)	90
Retail sale of bread, cakes, flour confectionery and sugar confectionery in specialised stores	30
Retail sale of tobacco products in specialised stores	30
Retail sale of footwear and leather goods in specialised stores	30
Retail sale of clothing in specialised stores	20
Dispensing chemist in specialised stores	10
Food and beverage service activities	10
All other sectors	0

The concentration of watch and jewellery stores in Schwanenplatz along with the large number of coaches and group tourists, have resulted in high density tourism, which is "overtourism" in the eyes of many.

The challenges of overtourism in the city of Lucerne

In recent years, the strong growth of tourism in Lucerne, particularly of group tourism, has heightened the debate about excessive tourism in the city. A key issue is traffic, particularly in summer. Summer is the busiest period, with most travellers arriving in July and August. The great majority of group travellers arrive by tour coach. After their passengers are dropped off, the coaches are driven to a less centrally-located parking area. Then after a wait of two to three hours, the coaches are driven back to the centre to collect their passengers. The movements of large numbers of buses, with up to 342 movements per day in summer, lead to heavy tourist traffic in the city centre, causing congestion and parking problems for the residents and other visitors.

Another issue is that city residents are not seeing the benefits of the large numbers of tourists. Although the value added by group tourism is relatively high, the benefits are concentrated mostly in watch and jewellery stores and souvenir shops.

Furthermore, the new souvenir shops that have opened in response to tourist demand have displaced traditional shops aimed at Lucerne's ordinary residents; these shops are therefore declining in number (cf. Blumer, 2017; Radio Pilatus, 2017). The demise of local stores, long waiting times in the shops, rising rents and the feeling that the public space is being lost to tourists have created resentment among some local residents.

In addition, due to the limited time and packed nature of tour programmes, there is hardly any interaction between the travellers and local residents. Ohnmacht und Ponnapureddy (2017) suggest that the shift towards mass tourism has reduced close contact between the providers of tourism services and their consumers. In their study of Lucerne, they describe a shift "away from social interaction and experience to isolated touristic pathways" (Ohnmacht und Ponnapureddy, 2017: 7), arguing that this is one reason for the increase in the culture gap between local residents and tourists in recent times.

Frank (2016) came to a similar conclusion in her study of Indian tourists in Engelberg, a destination close to Lucerne that is often visited by the same groups. She argues that tourists co-produce what is called a "dwelling-in-motion" together with the service and sales personnel and the local residents. She claims that the interactions between these actors are rather cold, as they are still rooted in colonial structures. Furthermore, Indian package tourists have little time to interact with the local population and lack interest in doing so after long days spent on excursions. Indeed, they are more interested in confirming their pre-conceived images of pristine mountain settings, fuelled by Bollywood films. Conversely, local residents have an astonishingly stable image of their guests, even though the first package tourists from India arrived in Engelberg more than 15 years ago (Frank, 2016).

In general, group tourists stay in the city for only a short period and are focused on visiting the most relevant sights and on the shopping experience. In addition, they often extend their stay in the region with an excursion to a nearby mountain such as Rigi, Titlis or Pilatus or a cruise on Lake Lucerne, leading to some of these popular neighbouring destinations struggling with similar signs of overtourism. This development has also been enhanced by the fact that Asia is treated as a priority market in the marketing activities of the Destination Management Organizations. Nevertheless, the problem seems to be especially severe in the limited space of the rather small city of Lucerne and the limited possibilities to regulate tourism in its complex city environment. It can therefore be concluded that there are many different challenges from tourism in Lucerne, the traffic and parking problems bringing the issue to light the most.

Innovative responses by local residents

In recent years more and more voices have risen to condemn further growth in tourism and to demand better control of the development of tourism. Local resentment is expressed through newspaper articles, letters to the editor and political initiatives (cf. Kaufmann, 2018; Schaber, 2018; Metz, 2018). The debate over the direction of Lucerne's tourism industry is also expressed through the cultural domain. The following two examples of innovative cultural initiatives demonstrate this.

The Kleintheater of Lucerne is a small independent theatre company that celebrated its fiftieth anniversary in 2017. For this occasion, it developed a special show that commented satirically on tourism issues in the city. Several story threads were woven together in the comedy, *Visit Pyöngyang!* In this play, Lucerne initially calls on tourists to visit, and they come, including Kim Jong-un, the leader of North Korea, who eventually proclaims a city partnership between Lucerne and Pyongyang. The play expresses the complexity of the dilemma the city currently faces, illustrating that when something is called for, one often receives more than one expected. The play shows government officials struggling to find effective strategies and unable to cope with the demanding situation. Tour coaches were used as a key element to illustrate the issues. Indeed, the advertisement for the play (see Fig. 12.2) depicts the actors posing in front of a group of tourists who are standing next to a coach parked in the city centre.

Fig. 12.2: Actors in front of a tourist group and coach (photo credit: Ingo Höhn).

Another cultural event that expresses the residents' views on overtourism is the "Invictis Pax Minifestival", which has taken place every August since 2012. This festival is held next to the Lion Monument, one of Lucerne's main tourist attractions. It is organised every year by an adjacent bar and coffee lounge called

"Alpineùm" and by the local residents' association. The festival is not aimed at tourists, but is consciously organised by residents for residents. The festival is free of charge and fulfils two main functions on its specific site. First, it provides the densely-populated tourist site with a new purpose and meaning. During the festival the local residents reclaim the site and occupy it for a leisure activity of their own. Second, by celebrating local musicians on the stage, the festival creates a platform for local expression and fosters regional identity. And by giving a voice to young and emerging talents who are rooted in the city of Lucerne, it provides an opportunity for an exchange of regional culture between the musicians and their audience. As there is no entry fee and no dedicated entry gates, everyone is free to join in or to simply pass by. This sometimes results in a strange situation in which bewildered tourists have to find their way through the local masses to get to the Lion Monument. This reverses the situation that residents perceive occurs throughout the rest of the year.

Measures to mitigate overtourism

Tourism representatives are well aware of the current tensions and are in close and continuous collaboration with representatives from government, business and society in order to analyse the problem and reach possible solutions. As the issues cover aspects of local life such as traffic, housing and public area planning, not simply tourism, an interdisciplinary approach must be adopted.

In recent years the discussion has mostly been about the Schwanenplatz and the tour coaches visiting it. City officials commissioned a study to analyse this "tour-coach problem" and to outline scenarios for the future management of the situation (Interface, 2018). The study identified three reasons for the traffic bottleneck within the city centre. First, Lucerne has experienced general growth in its population, leading to a higher density of transportation generally. This makes traffic flows more vulnerable to disruption. Second, the city residents' demands regarding the quality of public space have evolved. In particular, centrally-located public locations are expected to be openly accessible to all people and to be designed attractively. Third, the number of tour coaches has grown, which has caused problems, particularly at pick-up and drop-off places and parking areas, as well as on the roads between them (Interface, 2018).

The study proposed several solutions, ranging from a new parking terminal outside the city connected to the centre by train, to several options for underground car parks within the central perimeter of the city. Other measures being discussed by the community include taxes and regulation of tour coaches and entry fees for the most popular sights. Other options, like a new metro line, have created controversy in the city parliament and have so far failed to obtain political approval. Various political interests and the high levels of financial investment needed have led to an impasse in which no immediate solutions are identifiable. Meanwhile, the watch and jewellery stores at the Schwanenplatz have hired private security personnel to watch the busiest areas and to help keep the traffic under control, in order to prevent accidents at peak times. Due to the ongoing political debate, little has been decided, let alone implemented. The only measure implemented so far is a new coach management plan at Schwanenplatz. Coaches are now only allowed to drop off their passengers there. They have to pick them up at another location a few minutes away.

Public pressure is increasing. Two recent political initiatives illustrate the trends in the political debates. In September 2017, the Young Socialist Party (JUSO) launched a referendum initiative[1] to transform a coach parking lot into an urban public park. The parking lot is situated at a central location on the shores of Lake Lucerne and as of 2018 was being used exclusively by tour coaches.

In the debate, representatives of an opposing committee made it clear that centrally-located coach parking lots are vital for the tourism industry. Various tourism stakeholders and associated interest groups (such as the Lucerne Tourism Board, the Lucerne City Association and the Lake Lucerne Cruise Ship Company, among others) objected to the initiative.

The initiative committee used specific visual language in its campaign. It modified one of the posters that had been used at the turn of the 20th century to advertise the natural beauty of Swiss holiday destinations by inserting lines of tour coaches obstructing the view (see Fig. 12.3). In doing so, they deliberately linked the initiative to the ongoing overtourism debate.

The JUSO initiative was adopted, with 51.6% of the citizens of Lucerne voting for it. Accordingly, some vehicles will be banned from the specified parking area from 2019 onwards, thus adding more green space to the existing park nearby (Wydler, 2017). The result of the vote can be interpreted not only as confirmation of the demand for a public park, but also as a veto of the current model of tourism development (Inseli Komitee, 2017; Wydler, 2017). It remains unclear, however, where alternative parking lots for coaches will be located, as all existing possibilities have been exhausted, and new parking locations are not easy to find.

Two months after the successful vote against the coach park, Lucerne's Green Party asked the city government to review its tourism strategy and develop a new, forward-looking concept. A parliamentary motion submitted in November 2017 explicitly asked for a "Tourism Vision Lucerne 2030" to be drawn up in close collaboration with the Lucerne Tourism Board and with the wide participation of the local population, as well as other stakeholders (Green Party, 2017). The motion states that the impact of tourism, and consequently the degree of its acceptance by the

---

1 A popular initiative is an instrument of direct democracy in Switzerland. It allows citizens to propose changes to constitution on a federal, cantonal or municipal level. A vote is organised for every proposition of modification that collects enough valid signatures. This initiative (municipal level) needed only eight hundred signatures from residents.

Fig. 12.3: Stop the tour coach chaos; sign the initiative here (photo credit: Erich Brechbuehl).

local population, is currently a matter of debate and that city officials need to come up with new solutions to monitor and measure tourism better. In addition, the government must consider introducing restrictions on tourist apartments, coach parking lots and hotel capacities and consider using pricing models to balance tourism flows better, both in terms of time and space. Discussions are planned on whether tourism development should focus on quality or quantity.

A new target group: free independent travellers

Other solutions to overtourism are being discussed within the local Lucerne tourism industry. One suggestion is to become less dependent on group travellers by targeting other customer segments. Accordingly, a consortium of regional and national tourism actors, including several local tourism boards, hotels, transport providers and leisure and cultural institutions, are jointly evaluating the potential of encouraging so-called "free independent travellers" (FIT). This is being evaluated in a project supported by the Institute of Tourism of the Lucerne University of Applied Science and Arts that aims to reduce the predominance of group travel and foster a more compatible form of tourism consisting of individual guests who stay longer, spend more, visit different areas and interact more with the local people (Stettler et al., 2018).

The project does not aim to restrict or ban group tourism but instead seeks to attract individual travellers. Individual travellers move around in smaller groups, care more about the specifics of the destination they are visiting, and have a more balanced spending pattern and a greater interest in interacting with the local population. Attracting individual travellers is expected to improve the quality of tourism in Lucerne and its surroundings. While attracting additional guests does nothing to ease the crowding at the most popular sights and public spaces, the hope is that attracting a new segment that behaves differently (e.g. not using large tour coaches to the same extent, walking in smaller groups and having less fixed itineraries), will allow tourism to develop in a new direction and improve the quality of the host–guest relationship. The FIT approach differs from other approaches seen in comparable cities.

The project began at the end of 2016. In the initial phase, the project is targeting FIT in the Chinese outbound market, as this is one of the fastest growing markets, with great potential to attract individual travellers in the future, but the same measures could subsequently be applied to other source markets if they prove to have potential.

The project was initiated by the Lucerne Tourism Board and integrates other regional destination management organisations, such as Engelberg-Titl is Tourism and Andermatt Tourism. Local, regional and national tourism stakeholders involved in the project include hotels (e.g. the Bürgenstock Resort, the Radisson Lucerne and a Chinese hotel investment project based in Engelberg, Lucerne and Melchsee Frutt), transport companies (e.g. the Lake Lucerne Cruise Ship Company and Titlis Cable Cars), train companies (e.g. Zentralbahn and Matterhorn-Gotthard-Bahn), cultural institutions (e.g. the Lucerne Festival), watch and jewellery stores (e.g. Bucherer) and others (e.g. the Grand Casino). Nationally, various organisations are supporting the project with their expertise, including the Switzerland Tourism Board, the Switzerland Travel Centre, Switzerland Travel Services and the Swiss Travel Association (Stettler et al., 2018).

The inclusion of a variety of stakeholders allows the problems to be understood from different perspectives and for ideas to be developed that extend beyond traditional boundaries and concepts. The project will be implemented over two years and is supported by Switzerland's State Secretariat for Economic Affairs, which encourages innovation in tourism through a dedicated programme to enhance cooperation in the sector (Stettler et al., 2018).

New ways of targeting FIT were discussed in workshops and bilateral meetings that were initiated and conducted by the Lucerne University of Applied Science and Arts (Stettler et al., 2017). One goal of the workshops and meetings was to achieve a common understanding of the tourism situation in Lucerne and its region, and another goal was to understand the travel behaviour, motives and itineraries of free and independent visitors from the source market, China. Of particular interest was the difference between individual travellers and group travellers. It is believed that individual travellers stay longer at a destination and seek more experience-oriented travel activities.

The first step of the project involved segmenting the FIT category in accordance with individual interests, and creating detailed profiles by combining knowledge of travel behaviour, modes of transport, spending patterns, information and distribution channels and other specific travel characteristics. In a further step, the project partners jointly developed concrete tourism offerings aimed at the needs and desires of individual travellers. These modular packages, consisting of a fixed part (basic transport and accommodation) and an optional part (additional excursions and activities addressing individual interests) offer new and unconventional tourism itineraries. These not only include well-known sights and activities, but also offer "hidden gems" off the beaten track. The aim of providing flexibility in these packages is to allow more time for spontaneous interactions and personal encounters. The specially-designed FIT travel packages address the requisites of this type of traveller and contribute to a more even spread of tourists across the entire region.

These special FIT packages are now being promoted and distributed on a trial basis by Switzerland Travel Centre on dedicated Chinese online channels. The project team will closely follow the bookings and empirically analyse visitor behaviour. Ongoing monitoring will enable better-designed tourism packages to be offered in future so as to address visitors' needs and wants more precisely, while simultaneously respecting the needs and wants of the local population (Stettler et al., 2018).

Where will tourism be in 2030?

A key issue in the debate over overtourism in Lucerne is group tours. They represent the phenomenon of mass tourism like none other and symbolise the current development model of supposedly unlimited growth.

These tours bring large groups of tourists who travel together on coaches. As noted above, group tourists tend to stay only for short periods of time at the destination and generally show stereotypical tourist behaviour, with hardly any interaction with local residents. Tourists arriving in tour coaches pass through rather than really visit their destinations. They generate hardly any value-added in the accommodation and food sector, but spend a lot on watches and souvenirs. The coaches have a serious impact because of their effect on local traffic and parking. These and other issues (e.g. closure of shops targeting residents, etc.) are causing resentment among the local population.

The example of Lucerne shows that tourism development in the city has now reached a turning point. While some stakeholders are eager for the tourism industry to continue to grow in size, enabling them to continue to gain lucrative revenues in both existing and new markets, others seek qualitative growth. The issue is controversial, and not many remedial measures have been implemented so far.

As discussed above, a project is underway in Lucerne to shift the focus of tourism development away from group tourism towards attracting free independent travellers. The assumption is that a different type of tourism would find more acceptance among the local population and reduce the negative effects of tourism. Future research should examine the motives and behaviour of this new segment in greater depth and, in particular, how Lucerne can provide the travel experiences to match the needs of this segment. While it will be interesting to see whether the new tourism products and marketing activities will lead to tourism becoming more acceptable to local residents, it should be remembered that this is a long-term measure and that the efforts made now could still be outweighed by the strong growth of group tours, especially among visitors from China (a growing market).

Lucerne as a destination will have to decide the direction of its future tourism development. Until now, it has mainly been the destination management organisation and some big tourism players, like the watch companies, that have determined the direction of tourism development in Lucerne. Future decision-making must be with the inclusive participation of all involved stakeholders.

The Swiss political system allows for public votes on specific issues, thus giving its citizens a say in current developments. The media play a crucial role in shaping and stimulating the public debate. Many complex questions are interwoven together and concern not only tourism, but also other dimensions of living together in urban spaces. Given the debate and the strong feelings on the subject, the needs of Lucerne's residents will have to be taken into account when determining the future direction of tourism development in Lucerne. This process has only just started and will not end any time soon. Much will depend on "Tourism Vision Lucerne 2030," which will be drawn up in the near future. This process will provide an important opportunity to unite different opinions and build the basis for the sustainable development of tourism in the city of Lucerne.

References

Acklin, C., Barth, M., Weber, F., Eicke, M. (2013) *Chinesische Touristen in Luzern*. HSLU. Lucerne.

Aschwanden, E. (2018) Barcelona, Venedig, Luzern – die Angst vor dem «Overtourism» wächst. *Neue Zürcher Zeitung*, 2 August. https://www.nzz.ch/schweiz/barcelona-prag-luzern-in-der-innerschweiz-werden-tourismuskritische-stimmen-lauter-ld.1406105 (Accessed 24 September 2018.)

Blumer, F. (2017) Luzerner meiden ihre Altstadt. *Blick*, 30 July. https://www.blick.ch/news/schweiz/einheimische-leiden-unter-dem-touristenstrom-luzerner-meiden-ihre-altstadt-id7068977.html (Accessed 24 September.)

Bürgi, A. (2016) *Eine touristische Bilderfabrik. Vergnügen und Belehrung am Luzerner Löwenplatz, 1850–1914*. Zürich: Chronos.

Chou, C-M., Hsieh, S. F., Tseng, H. P. (2014) The crowding-out effects of Chinese tourists on inbound tourism in Taiwan. *Tourism Economics*, 20 (6): 1235–1251.

Federal Statistical Office of Switzerland (2018) Overnight statistics. Neuchâtel. www.statistik. admin.ch

Frank, S. (2016) Dwelling-in-motion: Indian Bollywood tourists and their hosts in the Swiss Alps. *Cultural Studies*, 30 (3): 506–531.

Green Party (2017) Tourism Vision Lucerne 2030. Political Motion. Lucerne. http://www.gruene-lu zern.ch/?p=artikel&id=201711271112 (Accessed 25 September 2018.)

Hanser Consulting AG (2018) *Gruppentourismus in Luzern. Analyse der volkswirtschaftlichen Bedeutung.* Schlussbericht.

Hanser und Partner AG (2015) *Touristische Wertschöpfung im Kanton Luzern. Schlussbericht zuhanden der Luzern Tourismus AG und der Dienstelle Raum und Wirtschaft des Kantons Luzern.* Lucerne.

Hug, C. (2013) Big Business in Luzerns Chinatown. *zentralplus*, 17 October. https://www.zentral plus.ch/de/news/wirtschaft/75182/Big-Business-in-Luzerns-Chinatown.htm (Accessed 24 September 2018.)

Inseli Komitee (2017) Unser Inseli für alle. Lucerne. http://www.inseli-initiative-nein.ch/worum. html (Accessed 25 September 2018.)

Interface (2018) Einen Schritt voraus wagen. Ein mittel- und langfristiger Ansatz zur Lösung des Carproblems in der Luzerner Innenstadt.

Kaufmann, H. (2018) Tourismus: Wie wir unsere Gäste in Luzern empfangen sollten. Lucerne. https://www.luzernerzeitung.ch/meinung/leserbriefe/tourismus-wie-wir-unsere-gaste-in-lu zern-empfangen-sollten-ld.1027487 (Accessed 25 September 2018.)

Li, X. (Ed.) (2016) *Chinese outbound tourism 2.0*. Advances in hospitality and tourism book series, Oakville, ON, Waretown, NJ: Apple Academic Press.

Luzern Tourismus (2018) Die Luzern Tourismus AG – Facts & Figures. https://www.luzern.com (Accessed 24 September 2018.)

Metz, K. (2018) Luzern: Lebensqualität und die Zweistunden-Besucher. *Luzerner Zeitung*, 16 August. https://www.luzernerzeitung.ch/meinung/leserbriefe/luzern-lebensqualitat-und-die-zweistunden-besucher-ld.1045524 (Accessed 25 September 2018.)

Ohnmacht, T. and Ponnapureddy, S. (2017) Tourism mobilities and the hospitality industry: From pilgrimage to mass tourism and patterns of encounter between locals and tourists. 2nd International Conference on Tourism and Business, ICTB, Luzern.

Pilatus (2018) Die steilste Zahnradbahn der Welt und ihre Geschichte. https://www.pilatus.ch/en tdecken/zahnradbahn/geschichte/ (Accessed 24 September 2018.)

PwC – Lodging & Tourism Clients Group (2014) Studie zum Carverkehr in der Luzerner Innenstadt. Luzern Tourismus.

Radio Pilatus (2017) Stadt Luzern soll Ladenbesitzer unterstützen. Luzern bleibt ein schwieriges Pflaster für die Geschäfte. *Radio Pilatus*, 17 November.https://www.radiopilatus.ch/artikel/148862/stadt-luzern-soll-ladenbesitzer-unterstuetzen (Accessed 24 September 2018.)

Rigi (2018) Bahngeschichte. https://www.rigi.ch/Information/Bergbahnen/Rigi-Bahnen/Ueber-die-RIGI-BAHNEN-AG/Bergbahnen/Bahngeschichte (25 September 2018.)

Schaber, L. (2018) Stadt Luzern: Wie man die Probleme mit dem Cartourismus lösen könnte. *Tagblatt*, 28 August. https://www.tagblatt.ch/meinung/leserbriefe/stadt-luzern-wie-man-die-probleme-mit-dem-cartourismus-losen-konnte-ld.1048465 (Accessed 25 September 2018.)

SGV (2018) Geschichte SGV Gruppe. https://www.sgvgruppe.ch/sgv-gruppe/geschichte-sgv-gruppe/ (Accessed 24 September 2018.)

SRF (2013) Alex Wang sorgt für Boom chinesischer Touristen in Luzern. *SRF*, 10 May. https://www.srf.ch/news/regional/zentralschweiz/alex-wang-sorgt-fuer-boom-chine sischer-touristen-in-luzern (Accessed 25 September 2018.)

Stettler, J., Eggli, F., Huck, L. (2018) Chinesische Individualreisende: Chancen und Potenziale für die Zentralschweiz. Hochschule Luzern. https://www.hslu.ch/en/lucerne-university-of-applied-sciences-and-arts/research/projects/detail/?pid=3940 (Accessed 25 September 2018.)

Stettler, J., Egli, A., Zemp, M., Eggli, F. and Huck, L. (2017) Innotour-Projekt: "Outbound-Reisemarkt China": Beschreibung, Herausforderungen und Handlungsmöglichkeiten. ITW Working Paper. Lucerne University of Applied Sciences and Arts, Lucerne. Institute of Tourism.

Towner, J. (1985) The grand tour: A key phase in the history of tourism. *Annals of Tourism Research*, 12 (3): 297–333.

UNWTO (2017) *Penetrating the Chinese Outbound Tourism Market – Successful Practices and Solutions*. World Tourism Organization (UNWTO).

Wydler, J. (2017) Fertig Blechlawine: Cars werden vom Inseli verbannt. *zentralplus*, 24 September. https://www.zentralplus.ch/de/news/politik/5547773/Fertig-Blechlawine-Cars-werden-vom-Inseli-verbannt.htm (Accessed 25 September 2018.)

Jahanzeeb Qurashi

13 The Hajj: crowding and congestion problems for pilgrims and hosts

Introduction

The Hajj is the fifth pillar of Islam and is considered to be the largest annual religious pilgrimage event in the world. The Hajj journey is completed over a period of five days and consists of several religious rituals with multifarious activities (Mahmoud and Plumb, 2010).

The divine city of Makkah (Mecca) has hosted the annual pilgrimage for more than 14 centuries (Gwyn, 1989). Makkah is considered the most sacred city in the Muslim world. It is the capital city of one of the 13 regions of the Kingdom of Saudi Arabia and has over 2 million inhabitants (Mahmoud and Plumb, 2010). The holy city of Makkah's importance far outweighs its size on account of its status as the capital of Islam and its privilege of hosting the Hajj.

The city is bordered by the sacred area called Haram, which the large crowd of pilgrims visits to accomplish the diverse, multifaceted rites of the Hajj. The actions of pilgrims include the circumambulation of the Kaaba (black cube) seven times; running and walking between the Hills of Al-Safa and Al-Marwah; staying for a day under tents or in the sun in the field of Arafat; spending a night in the rocky field of Muzdalifah to collect pebbles to stone the three devils; and staying in the tent city of Mina, conducting activities including the stoning of the devils and the sacrificing of animals (Robinson, 1999).

Over 2 million pilgrims from across the globe gather for the Hajj every year (Saudi Arabian Commission for Tourism and Antiquities, 2016), making the Hajj one of the largest annual religious tourism events worldwide. The excessive number of pilgrims during the Hajj period is an indication of overtourism. Because this large number of visitors converges on Makkah in a short space of time, the Hajj is a hazardous event. Despite the peaceful nature of the Hajj, the congestion and the emotions of the crowd, with pilgrims full of exhilaration, anxiety, fear, religious passion and aggression, have led to crowd crushes, resulting in the deaths of thousands of pilgrims (Al Jazeera, 2015). Managing the crowds and congestion has become a massive challenge, not only for the pilgrims but for the government of the Kingdom of Saudi Arabia (KSA).

This chapter will begin with a discussion of the ideology behind the Hajj and its connection with Makkah, and then will examine how the host, the Kingdom of Saudi Arabia (KSA), has turned the destination into a religious tourism hub. The chapter will also examine the challenges related to overtourism and how local Saudi services are working to address the issues of crowds and congestion.

https://doi.org/10.1515/9783110607369-013

The ancient Hajj and current Makkah

The ideology behind the Hajj dates back to when the Prophet Ibrahim peace be upon him (PBUH) was given the task of leading mankind and was ordered by Allah (God) to go to Makkah (Johnson, 2010: 42). The day the Prophet Ibrahim (PBUH) arrived in Makkah, Allah commanded him to abandon his wife, the Prophet Hagar (PBUH), and his first-born son Ishmael (PBUH) in a deserted, rocky valley. The Prophet Ibrahim (PBUH) obeyed. Soon, their stock of dates and water was exhausted; both mother and son became thirsty. Prophet Hagar (PBUH) ran seven times between the sacred hills of Al-Safa and Al-Marwah located within the current city of Makkah, but found nothing. However, close to where Prophet Ishmael (PBUH) was resting, water sprang from the earth by the command of Allah. This source of water became the miracle holy water of "Zam Zam" in Makkah, and still runs today.

Allah was highly pleased with the commitment of the Prophet Ibrahim (PBUH) and commanded him to construct the house of Allah, called the Kaaba, a cubical structure made of black stone in the Grand Mosque of Makkah (O'Connor, 2010: 11–13). The Kaaba has a vital role in the lives of Muslims; it represents the third pillar of Islam, or "Salah", which means praying five times a day facing towards the Kaaba wherever they are in the world. The fifth pillar of Islam, the Hajj, could not be performed without the Kaaba, as pilgrims have to perform a circumambulation of it seven times. Given the religious emblematic value of the Kaaba, no pilgrim should endow it with the power to benefit or to hurt (Sardar et al., 1978). After the completion of the Kaaba, Allah ordered the Prophet Ibrahim (PBUH) to call on mankind to pay pilgrimage, to visit Makkah and the Kaaba.

With the passage of time, both the method and the goal of the Hajj were changed. Idolatry spread throughout Arabia, and the Kaaba lost its purity and idols were placed inside it (Sardar et al., 1978). In 629 A.D, the Prophet Mohammed (PBUH) returned to Makkah as a pilgrim and destroyed all the idols in the city (Long, 1979: 162). This act of purification cleansed the Abrahamic holy sites of pagan Gods and rituals and provided the basis of Islam in Makkah. Later, the Hajj was declared and over time became the largest Islamic religious ritual practice in the world.

The ancient desert city of Makkah today displays a dazzling array of towers, shopping malls, luxury hotels and modern technology (Taylor, 2011). The KSA government has invested 88 billion United States dollars (USD) into religious tourism planning, aiming to boost the hospitality, tourism and telecommunications infrastructure of the two holy cities: Makkah and Madinah (Travel Talk Middle East, 2010). Despite Makkah's modernisation, however, challenges arise from the Hajj every year due to the enormous numbers of pilgrims.

According to Smith (2016), the tourism industry as a whole currently generates about 2.4% of Saudi Arabia's gross domestic product (GDP), a contribution which is expected to rise to 5.7% by 2020. Religious tourism is one of the main drivers of growth of the tourism industry in the KSA. According to a report by Jeddah Chamber of Commerce (2016), in 2015 the total tourism industry was valued at USD 21.33 billion, with the religious tourism sector accounting for USD 5.68 billion. The report suggests that the tourism sector has the potential to create 400,000 more jobs by 2020 (Jeddah Chamber of Commerce, 2016).

The country attracted 19 million religious visitors in 2015, including 2.95 million Hajj visitors and 14.05 million Umrah (pilgrimage to Makkah outside the Hajj period) visitors. Tab. 13.1 presents the annual numbers of Hajj pilgrims between 2005 and 2009 and between 2012 and 2017. The sharp drops in the numbers of pilgrims in 2013 and 2016 are believed to be related to the extensive construction projects in Makkah, negative publicity surrounding construction-related incidents and (in the case of the 2016 decline) the deaths caused by a pilgrim stampede in 2015. Approximately 2.93 million Muslims took part in circumambulation around Kaaba in 2011 (Mintel, 2012) and in 2012 more than 3 million pilgrims took part in circumambulation (Huda, 2016).

Tab. 13.1: Numbers of Hajj pilgrims (millions), 2005–2009 and 2012–2017 (source: Saudi Arabian Commission for Tourism and Antiquities, 2016).

2005: 2.26	2012: 3.16
2006: 2.38	2013: 1.98
2007: 2.45	2014: 2.90
2008: 2.41	2015: 2.95
2009: 2.31	2016: 1.8
2010: 2.79	2017: 2
2011: 2.93	

The Hajj system consists of subsystems that each cater for the mass of pilgrims. In the physical sector, these range from wide-open valleys – Arafat, for example – to narrow routes – the movement between Arafat and Muzdalefa, for example. In the domain of activities, they vary from temporary and locally diffused actions (the shaving of the head after the Hajj, the sacrifice, and ritual ablutions) to ones that are exactly defined in time and/or space, for instance the Tawaf (circumambulation of the Kaaba) (Alaa, 1992).

After performing Hajj rituals at Mina, Arafat and Muzdalifa, the pilgrims return to the Grand Mosque Al-Haram for the Tawaf Al-Ifada, which consists of seven laps around the Kaaba, which is situated in the centre of the Mataf (area around the black cube) (Rinschede, 1992). The Grand Mosque consists of two significant zones: 1) the Mataf (area of circumambulation) and 2) the zone of the sacred hills of Al-Safa and Al-Marwah for Sa'I, in which pilgrims walk and run between the two hills seven times and cover a distance of approximately 3.15 km. The various stages of the Hajj are presented in Fig. 13.1.

As a result of overtourism, the Hajj has become the world's most commoditised, commodified and capitalised religious tourism journey (Qurashi, 2017). Shepherd

Step-by-step guide to the Hajj

1) Point of start (Tawaf) from Black Stone

2) Welcome circumambulation (Tawaf)

3) Performing Sai between two holy mountains (Al-Safa and Al Marwa)

4) Departure to Mina

5) Day at mount Arafat

6) Night at Rocky field of Muzdalifha

7) Devil stoning bridges at Mina

8) Sacrificing animal at Mina

9) Hair trimming and removal of official dress (Ihram) of Hajj

10) Return to Grand Mosque for Tawaf and Sai

11) Going back to Mina same day for max five days (Stoning Devil)

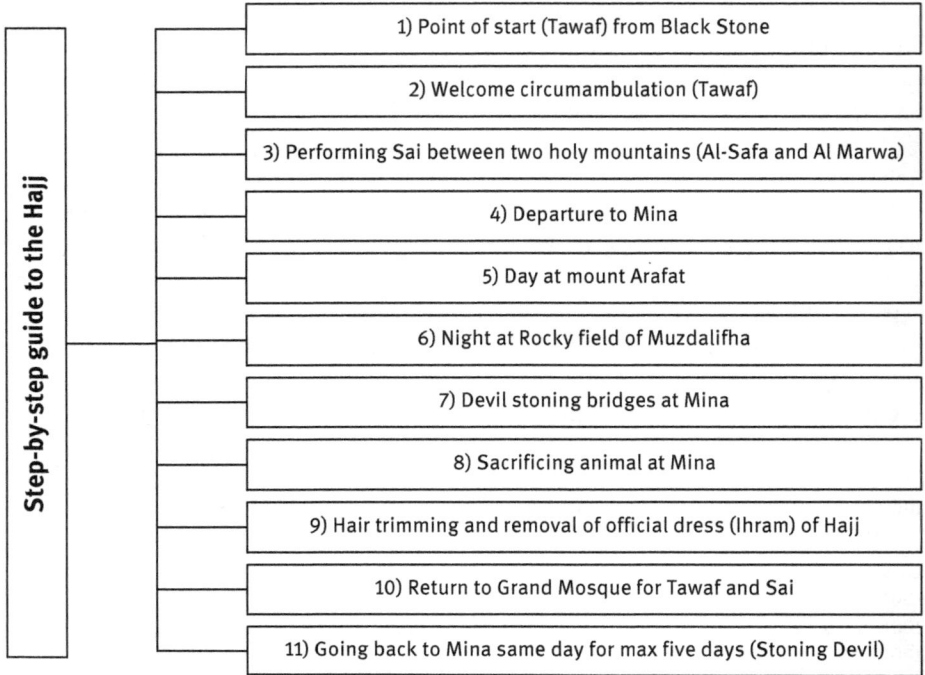

Fig. 13.1: Step-by-step guide to the Hajj (photo credit: Jahanzeeb Qurashi).

(2000) observed that what was formerly unadulterated and authentic has become damaged and commodified. The main concern with overtourism, however, is that the immense crowding leads to the deaths of pilgrims every year. The following section considers the challenges faced during the Hajj due to overtourism.

Challenges during the Hajj

Between 2002 and 2015, approximately 23 million overseas pilgrims visited Makkah for the Hajj. During that period, about 30,000 casualties were recorded among overseas visitors in the Hajj season. These deaths were the result of various factors, including: stampedes and crowd suffocation, heat and fatigue, and construction accidents. The death rates for eight of the largest nations participating in the Hajj for the period 2002 to 2015, excluding Saudi Arabia, are presented in Tab. 13.2. Despite these setbacks, however, overtourism of Makkah continues at pace, and there is a need to understand the flow of pilgrims; the narrow places of Hajj and the fluctuations in the density of pilgrims during Hajj, which consequently affect the cause of accidents due to overtourism.

Tab. 13.2: Death rates for eight of the largest nations participating in the Hajj (2002–2015) (source: Kingdom of Saudi Arabia, Ministry of Health, 2016).

Country	Hajj death rates	Total pilgrims	Hajj deaths
Iran	6.30	1,173,307	738
Turkey	7.20	1,291,338	935
Indonesia	15.83	2,770,000	4,386
Pakistan	16.80	2,127,112	3,559
Bangladesh	17.28	1,032,088	1,783
India	18.91	1,480,186	2,803
Nigeria	17.60	1,123,000	1,988
Egypt	23.52	1,000,500	2,353

*Local Saudi death rate is not available

Congestion during the Hajj occurs at the narrow passes in the system, for instance: at the sites of the Tawaf and Sa'I (walking and running between the hills of Al-Safa and Al-Marwah) before the ninth day of the Hajj month when the pilgrims offer the Tawaf Al-Qudum (welcome circumambulation of the black cube), and additional Tawafs during their visit to Makkah. Other sites of congestion are during the Nafra (process includes the movement of pilgrims from Arafat to Muzdalifa before sunrise using certain limited routes), including at its starting places – the pedestrian and vehicle bridges in front of Arafat. Congestion also occurs on the Jamarat Bridge (Devil's Bridge); at its eastern entrance on the morning of the tenth day, and in the afternoon of the eleventh and twelfth days of the Hajj month. Another site of congestion is the road between Mina and Makkah on the tenth and twelfth days; and again from the tenth day of the month at the sites of Tawaf and Sa'I, when the pilgrims perform Tawaf Al-Wada (farewell circumambulation) and other Tawafs (Owaidah, 2015).

The sizes of the crowds of pilgrims at any particular point change constantly, depending on the day and on the speed and compactness of the pedestrians. Pilgrims walk individually and in groups (the majority). In the early stage of the Hajj, pilgrims walk at an average speed of 40 metres per minute, but when compaction occurs, with the pilgrims touching each other, freedom of movement is blocked and the entire crowd can come to a halt. If not addressed, this can result in chaos (Sarmady et al., 2011).

During the Tawaf, crowd movement is fundamentally in a circular movement around the Kaaba. However, the wall of Al-Hateem, an extension of the Kaaba, can disrupt this circular movement. This interruption of the counter-clockwise Tawaf motion causes a compressed and mobbed area near Al-Hateem. This congestion, combined with the crowds formed by the attraction on the east side of the Kaaba, causes a high density on that side of the Kaaba, while on the other side it is less crowded. Due to heightened emotion during the circumambulation, there is much contact between pilgrims and pushing among the crowd, which sometimes leads to suffocation (Sarmady et al., 2011). Figure 13.2 illustrates the crowd size.

Fig. 13.2: Circumambulation of Kaaba (photo credit: Jahanzeeb Qurashi).

The ritual of stoning the three devils is currently the most dangerous ritual of the Hajj. It is carried out on Jamarat Bridge. A new Jamarat Bridge was built in 1975, with pillars that penetrated three openings in the bridge, thus permitting pilgrims to throw pebbles from ground level or from the bridge (The Hajj, 2015). Prior to that, pillars were approached only from the ground level, and the ritual was conducted in a less coordinated manner. Despite this new design, more than 1,000 pilgrims died during stampedes on the Jamarat Bridge between 1994 and 2006 (The Guardian, 2006). This occurred even though movement was regulated, with pilgrims given access to the bridge at different times in accordance with their tent zones.

Mitigation of overtourism, successes and challenges

Following an incident on the Jamarat Bridge in 2004, new crowd management measures were applied to the bridge's design. Furthermore, the form of the Jamarat pillars was altered from spherical pillars to larger oval walls. This augmented the surface area and enabled a better-organized arrangement, avoiding any weak points. Despite these efforts, however, another stampede occurred in 2006 in which 380 pilgrims were killed and 289 injured. Following these tragic incidents on Jamarat Bridge, rather than reducing the number of pilgrims, the Saudi authorities altered the design of the bridge again (Ngai et al., 2009). Indeed, the Saudi government destroyed the bridge and built a new one. This was done in cooperation with domestic and international professionals in crowd safety and congestion.

In 2007, the new bridge was opened. It is over 950 metres long and 80 metres wide, with five levels. Each level is 12 metres in height, with a capacity of 300,000 pilgrims per hour along its length (Jeavans, 2015). Anticipating future upsurges in the number of pilgrims, the bridge was designed to accommodate five million pilgrims. The government increased the number of entrances and exits, permitting pilgrims to move freely and safely.

Previously, the paths to and from the bridge had permitted bidirectional movement of pilgrims, which led to obstacles and interruptions in the flow. The new design altered this to a unidirectional system, minimizing obstructions. However, in 2015 a stampede on the new bridge claimed the lives of 769 pilgrims and injured 934. This time, the authorities did not criticize the design of the bridge but rather the crowd's psychological attitude and physical behaviour. Despite the high-tech structure and massive capacity of the bridge, further disasters remain a possibility (Saudi Health Ministry, 2015).

As well as redesigning the bridge, the Saudi government has applied risk management systems to mitigate hazards that arise as a result of overtourism during the Hajj period. For example, following a fire in 1997 the Saudi government changed the ordinary tents of Mina to fireproof ones (Gibaldi, 2009: 17). Figure 13.3 shows the five levels of the new Jamaraat Bridge and the fireproof tents in Mina.

The Grand Mosque, with the Holy Kaaba at its centre, has witnessed successive expansions, beginning in the era of the Caliph Umar ibn al-Khattab, who carried out the first expansion in the year 638. In 1925, the late King Abdul Aziz Al Saud, founder of the Kingdom of Saudi Arabia, ordered a full renovation and modernisation of the Holy Mosque, including area expansion. In view of the increasing numbers of pilgrims and the high summer temperatures, the late King Abdul Aziz sought to not only expand the Grand Mosque Al-Haram but to also install air conditioning. Expansion operations continued in the reign of the late King Saud (1953–1964). Between 1955 and 1961, the Grand Mosque was expanded to a total area of 152,000 square meters, with a capacity of 400,000 worshippers. Further expansion operations were undertaken during the reign of the late King Fahd (1982–2005), beginning in 1988.

As of 2016, the total area of the Grand Mosque had reached 356,000 square meters (Royal Embassy of Saudi Arabia Italy, 2016). According to Redfern (2010: 32) the capacity of the Grand Mosque is 700,000 pilgrims offering prayers. Plans exist to raise the capacity to 2 million (Reuters, 2011). The development will be spread over

Fig. 13.3: The new Jamaraat Bridge and fireproof tents (photo credit: Jahanzeeb Qurashi).

an area of 1,020,500 square meters, with the mosque building itself occupying an area of 614,800 square meters. The project will involve expansion of the northern side to 1,250,000 square meters of land (BNC for Stone & Surface Middle East, 2017). Expansion efforts will extend to the hills of Al-Safa and Al-Marwah, with plans to increase the area from 29,000 square meters to 87,000 square meters. This will allow more than 100,000 pilgrims to run between the two holy hills. Figure 13.4 presents a model of the Grand Mosque and shows the area that will be expanded.

Transport of pilgrims during the Hajj is one of the biggest issues facing authorities in Makkah. On arrival, the pilgrims are taken from Jeddah to Makkah or from Madinah to Makkah, and they mostly depart in the same order as they arrived. On the ninth day of the Hajj month, the pilgrims are transported directly to their tents in Arafat or left in the open. Then buses load the pilgrims and take them to Muzdalifa before sunset. The pilgrims depart in a mass departure to Madinah or Jeddah on the twelfth day of the Hajj month.

Approximately 19,000 government buses took part in the Hajj in 2016. These buses are guided and controlled by Saudi pilgrim guides called Mutawiffun. Apart from government buses, between 50,000 and 60,000 private vehicles participate in Hajj operations leaving Arafat. With such high numbers of vehicles, congestion inevitably results, particularly on the final day of the Hajj, and this takes hours to clear. There have been reports of vehicles covering a distance of only six kilometres in a period of 12 to 17 hours, with their engines remaining running throughout to operate the air conditioning.

Fig. 13.4: Plan for the expansion of the Grand Mosque in Makkah (photo credit: Jahanzeeb Qurashi).

To overcome this traffic congestion issue, Saudi Arabia has built a network of roads, bridges, crossings, motorways and other traffic features in the holy venues. In addition to an airport rail link (discussed below), a high-speed rail link is planned between the two holy cities, Makkah and Medina, which will be supported by the local mass rapid transit system within Makkah, which links the holy places of Mina, Arafat and Muzdalifa. In 2010 an 18-kilometre southern line of the Al-Mashaar and Al-Mugadassah metro opened, with nine stations, connecting the holy places of Mina, Muzdalifah and Arafat. Additional extensions to the mass-transit system will link sites with the Grand Mosque of Al-Haram (Railway Gazette International, 2010).

In 2006 the KSA launched plans to extend, in several phases, Jeddah's airport, so as to better cope with the large number of visitors passing through the airport during the Hajj. The first phase will increase the capacity from 15 million to 30 million passengers annually. This phase will include constructing a high-speed train link from Jeddah airport to Makkah (Abdel-Razzaq, 2017).

At the same time, the Saudi government is developing a new city, "King Abdul Aziz Economic City", some 72 kilometres from Makkah, with a 14 square kilometre seaport which will have the capacity for 300,000 pilgrims arriving by sea. Most of these pilgrims will come from the Middle East, South Asia, South East Asia and Africa (Jafari, 2010: 101). The new city will contain a business district, residential areas, an educational zone and seaside resorts. The main focus of the city is to facilitate pilgrim movement and promote religious tourism, but it will also promote commercial tourism through adding further dimensions to the Kingdom's tourism infrastructure.

As well as developing and expanding infrastructure to address congestion during the Hajj, the Saudi government has also imposed a Hajj quota system on nations with the highest pilgrim attendance. Furthermore, pilgrims can only perform the Hajj once every five years. The pilgrims who participate in the Hajj come from all over the world and bring germs and viruses with them. Given the large numbers of pilgrims, this poses a health risk. The Saudi government has therefore introduced measures to prevent the transmission of airborne diseases and other communicable diseases. It has placed public health officers at every entry point of Saudi Arabia and has introduced medical scanning equipment at all ports. Health facilities and attendants have also been placed at the various Hajj venues to ensure that any pilgrims who are ill are easily taken care of. Free medical care is available at these facilities, which are fully equipped with medical material and personnel, giving the pilgrims the best possible medical attention. As a result of standby emergency teams, casualties have decreased, and responses to emergencies are faster (Sheikh et al., 2008). The government has also improved the local hospitals, by supplying them with modern equipment and ensuring an adequate supply of medical personnel. This preventative approach seeks to avoid the mass spread of disease and epidemics (Ljioui and Emmerich, 2008).

Psychological and physical aspects of Hajj crowding

Saudi Hajj authorities spent more than $35 billion USD in the twenty-year period between 1992 and 2012 on redesigning the infrastructure of the Hajj to ensure the safety of pilgrims (Vijayanand, 2012). Although new infrastructure and facilities have eased congestion of pilgrims and vehicles, risks remain and tragedies still occur. The massive numbers of people that perform the rituals mean that large crowds will always be a key feature of the Hajj. Unfortunately, crowd crushes claim the lives of pilgrims almost every year during the Hajj.

Until now, this chapter has addressed the reasons large crowds form during the Hajj, but investigation is required into the reasons why catastrophes occur in these crowds. Any effort to reduce the risks associated with these crowds must be based on an understanding of crowd behaviour. The remainder of this chapter will examine the psychological and physical aspects of Hajj crowd behaviour.

Crowds are usually physical (a group of people in one location), but can also be psychological (where people in a crowd share a common social identity) (Templeton et al., 2015). At any particular event, the members of the group may have a collective identity, whether because they are Muslims, football fans, music fans or others. When there is a collective identity, this affects the behaviour of the crowd, including crowd movement, flow and congestion (Curtis et al., 2011). Silverman et al., 2005 observed that people in a "psychological crowd" (with a collective identity) walk together closely and walk additional distances to stay together, compared with a crowd in which there is not a clear shared identity. Furthermore, when there is a collective identity, the emotional state of a group might mean that the crowd is easier to manage, even if it is compact or moving slowly, because people feel safe within the group (Templeton et al., 2015). But when there are numerous identities within a crowd, this may cause issues.

In terms of the Hajj, this raises certain questions. Do the physical crowds in Makkah comprise more than one psychological crowd – for instance Sunni and Shia pilgrims? Do these different psychological crowds behave differently? The answers to such question have critical importance due to the diversity of rituals the Hajj pilgrimage comprises, and have vital implications for planning and simulations of the Hajj. For instance, if one group of pilgrims may prefer to worship under the open sky, this will affect their behaviour and that of the overall crowd.

The Saudi authorities use computer-based models to study and predict crowd behaviour, such as the cellular automata model, force-based methods, matrix-based models and rule-based models, which are the most common methods used to simulate crowd complex movements and behaviour during the time of congestion. Matrix-based systems divide environments into cells and make use of cellular automata to model the movements of entities between cells. In rule-based models, items like birds and animals are simulated in the form of a flock and interact based on their perceptions of the environment. Each model above has its own strengths and weaknesses to monitor crowd movements and depending on the specific requirements and situation being simulated, one model may be more suitable than another. The social forces model, for instance, produces smoother movements in comparison to cell-based methods, due to its continuous nature. However, due to the computational complexity of that model, simulations based on it require high processing power. For instance, for huge crowds like the one in the court of the Grand Mosque, which can reach 300,000 pilgrims, it is not practical to use this method unless someone incorporates a parallel processing technique. Therefore, despite research demonstrating that there are often small psychological groups within physical crowds, and extensive research showing that collective behaviour requires individuals to see themselves as part of a large psychological crowd or group, most such models treat crowds as consisting of simply many individuals within a mass. Such models, which treat the crowd as a homogeneous unit, are not able to predict how large groups of pilgrims will fragment, with some groups extricating themselves from other groups and creating mass contraflows (Templeton, 2015).

As yet, computer modellers have not created models that adequately simulate certain key psychological features of large crowd behaviour. Furthermore, the models they use do not monitor the compactness and flow of crowds in real time (Sarmady et al., 2011). Therefore, the existing models cannot accurately predict crowd movement. But instead of using better computer models to understand Hajj crowd behaviour, it would be useful to examine the different psychological groups within the Hajj crowd and use knowledge gained from such studies to make predictions about overall crowd behaviour. This is a valuable area for further research.

Conclusion

Taking all the above discussion into account, it is clear that the intense overtourism of the Hajj presents many challenges for the Saudi authorities. These challenges are expected to increase in the future as it is predicted that the Hajj crowd will increase to 6 million by 2030 (Gulf News, 2018). The KSA is attempting to manage these challenges through social and technical measures. Currently the Saudi government is working on Vision 2030, which not only seeks to boost the country's economy but also offers strategies to address overtourism within both holy cities. These strategies involve using advanced smart media technologies and contemporary tourism infrastructure design. Other elements include advanced and sophisticated measures to address issues associated with the transportation of pilgrims, pilgrims' food, accommodation and other supplies, and the environmental issues of the Hajj.

References

Abdel-Razzaq, J. (2017) King Abdulaziz International Airport expansion 88% complete, *Construction Week Online.Com*, 4 June. http://www.constructionweekonline.com/article-44711-king-abdulaziz-international-airport-expansion-88-complete/ (Accessed 12 December 2017.)

Al Arabiya News. (2012) Saudi Arabia declares Hajj 2012 one of the most successful, *Al Arabiya*, 29 October. http://en.ammonnews.net/article.aspx?articleNO=18662 (Accessed 5 May 2016).

Al-Azraqi, A. M. (1965), *Akbar Makkah*, p. 281. In Alken, I. A. (1995) The Hajj: Past, Present and Future. PhD Thesis University of Leeds, UK. Institute of Communication Studies.

Al Jazeera (2015) Saudi Arabia orders probe into deadly Hajj stampede. *Al Jazeera*, 25 September. https://www.aljazeera.com/news/2015/09/saudi-arabia-orders-probe-deadly-hajj-stampede-150924164022374.html (Accessed 5 May 2016).

Al-Sarif, A., Makkawa al-Madina, ftallahiliyyawa Al-Rasül, A. (2011), A survey of geographical references, pp. 111–112. In D. Gibson, *Quranic Geography*. Surrey, Canada: Independent Scholar's Press.

Alaa, S. (1992) Unresolved problem of the Hajj in the city of Makkah in Saudi Arabia, Master's degree thesis, University of Arizona. http://arizona.openrepository.com/arizona/handle/10150/559272 (Accessed 3 June 2017).

Bucks, J. (2015) The Hajj crush: 'It was the closest thing to hell on earth', *The Guardian*, 23 December. https://www.theguardian.com/news/2015/dec/23/hajj-crush-pilgrimage-mecca-stampede-saudi-arabia-mina-valley (Accessed 30 June 2017).

BNC for Stone & Surface Middle East (2017) Mega Ongoing Projects.https://www.stoneandsurfacesaudi.com/market-intelligence/industry-reports (Accessed 12 December 2017.)

Curtis, S., Guy, S. J., Narain, R., Patil, S., Lin, M. C. and Manocha, D. (2011) Simulation and analysis of large crowds, University of North Carolina at Chapel Hill. http://gamma.cs.unc.edu/LARGE (Accessed 3 May 2017.)

Gibaldi, J. (2009) *MLA handbook for writers of research papers*. New York: Morden Language Association of America.

Gulf News Saudi Arabia (2017) Haj pilgrim spending jumps by 70 per cent. *Gulf News*, 3 September. https://gulfnews.com/news/gulf/saudi-arabia/haj-pilgrim-spending-jumps-by-70-per-cent-1. 2084376 (Accessed 30 July 2018.)

Gulf News Saudi Arabia (2018) 'Green Haj' slowly takes root in Makkah. https://gulfnews.com/world/gulf/saudi/green-haj-slowly-takes-root-in-makkah-1.2269892 (Accessed 12 December 2018.)

Gwyn, R. (1989) The centrality of Islam: Space, form and process. *GeoJournal*, 18 (4): 351–359.

Huda (2016) Hajj Pilgrimage Statistics. https://www.thoughtco.com/hajj-by-the-numbers-2004319 (Accessed 6 June 2017.)

Ijioui, R., Emmerich, H. and Ceyp, M. (2008) *Strategies and tactics in supply chain management*. Berlin: Springer.

Jeddah Chamber of Commerce (2016) *Tourism in Saudi Arabia*. http://www.jeg.org.sa/data/modules/contents/uploads/infopdf/2867.pdf (Accessed 28 May 2017.)

Jeavans, C. (2015) Hajj: Jamarat Bridge, a deadly pinch point. *BBC News*, 25 September. http://www.bbc.co.uk/news/world-middle-east-34361122 (Accessed 10 May 2017.)

Johnson, D. J. (2010) Tourism in Saudi Arabia. In N. Scott and J. Jafri (Eds.) *Tourism in the Muslim world. Bridging tourism theory and practice*, Vol. 2, Bingley, UK: Emerald Group Publishing, pp. 91–106.

Kahhdla, R, O. (1964) *Jugrafyat Sibh Jaztrat al-'Arab*, 2nd edition.Kingdom of Saudi Arabia, Ministry of Health. (2016) Statement of Deaths during Period from 1423 to 1437. http://www.al-akhbar.com (Accessed 15 February 2017.)

Long, D. E. (1979) *The Hajj Today: A Survey of the Contemporary Mecca Pilgrimage*, Albany: State University of New York Press.

Mahmoud, B. C. and Plumb, C. (2010) *Real value in a changing world*. Berlin: Jones Lang Lasalle. http://www.jll.de/germany/en-gb/Documents/JLL-service-brochure.pdf (Accessed 10 July 2018.)

Mintel (2012) Religious and Pilgrimage Tourism International. *Mintel*, February. http://store.mintel.com/religious-and-pilgrimage-tourism-international-february-2012 (Accessed 4 August 2016.)

Ngai, K. M., Burkle, F. M., Hsu, A. and Hsu, E. B. (2009) Human stampedes: a systemic review of historical and peer-reviewed sources. *Disaster Medicine and Public Health Preparedness*, 3 (4): 191–195.

O'Connor, P. J. (2010) *The modern Hajj: Themes of modernity, the Saudi State, International pilgrims, and the British experience*. Saarbrücken, Germany: Lambert Academic Publishing.

Owaidah, A. A. (2015) Hajj crowd management via a mobile augmented reality application: A case of the Hajj event, Saudi Arabia. Master's thesis, University of Glasgow.http://theses.gla.ac.uk/6330/ (Accessed 11 February 2017.)

Qurashi, J. (2017) Commodification of Islamic religious tourism: From spiritual to touristic experience. *International Journal of Religious Tourism and Pilgrimage*, 5 (1): 89–104.

Railway Gazette International (2010) Railway Gazette International 12 (10), 22 November. http://archiv.railwaygazette.com/railway-gazette-international.html (Accessed 5 August 2014.)

Redfern, B. (2010) A holy city in transition, *Middle East Economic Digest*, 54 (40). http://connection.ebscohost.com/c/articles/54574463/holy-city-transition (Accessed 4 May 2017.)

Rinschede, G. (1992) Forms of religious tourism. *Annals of Tourism Research*, 19: 51–67.

Robinson, N. (1999) *Islam: A Concise Introduction*. Washington, DC: Georgetown University Press.

Royal Embassy of Saudi Arabia, Italy (2016) Exploring the Kingdom of Saudi Arabia http://www.arabia-saudita.it/files/news/2016/10/september_e-newsletter.pdf (Accessed27 July 2018.).

Reuters (2011) Saudi Arabia starts Mecca mosque expansion, *Reuters*, 20 August. https://ca.reuters.com/article/topNews/idCATRE77J0W520110820?sp=true (Accessed 4 May 2017.)

Salaman, B. (2009) Kingdom Eyes SR101 bn revenue from tourism. *Arab News*, 3 May. https://www.highbeam.com/doc/1G1-198979027.html (Accessed 5 August 2014.)

Sardar, Z. and Badawi, M. A. Z. (Eds.) (1978) *Hajj studies*, London: Croom Helem.

Sarmady, S., Haron, F. and Talib, A. Z. (2011) A cellular automata model for circular movements of pedestrians during Tawaf, *Simulation Modelling Practice and Theory*, 19 (3): 969–985.

Saudi Health Ministry (2015) Mina's EOC helped save lives of tens of stampede victims. *MOH News*, 25 September. http://www.moh.gov.sa/en/Ministry/MediaCenter/News/Pages/News-2015-09-25-007.aspx (Accessed 6 May 2017.)

Saudi Arabian Commission for Tourism and Antiquities (2016) https://www.statista.com/statistics/617696/saudi-arabia-total-hajj-pilgrims/ (Accessed 6 August 2017.)

Scott, N. and Jafri, J. (Eds.) (2010) *Tourism in the Muslim world: Bridging tourism theory and practice*, Vol. 2.Bingley, UK: Emerald Group Publishing.

Sheikh, A. and Gatrad, A. R. (2008) *Caring for Muslim Patients*, 2nd edn. New York: Radcliffe.

Shepherd, R. J. (2002) Commodification, culture and tourism. *Tourist Studies*, 2 (2): 183–201.

Silverman, B. G, Badler, N. I., Pelechano, N. and O'Brien, K. (2005) Crowd simulation incorporating agent psychological models, roles and communication. Center for Human Modeling and Simulation, University of Pennsylvania. https://repository.upenn.edu/hms/29/ (Accessed 6 May 2017.)

Taylor, J. (2011) Mecca for the rich: Islam's holiest site 'turning into Vegas', *The Independent*, 24 September. https://www.independent.co.uk/news/world/middle-east/mecca-for-the-rich-is lams-holiest-site-turning-into-vegas-2360114.html (Accessed 6 July 2018.)

Templeton, A. and Drury, J. (2015) Analysis: Here's how to make the Hajj safer – by better understanding crowd psychology. *The Conversation*, 28 September. https://theconversation.com/heres-how-to-make-the-hajj-safer-by-better-understanding-crowd-psychology-48128 (Accessed 26 March 2016.)

Templeton, A., Drury, J. and Philippides, A. (2015) From mindless masses to small groups: Conceptualizing collective behavior in crowd modeling. *Review of General Psychology*, 19 (3): 215–229.

The Guardian (2006) A history of Hajj tragedies, *The Guardian*, 13 January. www.theguardian.com/world/2006/jan/13/saudiarabia (Accessed 10 April 2018.)

The Hajj (2015) The Jamarat Bridge project: An exceptional achievement of crowd control. http://www.kapl-hajj.org/jamarat_bridge.php (Accessed 14 March 2018.)

Travel Talk – Middle East (2010) Religious tourism sets pace in Middle East. *Travel Talk*. https://travtalkmiddleeast.com/ (Accessed 6 June 2017.)

Vijayanand, S. (2012) Socio-economic impact in pilgrimage tourism. *International Journal of Multidisciplinary Research*, 2 (1): 329–343.

World Travel and Tourism Council (2017) *Travel & Tourism Economic Impact 2017: Saudi Arabia*, https://www.wttc.org/ (Accessed 15 April 2018.)

Richard W. Butler

14 Overtourism in rural settings: the Scottish highlands and islands

Introduction

Much of the attention and concern expressed about overtourism in recent years has been in the context of urban tourist destinations, perhaps reflecting the large numbers of tourists who visit urban centres such as Venice (Chapter 10) and Barcelona (Chapter 9). However, the problems of overtourism may be equally, or even more difficult, to mitigate and prevent in rural settings, particularly in remote and insular areas where small numbers of residents may feel overwhelmed by an influx of large numbers of tourists.

Small rural settlements generally have a tranquil and slow pace of life, and find the arrival of large numbers of visitors from outside their immediate area disturbing, if not threatening, to their established traditional patterns of life. Doxey's (1975) well-known Irridex originated in rural and small town settings (the Caribbean islands and Niagara-on-the-Lake, Ontario) where local residents had objected to the relatively rapid growth in tourist numbers and to what was perceived to be excessive numbers of visitors.

Issues related to overtourism may be exacerbated in rural settings by the fact that transportation modes in such settings are often limited in capacity and infrequent in service, and can therefore be "taken over" by tourists, who are then in competition with locals for the services. In the context of islands this is a particularly important and sensitive issue, even where services are provided in the tourist season to accommodate the added numbers of visitors (Brougham and Butler, 1981). The point made by Wall (Chapter 3), that tourism can be seen as a form of urbanisation, is of particular relevance in this context, as many of the requirements of tourists in terms of transportation, food and beverages and services will be found more widely in urban rather than rural settings. At the same time, there is no doubt that at least some residents of rural areas welcome tourists as they enjoy meeting new people and the interaction involved (Brougham and Butler, 1981).

This chapter explores the rapid growth in tourist numbers in parts of northern Scotland. This growth has been accompanied by media reports of overtourism, congestion, crowding and resident discontent in these locations. Two areas are examined in some detail, the Isle of Skye and the north-west Highlands, both of which have seen significant increases in tourist visitation following publicity and promotional efforts of regional and national agencies, often without consultation with, or advice from, residents.

https://doi.org/10.1515/9783110607369-014

The Scottish highlands and islands

Scotland has had a relatively long (a century and a half) history of tourism, with a tourist industry that is well established and which has been based heavily upon its scenery, cultural heritage, sporting opportunities and royal connections (Butler, 1998; Gold and Gold, 1995). The transformation in the public perception of northern Scotland from being a wilderness unwelcoming to visitors into being a Victorian pleasure ground frequented by royalty, artists, poets, writers and scientists was mainly due to two forces. One was the writings of Sir Walter Scott, who created a romantic image of the Highlands that finds echoes even today in film and television productions such as *Rob Roy, Braveheart, Highlander, Outlander* and *Victoria*, and the second was the establishment of a royal residence at Balmoral by Queen Victoria and Prince Albert in 1853, which gave establishment approval to a holiday in Scotland. The global popularity of Scott's writings and the well-publicised love of the Highlands by successive royal families (Butler, 2008) established northern Scotland as a key holiday destination, first for the upper classes, sporting families and romantic-minded individuals, and subsequently for many others. The art of Turner and Landseer and the writings of Burns, Southey, Wordsworth, Johnson and Boswell, and Victoria herself in her journals (Chapman, 1979; Millar, 1985) all strengthened an image of mountains, lochs, castles and a cultural heritage of romance and fierceness that still dominates the touristic image of Scotland. While current political fashion is to stress the modernity and youthful appeal of Scotland (MacLellan, 2017), there is little doubt that it is the scenery and its associated images that draws most visitors to Scotland, particularly in the key summer season.

Visits to some of the National Trust for Scotland (NTS) properties in northern Scotland have grown rapidly in numbers in recent years, in part due to their links to films and television programmes. For example, the NTS site at Culloden Battlefield (*Outlander*) saw visitor numbers rise from 89,000 in 2007 to 183,000 (plus 82,000 school children) in 2017, and NTS sites as a whole have seen a rise from 2.65 million visitors in 2015/16 to 2.99 million in 2016/17, and then to 3.69 million in 2017/18 (NTS, 2018).

The Highlands and Islands of Scotland are both blessed and cursed by geography, in that the scenic mountainous terrain makes transport opportunities limited and confines road and rail networks to a few routes through mountain passes to small settlements, especially coastal transport hubs. Access through the area has long been noted as difficult, and despite military and civilian efforts from the mid-18th century, the basic road and later rail network has not changed appreciably in layout for 200 years (Butler, 1973). In the past few decades, new road bridges in particular have eased what used to be ferry bottlenecks for road traffic, and air services have relieved a little of the pressure on roads, but recent publicity and promotion (e.g. of the North Coast 500 route) has undone many of the benefits gained by locals from these improvements.

Based on images in tartan-fringed publicity material produced by tourist associations, from Visit Scotland to those at the local level (see, for example, the Visit Scotland website), visitors can expect to see impressive scenery, historic buildings and other ancient sites, and the image portrayed has always been of virtually empty landscapes and wilderness. This image clashes with the reality today of queues of cars for ferries and of passengers for trains, as well as "full" and "no vacancy" signs at car parks (Fig. 14.1) and at accommodation establishments. This indicates that overtourism, epitomised by large numbers of tourists and general congestion, has become a problem in terms of maintaining the image of Scotland presented in the promotional material.

Fig 14.1: Carpark full (photo credit: Richard D. Butler).

Isle of Skye

The Isle of Skye is a major destination in northwestern Scotland, made famous by its associations with Bonnie Prince Charlie and Flora MacDonald (encapsulated in the romantic Victorian era *Skye Boat Song*, used in the opening sequences of the film *Outlander*). The island also has Dunvegan Castle (seat of the Macleod Clan), two whisky distilleries impressive mountains and scenic volcanic landscapes. It is also a connecting point for travel to the Outer Hebrides and St Kilda. Settlements in Skye are small and many of the island residents live in scattered crofting townships or small villages.

Skye was not connected by road to mainland Scotland until 1994, and at the time there was considerable opposition to the construction of the bridge, mainly on the grounds that it would allow travel on Sundays. At the time, no ferries and few services were open on Skye on Sundays, as the Presbyterian Church had considerable influence on the pattern of life on the island and insisted on Sunday as a day of rest. Thus, tourists could not enter or leave the island after the last ferry on Saturday until the first one on Monday. Also, many of the residents of Skye are Gaelic speakers, some having Gaelic as their first language, and tourism was seen as a threat to the language (Butler and Brougham, 1977). The bridge meant this pattern was changed radically, allowing not only freedom of access over weekends, but a much easier and free-of-charge (since 2004) means of accessing the island for residents and visitors (McQuaid and Greig, 2007). The opening of the bridge was of great significance in the growth of tourism to Skye. In 1971, the car ferries carried around 300,000 vehicles but in the bridge's first year of operation (1994/95) around 612,000 vehicles crossed it. Between 2006 and 2014, traffic flows rose by over 35% (Ross, 2017).

As several of the key attractions on Skye are landscape features with no facilities or entry arrangements, there are few official numbers of visitors recorded. Tourist numbers can, however, be estimated based on vehicle numbers and ferry traffic on routes to Skye (Tab. 14.1),[1] which show considerable rises in total numbers, particularly in summer coach traffic over the decade between 2008 and 2017 (Tab. 14.2).

Tab. 14.1: Annual Ferry Traffic from Mallaig to Armadale (Isle of Skye) 2008–2017 (source: A. Redhead; CalMac.co.uk).

Year	Passengers Mallaig to Armadale	Percentage change from previous year	Cars Mallaig to Armadale	Percentage change from previous years	Coaches Mallaig to Armadale	Percentage change from previous year
2008	187,507	−1.6	46,597	−0.7	1,227	−5.8
2009	208,840	11.3	54,336	16.6	1,194	−2.7
2010	212,117	1.7	51,853	−4.6	1,499	25.5
2011	220,782	3.9	52,441	1.1	1,615	7.7
2012	217,274	−1.6	50,324	−4.0	1,740	7.3
2013	237,445	9.2	52,360	4.0	2,103	20.9
2014	239,453	0.9	53,156	1.5	2,106	0.1
2015	247,613	3.4	54,927	3.3	2,289	8.0
2016	250,764	1.3	61,797	12.5	1,942	−15.0
2017	285,483	13.8	70,009	13.3	2,337	20.3

1 Thanks are due to A. Redhead, CalMac.co.uk for data on the Mallaig-Armadale Ferry which was used in Table 14.2 and 14.3.

Tab. 14.2: Seasonality of vehicle traffic Mallaig to Armadale Ferry, 2008 and 2017 (source: A. Redhead; CalMac.co.uk).

Month	2008	2017	2008	2017
	Passengers		Coaches	
Jan	309	646	1	0
Feb	407	723	0	0
Mar	2,408	1,950	3	1
Apr	5,496	12,734	52	87
May	12,307	21,677	135	323
June	14,544	25,076	207	481
July	21,518	30,010	291	460
Aug	22,987	31,367	360	526
Sep	11,981	20,636	194	376
Oct	3,715	7,172	58	82
Nov	477	1,190	2	0
Dec	504	891	0	1

The growth in passenger numbers in what used to be shoulder months of June and September (Tab. 14.2) indicates that pressure on Skye is not only higher overall but for a longer period than before, thus shortening the period during which residents are free from the pressure of tourist visitation.

While the Isle of Skye in general has long been a scenic tourist destination, in recent years specific locations have become the focus of attention, particularly because of photos spread via social media. These locations include the "Fairy Pools", "Fairy Glen", Dunvegan Castle and the Quiraing.

The Quiraing is a volcanic region in northern Skye (see Fig. 14.2) that has been featured in *Game of Thrones* and other programmes, and has become a site of considerable interest, with many tourists now visiting it. This has led to traffic jams on the single-track road that traverses the steep slopes of the area. Other sites, such as that overlooking Kilt Rock and the footpaths to local landmarks have also recently become scenes of congestion and traffic problems. Most of these sites have few, if any, tourist facilities and no, or very limited and inadequate, parking spaces. Considerable numbers of visitors have been recorded at relatively isolated sites, some involving a walk of a few miles to reach and return to one's car. In August 2018, a resident of Skye reported that each day there were "around a thousand people at the Fairy Pools" even when it rained (Dickinson, 2018). Such was the level of crowding on Skye in 2017, that local police issued advice to tourists not to visit the island unless accommodation had been booked in advance (Rudgard, 2017).

As a result of the large numbers of visitors, foot trails are becoming crowded and eroded, and there is increasing pollution due to the absence of toilets. More

Fig. 14.2: Quirang, Isle of Skye and single track road (photo credit: Nick Fox).

generally, problems have arisen from a lack of information on facilities and services (BBC News, 2017).

In response to the increased numbers of visitors and consequent traffic jams, a number of enterprises have begun operations to cater to tourist transport needs. Such organisations offer mini-bus tours to the Fairy Glen and the Quiraing, noting on their websites the difficulty of car access and parking at such sites (see, for example, Skye Minibus Tours).

The issue of authenticity (see Chapter 4) has arisen in the Isle of Skye as not all of the attractions are "authentic", as in original to the region. The "Fairy Glen" and "Fairy Pools" were not traditionally called such; that nomenclature has only recently been applied (Ross, 2018). Furthermore, new, arguable "inauthentic", rituals have become popular with tourists. The stacking of stones by tourists has raised concerns among residents about environmental damage to the crofts (Whitehead, 2018). Worry over such rituals is expressed in the Isle of Skye website:

> In recent years' [sic] visitors have started to move the rocks to create spirals on the ground. We have been told that some of the bus tour guides have made up and encouraged some rituals involving walking the spirals then leaving a coin or token in the centre as an offering to the fairies for good luck. The locals on Skye have repeatedly removed these stone spirals in an attempt to keep the Glen in its [sic] natural state. We hope that all visitors would respect the country code. To visit & [sic] enjoy, but not make adjustments and certainly not leave anything behind, even if you think it may give you good luck. (Isle of Skye, n.d.)

In September 2018 the issue of stone spirals made the national press, with several articles and letters in *The Times* newspaper (The Cameron, G) noting the actions of locals in demolishing the piles of stones and them being remonstrated by tourists for doing so.

Attitudes on Skye run a gamut from strong support for current tourist numbers to strong opposition to them. The inappropriate behaviour of tourists is an issue for many local residents. For example, in one case, a tour bus that was trying to park disturbed a funeral, causing the mourners great distress. "One mourner wrote to the tour company, urging them to stay off Skye" (Carrell, 2017). Common to most criticisms by residents is the sense that the problem of overtourism on the island is outside the control of Skye and that the island is subject to significant tourism growth because of those external factors (Carrell, 2017; Shaw, 2017).

While the pressures on roads, car parks, toilets and accommodation are severe enough to warrant warnings by the local police not to visit Skye without prior booking of accommodation, other local agencies and representatives continue to stress the importance of tourism to the local economy and the need to maintain a positive and welcoming attitude towards visitors (West Highlands Free Press, 2018). Likewise, while a significant number of residents have expressed concerns about overtourism, individual attractions on Skye continue to actively promote tourism and visitation to their properties. For example, the Dunvegan Estate, owners of Dunvegan Castle, has allowed used the estate for film and television productions, including *Highlander, 47 Ronin, Made of Honour, Macbeth,* and an episode of *The Island* (Dunvegan Castle, n.d.). Skye was also the setting for a Peugeot car advertisement filmed in 2017 and the backdrop for a Supertramp advertisement, both supported by Visit Scotland, and was featured in other pop music and extreme sports videos.

The issue of overtourism is not only being felt on the Isle of Skye, but also on the access routes to Skye. One of the two main routes to Skye, from Fort William to the port of Mallaig (for the ferry to Armadale in southern Skye), known as the "Road to the Isles", is particularly suffering. This area has the distinction of having featured in several of the *Harry Potter* films. Scenes featuring the "Hogwarts Express" train were filmed on the rail route parallel to the road. A restored steam train (Fig. 14.3) runs on this route with a stop at the Glenfinnan Viaduct (illustrated in the films) on the outward journey to Mallaig.

Many road tourists choose to stop at the National Trust for Scotland (NTS) site at Glenfinnan (where Bonnie Prince Charlie raised his standard in 1745, which also has connections to the *Outlander* books and television programmes) from where one can view the viaduct and the train. The car park is therefore often full, resulting in chaotic parking by visitors on or near the road and a dangerous situation, with pedestrians walking on the road (BBC News, 2018). However, while the NTS has concerns about the impact of tourism, it still advertises the *Harry Potter* connection on its website (National Trust for Scotland, n.d.).

Fig. 14.3: Hogwart's Express' approaching Glenfinnan Viaduct, Scottish Highlands (photo credit: Joanna Lorrainerhodes).

The appeal of the Isle of Skye is not likely to diminish in the years ahead, as its culture, history, and landscape, real and fictional, are almost certain to remain highly attractive to tourists, therefore the problem of overtourism is likely to remain in the foreseeable future.

North Coast 500

The second example of overtourism in rural areas relates to a new tourist attraction that consists of a route extending some 500 miles around the west, north and east coasts of Scotland, beginning and ending in Inverness. The "North Coast 500" is the name given to this route, which uses existing roads serving local communities and which, before its promotion, carried very limited traffic. The route runs through some of the most impressive mountain and wild scenery in Scotland.

> The concept of the North Coast 500 was launched in March 2015 by the Tourism Project Board of the North Highland Initiative (NHI). [...] The initiative was supported by Visit Scotland and Highlands & Islands Enterprise. [...] It has been described as "Scotland's Route 66". (Wikipedia, n.d.)

The route is, therefore, a completely fabricated attraction, "created" to attract more tourism to the area, but apparently without much thought being given to the capacity of the roads involved to carry the additional traffic, nor to the absence of tourist facilities in many locations, and the very limited accommodation and food and beverage opportunities. It has been called "Scotland's Route 66" to make a comparison with the iconic highway route in the United States, clearly with one eye to the American market, and has been very successful in creating a market among foreign visitors to Scotland in particular.

The official Visit Scotland website promotes the route and references a recent (2017) movie, *Edie*, which was filmed in the area and is a co-sponsor of the route. The route's own website describes it as the "ultimate road trip showcasing fairy-tale castles, white sand beaches and historical ruins" (North Coast 500, n.d.). This website has several links to other products, including clothing and Aston Martin cars, as well as advertising its own online shop, and memberships (ranging from 15 to 300 British pounds a year) that offer various inducements and products. These promotional efforts have obviously been successful, as it was reported that the North Coast 500 had attracted 29,000 additional tourists to the area, with a 26% annual rise in visitors and a 48% increase in spend from North America alone in the period between June 2016 and June 2017 (Brooks, 2017). How reliable such figures are is hard to determine but there has undoubtedly been a noticeable rise in numbers of visitors using the roads involved. Visit Scotland noted visitor numbers at its information centres had increased by 30% in Ullapool, 27% in Durness and 25% in Thurso (all communities along the route) since the route was designated (BBC News, 2016). As an example of creating a tourist market for something that existed for many years but was utilised by few tourists, North Coast 500 is an outstanding success in terms of increased numbers of visitors.

Various problems have arisen on the route, however, particularly with regard to inexperienced drivers using the route, parts of which are single-track roads, with frequent small lay-bys designated as passing places (as visible in Fig. 14.2). Such conditions require careful attention and patience on the part of drivers. Multiple instances of inappropriate behaviour have been recorded on the route, such as racing oncoming vehicles to passing places, failing to allow following traffic to overtake, using large trailers and campervans unsuitable for the road, rogue camping and stopping overnight in passing bays (Heavywhalley, 2017). Locals have also expressed concern over the impact heavy traffic on the route could have on access by emergency and service vehicles, as well as on local and business traffic (Harrison, 2018). The North Coast 500 website notes that "If you cannot accurately reverse your vehicle several hundred yards on a narrow single track – you cannot safely drive over a road such as this" (North Coast 500, n.d.), but there is only one road sign along the route warning that it is not suitable for inexperienced drivers (Heavywhalley, 2017).

Despite the issues caused by overtourism on the route, there seems little chance of promotional efforts being reduced in the immediate future as proponents of the project express enthusiasm over recognition of the route as one of the top six coastal routes in the world and plan to continue to promote it because "the north Highlands of Scotland is an unrivalled, unspoilt, stunning area that just begs to be experienced" (Kerr, 2015). This is a statement somewhat at odds with local opinions along the route (Heavywhalley, 2017)

The success of the North Coast 500 in stimulating tourism in a relatively remote part of Scotland is indicative both of the power of the media to draw attention to phenomena and the willingness of the public to be persuaded to participate in specific behaviour. The website of the North Coast 500 has many photographs sent in by those who have driven the route, very few showing the actual road or landscape, most being photographs of the participants themselves (North Coast 500, n.d.).

What is disconcerting, and depressingly common in many locations experiencing overtourism, is the apparent disregard for the existing residents of the area. In this specific case, there has been a lack of consideration of the pressure that the increased traffic, generated by drivers inexperienced on these types of roads, would have on the facilities, services and local accessibility of the area. This indicates a lack of appreciation of the importance of the road to local residents, who find the additional, often inappropriate, traffic disturbing and hazardous, with potential impacts on emergency services.

As with the Isle of Skye, the North Coast 500 reveals the tension that can develop between those supporting the considerable economic benefits (to the region in general and to some specific residents) from tourism, and the considerable costs that can accrue to other locals in terms of lost time, inconvenience and disturbance (Fig. 14.4 shows a car park full of visitors' cars despite a sign requesting space for a

Fig. 14.4: Carpark overfull, despite request for space for church event (photo Credit: Richard D. Butler).

church event). In addition, the marketing of the route overlooks the loss of quality of experience for visitors who might have desired a slow, scenic, empty road, as portrayed in much of the publicity for both the route and northern Scotland more generally. As in many cases, including several discussed in this volume, promotion and development of tourism on the North Coast 500 route has taken place with little consultation or consideration of local preferences and needs. This clearly indicates that overtourism is a relative concept and phenomenon, and needs to be considered in the specific context in which development is taking place.

Conclusion

The effects of overtourism on rural destinations can be just as problematic, or even more so, than those experienced in urban settings, even when the numbers of tourists involved are smaller. Urban destinations are used to experiencing large numbers of people, residents as well as tourists, throughout the year as urban tourism is much less seasonal than that in rural areas (Butler 2001). The specific issues of overtourism in urban settings are mostly due to the worsening of existing problems (congestion, parking, traffic, noise, litter and pollution). In rural areas, however, such as those discussed in this chapter, tourism and particularly overtourism often create new problems not experienced before, because tourism represents a very different situation and experience to the norm for many residents of rural areas.

The two rural locations discussed here reveal a variety of symptoms and causes of overtourism. In the case of the Isle of Skye, a well-established tourist destination began to receive significantly larger tourist numbers initially because of a major improvement in access, the Skye Road Bridge. More recently, the appeal of Skye has been increased by the expansion and addition of tourist services and facilities, but more specifically by major media attention. Film and television media have used Skye and its vicinity as the setting for adventure and drama, and to advertise products, thereby bringing the island to international attention, and social media has greatly increased that attention and has also altered tourist behaviour, to the chagrin of many local residents. The North Coast 500 is an example of a tourist attraction (one of the "lines" of Wall, Chapter 3, albeit 500 miles long) that has been created and publicised based on an existing local facility (minor roads), and which has resulted in overuse of the roads and inconvenience for local residents.

In both cases, local enterprises and local government agencies have supported, and in some cases actively promoted, the areas, despite opposition and discontent among local residents. This has been because of the benefits gained, in terms of income, taxation generation and job creation, for rural locations needing such stimuli to halt depopulation and economic stagnation or decline. The two examples illustrate the universal tendency for economic gains to be given priority over social and environmental concerns. Whether the local negative reactions and lack of adequate facilities for visitors and residents alike will in turn negatively affect tourism itself remains to be seen, but at present, little is being done to mitigate these impacts.

Complaints about tourists and tourism are not new in Scotland (Brougham and Butler, 1981), but tourist numbers and the number of complaints about them in 2018 were at levels not previously experienced. There are signs that overtourism is being experienced in other parts of rural Scotland, or may be experienced in the near future. The Orkney Islands, for example, lying off the north coast of Scotland, has rapidly become a major cruise destination. While in 2011 Orkney received 61 ships and 36,000 passengers, in 2018 Orkney was forecast to receive 140 ships and over 130,000 passengers on the main island, mostly concentrated in the small town of Kirkwall (7420 people) (Brocklehurst, 2017). The rapid rise in numbers of ships and passengers (more than doubling since 2013) has been accompanied by inappropriate behaviour by cruise ship visitors, including disturbing church services and attempting to open the lid of a coffin at a funeral, which resulted in a ban on tourists attending local funerals (Horne, 2016a; Horne, 2016b). While Orkney has imposed a maximum number of cruise passengers allowed in any one year, this has not reduced the impacts of overtourism, and resentment about numbers and disturbance is growing, despite the economic benefits tourism brings (BBC One: 2018).

Growing discontent among residents with tourist numbers, congestion on ferries and roads, and inability to find accommodation or parking spaces at specific attractions will possibly result in a backlash and a subsequent decline in tourist numbers to more traditional levels. Some residents of Skye are clearly of that opinion:

> Just give it a couple of years and it will blow over. Sadly just in time for the new carparks, hotels etc. to be ready, the next 'big thing' will come along and the box ticking tourists will move on and much of the new "normal" tourism will be left derelict. Balamory, Harry Potter, Outlander, Game of Thrones, NC500. Which will last? M. Wilson. (The Telegraph, n.d.)

The most likely outcome is no action by any specific agency to combat overtourism beyond bland comments about the economic benefits of tourism and people needing to adjust to higher levels of visitation. It will most likely be business-as-usual. A hostile attitude among Europeans following the expected Brexit in April 2019 may deter some European visitors in the short term, but long haul tourism is likely to be unaffected and will probably continue on a growth pattern, with North American and Asian visitors continuing to increase in numbers. Overtourism, as experienced in 2017 and 2018, may well be the norm for the next decade or longer.

There are few solutions or mitigation measures that are likely to be effective in the medium to long term that are also without any permanent or significant negative effects on the overall appeal of the areas discussed above. To reduce visitor numbers to islands, ferry services could be reduced or maintained at current levels, but few other alternative actions to reduce overtourism exist. In general, there is no readily available measure to reduce tourism numbers apart from reducing publicity, and that would inevitably receive opposition from national level agencies and departments, if not at the local level also. Encouraging tourists to visit at alternative time periods is relatively pointless, as outside the May to September period climatic conditions are generally not conducive for most visitors and their normal activities, and most services and facilities are either closed or are on "off-season" programmes. Suggesting that tourists visit other locations within Scotland is ineffective as it merely moves the problem to other areas, and such suggestions are unlikely to be followed by tourists as the main features they want to visit are in specific locations and no real alternatives exist. There is, for example, no alternative route to the North Coast 500, and no other island that has the mystique and romance of Skye. The most likely forces to lower tourist numbers in the foreseeable future are bad weather, continued reports of overcrowding, ferry breakdowns and road congestion, most of which are generally uncontrollable, and generally undesired by all involved, residents, agencies and tourists alike.

References

BBC One (2018) Orkney: When the boat comes in, *BBC One*, 28 June. https://www.bbc.co.uk/pro grammes/b0903s71 (Accessed 5 September 2018.)

BBC News (2016) North Coast 500 increased tourist visits, says VisitScotland, *BBC News*, 13 December. https://www.bbc.com/news/uk-scotland-highlands-islands-38299896 (Accessed 5 September 2018.)

BBC News (2017) Skye needs 30-year tourism strategy, say islanders, *BBC News*, 26 June. https://www.bbc.com/news/uk-scotland-highlands-islands-40382450 (Accessed 20 August 2018.)

BBC News (2018) Muggles of the Glen: Where Potter fans gather in their hundreds, *BBC News*, 31 August. https://www.bbc.com/news/uk-scotland-highlands-islands-45359275 (Accessed 30 October 2018.)

Brocklehurst, S. (2017) Orkney copes with cruise ship invasion, *BBC News*, 31 July. https://www.bbc.com/news/uk-scotland-40731839 (Accessed 5 September 2018.)

Brooks, L. (2017) Scottish Highlands feel the strain as tourism surge causes disruption. *The Guardian*, 1 November. https://www.theguardian.com/uk-news/2017/nov/01/scotland-feels-the-strain-as-tourism-causes-disruption-across-the-highlands (Accessed 5 September 2018.)

Brougham, J. E. and Butler, R. W. (1981) The Application of Segregation Analysis to Explain Resident Attitudes to Social Impacts of Tourism, *Annals of Tourism Research*, 8 (IV), 569–590.

Butler, R. W. (1973) *The Tourism Industry in the Highlands and Islands*, PhD thesis, University of Glasgow: Glasgow.

Butler, R. W. (1998) Tartan mythology: the traditional tourist image of Scotland. In G. Ringer (Ed.), *Destinations Cultural Landscapes of Tourism*, London: Routledge, pp.121–139

Butler, R. W. (2001) Seasonality in Tourism Issues and Implications. In T. G. Baum, and S. Lundtopr (Eds.), *Seasonality in Tourism*, Oxford: Elsevier, pp.5–22.

Butler, R. W. (2008) The History and Development of Royal Tourism in Scotland Balmoral the ultimate holiday home? In Long, P. and Palmer, N. J. (Eds.), *Royal Tourism: Excursions Around Monarchy,* Clevedon: Channelview Publications, pp. 51–61.

Butler, R. W. and Brougham, J. E. (1977) *The Social and Cultural Impact of Tourism: A Case Study of Sleat, Isle of Skye.* Edinburgh: Scottish Tourist Board.

Cameron, G. (2018) Record is good reason to roll out the barrels, *The Times*, 1 August, https://www.thetimes.co.uk/article/scotch-whisky-record-is-good-reason-to-roll-out-the-barrels-j0mc6ml2p.

Carrell, S. (2017) Skye islanders call for help with overcrowding after tourism surge, *The Guardian*, 9 August. https://www.theguardian.com/uk-news/2017/aug/09/skye-islanders-call-for-help-with-overcrowding-after-tourism-surge (Accessed 21 August 2018.)

Chapman, R. W. (1979) *Johnson and Boswell Journey to the Western Islands and A Tour to the Hebrides*, Oxford: Oxford University Press.

Department for Transport (2016) Traffic counts. www.dft.gov.uk/traffic-counts/cp.php?la=High land#countpointstables (Accessed 20 August 2018.)

Dickinson, G. (2018) Has tourism killed Skye? *The Telegraph*, 19 August. https://www.telegraph.co.uk/travel/destinations/europe/united-kingdom/scotland/articles/tourism-skye-crowded/ (Accessed 30 October 2018.)

Doxey, G. V. (1975) A causation theory of visitor-residents irritants. Methodology and research inferences. pp. 195–198. San Diego: Travel Research Association Proceedings of the Travel Research Association 6th Annual Conference.

Dunvegan Castle (n.d.) Film and TV. www.dunvegancastle.com/the-estate/film-tv (Accessed 18 August 2018.)

Garavelli, D. (2018) Insight: Visitor numbers drive Highlands into tourist trap, *The Scotsman*, 21 July, pp. 26–29.

Gold, J. R. and Gold, M. M. (1995) *Imagining Scotland*, Aldershot: Gower Press.

Harrison, J. (2014) Orkney best for quality of life, *The Herald*, 20 December.

Harrison, J. (2018) Locals find living round NC500 brings problems as well as profits, *The Herald*, 7 June. https://www.heraldscotland.com/news/16275031.locals-find-living-round-nc500-brings-problems-as-well-as-profits/ (Accessed 30 October 2018.)

Heavywhalley (2017) Race Track or Tourist Magnet? The North Coast 500. Any thoughts? https://heavywhalley.wordpress.com/2017/05/24/race-track-or-tourist-magnet-the-north-coast-500-any-thoughts/ (Accessed 30 October 2018.)

Horne, M. (2016a) Snap-happy tourists disrupt funerals at island cathedral *The Times*, 8 August, p. 19.

Horne, M. (2016b) Cathedral bans tourists from funerals after selfies taken, *The Times* 10 August, p. 22.

Horne, M. (2018a) Heritage sites at risk from new developments, trust chief warns, *The Times* 31 July, p. 16.

Horne, M. (2018b) Overseas tourists 'are scared off by tightfisted locals', *The Times*, 6 August, p. 21.

Isle of Skye (n.d.) Fairy Glen. https://www.isleofskye.com/skye-guide/skye-places/fairy-glen (Accessed 30 October 2018.)

Kerr, D. (2015) North Coast 500 named in top five coastal routes in the world, *The Press and Journal*, 6 August. https://www.pressandjournal.co.uk/fp/news/highlands/657962/north-coast-500-named-in-top-five-coastal-routes-in-the-world/ (Accessed 21 August 2018.)

Macaskill, M. (2018) Drive the scenic NorthCoast500 and risk 'running into a pothole', *The Times*, 26 August, p. 6.

Macdonald, L. (2018) Swerve the crowds on Skye this summer by heading north to Staffin, *The Telegraph*, 27 July. https://www.telegraph.co.uk/travel/destinations/europe/united-kingdom/ articles/great-british-getaways-staffin/ (Accessed 1 September 2018.)

MacLellan, R. (2017) Political Change and Tourism in Scotland: Nationalism, devolution and autonomy. In R. W. Butler and W. Suntikul (Eds.), *Tourism and Political Change Second Edition*. Oxford: Goodfellow Publishers, pp 90–102.

McQuaid, R. W. and Greig, M. (2007) The Bridge to Skye, Scotland. In G. Baldacchino (Ed.), *Bridging Islands: The Impact of Fixed Links*. PEI, Canada: Acorn Press, pp. 185–202. https://www.researchgate.net/publication/301200720_'The_Bridge_to_Skye_Scotland_-_PFI' (Accessed 21 August 2018.)

Millar, D. (1985) *Queen Victoria's Life in the Scottish Highlands*. London: Phillip Wilson.

Munro, A. (2015) Huge drive to promote 'Scotland's Route 66', *The Scotsman*, 2 March. https://www.scotsman.com/news/transport/huge-drive-to-promote-scotland-s-route-66-1-3705709 (Accessed 31 August 2018.)

National Trust for Scotland (n.d.) The Highlands Glenfinnan Monument. https://www.nts.org.uk/ visit/places/glenfinnan-monument (Accessed 20 August 2018.)

North Coast 500 (n.d.) FAQ: Is the road suitable for motorhomes/caravans? https://www.northcoast500.com/about-nc500/faq/ (Accessed 31 August 2018.)

Orkney Islands Council (2015) New record for cruise ship port calls, 17 November. http://www.orkney. gov.uk/OIC-News/New-record-for-cruise-ship-port-calls.htm (Accessed 5 September 2018.)

Ross, C. (2017) Talks with minister due over surge in visitors to Skye, *The Press and Journal*, 17 January. www.pressandjournal.co.uk/fp/news/islands/inner-hebrides/1142419/talks-with-minister-dueover-surge -in-visitors-to skye (Accessed 21 August 2018) .

Ross, L. (2018) Locals rebel against tourist trend, *The Times*, 18 September, p. 18.

Rudgard, O. (2017) Don't come to Skye unless you have a room for the night, say local police, *The Telegraph*, 9 August. https://www.telegraph.co.uk/news/2017/08/09/dont-come-skye-un less-have-room-night-say-police/ (Accessed 1 August 2018.)

Scotland's Route 66 (n.d.) www.scotlandsroute66.co.uk (Accessed 31 August 2018.)

Shaw, J. (2017) Is Skye reaching the limit for tourists? *BBC News*, 9 August. https://www.bbc.com/ news/uk-scotland-40874488 (Accessed 30 October 2018.)

Skye Connect (n.d.) About. https://www.skye-connect.com/about (Accessed 5 September 2018.)

The Telegraph (n.d.) www.telegraph.co.uk

Visit Scotland (n.d.) North Coast 500. https://www.visitscotland.com/see-do/tours/driving-road-trips/ north-coast-500/ (Accessed 31 August 2018.)

West Highland Free Press (2018) Skye is "well and truly open for business", say local firms, *West Highland Free Press*, 3 August. www.whfp.com/2018/08/03/skye-is-well-and-truly-open-for-business-say-local-firms (Accessed 5 September 5 2018.)

Whitehead, J. Scottish Highlands at risk of erosion by tourists seeking 'perfect picture', warn activists, *The Independent*, 18 September. https://www.independent.co.uk/travel/news-and-advice/scot tish-highlands-erosion-instagram-isle-of-skye-iona-orkney-the-bfg-film-trail-a8542661.html (Accessed 30 October 2018.)

Wikipedia (n.d.) North Coast 500. https://en.wikipedia.org/wiki/North_Coast_500 (Accessed 31 August 2018.)

PART III: **Challenges**

The third part of the book deals with the level of involvement, or lack thereof, of the various stakeholders in tourist destinations. These three chapters examine in some detail the nature and potential roles of stakeholders at various levels of governance, beginning with a chapter by Jamieson and Jamieson (Chapter 15) which observes that the differences between destinations means that there is no single management approach that is likely to work effectively in all situations. Furthermore, in general, local municipalities have a poor record in implementing and coordinating actions to address the enablers of overtourism. The chapter discusses several ways in which overtourism can be addressed at the local or municipal level. In a similar vein, the chapter by Becken and Simmons, discusses stakeholder management (Chapter 16). The authors note that part of the difficulty in resolving the enablers of overtourism and the issues created by it is the number and range of potential interested parties. Additionally, not all of these parties assume the roles and implement the actions that might be expected of them. The various responses of these actors are not necessarily appropriate or effective, partly because they often compete with and oppose each other. This part concludes with a chapter by Joppe (Chapter 17), which provides a strong, critical review of the field of planning and governance and resulting policy formulation, concluding that there has been little effective integration, action or identification of the issues and potential solutions at the various levels of governance.

This part and the earlier ones make it clear that overtourism comes about at least in part because of a lack of anticipation of the problems, a lack of long term planning (which is almost inevitable when the main motive is short-term economic growth and all forms of governance have a short election cycle), and a general lack of agreement on key issues. These problems are compounded by a common failure to determine, acknowledge and incorporate the concerns of residents of municipalities and destinations about the level and nature of tourism development. While the chapters demonstrate the ability of decision makers to commission plans and to formulate policies, they also reveal a disturbing inability or unwillingness to implement these plans and policies, and thereby avoid and mitigate the problems resulting from overtourism. Thus, while some stakeholders may "talk the talk", very few "walk the walk" when this would mean challenging the priority of economic growth. These points are taken up in the final chapter of the volume.

Walter Jamieson and Michelle Jamieson

15 Managing overtourism at the municipal/ destination level

Introduction

A significant portion of the recent discussion around overtourism has centred on the opposition of residents to tourism levels that are overwhelming their communities. Resident concerns focus on issues such as congestion, rising housing and land costs, inadequate solid waste management, reduced water availability, inadequate water treatment, and unequal access to destination resources. In the discussion of overtourism there is also recognition that the lack of planning and management in many destinations has resulted in a "degraded tourist experience, overloaded infrastructure, damage to nature, and threats to culture and heritage" (WTTC and McKinsey & Company, 2017: 8). The concerns of residents and tourists are being addressed by measures that have been explored in previous chapters.

This book has explored the factors contributing to the manifestation of overtourism. Researchers of the subject would agree that overtourism is a result of tourism development that is driven by numbers rather than by an informed planning and policy approach. An informed approach utilises data on resident sentiment, carrying capacity, infrastructure, culture and environmental capacities to better understand the parameters of time and space in which tourism activities should be developed (Postma and Schumecker, 2017), especially in relation to the question of how many tourists are too many (Tourtellot, 2017). In Chapter 17, Joppe eloquently makes the argument for a transformation of tourism policy and practice to approaches that are based on equitable, sustainable, resilient and diversity principles.

Planners and policy makers might argue that overtourism is partly a result of inadequate planning and management strategies that have not effectively dealt with tourism numbers. The reality is that there are many destinations that have had large scale and ambitious master plans but do not consider limiting visitor numbers. This is true, but a key challenge is that plans and strategies are rarely implemented. This is a significant issue in destination planning and management. A survey conducted by the United Nations World Tourism Organization (UNWTO) in 1979 found that of 1619 tourism plans, only half had ever been put into place (Yuksel and Yuksel, 2000). Reasons for lack of implementation include a lack of buy-in from key stakeholders, scarce financial and human resources to carry out the plans, and poor levels of capacity for those responsible for plan implementation (Jamieson and Jamieson, 2016). The lack of implementation can also be traced to the cumbersome process of developing tourism master plans, with the quest to be comprehensive and, in most cases, a numbers-focused ideology. Many of such plans are flawed given that they

https://doi.org/10.1515/9783110607369-015

are centred on "the idea that action should only be taken after all the answers and the resources have been found" (Lydon, 2012). This lack of success with present planning approaches should not lead to the conclusion that planning cannot be effective in dealing with the issue of overtourism, but rather that tourism planning models must be re-examined.

Given the pace of tourism growth (UNWTO, 2017), there is not the luxury of waiting until a transformation takes place. There is an urgent need to ensure that tourism development overcapacity is dealt with immediately within existing legislative and ideological constraints at the municipal or destination level. Key directions that can be pursued to address the overtourism phenomenon include:

- changing the mindset of those responsible for guiding tourism development in destinations,
- developing a better understanding of the nature of destinations,
- managing overtourism in a destination context,
- assessing the role of destination marketing (or management) organisations (DMOs) in managing overtourism,
- identifying the role of local government in managing overtourism and
- better managing visitors within destinations.

A change in mindset

A shift is needed in mentality, from the "silo" – "it's not my job" – approach to one of responsible and informed co-management that involves the public, private and non-profit sectors at all levels of management. As discussed elsewhere in this book, this is an integrated, whole-of-government approach that recognises the interconnected nature of destination plans, strategies and solutions. Another essential change is in the mindset regarding tourism numbers; destinations must focus on maintaining or enhancing the quality of the tourism experience, as well as residents' quality of life and environmental sustainability, rather than on maximising the quantity of tourists.

This mindset change is already in place in several destinations. For example, a three-hour time limit has been set for visitors at the Taj Mahal, India; permits are now required to hike to the top of Half Dome at Yosemite National Park, United States; tourists have been banned from visiting the popular daytrip location of the Koh Khai Islands in Thailand; and the number of cruise passengers allowed on land each day in Santorini, Greece, has been limited (Gupana, 2018).

The challenge is for this mindset change to become common practice. This could occur by, for example, pursuing the following approach:

> An essential first step is to move from measures of success that celebrate tourism arrivals and tourism spend figures to ones that are tied to the overall development objectives – social,

cultural, environmental – of a destination. This clearly is a difficult task given the reality as well as the perception of the important economic contributions that tourism makes to destinations. As is well recognized it is much easier to make the case for success of tourism in a destination by celebrating a growth in visitor numbers or the contribution of tourism to the local GDP than celebrating the attainment of important social, cultural and environmental objectives. While many have attempted to accomplish this, including the authors, it is important to continue to "define metrics that allow for an understanding of the role of tourism in providing benefits and the costs of increased" tourism to ensure that destinations are more effectively planned and managed, especially in light of the significant impact of overtourism.[1] These fine-grained metrics can include: "whether tourism is being directed to areas of greatest economic needs, average revenue per tourist, tourism receipts per capita, receipts per job, CO_2 emissions per unit of tourism receipts" (Jamieson and Jamieson, 2016: 15).

A clear example of this mindset shift is in Croatia where the tourism strategy focuses on sustainability and not on mass tourism, in recognition of the overwhelming issues that have been experienced as a result of a 7% year-on-year increase in visitor numbers (Blake, 2018).

In most destinations, bringing about this mindset change will be a difficult undertaking that will require organisations and individuals to develop leadership skills, team work and problem-solving skills, and be trained in creative thinking (Garvin, 1993; Van Laar et al., 2017). A willingness to look at different ways of organising teams and bureaucracies is seen as another essential element of making change occur. Sceptics often argue that bureaucracies can never respond in a positive way to change, but as Landry and Caust (2017) explain, the lack of responsiveness may not be due to the nature of bureaucracies themselves but rather a result of the way that they are managed. They call for "creative bureaucracies" and argue that it is necessary to create in bureaucracies a positive, respectful atmosphere, and an ethos of sharing and helping out. This is a topic unto itself but is indicative of the kind of changes that must occur in dealing with many tourism issues, especially overtourism, with its multifaceted dimensions (Landry and Caust, 2017)

The nature of destinations

In order to effectively manage overtourism, it must be recognised that there are many different types of destinations. The president and CEO of the World Travel and Tourism Council (WTTC), Gloria Guevara, has stated, "there is no one solution for all, every destination is different" (Pylas, 2017). That is, each set of unique circumstances

---

1 The authors have been successful in including finer grained metrics in their tourism planning work, in particular in the development of the first ASEAN Tourism Marketing Strategy 2012–2015 available at https://www.asean.org/wp-content/uploads/images/2012/publications/ATMS% 202012_2015_FA.pdf.

will require different planning and management responses. Approaches to managing overtourism therefore vary depending on destination conditions and objectives (Postma and Schumecker, 2017). While this may be apparent, much of the discussion of destination management appears to work on the basis that there is only one type of destination.

Destinations tend to vary in seven main ways. One difference is in terms of whether a destination is urban or rural. While many rural areas have declining populations, urban areas in many parts of the world are growing very quickly and as of 2018 have more than half of the global population. It is estimated that by 2050 70% of the world's population will live in urban areas (UNWTO, 2018). Efforts to manage significant population increases in urban areas are complicated by huge influxes of tourists, which put pressure on natural resources and infrastructure, and often have negative impacts on local mobility and social and cultural systems.

Another key difference between destinations is in terms of their primary function. While some destinations are largely devoted to tourism, others serve multiple functions, which therefore dictate other government priorities and strategies. A third major difference between destinations is the nature and quality of tourism governance. Some destinations may have the necessary legislative and regulatory power and capacity to determine the future of their community from a tourism perspective, while others, either due to a lack of legislative power or political will, may choose not to exercise planning or management control of overtourism in their destinations. Countries with low governance capacity face far more challenges in managing overtourism than others, especially if they also lack the necessary regulatory and financial resources to deal with rapid rates of tourism growth and related social and environmental challenges.

A further difference between destinations is in the level of development pressures they experience. Some destinations may experience significant pressures, both from overall urban development as well as tourism, while others may not. A fifth difference is that some destinations are seasonal while others are year-round destinations. While some destinations may experience overtourism for a limited period of time each year (e.g. a ski resort), others have a year-round overtourism issue (e.g. a tropical island). Another difference between destinations is in the nature and mix of economic activity. While destinations that have mixed economies may be in a position to limit the level of visitors and replace tourism jobs and revenue with other types of economic activity, other destinations have limited economic choices. Such destinations are often over reliant on tourism, so are hard-pressed to limit tourism numbers. For example, Bermuda does not face the same pressures as other Caribbean islands as it has other economic sectors besides tourism, such as the banking sector. Another key difference between destinations is in the level of acceptance and readiness for tourism of the local residents. Residents differ in their perspectives, with more residents who are likely to support larger tourism numbers if such numbers are introduced gradually over a period of time.

Managing overtourism within the destination context

Most urban and regional planners and managers have long recognized that destinations are complex systems with various types of stakeholders. Given this complexity, those responsible for addressing overtourism and influencing the future direction of tourism need to move from simplistic solutions to ones that are realistic within the realm of what municipalities can accomplish (Crawford, 2016). Academics and tourism policy makers often see tourism as being separate from the responsibilities, issues, interests and operations that local level governments must contend with, but tourism is also one of the responsibilities of local governments. This tendency to deal with tourism in isolation is compounded by the fact that tourism is often not seen as a major policy and planning issue in many municipal plans and often the only governance of tourism activity is through tourism marketing organisations. For example, tourism is only mentioned twice in a recent Toronto downtown plan (Toronto City Planning, 2017). This must change. Tourism planners and developers must fit tourism into the larger policy and management process (Jamieson, 2012).

A better understanding of tourism's place in the municipal/local government context requires taking into account the many overtourism-related destination challenges that a municipality/local government must deal with. Many of these have been discussed in previous chapters, but such challenges also include elements from the Resilient Cities Report (ICLEI, 2018) and the World Economic Forum's "Mapping Global Transformations", which is an effort to explore and make sense of the complex forces driving transformational change across economies, industries, global issues (WEF, n.d.). These elements include:
- how to finance the delivery of the various services and infrastructure that tourism requires and that are impacted by tourism,
- how to manage environmental pressures, including providing clean and free drinking water and solid waste management, and developing resilient destinations in response to climate change,
- how to manage the expectations and activities of land owners and developers and other tourism private-sector stakeholders, while attempting to restrict the number of visitors,
- how to deal with continuing and, in some cases, accelerating population growth, which is exacerbated by rapidly rising tourism levels that often exceed the capacity of the destination to safely and responsibly accommodate these numbers,
- how to assess the real costs of tourism to a destination as part of assessing the value of tourism to the residents,

- how to address the reality that even with significant tourism activity many local people often do not benefit from tourism due to leakages and
- how to ensure the political will in a destination to balance revenue generation and responsible development.

The role of the DMO in managing overtourism

As advocated earlier in this chapter, destinations must not only realign their metrics but must also introduce policies and strategies to responsibly manage visitor numbers. For many destinations, the destination marketing organisations or destination management organisations (DMOs) are differentiated based on the focus of the organization's activities. Whether their focus is marketing or management, both types of DMOs most often have dedicated staff and funding to deal with tourism within their jurisdictions. As Dredge (2016: 348) stated, "what they have in common is that both of them are a type of policy tool used to stimulate tourism growth, where the emphasis on marketing or management is simply a reflection of the dominant political discourse about whether tourism should be solely market-driven, or driven by a mix of marketing/management approach".

Many destinations have recognised the limitations of traditional DMOs, and see the need for a shift from simply marketing the destination to also playing a vital role in developing and managing the destination. This recognition has resulted in the creation of Destination Development, Marketing and Management Organisations (DDMMO) (European Cities Marketing, 2018). As their name implies, DDMMOs have expanded the mandate of DMOs to encompass planning and management responsibilities, which include: social sustainability, heritage conservation, place making, liveability and localism, partnerships, new funding approaches, the sharing economy, smart cities and crisis management and recovery. While DDMMOs may not be the appropriate structure in all situations, they do move the management and planning of destinations towards an integrated approach by being involved not only in marketing but also in management and development activities.

Given the limitations of DMOs, even those with an expanded DDMMO mandate, a short term role of a DMO – whether it is marketing or management focused – in helping to manage overtourism, should be to focus on "de-marketing" a destination, both by changing the destination's marketing message to appeal to different market segments, which may offer higher economic spend for a smaller number of visitors, and by making potential visitors aware of the pressure visitors place on the resources of the destination and on the resulting experience (Place Brand Observer, 2017; Aleksandrov, 2014). DMOs can also make potential visitors aware of experiences in neighbouring destinations that are less pressured by visitor numbers and that offer a similar, if not the same, experience. It could be argued, however, that given that destinations differ considerably and face many social, economic and political issues, and given the need for an integrated approach, which is often beyond the mandate of tourism authorities in a destination, the traditional DMO – and even the expanded DDMMO –often cannot provide sufficient and effective resolutions to overtourism (UNWTO, 2018; Dredge, 2016).

The role of local government in managing overtourism

In many situations, the planning and management of tourism at the local level, including the issue of overtourism, may be best situated within local level governments, which have the regulatory powers and, in most cases, the necessary skills and resources to ensure responsible tourism development. An OECD (2012) report recognised, however, that it is very difficult for ministries and government agencies to accept the rationale and advantage of working together on tourism development. It states that "there is a need to strengthen institutional governance mechanisms, so that more effective tourism-related policies can be developed, and to make changes in the organisation of government institutions to maintain competitive advantage" (OECD, 2012: 14).

Figure 15.1 illustrates the public-sector activities that are essential in a whole-of-government approach. It is inconceivable that a complex issue like overtourism can be responsibly dealt with without cooperation between many of these areas of activity.

This whole-of-government approach is best understood by looking at one of the key, if not always effective, strategies put forward for dealing with overtourism: distributing tourism activity over larger areas and thereby relieving the pressure on key attractions and tourism areas. While conceptually fairly straightforward, implementing a policy that requires distributing tourism activity to other jurisdictions and planning systems presents challenges. Questions that arise from this policy include: Do these other jurisdictions and destinations want more tourism? Do they understand the impact of increased tourism levels? Do they have the capacity to absorb more tourism? Will these destinations be able to meet the expectations of tourists? Will the local residents have the capacity to benefit from this increase tourism activity? Such questions clearly illustrate the need for an integrated approach and resolution within a local government context, with the clear realisation that the destination is willing to reduce its visitor numbers.

Along with concerns about the willingness and ability of other destinations to absorb redirected tourism is the question of what will happen (after congestion in the destination is eased) to the individuals and businesses that depend on tourism for their livelihoods. Except in cases where destinations have multiple economic opportunities, limiting tourism activity will have immediate economic impacts on residents as well as on the larger supply chain. Economic development activities,

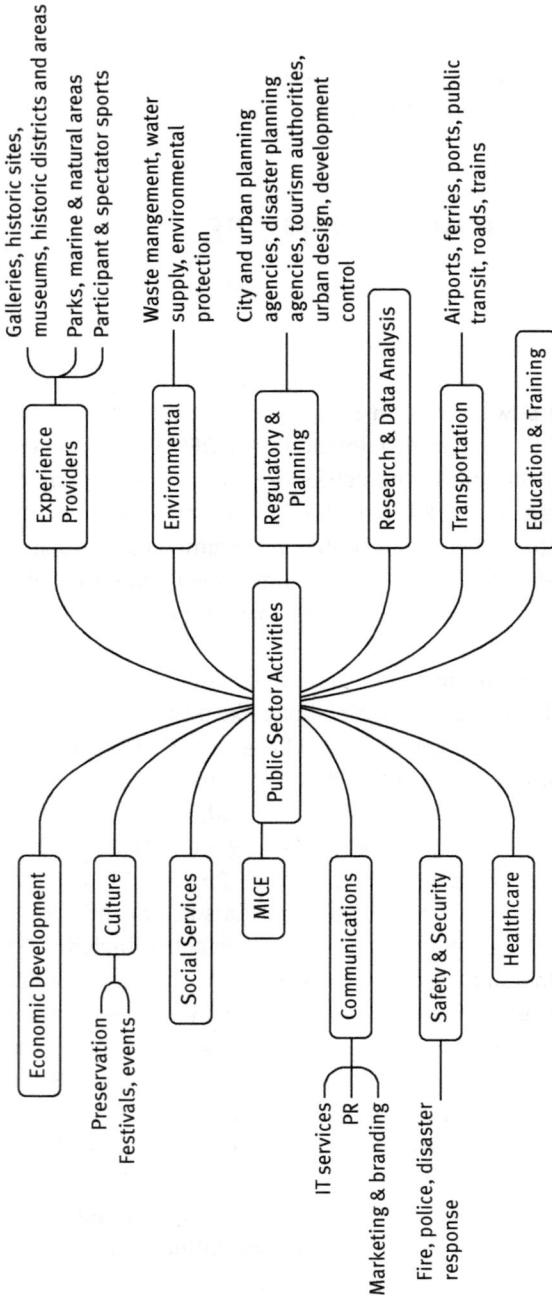

Fig. 15.1: Local government responsibilities.

along with other activities listed in Fig. 15.1, to find other livelihoods and sources of income for individuals and businesses will therefore be essential.

Should a destination agree to redistribution of tourism, government agencies will have to work together, often across jurisdictions, and regulatory and planning systems will need to interface to ensure minimal impact on the livelihoods of people in the originating destination and in the area where tourism is redirected. Organisational and individual capacities will have to be developed to ensure full opportunities for participation in the large tourism economy, which may take time to implement. Only a whole-of-government approach can responsibly implement a policy of redistribution of visitor activity. The best example of a whole-of-government approach is that of Singapore, where tourism is discussed and developed within a larger context (Smartgov.consulting, n.d.).

Visitor management

As noted earlier, while transformation will be necessary to ensure responsible development in tourism destinations, it is possible to better manage tourism numbers within existing legislative and ideological frameworks. As discussed by Wall in Chapter 3, there are a number of visitor management models and approaches which can ensure that natural environments and systems are protected, cultural sites maintain their integrity, the quality of the visitor experience is maximised and the quality of life and the livelihoods of the residents of a destination are maintained.

Many destinations' policy and marketing strategies have implicitly or explicitly worked on the assumption that any destination can absorb more tourists if the destination is well-managed. This is only partially true, however, given the finite capacity of spatial and infrastructure dimensions. Furthermore, for some destinations, it may not be the actual numbers of tourists but the behaviour of the visitors that is of concern, both for residents and other tourists (Postma and Schumecer, 2017).

Destinations dealing with overtourism can potentially lessen the impact of visitors through increasing the number and quality of visitor experiences. However, visitor managers must recognise that tourists will still want to experience key attractions. That is why sometimes the only resolution to the overtourism problem is policies and procedures that limit people coming to an area. This policy has been implemented by several highly desirable destinations, such as the Cinque Terre, Italy, where the government has limited visit numbers per year; Machu Picchu, Peru, which not only limits the number of tourists but also the time they can spend at the site; and Venice, Italy, which no longer allows cruise ships to use the city's terminal, so cruise ships must use one further away (Jet, 2018).

The development of visitor use management plans

In order to be more effective in managing overtourism, destinations need to be much more oriented to ensuring that short-term and medium-term goals are adaptive and flexible, allowing for swift implementation (Jamieson and Jamieson, 2016). Ideally, plans should be implemented. Therefore, implementation is one of the most practical aspects to be considered (Lai et al., 2006). However, planners are challenged by the fact that their choices "are nuanced and have to balance idealism [what ought to happen by and for society] with pragmatism [what can happen with private-sector investment]" (as quoted in Lai et al., 2006: 1171). A gap is seen between planning and implementation, which has led to the failure of tourism plans (Lai et al., 2006).

One immediate tactical approach for destinations dealing with overtourism is the development of visitor-use management plans, which are essentially planning and management tools. Some are restrictive in nature, while others are "softer" and deal with modifying behaviour. Visitor-use management plans can usually be implemented without legislative or regulatory changes but, when dealing with carrying capacity issues, political will is required to carry out these plans. Most visitor-use management planning processes share common characteristics. Figure 15.2 illustrates the essential stages of the visitor use management planning process.

While most of the stages in the planning process are self-evident, it is necessary to expand on Stage 6: Development of management strategies. Table 15.1 outlines the key actions involved in developing a visitor-use management strategy.

An interesting approach to managing visitor numbers is that taken by Disney, which is aware of the implications that overcrowding can have on a destination and on overall visitor satisfaction, and which therefore focuses on the visitor experience. Disney CEO, Bob Iger, has said he is willing to sacrifice visitor numbers to improve the experience for visitors. This reflects an understanding of the capacity of an area. To address overcrowding, Disney has implemented supply and demand pricing, which better distributes attendance throughout the year, allowing for a safer and more enjoyable experience for guests (Sampson, 2018). Notwithstanding the fact that it is a privately owned and managed entity,[2] other destinations can learn from Disney. It applies many of the same principles that deal with time and space of tourism in a destination and considers how to best manage those dimensions of a destination (Postma and Schumecker, 2017).

---

2 While Disney is a man-made attraction, as a destination it operates, in most instances, in a similar manner to a city or other destinations.

1	Assessment of the role of tourism in the overall municipal/local government agenda.
2	Guidance from tourism policies and plans, including desired outcomes.
3	Defining objectives for the visitor use management planning process.
4	An assessment of the existing tourism situation as it relates to visit use and, in particular, overtourism.
5	Defining indicators of success and visitor number thresholds.
6	Development of management strategies.
7	Ongoing monitoring and research related to indicators of success thresholds.
8	Adjusting visitor use management strategies.

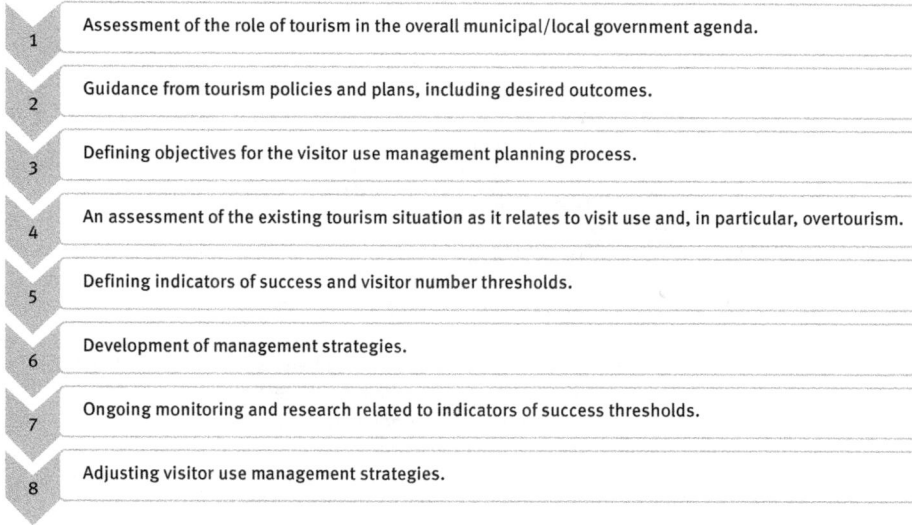

Fig. 15.2: Visitor use management planning process (adapted from Stein and Berhman, 2015).

Tab. 15.1: Actions necessary to define a visitor-use management strategy.

The development of pre-visit procedures and policies	– Before the visitor arrives at a destination there is a need to set expectations about the nature of visitor experience and community expectations regarding visitors behaviour through appropriate social media, advertising and promotion. – The development of registration and pre-booking policies and procedures for health-visited sites and attraction.
The development of an information and communication strategy	– The interpretation of local and cultural values – The provision cultural guidelines – Advertising visitors to accept differences and adopt customs – The identification of appropriate behaviour when photographing, purchasing goods and tipping – The provision of appropriate information and interpretation through literature, briefings, interpreters and interpretive programmes – The development of visitors or information centres to provide orientation to the visitor and to ensure that the visitor is aware of the full potential of a destination, aside from the most popular sites and attractions – The introduction of smart technologies both for managing tourism flows and making visitors aware of areas of congestion and possible alternative experiences

(continued)

Tab. 15.1 (continued)

Physical design and constraints	– The introduction of barriers to limit visitor access – Physical changes to a destination, including the hardening of pathways and trails – The introduction of raised footpaths to preserve natural vegetation
Restrictions/controls	– Prohibiting diret access to natural and cultural fragile elements of a destination through the development of zoning systems – The implementation of pricing policies – Limiting group sizes and access times – Control of the total number of visitors at any one time to avoid congestion and deterioration of destination resources – Limiting the number of cruise arrivals – Time ticket admission
Mobility/movement	– Identification of logical access and exit points – The design of visitor flows that respect residents while enhancing the visitor experience – Developing wayfinding strategies that help guide visitors through a destination – Developing mobility strategies to move people, especially those with mobility challenges, within tourism areas
Developing new experiences	– The development of new routes and packages. For example, Australia's restaurant campaign encourages visitors to explore secondary markets through the development of food themes and packages.
Providing incentives	– The provision of tax credits and grants to attraction/activities that relocate away from central tourism areas into areas in need of tourism development – The provision of incentives for tourists to visit other areas. For example, New York provides incentives to get visitors out of Manhattan and into other areas. – The provision of incentives for visitors to travel at off-peak times
Place making (PPS, n.d.)	– The evaluation of spaces and issues from the perspective of the residents and visitors on issues of overcrowding – Carrying out short-term experiments to see what works and doesn't work in terms of the physical and management dimensions of a place – Carrying out ongoing evaluation – Tactical place making, which involves a series of temporary and experimental initiatives to test new ideas. Examples: closing a street to identify the impacts of a street closure or widening a sidewalk to observe the impact of the intervention on visitor behaviour

Tab. 15.1 (continued)

The development of new and existing experiences	– Ongoing evaluation of visitor use and assessment of experiences – Development of storylines and interpretive themes for new experiences in other destinations that compliment those offered in destinations under overcrowding stress – Understanding of visitor behaviour through experience mapping
The development and ongoing assessment of key success metrics (Jamieson and Engelhardt, 2018)	Examples of key success metrics: – Local involvement in destination planning – Energy availability at peak tourism seasons – Perceptions of crowding on the part of residents – Perceptions of crowding on the part of visitors – Water availability in peak seasons – Increase in crime levels during peak seasons – Increase in cost of housing – Resident satisfaction with the quality of life of the heritage area

The way forward

Managing overtourism in a comprehensive way will require a mindset change on the part of all stakeholders, particularly among those working in the public sector. Given the nature of the tourism industry and its goals and objectives, addressing the key sources of overtourism will also require significant policy changes.

To overcome overtourism, this chapter has proposed that those involved in tourism must understand that managing tourism is part of the larger process of planning and management of local government areas and a whole-of-government approach is needed, as well as a shift from focusing on quantity to emphasising quality for both visitors and residents. In many instances DMOs do not have the mandates or capacity to address the complex issues, and management of overtourism therefore needs to be responsibility of the public sector.

There is a need for ongoing development and evaluation work to help destinations determine their carrying capacities in order for social, cultural and economic objectives to be met while maintaining the quality of life for residents and the integrity of the destination's environment. Simplistic and restrictive measures should be avoided. For destinations to be able to effectively deal with overtourism they must take an integrated and strategic approach. As Rochelle Turner, Research Director at the WTTC, has argued, destinations need "a vision of what they want to be, and how that vision then can be supported through planning, and through consultation with the people that live and work in those destinations" (CBC, 2018).

References

Aleksandrov, K. (2014) The role of DMO for sustainable development of a tourist destination: Bulgaria case study, *Journal of Tourism Research*, 9: 198–209.

Blake, E. (2018) Croatian tourism to face challenging year, although visitors are on the up, *Express Daily*, 10 April. https://www.express.co.uk/travel/articles/944078/croatia-tourism-minister-strategy-sustainability-overtourism-dubrovnik (Accessed 20 November 2018.)

CBC (2018) Too many tourists? Rethink how you travel or risk ruining destinations, says expert, *CBC Radio*, 6 August. https://www.cbc.ca/radio/thecurrent/the-current-for-august-6-2018-1.4775303/too-many-tourists-rethink-how-you-travel-or-risk-ruining-destinations-says-expert-1.4775306

Crawford, R. (2016) What can complexity theory tell us about urban planning? Research note 2016/2, New Zealand Productivity Commission.

Dredge, D. (2016) Are DMOs on a path to redundancy? *Tourism Recreation Research*, 41 (3): 348–353.

European Cities Marketing (2018) Managing tourism growth in Europe: The ECM toolbox. https://www.ucm.es/data/cont/media/www/pag-107272/2018-Managing%20Tourism%20Growth%20in%20Europe%20The%20ECM%20Toolbox.pdf(Accessed 20 November 2018.)

Garvin, D. (1993) Building a learning organization, *Harvard Business Review*, July-August. https://hbr.org/1993/07/building-a-learning-organization (Accessed 20 November 2018.)

Gupana, S. (2018). 11 overrun destinations that are trying to curb tourism, *Matador Network*, 16 May. https://matadornetwork.com/read/11-overrun-destinations-trying-curb-tourism/ (Accessed 20 November 2018.)

ICLIE (2018) *Resilient Cities Report 2018: Tracking local progress on the resilience targets of SDG 11*. Bonn: ICLEI World Secretariat.

Jamieson, W. (2012) The urban design and tourism interface -The complementary role of urban design in tourism development. In V. Horayangkura, W. Jamieson and P. Mallikamarl (Eds.), *The design and development of sustainable cities: International and Thai perspectives on urban design in the 21st century*. Bangkok: Thammasat University.

Jamieson, W. and Engelhardt, R. (2018) *The planning and management of responsible urban heritage destinations in Asia: Dealing with Asian urbanization and tourism forces*. Oxford: Goodfellow Publishers.

Jamieson, W. and Jamieson, M. (2016) Urban destination level tactical tourism planning in developing economies. Tourism Development Journal, 14 (1).

Jet, J. (2018) How is overtourism impacting travel to popular destinations? *Forbes*, 20 August. https://www.forbes.com/sites/johnnyjet/2018/08/20/how-is-overtourism-impacting-travel-to-popular-destinations/#77d39d335b84 (Accessed 20 November 2018.)

Lai, K., Li, Y. and Feng, X. (2006) Gap between tourism planning and implementation: A case of China. *Tourism Management*, 27: 1171–1180.

Landry, C. and Caust, M. (2017) *The creative bureaucracy & its radical common sense*. Gloucestershire, UK: Comedia.

OECD (2012) *OECD Tourism Trends and Policies 2012*. Paris: OECD. http://dx.doi.org/10.1787/tour-2012-en (Accessed 20 November 2018.)

Peltier, D. (2018) London uses mobile gaming app to help tackle overtourism, Skift, 27 June. https://skift.com/2018/06/27/london-uses-mobile-gaming-app-to-help-tackle-overtourism/ (Accessed 20 November 2018.)

Place Brand Observer (2017) How overtourism affects destination reputation and competitiveness: Issues, strategies and solutions, *Place Brand Observer*, 17 October. https://placebrandobserver.com/overtourism-issues-strategies-solutions (Accessed 20 November 2018.)

Postma, A. and Schmuecker, D. (2017) Understanding and overcoming negative impacts of tourism in city destinations: Conceptual model and strategic framework, *Journal of Tourism Futures*, 3 (2): 144–156.

Project for Public Spaces (n.d.) What is placemaking? https://www.pps.org/article/what-is-place making (Accessed 20 November 2018.)

Pylas, P. (2017) Managing overtourism an increasing feature of global travel, CTV News, 15 November. https://www.ctvnews.ca/lifestyle/managing-overtourism-an-increasing-feature-of-global-travel-1.3678953 (Accessed 20 November 2018.)

Sampson, H. (2018) Disney World's latest pricing changes take aim at crowd control, *Skift*, 26 September. https://skift.com/2018/09/26/disney-worlds-latest-pricing-changes-take-aim-at-crowd-control/ (Accessed 20 November 2018.)

Smartgov.consulting (n.d.) Whole-of-government approach? http://smartgov.consulting/eng/whole-government-approach

Stein, J. and Berhman, W. (2015) Integrating visitor use management and commercial services, 1 April. http://www.georgewright.org/stein_gws2015_ppt.pdf (Accessed 20 November 2018.)

Lydon, M. (Ed.) (2012). *Tactical urbanism 2: Short-term action, long-term change.* https://issuu.com/streetplanscollaborative/docs/tactical_urbanism_vol_2_final (Accessed 20 November 2018.)

Tourtellot, J. (2017) "Overtourism" plagues great destinations; Here's why, National Geographic, 2 October. https://blog.nationalgeographic.org/2017/10/29/overtourism-plagues-great-desti nations-heres-why/ (Accessed 20 November 2018.)

Toronto City Planning (2017) Proposed Downtown Plan. https://www.toronto.ca/wp-content/up loads/2017/10/9902-CityPlanning-TOcore-Proposed-Downtown-Plan.pdf (Accessed 20 November 2018.)

UNWTO (2017) *UNWTO Tourism Highlights.* Madrid: UNWTO. https://www.e-unwto.org/doi/pdf/10.18111/9789284419029 (Accessed 20 November 2018.)

UNWTO (2018) *'Overtourism'? Understanding and managing urban tourism growth beyond perceptions.* Madrid: UNWTO. https://www.e-unwto.org/doi/pdf/10.18111/9789284420070

Van Laar, E., Van Deursen, A. J. A. M., Van Dijk, J. A. G. M. and De Haan, J. (2017) The relation between 21st-century skills and digital skills: A systematic literature review. *Computers in Human Behavior*, 72: 577–588.

World Economic Forum (WEF) (n. d.) Mapping global transformations. https://www.weforum.org/about/transformation-maps (Accessed 20 November 2018.)

WTTC and McKinsey & Company (2017) *Coping with success: Managing overcrowding in tourism destinations.* New York: McKinsey & Company. https://www.wttc.org/-/media/files/reports/policy-research/coping-with-success—managing-overcrowding-in-tourism-destinations-2017.pdf (Accessed 20 November 2018.)

Yuksel, F. and Yuksel, A. (2000) Tourism plan formulation and implementation: The role of inter-organisational relations. Paper presented at the First International Joint Symposium on Business Administration: Challenges for Business Administration in the New Millennium.

Zelenka, J. and Kacetl, J. (2014) The concept of carrying capacity in tourism, *Amfiteatru Economic Journal*, 16 (36): 641–654.

Susanne Becken and David G. Simmons

16 Stakeholder management: different interests and different actions

Introduction

Who are key stakeholders in tourism and who among them are addressing issues of overtourism? The answers depend on the role of the state and the general approaches to governance in the particular destination. In the member countries of the Organisation for Economic Co-operation and Development (OECD), for example, development builds on three dimensions, namely effective and accountable governance, growth and social cohesion (including well-being and equity). Other countries, such as China, are transforming from communist to market-oriented economies (albeit state-controlled), and this change is bringing with it key challenges such as economic inequality and environmental degradation. Such challenges have led to a call for new arrangements and the participation in decision making of all stakeholders, including local communities, to achieve positive outcomes from development, including from tourism development (Lin and Simmons, 2017; Su et al., 2014).

Tourism is rife with market failures (Simmons, 2017) and, as such, has experienced boom and bust cycles commonly seen in other resource-based sectors, such as mining (for a comparison of mining and tourism see Moyle, Moyle and Becken, 2018; for examples of booms and busts in the history of a tourism destination see McAloon et al., 1998). Put simply, market failure is when the outcome of market forces is unsatisfactory from the perspective of society. One type of market failure is when the market fails to price, or include all costs associated with production or consumption, resulting in "externalities" (e.g. pollution). Addressing such externalities requires suitable governance arrangements, such as the intervention by the government in the form of legislation or taxes (UNWTO and Griffith University, 2017)

The prevailing market-oriented paradigm has also shaped perspectives on investment, development, marketing and regulations relating to tourism, resulting in phenomenal tourist growth rates and increasing pressures on destinations, at least in some parts of the world. Under the free market philosophy, tourism destinations face the dilemma of trying to meet local needs (clean air, clean water, etc.) while also adhering to the demands of the global capitalist society. This dilemma highlights the need for governance and management to be integrated within the lens of sustainable tourism. The successful creation of sustainable development outcomes for destinations and all their stakeholders results from a balanced link of formal (public, economic and non-economic institutions) and informal (social capital) institutions (Platje, 2008; Shen et al., 2008). These must be enforced via robust institutional governance, which is participatory and inclusive of all stakeholders.

https://doi.org/10.1515/9783110607369-016

Thus, understanding the needs of all stakeholders involved is a key point in the management of overtourism.

The almost unquestioned rise of the neoliberal economic agenda (Becken, 2016; Simmons, 2017), with its associated policies regarding free trade and minimisation of government intervention in markets, has in many cases led to the public sector having less influence on resource management. This raises questions around who the dominant stakeholders in tourism development are, and whether there is need for a renewed strengthening of public sector organisations, the participation of other stakeholders in decision making, and/or novel types of partnerships to address some of the challenges that tourism growth poses. This chapter will discuss the roles of the various stakeholders involved in managing "overtourism", and their actions and attempts in addressing the issues and creating new opportunities.

Stakeholder models

Tourism is a complex system that involves many stakeholders at a variety of scales. Some are tightly constituted (with legal or quasi legal standing) while others are disparate groups or individuals, for example leaders of various groups in destination communities. A "stakeholder" is commonly defined as any individual, group, or organization, who may affect, be affected by or perceive itself to be affected by, a decision, activity or outcome of a project (Freeman, 1984). For the United Nations World Tourism Organization (UNWTO) (1998), this definition is sufficiently broad to include the press and media.

Figure 16.1 illustrates the key stakeholders, in both the public and private sectors, who represent important aspects of the tourism value chain and production system. On the industry side, tourism is composed of multiple sub-sectors, including core industries such as attractions, accommodation and tourism transport (see the Tourism Satellite Account method for ways of measuring the importance of these industries). Micro-businesses and small and medium-sized enterprises often also form an integral part of the tourism industry, and of the community, and have interests beyond their own financial bottom line. Industry stakeholders need not be physically present in a destination and can include online booking agents, virtual p2p platforms (such as Airbnb) and social media commentators. The tourism industry is supported by many other industries and sectors (e.g. the agricultural sector, food manufacturing industries, the recreation industry and the non-tourism transportation sector) and linkages can be measured through economic modelling (e.g. Khanal et al., 2014).

Figure 16.1 shows that the public-sector stakeholders involved in tourism are diverse and operate at multiple levels, including central, regional and local. Aside from dedicated ministries of tourism, other ministries and departments also have tourism as a core business, for example immigration and transport, and yet others

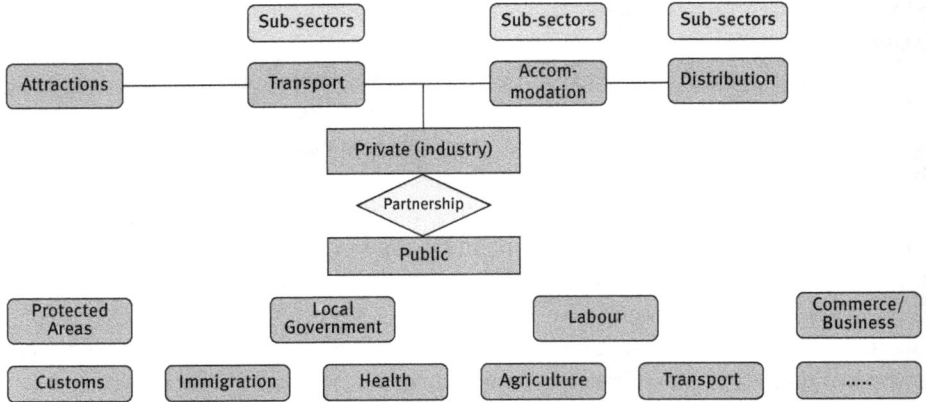

Fig. 16.1: Key private and public sector stakeholders involved in tourism.

have tourism as a key policy consideration (e.g. conservation, regional development and employment).

The segmenting of stakeholders into different sectors and organizations, as illustrated in Fig. 16.1, while useful in identifying the various types of tourism stakeholders, omits several key players involved in tourism. Other important stakeholders include residents who are not involved in tourism but are affected by it, and cultural and ethnic groups, advocacy groups, NGOs and other institutions that represent particular views relevant to community well-being. Well-being is a multidimensional concept that comprises material conditions and quality of life, and it likely to differ between cultural groups.

An enhanced way of conceptualizing tourism stakeholders is via the VICE model (Sleeman and Simmons, 2004), shown in Fig. 16.2. The VICE model puts visitors at the core of the tourism "production-scape" and, as a result, highlights the need to protect the essential tourist experience. In this model, visitors are the key stakeholders, and they bring with them expectations, needs and "measures of success".

The model conceptualizes interactions between the visitor, as the consumer of tourism, and the other stakeholders, which are represented as the "industry", the "community" and the "environment". In so doing, the model focuses the discussion on (local) development and away from an intensely commercial model. Moving away from growth-focused approaches and narrow measures such as Gross Domestic Product (GDP), towards measures of societal well-being and environmental health is reflected in frameworks such as the Human Development Index and the Genuine Progress Indicators (OECD, 2001).

While government agencies do not directly appear in the VICE model, they are indirectly represented through their functions in support of the visitor experience (e.g. national tourism boards), the industry (e.g. ministries of economic affairs and

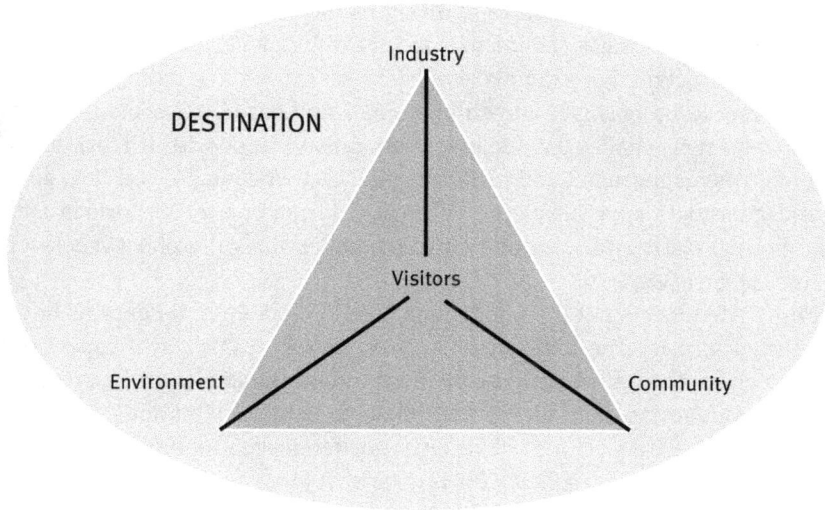

Fig. 16.2: The VICE model of tourism development (source: Sleeman and Simmons, 2004).

development, and chambers of commerce), the community (local government councils) and the environment (ministries of the environment and protected area agencies). The VICE model gives a voice to stakeholders that are not necessarily included in the tourism production process and it highlights the ultimate goal of protecting local social, cultural and environmental assets while attending to local community well-being.

Geography and scale are important in that there are many individual sites and destinations that make up travellers' itineraries (which may or may not become "hotspots"). Given that destinations and their stakeholders compete for the economic opportunities that are perceived to arise from tourist visitation, it might be anticipated that agreement between stakeholders on short-term development objectives, growth or market trajectories may be difficult to reach.

Different interests?

Stakeholders have different roles and, depending on the governance arrangements, they differ in their interests, and some may be excluded from participating in decision-making about tourism. Given that goals differ inherently or can begin to diverge over time, tourism development, in all phases of its lifecycle, can lead to conflict.

Overtourism is a prominent example of diverging interests. Stakeholders operate at different levels – macro, meso and micro – and the different perspectives that arise from this can cause friction. For example, while tourism growth at a national scale is perceived by many to be positive, growth at a small number of hot spots presents significant management challenges. Clearly, overtourism brings with it tensions in the context of crisis management and resilience building, where top-down (e.g. government) and grassroots approaches (e.g. by non-governmental organisations and community groups) clash and unresolved friction undermines the effectiveness of interventions (Larsen et al., 2011).

The group: "visitors" is not a homogenous one. For example, it contains both domestic visitors and international visitors. The UNWTO (2018) in a report on overtourism in cities distinguishes domestic from international visitors because of their differing motivations, behaviours and impacts. Some destinations, such as Amsterdam, recognise that visitors have differing requirements and behaviour, so have implemented specific policies for the various types of visitors, including policies to deal with inappropriate visitor behaviour, so as to protect residents and other visitor groups (see WTTC and McKinsey & Company, 2017).

The differences between the main goals of the stakeholders are probably most evident when comparing their key performance indicators (KPIs). These help to define and measure progress toward defined objectives. Table 16.1 lists many of the stakeholders that heavily shape tourism development. These include external investors and developers, as they play a key role in determining the extent of tourism growth in a destination and the type of tourism that unfolds. As well as listing the key tourism stakeholders, their roles and activities, Tab. 16.1 lists the types of KPIs (measures of success) the stakeholders might typically have. As indicated above, there are many other important players that are not presented in the table. In New Zealand, for example, an earlier study on public sector yield highlighted that the single largest cost driver arises from the provision of site access and activities by the Department of Conservation (DOC). The research on "public sector yield" found that while the DOC receives revenues from tourists (e.g. hut fees), it provided services to tourism at an estimate net cost of $79 million in 2005 (Simmons, Becken and Cullen, 2007). The marketing budget of Tourism New Zealand in the same year was $82 million (TNZ, 2006).

Juxtaposing the KPIs of the different stakeholders (Tab. 16.1) shows that stakeholders often have opposing goals. While some (e.g. national governments, investors, airlines and airports) seek to maximise tourism growth, others (e.g. local governments, community groups and visitors who want more authentic experiences) seek to maximise community well-being and/or environmental well-being. The goals of the latter group of stakeholders imply managed, if not contained, growth of tourism, and the possibility of proactively promoting de-growth to reach a desired level of tourism activity. An example of such de-growth can be observed in Mallorca, Spain, where

Tab. 16.1: Key stakeholders, their roles and interests, and how they measure success.

Stakeholders	Roles	Examples of activities	Measures of success (KPIs)
National-level government (e.g. Ministry of Tourism)	Develop policy and legislation	– Allocate budget for marketing – Promote investment in tourism – Frameworks for training and education – Coordinate tourism-relevant activities across Government	– Visitor arrivals – Contribution of tourism to GDP – Tourism employment – Tax take from tourism
National Tourism Board	Marketing (typically international)	– Develop promotional material of key attractions – Advertise the country – May partner with other stakeholders (e.g. private sector) on specific campaigns	– Visitor arrivals – Visitor expenditure
Local-level government (e.g. local council)	Local level planning, operations, and community well-being	– Land use planning – Regulation of business operations – Regulate aspects of environmental/resource management – Invest in recreational facilities, events	– Local visitor expenditure – Resident satisfaction – Budget
International investors	Provide capital	– Make investment decisions – May partner with local actors	– Return on investment – Shareholder return
Airlines and airports	Provide access to destinations	– Invest in assets and operations (e.g. new aircraft, airport extensions) – Partner with Government (e.g. joint campaigns, co-investment)	– Profitability – Shareholder return – Company value – Corporate Social Responsibility (CSR) – Potential industry leader
Large (national) companies	Produce service	– Invest in the company – Create partnerships for specific purposes – Employee training and retention – Manage environmental impact – CSR activities, donations, investment	– Profitability – Shareholder return – Company value – Customer and employee satisfaction and other CSR

Tab. 16.1 (continued)

Stakeholders	Roles	Examples of activities	Measures of success (KPIs)
Smaller (local) tourism businesses	Produce Service	– Business operations (accommodation, activities) – Staff training – Local sector advocacy	– Profitability – "Lifestyle" – Capital growth (most evident through on-selling) – Contribution to local community
National-level industry associations	Represent industry	– Advocacy and input into policy decisions – Produce industry guidelines and/or standards (e.g. code of conduct)	– Sector standing – Sector growth – Stakeholder management
Regional tourism organisations	Marketing	– Develop promotional material of key attractions and areas – Promote the region – Sector advocacy at regional / local scales – May partner with other stakeholders (e.g. private sector) on specific campaigns	– Visitor arrivals – Visitor expenditure – Local understanding of sector
Community	Hosts Investors Employees	– Employment – Recreation and leisure in common (touristic) places	– Well-beings –social and environmental – Protection and development of amenity – Livelihoods (including the development / retention of community services)
NGOs	Cause advocacy	– Protection of natural assets – Advocacy for poor or marginal groups	– Designation of protected areas – Skill development – Lead to change
Visitors	Enjoyment or other values	– Engage in a wide range of activities at the destination (and spend money) – Interact with local community and environment	– Satisfaction – Health, safety, well-being

the government recently introduced a new law to cap the number of beds available to visitors (at 623,624 beds) with a plan to reduce this by 120,000 over the next few years (Summers, 2017). This will be achieved by various means, including not issuing any new licenses to Airbnb owners for one year.

International actors today exert considerable exogenous influence on destinations. Airlines, cruise ships and other international transport services are particularly powerful. For example, when airlines choose to fly to a particular destination it can open up a pipeline of tourist flows that are difficult to control (see Chapter 11). In the case of Mallorca, referred to above, the plan to control bed capacity will require also controlling airline capacity and/or schedules, such that only the visitors who have accommodation can book a flight to Mallorca. Restricting bed numbers alone would result in a mismatch between accommodation and transport providers. In 2016, there were an average of 800 flights a day at Palma Airport in Mallorca during the peak season (Morey, 2016), with a record number of passengers (more than 180,000) using the airport in one day. This is a large number relative to the island's residential population of about 860,000 (AbcMallorca, no date). Putting upper limits or "caps" in place is not always easy, as the destination sits within a broader system of tourism development.

As noted by Keller (1987), the development cycle usually entails a shift from local entrepreneur interests in the early stages to increasingly exogenous sources of capital in the subsequent growth phases, precipitating a loss of control from the (peripheral) destination to the industrial cores of the region, the country or the global level. The evolution depends on whether local authorities have managed to influence development, for example by imposing limits to growth and/or to external investment, and – perhaps simultaneously – empowering local groups to contribute to or drive the decision-making process. The idea of co-management is relevant here as it presents a governance system that combine "states" and "communities" that, in turn, endow decentralised decision-making with a greater sense of accountability (Carlsson and Berkes, 2005). The involvement of traditional owners in the management of the Great Barrier Reef is a good example of co-management.

It is important to note that the existing KPIs are not necessarily suitable in terms of achieving sustainable development outcomes. While governments, for example, currently measure tourism success by calculating the economic contributions of tourism to central funds (most notably through goods and services taxes, value added taxes and tourism business taxes), if they were to change their KPIs to include social and environmental measures, the outcomes would be very different. Growing numbers of visitors impose increasing costs on, for example, public sector services (e.g. roads, waste management and safety/security, see Simmons et al., 2007) and on society and the environment (e.g. biosecurity and biodiversity). While many such factors were previously excluded as external costs, these are increasingly included in government accounting sheets. A prominent example is the cost of carbon (see Fig. 16.3 for an example from New Zealand), which, when incorporated into accounting sheets allows one to calculate the true financial costs of consumption of carbon-producing products, such as cars, to the government, society and companies. As tourism grows, these costs rise. Figure 16.3 illustrates the near doubling of carbon dioxide emissions from tourist transport and accommodation activities in New Zealand between 2008 and 2017.

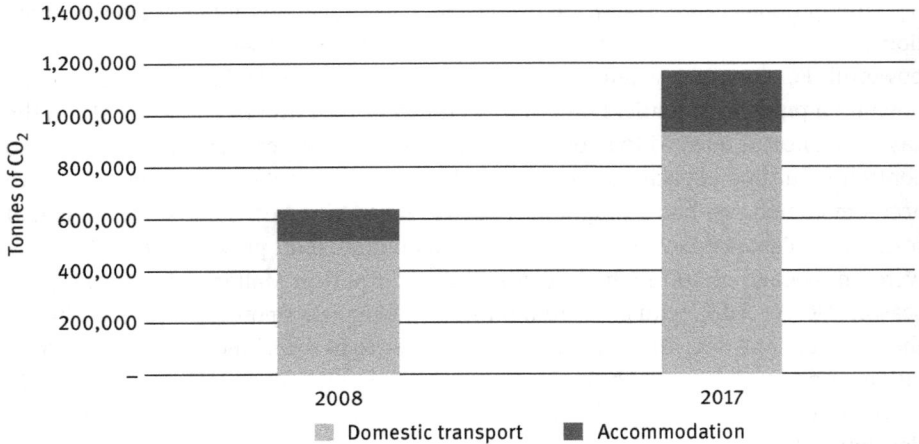

Fig. 16.3: Carbon dioxide emissions from international tourists' transport and accommodation activities within New Zealand, 2008 and 2017 (source: own calculations, building on Becken, 2009).

Alternative accounting frameworks are emerging that allow measurement of various aspects of well-being and prosperity of society beyond simplistic economic measures. The New Zealand Treasury for example, drawing on the OECD Better Life Initiative (e.g. OCED, 2017), is currently developing a "Living Standards Dashboard" that considers four types of capital (physical, financial, human and natural) and these will serve as a basis for developing indicators that inform policy making, with the overall goal of improved well-being for all New Zealanders (Smith, 2018). Such shifts in paradigms and measurements will have knock-on effects on the tourism industry and its stakeholders.

Moreover, new stakeholders are emerging. The giving of the right of personhood, represented by a committee, to Whanganui River in New Zealand (and later to Ganges River in India) means that nature has become a legal actor able to sue against violations of its rights (Tanasescu, 2017) (ABC Australia, 2017).

Overcoming the challenges

Addressing the challenges related to excessive tourism growth is partly a governance problem (see Chapter 17). Good governance implies having a strategic vision of what constitutes appropriate tourism development, which reflects the complexities of the respective destination, including the cultural context, social fabric and environmental constraints, and involves working towards achieving that vision. Good governance ensures equitable and transparent participation by stakeholders, following specified rules of law and engagement, and subject to accountability (UNWTO and Griffith University, 2017). However, our understanding of good governance must move beyond acknowledging key stakeholders and their roles, and recognise the agency of stakeholders in the system and their ability to influence decision making. In particular, this relates to the agency of informal stakeholders, which "operate within the institutional, legal and administrative structures and officially accepted and mandated mechanisms within the public, private sector, and civil society" (Larsen et al., 2011: 488). Research on tsunami recovery in Thailand has shown that it is exactly those informal actors (e.g. land owners, leading families) that draw on established systemic legitimacy to influence decision making, often to their benefit and not always to that of the broader community (Larsen et al., 2011). Clearly, Keller's (1987) set of questions "Development for whom?", "Development by whom?" and "Development for what?" are still highly relevant today.

The following section presents some suggestions regarding how the governance of the tourism system and the stakeholders within it can be strengthened to achieve sustainable tourismThe following section presents some suggestions how the governance of the tourism system and the stakeholders within it can be strengthened to achieve sustainable tourism development within recognized limits of capacity.

Strategy before promotion

The overtourism debate has brought to the forefront the historical emphasis on tourism promotion and marketing and the neglect of sound strategies and resources for tourism management. Accordingly, many destinations now recognize that more marketing and more tourism are not necessarily better. This is reflected in the trend to change destination marketing organisations into destination management organisations (WTTC and McKinsey & Company, 2017). Demonstrating this shift, Visit Norway has rebranded itself as Innovation Norway (2018). It now performs various functions, including promotion, management of tourism and catalyzing innovation. The organisation is mindful that tourism marketing must be backed up by quality experiences on the ground, and in the case of Norway this relates closely to the sustainability of tourism (personal communication with Ms Bratland Holm, CEO Innovation Norway, 25 June 2018, https://www.visitnorway.com/about/sustainability/). Putting in place adequate strategies and systems, including for sustainability monitoring, is a priority for the organisation. According to Innovation Norway, promoting certified sustainable destinations is an important vehicle for "demonstrating their lasting commitment to providing the best possible experiences for their guests, while keeping the negative impact of tourism to a minimum" (Innovation Norway, 2018). However, the organisation will be challenged to achieve the desired outcomes, for reasons such as a lack of critical mass, deficiencies in certification schemes and the ongoing growth of tourism.

In a similar vein, the New Zealand Tourism 2025 strategy (Tourism Industry Aotearoa, 2014) is oriented towards "value over volume", is "targeting for value" and is seeking "visitor and community satisfaction". This theme has been taken up by the national tourism strategic plan, which lists as priorities the need to "broaden our measure of value from near-term growth to long-term sustainability" and to "work with Government and industry partners to sustain and improve the experience of visitors and host communities" (Tourism New Zealand, 2017a: 2). While annual reports continue to measure success in terms of growth of arrivals and tourist expenditure, in recent years reports have focused more on resident satisfaction (Tourism New Zealand, 2006; Tourism New Zealand, 2017b).

Strategies for managing overtourism are required at all levels, including at the local level. As Keller (1987) pointed out, local-level strategies are needed by destinations outside major urban centres. However, communities in "peripheral" destinations must connect with and maintain influence at the regional and national levels of decision making, so as to maintain control over development. Hence, it is essential to ensure that local tourism strategies are being developed, resourced and implemented.

Measurement

While "good governance" and the capacity of stakeholders and their relationships are difficult to measure (Larsen et al., 2011), it is possible to measure the outcomes of governance. The notion of measuring overtourism is necessary in order to recognise and monitor the problem. However, calculating the number of visitors alone is inadequate as the impacts of tourists depend on the context and the management responses (UNWTO, 2018). Proxies include the well-known Doxey index (visitors per head of population) and environmental footprints (e.g. energy, carbon, water, waste per visitor) (see Global Sustainable Tourism Dashboard, n.d.). Another approach is that by Becken and Simmons (2008) who developed a broad framework for assessing tourism yield (financial, economic, social and environmental) by various types of visitors in an attempt to define an "ideal visitor type", so as to refocus marketing efforts on tourists that best meet societal and sustainability goals.

Measuring residents' perceptions is an important aspect of gauging whether a destination is experiencing overtourism or not. The need to understand how residents perceive tourism is not new, and indeed it is one of the most researched areas in tourism, but the implementation of monitoring tools is relatively new and indicates growing government concern about the eroding "social license" of tourism. Both Australia and New Zealand, for example, undertake "Mood of the Nation" surveys to elicit residents' views of tourism (Tourism New Zealand, 2016; Blue Swan Daily, 2017). Beyond surveys, there is a growing interest in using crowdsourced data and other online approaches to gauge the sentiment of local communities. Social media, for example, can provide a powerful and cost effective mechanism for gathering data on support for tourism, for identifying hot spots and for monitoring specific incidents associated with intense tourism visitation (Becken et al., under review). Similarly, just-in-time geo-spatial data, deliverable, for example, via smart phones and watches, is emerging as a new tool to advise visitors of site congestion and alternatives, for example, in Amsterdam and Dubrovnic (WTTC and McKinsey & Company, 2017).

New partnerships

Overtourism and the failure of government to effectively control or manage tourism development have catalysed new types of partnerships, often initiated by non-governmental stakeholders. Today, many governance arrangements involve not only governments, but non-state actors, in public-private sector partnerships. A prominent example is the role that Air New Zealand (jointly owned by the government and the private sector) is playing in proactively seeking to influence the distribution of tourist flows in New Zealand. As a key determiner of access to destinations, the airline plays a critical role in shaping visitation patterns. Interventions by the airline can affect places suffering from excess tourism and also those that are currently struggling to attract tourism, and in the latter case aid the development of regional (and often remote) economies. Air New Zealand's efforts in the East Cape region of the North Island (the Tairawhiti) is particularly notable, as the airline is supporting the building of effective governance structures for tourism, recognising the leading role of Activate Tairawhiti, but also involving other stakeholders, including indigenous people represented through multiple *iwi* (Maori tribes). Assurance of ongoing air services and the building of local capacity have helped to attract financial investment by central government agencies. What sits behind this initiative is the idea that businesses, in this case a national carrier, are able to support a long-term vision for tourism that extends beyond the immediate market imperative.

A second example of the development of new tourism partnerships in the face of crisis comes from the Great Barrier Reef in Australia. By identifying values of nature (e.g. a strong desire for conservation) among tourism stakeholders, the local tourism operators and the tourism industry association have allied with international environmental conservation organisations and UNESCO to provide resistance to formal government organisations (state, federal and the Great Barrier Reef Marine Park Authority) and industries (most notably the shipping industry, which is involved in dredging for expansion of ports, and the agriculture industry, which is responsible for nutrient leaching into the ocean). The alliance has proved effective and has helped to both prevent further impacts and change government policy. This indicates that unified approaches by unlikely groups of advocates (stakeholders) have the potential to trigger change and shift the trajectory of development.

At the same time, some stakeholders in the tourism system have become "stakeholders" (Larsen et al., 2011) who seek to maintain status quo to cement their vested interests. These can include public sector stakeholders who are wittingly or unwittingly swayed by pressures or promises from outside actors that may not have community well-being at the heart of their activities. This type of behaviour has been observed in the context of disaster recovery in developing countries, and it is possible that tourism is also subject to the interests of a small number of key actors who benefit from a status quo and have little interest in changing it, and of those who lack full information and agree to decisions they may not fully comprehend in terms of community outcomes. This question certainly deserves further research.

Funding mechanisms

A key to successful tourism management lies in adequate resources and the power to deploy them. As indicated earlier, much of the financial benefit of tourism accrues at the national level through collecting taxes. It is only when the central government distributes these financial benefits to lower levels of government that the regions where much tourism occurs (and most of the negative social and environmental impacts occur) receive the necessary resources to address the challenges of overtourism. Investment in tourist destinations must therefore go beyond centrally-funded and coordinated infrastructure projects (e.g. see Ireland and New Zealand as recent cases of government funding of tourism infrastructure) and should instead be sufficient to cover everyday management activities and strategic planning.

Some countries have developed specific policies to increase the revenue from tourism, for example through additional taxes or border fees. Prominent examples are Botswana's "eco-tax" of 30 United States dollars (USD) per visitor to support conservation (DW, 2017) and the Balearic Islands' doubling of the tourist tax during the peak season (Majorca Daily Bulletin, 2018). An alternative to taxation is a minimum spend amount imposed on visitors. This is the approach taken by the Kingdom of Bhutan, which stipulates that each visitor spends at least 200 USD per day in the low season and at least 250 USD in the high season. This minimum spend includes a sustainable development fee of 65 USD per day (WTTC and McKinsey & Company, 2017).

Conclusion

As tourism has grown, so too has the list of stakeholders who have interest in its development and operation. Overtourism has brought into sharp focus the goals of these stakeholders. Analysis of the KPIs of key stakeholders indicates a common tendency to measure success in terms of tourism growth, most commonly as visitor arrivals. This sows the seeds of overtourism.

Overtourism is manifested at the local level, where pressures brought about by visitors can overwhelm local (physical and social) capacities. It is therefore at this level that overtourism must first be addressed. Tourism inevitably draws on local communities and shared resources. These can be physical and environmental assets such as parks and beaches as well as more general aspects of a destination, such as community goodwill. These are un-priced inputs into tourism production and consumption, however, which leads to their overuse. This type of market failure is inevitable and can only be addressed through regulatory mechanisms, such as taxes.

What is now required is a new set of communication and cooperative mechanisms across the tourism sector, and the empowerment of the stakeholders who can most effectively and legitimately implement these. This chapter argues that there are signs of new governance processes and initiatives to address questions created by overtourism. While some stakeholders, such as local communities and relevant sub-groups, have been marginalised in the past, today in many cases the needs and voices of these stakeholders are being given consideration alongside the national development agenda and global investment ventures and operations.

In some situations there is a stronger interest in government stakeholders stepping forward to address market failures (in this case, unpriced inputs and outputs in the tourism industry). Increased taxes to address tourism congestion and mitigate resource damage are being seen in a number of situations. Such activities fly in the face of the conventional global economic agenda. In other cases, business interests are undertaking their own investigations, for example into infrastructure requirements, which were traditionally the domain of government agencies.

At the same time, social media are providing new opportunities for both participatory decision making and consumer pressure, while new communication technologies, be they advisory or directive (such as Google Maps and TripAdvisor), are adding complexity to stakeholder engagement and management. What remains unclear is what particular forms of stakeholder engagement are likely to emerge in future to govern the continuing growth and expanding reach of tourism. In any event, it is increasingly clear to all stakeholders that the well-being of residents and visitors and the environmental integrity of destinations need to be placed at the centre of engagement and governance.

References

ABC Australia (2017) New Zealand's Whanganui River granted legal status as a person after 170-year battle, *ABC Australia*, 16 March. http://www.abc.net.au/news/2017-03-16/nz-whanganui-river-gets-legal-status-as-person-after-170-years/8358434?pfmredir=sm (Accessed 22 September 2018.)

AbcMallorca (no date). Mallorca at a glance. https://www.abc-mallorca.com/mallorca/ (Accessed 18 November 2018.)

Becken, S. (2009). *The carbon footprint of domestic tourism in New Zealand*. Hikurangi Foundation, Wellington. https://researcharchive.lincoln.ac.nz/bitstream/handle/10182/1216/becken_carbon_footprint.pdf;sequence=1 (Accessed 18 November 2018.)

Becken, S. (2016) Evidence of a low-carbon tourism paradigm? *Journal of Sustainable Tourism*, 25 (6): 832–850.

Becken, S. and Simmons, D. (2008) Using the concept of yield to assess the sustainability of different tourist types. *Ecological Economics*, 67: 420–429.

Becken, S., Alaei, A. and Wang, Y. (under review) Benefits and pitfalls of using Twitter to assess destination sentiment, *Journal of Hospitality and Tourism Technology*.

Blue Swan Daily (2017) Tourism Australia releases the results of the Mood of the Nation survey, 18 May. https://blueswandaily.com/tourism-australia-releases-the-results-of-the-mood-of-the-nation-survey/ (Accessed 15 November 2018.)

Butler, R. W. (1980) The concept of a tourist area cycle of evolution: Implications for management of resources, *The Canadian Geographer / Le Géographe canadien*, 24(1): 5–12.

Carlsson, L. and Berkes, F. (2005) Co-management: Concepts and methodological implications, *Journal of Environmental Management*, 75 (1): 65–76.

DW (2017) Botswana introduces a tourist tax, *DW*, 3 May 2017. https://www.dw.com/en/botswana-introduces-a-tourist-tax/a-38674173 (Accessed 15 November 2018.)

Freeman, R. E. (1984) *Strategic management: A stakeholder approach*, Boston: Pitman.

Global Sustainable Tourism Dashboard (n.d.) https://tourismdashboard.org/ (Accessed 15 November 2018.)

Innovation Norway (2018). Homepage. Available https://www.innovasjonnorge.no/en/start-page/

Keller, P.C. (1987) Stages of peripheral tourism development – Canada's northwest territories, *Tourism Management*, 8 (1): 20–32.

Khanal, B.R., Gan, C. and Becken, S. (2014). Tourism inter-industry linkages in the Lao PDR economy: An input output analysis, *Tourism Economics*, 20 (1): 171–194.

Larsen, R. K., Calgaro, E. and Thomalla, F. (2011) Governing resilience building in Thailand's tourism-dependent coastal communities: Conceptualising stakeholder agency in socio-ecological systems, *Global Environmental Change*, 21 (2): 481–491.

Liburd, J. and Becken, S. (2017) Values in nature conservation, tourism and UNESCO World Heritage Site stewardship, *Journal of Sustainable Tourism*, 25 (12): 1719–1735.

Lin, D. and Simmons, D. G. (2017) Structured inter-network collaboration: Public participation in tourism planning in Southern China, *Tourism Management*, 63: 315–328.

Majorca Daily Bulletin (2018) Balearic tourist tax rates from 1 May to 31 October 2018, *Majorca Daily Bulletin*, 1 May. https://www.majorcadailybulletin.com/news/local/2018/05/01/51735/tourist-tax-rates-from-may-october.html (Accessed 15 November 2018.)

McAloon, J., Simmons, D. G. and Fairweather, J. R. (1998) Kaikoura: Historical background, *Tourism Research and Education Centre Report* No. 1, Lincoln: Lincoln University, New Zealand.

Morey, J. (2016) Palma airport breaking records again, *Majorca Daily Bulletin*, 13 August. https://majorcadailybulletin.com/news/local/2017/07/29/48697/palma-airport-breaking-records-again.html (Accessed 22 September 2018.)

Moyle, C. J., Moyle, B. D. and Becken, S. (2017) A multi-sectoral model of tourism and resource sector transformation, *Tourism Recreation Research*, 42 (4): 422–435.

OECD (2001) The well-being of nations: The role of human and social capital. Paris: OECD Publishing.

OECD (2017) How's life? 2017: Measuring well-being. Paris: OECD Publishing.

Platje, J. (2008) "Institutional capital" as a factor of sustainable development - the importance of an institutional equilibrium, *Technological and Economic Development of Economy*, 14 (2): 144–150.

Rahman, M. S. -U., Simmons, D. G., Shone, M. C. and Ratna, N. (under review) Co-management of capitals for community wellbeing and sustainable tourism development: A conceptual framework. *Tourism Planning & Development*.

Shen, F., Hughey, K. F. D. and Simmons, D. G. (2008) Connecting the sustainable livelihoods approach and tourism: A review of the literature. *Journal of Hospitality and Tourism Management*, 15 (1): 19–31.

Simmons, D. G. (2017) Neoliberal politics and the fate of tourism. In R. Butler and W. Suntikul (Eds.), *Tourism and political change*, 2nd edition. Oxford, Goodfellow Publishers, pp. 9–24.

Simmons, D. G, Becken, S. and Cullen, R. (2007) Assessing tourism yield: An analysis of public sector costs and benefits. In J. Tribe and D. Airey (Eds.), *Developments in Tourism Research*, Advances in Tourism Research Series. Oxford: Elsevier, pp. 95–106.

Sleeman R. and Simmons D. G. (2004) *Tourism planning toolkit for local government*. Lincoln: Tourism Recreation Research and Education Centre, Lincoln University, New Zealand. http://www.china-up.com:8080/international/case/case/624.pdf (Accessed 15 November 2018.)

Smith, C. (2018) *Treasury living standards dashboard: Monitoring intergenerational wellbeing*. Kotata Insights. https://treasury.govt.nz/publications/commissioned-report/treasury-living-standards-dashboard-monitoring-intergenerational-wellbeing (Accessed 9 September 2018.)

Su, M. M., Wall, G. and Ma, Z. (2014). Assessing ecotourism from a multi-stakeholder perspective: Xingkai Lake National Nature Reserve, China. *Environmental Management*, 54 (5), 1190–1207.

Summers, H. (2017) Balearic Islands caps number of beds available for tourists, *The Guardian*, 10 August. https://www.theguardian.com/travel/2017/aug/10/balearic-islands-caps-number-of-beds-available-for-tourists (Accessed 12 September 2018.)

Tanasescu, M. (2017) When a river is a person: from Ecuador to New Zealand, nature gets its day in court, *The Conversation*, 19 June. http://theconversation.com/when-a-river-is-a-person-from-ecuador-to-new-zealand-nature-gets-its-day-in-court-79278 (Accessed 24 September 2018)

Tourism Industry Aotearoa (2014) *Tourism 2025: Growing value together: Whakatipu Uara Ngatahi*. http://www.tourism2025.org.nz/ (Accessed 15 November 2018.)

Tourism New Zealand (2006) Annual report 2005-2006. https://www.parliament.nz/resource/en-NZ/48DBHOH_PAP14524_1/eaa7885d17f2b3b4f328d5deca555289df30bfbd (Accessed 24 September 2018.)

Tourism New Zealand (2016) 'Mood of the nation' survey highlights tourism pressure points, 26 April. https://www.tourismnewzealand.com/news/mood-of-the-nation-survey-highlights-tourism-pressure-points/ (Accessed 15 November 2018.)

Tourism New Zealand (2017a) Four year strategic plan. https://www.tourismnewzealand.com/news/tourism-new-zealand-freshens-up-four-year-strategy/ (Accessed 15 November 2018.)

Tourism New Zealand (2017b) Annual report 2016/2017. https://www.tourismnewzealand.com/media/3191/2017-tnz-annual-report.pdf (Accessed 15 November 2018.)

United Nations World Tourism Organization (UNWTO) (1998). *Guide for local authorities on developing sustainable tourism*. Madrid: World Tourism Organization.

UNWTO (2018) Overtourism? Understanding and managing urban tourism growth beyond perceptions. Madrid: UNWTO.

UNWTO and Griffith University (2017) *Managing growth and sustainable tourism governance in Asia and the Pacific*. Madrid: UNWTO.

WTTC and McKinsey & Company (2017) *Coping with success: Managing overcrowding in tourism destinations*. London: World Travel and Tourism Council.

Marion Joppe

17 The roles of policy, planning and governance in preventing and managing overtourism

Introduction

Without a doubt, the backlash against tourism – whether due to overcrowding or an overabundance of negative impacts on residents such as rising costs, the disappearance of rental accommodation, or the spread of low quality jobs – is at least partly the result of a lack of political vision and will. Although many of the goods and services provided to satisfy tourism demand are delivered by the private sector, the public sector – composed of elected and appointed officials as well as bureaucrats – plays a key role in fostering and controlling the movement of tourists and the activities of the businesses that provide goods and services to tourists.

Balancing the needs of businesses, tourists and residents is the function of planning, and the decisions related to determining goals and selecting the methods to achieve them constitute policies. How decisions are reached, the processes used and the inclusion or exclusion of stakeholders is referred to as governance. This chapter will examine the role played by national level governments in addressing and preventing overtourism.

The growth of tourism

The 1950s saw the beginning of strong economic growth that led to a rapid expansion of the middle class, particularly in the United States. These middle class consumers were a key source of demand for travel-related services in the global economy over the next 50 years. International arrivals worldwide grew rapidly, rising from 25 million in 1950 to 166 million in 1970. As of 2018 we have surpassed 1.3 billion international visitors, with predictions of 2.4 billion by 2030 (Euromonitor International, 2018).

Today, 3.6 billion consumers are considered middle class, and this group is projected to reach 5.3 billion by 2030, with the growth occurring almost exclusively in Asia (Kharas and Hamel, 2018). With India and China accounting for half the middle class by then, it should not surprise anyone that these countries will dominate tourism demand in the years to come. As these new consumers join the ranks of international travellers, attracted by many of the same top destinations, it is little wonder that the pressure is often becoming too much for the local populations at those destinations.

https://doi.org/10.1515/9783110607369-017

In 1970s scholars began to speak out about the negative impacts of tourism. George Young, for instance, observed that a result of the over-development of the coast for tourist purposes was that the Mediterranean Sea had been damaged to the extent that in 1973 "every one of the 6,000 registered beaches in Italy was dangerously polluted and some beaches had bacteria counts five times higher than the safety limit" (1973: 157). Today, European cities are particularly impacted by tourists; their major attractions tend to be the historic centres, with their concentrations of old – even medieval – buildings and monuments, and plazas and narrow streets, which are quickly inundated by large crowds. This is the case of Barcelona, Venice, Prague and Lucerne, as described in the case studies (Chapters 9, 10, 11 and 12).

Whether listed in the Michelin Guide, Frommer's, Fodor's, Lonely Planet or any other off and online travel guides, the "must see" sites tend to be very similar. Word-of-mouth recommendations have always played a large part in tourism promotion and helped to put many "undiscovered" destinations on the dream list of visitors; electronic word-of-mouth recommendations on social media are no exception (see Chapter 5). Social media fuels travel and increases the desire of travellers to "discover" out of the way places, be the first to post about an achievement, connect with local residents or duplicate a famous image. Today, the amplification through social media of lesser-known destinations can have devastating consequences as such destinations are rarely equipped to handle a sudden onslaught of visitors (see Chapter 14).

The forces behind tourism policy

Since the early days of modern tourism, its development has been almost exclusively driven by the positive economic impacts associated with it. Therefore, at the national level the primary motivation for governments to foster tourism has tended to be to take advantage of tourism's prodigious ability to attract foreign exchange and investment, generate employment, provide tax revenues and assist with regional development. In post-war Europe, for example, governments incentivised the construction of high-end tourist accommodation to boost exports.

Although the primary motivation for governments to promote tourism is for its economic benefits, tourism is also recognised as a means to foster better mutual understanding and is therefore seen as contributing to preserving peace. "Peace", "security" and "quality of life" are the recurrent themes of declarations, treaties, acts and agreements at the international level. An example of this is the 1975 Helsinki Declaration (OSCE, 1975), which explicitly stated that the participating governments considered tourism as something that contributes to improving understanding among people, to increasing knowledge of the achievements of other countries and "to economic, social and cultural progress" (OSCE, 1975: 35). All politicians – regardless of political affiliation – ultimately promise their electorates that their policies and initiatives will improve their quality of life, whether they believe this can be achieved by easing the burden on corporate and individual taxpayers, investing in the creation of more jobs, or by creating support programmes for the more disadvantaged groups in society.

Since governments at all levels value tourism's economic contributions, they focus on increasing visitor numbers, specifically the figures for international overnight tourists, and on maximizing revenues derived from them. Tourism sector growth rates regularly exceed those of the global economy, and these are gleefully vaunted by all and sundry in the industry. For example, the World Tourism Organization noted that "International tourist arrivals (overnight visitors) increased 6% in January–June 2018 compared to the same period last year. [. . .] This represents a continuation of the strong results of 2017 (+7%) and exceeds the rate of 4% or higher growth recorded every year since 2010." (UNWTO, 2018b) Since both spending and length of stay can be directly correlated to distance travelled by source markets, tourism marketing plans tend to target long-haul tourists. Indeed, Weber et al. describe ideal tourists as "individual guests who stay longer, spend more, visit different areas and interact more with the local people" (Chapter 12: 179). Domestic tourism is also growing, and is easily five or six times as large as international tourism in terms of arrivals (Kester, 2013), and the combined pressure on societies and the environment of all these trips is making itself felt in every corner of the world.

The degree of involvement and the role that governments play in developing the loosely defined "tourism industry" depends heavily on a country's history, socio-economic development, the maturity of the industry and the political ideology of the ruling party. These factors will determine the extent to which their involvement is active or passive, and whether their actions will aim to control, support (financially or managerially), orient and/or plan the tourism market. In general, national and regional tourism policies tend to focus on improving understanding of the tourist markets and their potential, catering to their needs, and devising strategies to attract them.

Since there is no one industry called "tourism" – in spite of efforts to define it through Satellite Accounts (see Chapter 2) – but rather a complex, self-organizing network of relationships, akin to a swarm of bees or a school of fish with hundreds of thousands of individuals, it is very difficult for government to engage with relevant stakeholders. Therefore, tourism stakeholders tend to take an "association" approach: working with sector and functional associations and associations of associations. The "relevant stakeholders", however, tend to prioritise quantitative growth of tourism, not qualitative improvements in the quality of life of the resident population or in ecosystem health.

Policy documents at times address the barriers to international tourism, including lack of sufficient infrastructure (e.g. roads, rail, ports and airports), insufficient attractions, restrictive visa regulations and access limitations, but the commissioning organisation (ministry, department, etc.) actually has control over a very narrow scope of aspects. Therefore, tourism stakeholders have limited ability to influence policy in areas e.g. customs and immigration, health, education, economic development, transportation and natural resources remain marginalised

While tourism is seen as a tool in the arsenal for achieving policy goals, the policies that seek to increase the economic returns of tourism rarely seem to consider the downstream social and environmental consequences, such as congestion, undesirable tourist behaviour, crime, waste management issues and noise pollution, among others. While neoliberalism posits that the market will correct itself, an unfettered market can have devastating consequences when applied to tourism (Simmons, 2017). Examples of what results from ignoring or responding ineffectually to the fallout include the temporary closure by the Philippine government of the very popular Boracay Island (Chapter 7), the closure of Maya Bay in Thailand (Chapter 8) and the thousands of deaths annually during the Hajj in Saudi Arabia (Chapter 13). As long as success is measured in terms of increased visitors and receipts, one can expect more environmental damage and also more resentment, and even downright hostility, from local populations. Hence, tourism policy must include the checks and balances that allow the host community to share in the benefits to be derived from tourism, not just bear the costs.

Taking social and environmental factors into consideration in tourism policy making requires a "whole-of-government" approach, much as Barcelona has taken (Chapter 9), in which various government departments are brought together. This approach was recommended by the participants of the 2017 "High level meeting on tourism policies for sustainable and inclusive growth" hosted by the Organisation for Economic Co-operation and Development (OECD, 2017: 3). At this meeting, Portugal's Secretary of State for Tourism, Ana Mendes Godinho, stated that in her country, "'every minister is the minister of tourism' meaning [that] policy and regulatory decisions are considered carefully in how they might impact the tourism industry due to its vital importance to the country's economy" (TIAC, 2018). While a step in the right direction, this approach only considers the impact of each ministry on tourism and the actions by each ministry that will help sustain tourism, it does not consider the impacts of tourism on the other ministries and their portfolios.

The need for planning

Scholars have long identified the need for planning to ensure the integrated development of tourism that is responsive to community desires and needs, and the regular monitoring of key performance indicators covering all aspects of sustainability (see for instance Inskeep, 1991). While governments are increasingly happy to devolve tourism marketing to partnerships that involve public and quasi-public sector organisations and tourism business interests, they tend to keep a much firmer control over tourism development, with upper tier governments frequently overriding the wishes of local governments and communities that face the brunt of the impacts. Perhaps the best known examples of this are the hosting of hallmark events that often require billions of dollars in public infrastructure, ignoring the resident opposition to this profligate spending of tax revenues, partly in the name of enhancing the nation's image and increasing tourism (Dunn and McGuirk, 1999; Gursoy and Kendall, 2006; Giulianotti et al., 2015).

Butler (see Chapter 6) distinguishes between overtourism and overdevelopment and observes that overtourism leads to both a loss in quality of the experience for visitors and a loss of quality of life for residents, and that overtourism is largely due to the inadequacy of infrastructure, facilities and services. Ensuring that infrastructure, facilities and services are adequate to meet the needs of the increasing numbers of domestic and international visitors and those of the resident population (in a context of accelerating urbanisation) requires long-term planning.

The highly seasonal fluctuations in demand for services and facilities, experienced by most destinations, can aggravate any inadequacies. Governments can help spread demand by staggering school vacations, as Germany's Länder (regions) do (see, for example, School Holidays Europe, n.d.) or by requiring that some annual leave must be taken separately from the main holidays, as France did when it adopted a fifth week of paid vacation. Spreading demand geographically is another option in addressing overtourism, though more difficult as lack of transportation infrastructure and a lack of attractions tend to be barriers to dispersal, and both require significant investments to overcome.

Controlling supply to discourage demand is another option available to governments. Barcelona has taken the drastic step of halting further licensing and development of accommodation (Chapter 9), while Mallorca (Summers, 2017) has gone even further, with a planned reduction in the number of beds available. Many destinations are battling the spread of online short-term rental platforms, such as Airbnb, since the use of residential accommodation by tourists tends to lead to a shortage of affordable housing for residents.

Although governments can control development through regulation and licensing, to be effective they would need to be able to determine what constitutes an optimum capacity and identify when the limits to change that are acceptable to residents and visitors alike are approached. Walter Jamieson documents a number of the models that have been tested in this regard (Chapter 16).

Many issues associated with overtourism cannot be addressed at the macro level by upper tier governments as the conditions can vary vastly at the micro level, depending on the level of urbanisation, the amount and size of events and attractions, the diversity of the local population, the fragility of the natural environment, the public infrastructure in place, and ease of access, among others. At the same time, municipal governments have no say beyond their boundaries and are too often reliant on upper tier governments to help fund large infrastructure projects. Furthermore, a large portion of intra and intercontinental tourist flows are controlled by transport and tourism stakeholders, including airlines in terms of seat capacity and cost (see Chapter 11 on the impact of low-cost airlines on a destination), cruise lines in terms of ports of call, and tour operators. We see this playing out in several of the case studies: in Venice (Chapter 10), where the cruise port, outside the municipal borders, brings tens of thousands of day excursionists into the city each day; in Prague (Chapter 11), where the airport is being expanded to cope with demand even as the city centre is choking with visitors; and in Barcelona (Chapter 9), where the surrounding towns offer accommodation options, thus frustrating the efforts of the city government to control visitor numbers. These companies cannot easily be controlled and many companies, including transport and tour companies, can simply switch locations should the economic, social, environmental or political conditions in a destination no longer be optimal.

In theory at least, Barcelona is a "textbook case" of responsible tourism. The City of Barcelona was proactive by starting to plan strategically over a decade ago to "strengthen the balance between local residents and tourists while preserving the identity values of the city" (Chapter 9: 129), involving not only the community but also multiple municipal departments. It also decreased the focus on promotion and marketing by the local DMO, placing an emphasis on the management of tourism. And yet, the protests and antipathy towards tourists in Barcelona have increased to the point where the city finds itself in an almost intractable situation: those who stand to gain financially from the tourist trade do not want to see it curbed, but residents, especially those living in the areas where tourists congregate, feel crowded out and are dismayed by the drastic changes in their neighbourhoods. A survey by the city council in 2017 found that almost 60% of surveyed residents felt that "Barcelona is reaching the limit to its capacity for providing tourist services" (Ajuntament de Barcelona, 2017: 3). Yet every small "victory", like getting cruise liners to moor further away from the city and discovering thousands of illegally rented apartments, is countered by the strong year-over-year increases in visitation (e.g. a rise of 8.2% in the number of passengers on cruise ships docked at Barcelona Port between August 2017 and August 2018) (Ajuntament de Barcelona, n.d.).

Long-term planning at the national level is often decried as it is associated with communist regimes, yet many large-scale infrastructure programmes, such as the construction and expansion of major highways, rapid transit and high-speed rail, airports, etc., require planning 20 to 30 years into the future. While this type of planning will include forecasts for demand, sometimes even from tourists, they often do not consider how the improvements in access will shape and shift visitor demand (the market seizes those opportunities). Thus, there is almost no thought given to the impact on the quality of life of residents or on any changes to the identities of local communities that are an inevitable consequence. When growth is more rapid than the planning takes into account, we see not only an exacerbation of crowding, but also the failure of infrastructure, as in the case of deaths during the Hajj in Makkah (Chapter 13) where overcrowding has taken on extreme proportions. It is anticipated that the number of pilgrims will triple in the next decade, yet options for their dispersal in time and space are very limited due to the religious symbolism associated with certain sites in Makkah.

It is interesting to note that a recent publication by the UNWTO (2018a) on overtourism does not see any role for macro or meso-level planning in addressing the issue. At most, cities are encouraged to work with surrounding areas to promote alternative attractions and events and to disperse visitors seasonally, although it does call for "governance models that engage administrations at all levels (tourism and other relevant administrations), the private sector and local communities" (UNWTO, 2018: 10). There is no acknowledgement that the changing distribution of middle-class spending will have an effect on markets, and that established destinations will likely see increases in arrivals from Asia, particularly China and India, that outpace even the predicted middle class growth of 6% (Kharas and Hamel, 2018). This influx will add to the sense of overcrowding as such new entrants into the tourism market are more "visible" amongst the population, which could very well increase the sense of loss of identity of local residents at destinations, since there is a perception of greater social and cultural distance. This sentiment also correlates with the benefits and costs derived from tourism (Thyne, 2001; Zaidan, 2016) and is playing out in cities like Lucerne (Chapter 12).

Like "whole-of-government" policy and regulatory decisions, tourism strategies focus on how they impact on tourism. The foci tend to be: improving access and connectivity, streamlining visa and regulatory processes, expanding and upgrading product and experience offerings, ensuring sufficient labour including through temporary migration, and better research-driven marketing. All of these objectives will see an increase in numbers, possibly with some dispersal in time and space but with little space for resident voices, and none for those who are tourism-phobic. Furthermore, while it is generally recognised that "all strategies strongly benefit from more cooperation between administrations at multiple levels, also beyond tourism" (UNWTO, 2018: 10), such cooperation is very rarely the case.

Governance

"Governance determines who has power, who makes decisions, how other players make their voice heard and how account is rendered" (Institute on Governance, n. d.). The crux of the overtourism conundrum is that three of the four types of governance as defined by Hall (2011): *hierarchies* (state governance), *markets* (essentially private economic actors and their associations) and *networks* (dominated by various forms of public-private partnerships and associations) are dominated by actors that largely follow the dictums of a neoliberal agenda. Thus, these actors perpetuate the focus on economic growth and job creation, push for constant increases in tourist volumes and spending, and foster a business environment that is allowed to externalise social and environmental costs (Simmons, 2017).

Almost all the destinations suffering from overtourism have lost much of whatever power they had to control development and/or determine tourist flows to exogenous sources of capital (e.g. cruise lines, low cost airlines and international hotel chains). The neoliberal philosophy that took hold in the 1980's worked towards much greater liberalisation of trade, freedom of movement for capital, goods and services, deregulation and a reduction of government control and interventions as a means to increase economic growth. The signing of the General Agreement on Trade in Services (GATS) in 1995, followed by a myriad of regional trade agreements, forced the opening of more domestic markets to tourism development and foreign direct investment. The implications for tourism were problematic as these agreements reduced governmental autonomy in the delivery and provision of various social services and the management of resources. These agreements were signed at the national level and so the call that sustainable tourism development requires input from all stakeholders – formal (public, economic and non-economic institutions) and informal (social capital) institutions (see Chapter 18) – is fairly illusionary.

Governance through networks is particularly popular in tourism and can be found at every jurisdictional level, but more often than not, membership is "pay to play". This tends to limit participation to organisations that stand to gain from an increase in visitor numbers and spending. As regards the governance of marketing campaigns, which not only shape how a geographic region is portrayed but also who is targeted and the type of tourism that is promoted, the influence of the private sector leaves little room for other voices to be heard, be they residents or visitors.

Although it is recognised that governance requires government and non-government stakeholders to voluntarily collaborate through a complex web of both horizontal and vertical networks, private citizens and their associations in their capacity as taxpayers, workers and residents have little meaningful input into policy-making deliberations, especially at the regional and national levels. At best, they are "consulted" and requested to provide feedback on proposals that are fairly well advanced. Even their elected officials in local authorities can only exercise the powers granted to them by senior levels of government, severely constraining their ability to avoid the destruction of what are ultimately the primary attractors for tourists – the local environment and culture. And the negative impacts that inevitably accompany an ever-increasing number of international and domestic tourists are borne by local residents.

The governmental domains that impact tourism (e.g. the departments of transportation, natural resources, labour, health and safety, customs and immigration, consumer protection, culture, parks and recreation) tend to be hierarchical, with their own narrow agendas. Therefore, even when tourism agencies are inclined to drive positive social and environmental change by providing a more meaningful role for host communities, their counterparts at the national and state levels are rarely be open to including these voices. For example, a ban on climbing Uluru (formerly known as "Ayers Rock"), Australia, was achieved, after years of lobbying, by the Anangu people, the traditional owners, to whom Uluru has deep cultural meaning (Hitch and Hose, 2017), but the announcement of the ban by the Uluru-Kata Tjuta National Park Board of management engendered much controversy among businesses and national government officials, who are more interested in keeping the marketing draw Uluru represents than in respecting the wishes of the Anangu people. Similarly, tourists have been ignoring the many signs put up asking them not to climb this sacred site, contributing to the perceived disrespect for this "place of Law" (Wilson 2018, as quoted in Henschke, 2018, 1917).

Conclusion

Overtourism starts with short-term thinking on the part of politicians too focused on re-election and who have bought into the notion of unrestrained free-market capitalism, and is fostered by the ignorance of bureaucrats and the lack of courage to confront politicians about long term consequences, as well as by greed on the part of businesses, which are more concerned with grabbing as much as possible of the shared resources for their own profit while externalizing as many of the costs as possible.

The backlash to tourism did not happen overnight: it has built up slowly over decades (see, for example, Doxey, 1975). Today it is accelerating, however, as ever more people crowd into the same spaces. A piecemeal approach will not solve the problems. Piecemeal measures range from the ludicrous, e.g. stopping people taking beach sand in Sardinia (Street, 2018) and prohibiting street snacking in the historic district of Florence, Italy (O'Hare, 2018), to the extreme, e.g. banning new tourist shops in the centre of Amsterdam, Netherlands (Boztas, 2017). Addressing the issue of overtourism requires a transformation in how the capitalistic forces driving tourism's growth are harnessed. The focus must shift from raising tourist numbers and receipts to improving the quality of resident life and of tourism experiences, with a planning horizon that is at least 20 years into the future to anticipate the infrastructure, facilities and services needed by increasing local populations and visitor numbers.

This shift is gathering momentum, with the neoliberal market economy coming under increasing criticism in recent years, including from business leaders themselves, and viable alternative models and approaches being proposed. These include: "conscious capitalism", which proposes to "elevate humanity through business" (Conscious Capitalism, n.d.); social enterprises or cause-driven businesses, which aim to maximise improvements in social and environmental well-being; Bcorporations (a certification), which "consider the impact of their decisions on their workers, customers, suppliers, community, and the environment" (Bcorporation, n.d.); a "circular economy", which proponents say will "redefine growth, focusing on positive society-wide benefits. It entails gradually decoupling economic activity from the consumption of finite resources, and designing waste out of the system" (Ellen Macarthur Foundation, n.d.); and the "Economy for the Common Good", which "advocates a more ethical economic model, in which the wellbeing of people and the environment become the ultimate goal of business" (Economy for the Common Good, n.d.). All of these approaches challenge the short-term, profit-motivated approach to business that has greatly enriched humanity and driven the growth of the middle classes, but has been accompanied by environmental destruction, social stress and market failures.

With the world population fast approaching 9 billion, and with it likely to reach 11 billion by the turn of the century, and with more and more people having the means to travel domestically and/or internationally, we must recognise the pressure each of us exerts on the planet and societies in tourist destinations, and decide what we deem important and what we are willing to do without, and fundamentally change our mindsets and behaviour to ensure sustainability. Some paradigm shifts are already underway. Among young people, for instance, there is a tendency to be more minimalist, less focused on the acquisition of material goods and more interested in experiences, rather than traditional mass tourism.

Technology is touted by some as an enabler of making alternatives to traditional mass tourism more accessible, re-distributing arrivals temporally and geographically, and even as a substitute for physical travel, and technological solutions are being hotly pursued by many destinations as part of "smart cities" initiatives. Gretzel, and Scarpino Johns (2018) call for a smart tourism mindset to enhance destination resilience. This requires not only that the physical structures, means of transportation, electricity grid and utilities as well as closed circuit cameras all communicate with each other as well as with users, but that they do so with technologies that are "smart" in that they can adapt, sense, learn, anticipate and predict, and ultimately self-organise and even self-sustain (Derzko, 2007). The sharing and analysis of the data collected in this process would allow organisations to co-create value for consumers through the personalisation of recommendations and notifications. Boes, et al. emphasise "conceptualizing the smart tourism business ecosystem as involving a multitude of traditional and non-traditional stakeholders who, through participatory governance, are encouraged to co-create the smart tourism value propositions" (cited in Gretzel and Scarpino Johns, 2018: 7).

There is no magic solution to overtourism. Addressing the issues will require a combination of a compelling vision of well-being for the resident population and long-term strategic planning for tourism, managed using a governance model that is inclusive horizontally as well as vertically, and pays more attention to maximising social and environmental well-being than to the profit motive. While we can envision a future where smart cities will deliver offerings that allow for tourist, host and resident experience enhancement and sustainability goals at the destination level, this is a longer-term solution to addressing overtourism. It is also unclear to what extent this model is scalable to the regional or national levels, which play a large role in exacerbating the pressures at the local level.

References

Ajuntament de Barcelona (n.d.) Tourist activity. https://ajuntament.barcelona.cat/turisme/en/tourist-activity (Accessed 30 October 2018.)

Ajuntament de Barcelona (2017) Opinion of Barcelona's residents. Selected results of the Survey on Perception of Tourism in Barcelona. https://ajuntament.barcelona.cat/turisme/en/opinion-barcelonas-residents (Accessed 25 September 2018).

Bcorporation (n.d.) A global community of leaders. https://bcorporation.net/ (Accessed 30 October 2018.)

Boztas, S. (2017) Amsterdam bans new tourist shops to combat 'Disneyfication' of city, *The Telegraph*, 5 October. https://www.telegraph.co.uk/news/2017/10/05/amsterdam-bans-new-tourist-shopsto-combatdisneyfication-city/ (Accessed 30 October 2018.)

Conscious Capitalism (n.d.) Welcome to Conscious Capitalism. https://www.consciouscapitalism.org/ (Accessed 30 October 2018.)

Derzko, W. (2007) Smart technologies, Presentation at the Ontario Centers of Excellence, Discovery 07 To NEXT, Toronto, 1 May. http://archives.ocediscovery.com/2007/presentations/Session3WalterDrezkoFINAL.pdf

Doxey, G. V. (1975) A causation theory of visitor-resident irritants, methodology and research inferences. In Conference Proceedings: Sixth Annual Conference of Travel Research Association, San Diego, pp. 195–198.

Dunn, K. M. and McGuirk, P. M. (1999). Hallmark events. In R. Cashman and A. Hughes (Eds.), *Staging the Olympics: The event and its impact*. Sydney: University of Wollongong, http://ro.uow.edu.au/cgi/viewcontent.cgi?article=3275&context=sspapers (Accessed 30 October 2018.)

Ellen Macarthur Foundation (n.d.) What is a circular economy? https://www.ellenmacarthurfoundation.org/circular-economy/concept (Accessed 30 October 2018.)

Euromonitor International (2018) *Megatrends shaping the future of travel*. London: Euromonitor International.

Gursoy, D. and Kendall, K. W. (2006) Hosting mega events: Modeling locals' support. *Annals of Tourism Research*, 33 (3): 603–623.

Giulianotti, R., Armstrong, G., Hales, G. and Hobbs, D. (2015) Sport mega-events and public opposition: A sociological study of the London 2012 Olympics, *Journal of Sport and Social Issues*, 39 (2): 99–119.

Gretzel, U. and Scarpino Johns, M. (2018) Destination resilience and smart tourism destinations, *Tourism Review International*, 22 (3–4): 263–276.

Hall C. M. (2011) A typology of governance and its implications for tourism policy analysis, *Journal of Sustainable Tourism*, 19 (4–5): 437–457.

Henschke, R. (2018, June 28). Banning the Uluru climb: 'This rock means everything to us', BBC, https://www.bbc.com/news/world-australia-44365871 (Accessed 30 October 2018.)

Hitch, G. and Hose. N. (2017) Uluru climbs banned from October 2019 after unanimous board decision to 'close the playground', ABC News, 1 November. http://www.abc.net.au/news/2017-11-01/uluru-climbs-banned-after-unanimous-board-decision/9103512 (Accessed 5 November 2017.)

Inskeep, E. (1991) *Tourism planning: an integrated and sustainable development approach*. New York: Van Nostrand Reinhold.

Institute on Governance (n.d.) Defining governance. https://iog.ca/what-is-governance (Accessed 10 September 2018.)

Kester, J.G.C. (2013). 2012 International Tourism Results and Prospects for 2013, UNWTO News Conference HQ, Madrid, Spain 29 January 2013.

Kharas, H. and Hamel, K. (2018). A global tipping point: Half the world is now middle class or wealthier. The Brookings Institution, 27 September, https://www.brookings.edu/blog/future-development/2018/09/27/a-global-tipping-point-half-the-world-is-now-middle-class-or-wealthier/. (Accessed 28 September 2018.)

Norman, J. (2017) Why we are banning tourists from climbing Uluru, *The Conversation*, 6 November. https://theconversation.com/why-we-are-banning-tourists-from-climbing-uluru-86755 (Accessed 10 December 2017.)

O'Hare, M. (2018) Italy's Florence bans eating in the street, *CNN Travel*, 6 September. https://edition.cnn.com/travel/article/florence-street-eating-ban/index.html (Accessed 30 October 2018.)

Organisation for Economic Co-operation and Development (OECD) (2017) Meeting summary: High level meeting on tourism policies for sustainable and inclusive growth, 2–3 October, OECD, Paris. http://www.oecd.org/cfe/tourism/OECD_High-Level-Meeting-on-Tourism_Meeting-Summary.pdf (Accessed 30 October 2018.)

Organization for Security and Co-operation in Europe (OSCE) (1975) *Final Act of Helsinki*, Conference on Security and Co-operation in Europe, Helsinki. https://www.osce.org/helsinki-final-act (Accessed 30 October 2018.)

School Holidays Europe (n.d.) School Holidays Germany. https://www.schoolholidayseurope.eu/school-holidays-germany/#summer-holiday (Accessed 30 October 2018.)

Simmons, D. G. (2017) Neoliberal politics and the fate of tourism. In R. W. Butler and W. Suntikul (Eds.), *Tourism and Political Change* (Second Edition), Oxford: Goodfellow Publishers, pp. 9–24.

Summers, H. (2017) Balearic Islands caps number of beds available for tourists, *The Guardian*, 10 August. https://www.theguardian.com/travel/2017/aug/10/balearic-islands-caps-number-of-beds-available-for-tourists (Accessed 5 September 2018.)

Street, F. (2018) Sardinia fines sand thieves up to $3,480, *CNN Travel*, 9 August. https://edition.cnn.com/travel/article/sardinia-sand-theft-fines/index.html (Accessed 30 October 2018.)

Thyne, M. (2001) Social and cultural distance: Its effect on host tolerance of tourism, PhD Dissertation, Department of Tourism, University of Otago, New Zealand.

TIAC (2018) TIAC calls for whole-of-government approach to tourism, TIAC Talk Articles, 16 August. https://tinyurl.com/y83qcgk6 (Accessed 17 August 2018.)

United Nations (1948) Universal Declaration of Human Rights. http://www.un.org/en/universal-declaration-human-rights/ (Accessed 30 October 2018.)

UNWTO (2018) Overtourism'? Understanding and Managing Urban Tourism Growth beyond Perceptions, World Tourism Organization (UNWTO), the Centre of Expertise Leisure, Tourism & Hospitality (CELTH) of Breda University of Applied Sciences and the European Tourism Futures Institute (ETFI) of NHL Stenden, University of Applied Sciences. UNWTO: Madrid.

World Tourism Organization (UNWTO) (2013) *Domestic tourism in Asia and the Pacific*. Madrid: UNWTO.

World Tourism Organization (UNWTO) (2018a) *Overtourism? Understanding and managing urban tourism growth beyond perceptions*. Madrid: UNWTO.

World Tourism Organization (UNWTO) (2018b) *World Tourism Barometer*, 16 (4).

Young, G. (1973) *Tourism: Blessing or blight?* London: Pelican.

Zaidan, E. (2016) The impact of cultural distance on local residents perception of tourism development: The case of Dubai in UAE, *Tourism*, 64 (1): 109–126.

Rachel Dodds and Richard W. Butler

18 Conclusion

Destinations of all kinds face, and almost certainly will continue to experience, overtourism. Global tourism arrival figures will continue to grow and the ease of travelling will amplify the intensity of tourism. This is the crux of the issue and one that can be mitigated but perhaps not fully controlled. The characteristics and contributing factors may vary but destinations are facing similar situations. No one should forget nor deny that the sheer increase in the numbers of visitors and intensity of tourism is a key part of the problem.

Tourism is an industry that has historically been relatively poorly managed, has ignored sustainability principles and has instead prioritised maximising the numbers of visitors and economic gain over community and environmental considerations. Complaints about tourists, their numbers, their effects and their behaviour are long standing but have been ignored almost everywhere. All too often, local, regional and national governments turn a blind eye to the problems. Tourism is often ad lib, unplanned and municipalities and other tourism stakeholders are naïve in thinking that they can deal with overtourism *when it happens.*

The case studies presented in this volume are not claimed to be all-encompassing but they do provide a level of comparison for other destinations globally. These examples make it clear that overtourism is more of a relative problem than an absolute one, in that much depends on characteristics of affected destinations, their residents and the relative scale of tourism in those communities. In other words, overtourism is site specific. Like sustainable development, each place is unique, and different factors cause overtourism. In some places, smaller numbers can have with a noticeable and irritating impact, e.g. Skye (Chapter 14), while in other places larger numbers cause issues, usually with associated tourist behaviour problems, e.g. Barcelona and Venice (Chapters 9 and 10). In some places, the issues are very specific, e.g. the visible increase in tour buses in Lucerne (Chapter 12), inadequate facilities in Skye (Chapter 14), and the overcrowding in the small town centre of Prague (Chapter 11).

In all of the examples assessed, it is clear that economic priorities have overridden social and environmental concerns, thus making a mockery of claims of sustainable tourism and sustainable development. Nearly always, external forces are involved, in marketing, transporting and delivering tourists who have little involvement with local residents or facilities. Tourism businesses drive demand and supply tourism products and services, but they do not consider the impact of these products and services on other stakeholders. This inevitably results in an imbalance. Almost all of the private sector stakeholders involved in tourism development are focused solely on growth and this, when combined with the short term views of businesses and political authorities, inevitably results in the large scale development of tourism,

https://doi.org/10.1515/9783110607369-018

with scant regard to potential problems and negative impacts. This is despite the appearance of a large number of tourism plans and policies with a declared aim of sustainable development.

Much of the responsibility for the appearance of overtourism must rest with governments at all levels, from national agencies promoting tourism for the foreign exchange and regional authorities using tourism to generate employment, to local governments keen to gain local taxation benefits.

Clearly, overtourism is unsustainable and is not "responsible tourism" in any form, but it is also more than "mass tourism". Properly managed, mass tourism need not be excessively unsustainable and may be less harmful environmentally and socially on a per capita basis than some other forms of supposed "enlightened" tourism, which may involve long haul travel and considerable penetration of remote areas (e.g. "nature tourism"). Sustainability has been discussed for decades yet buy-in and application has been slow – possibly due to the concept being vague (Butler, 1993; 1998) or many people using the word "sustainable" as a term for financial viability rather than in a triple bottom line (environmental, social, economic) sense (Dodds and Butler, 2009). Fundamentally, making tourism more sustainable is about having a tourism industry that *thrives* rather than *grows*. Without this clear distinction, problems will continue.

It is rare that those responsible for driving tourist demand have the vision, authority and power to guide the tourism industry towards sustainable outcomes. Furthermore, even in centres such as Barcelona (Chapter 9), where there has been a relatively long history (over a decade) of policies and measures taken to control tourism development, protests against the excesses of overtourism are now being made with increasing vigour, even in 2018. In places such as Calvia, Spain (Dodds, 2007), where there has been true leadership, local power over all aspects of tourism is missing and therefore control and true governance are not being seen.

Solutions to overtourism issues

A multitude of actions have been proposed and tried by destinations to mitigate the effects of overtourism, with varying success. While a few destinations, for example Whistler, Canada, have introduced measures aimed at developing a sustainable future based on tourism (Sheppard, 2017; Gill and Williams, 2018), in almost every case the measures have only been instituted after destinations have been negatively affected by overtourism, and mostly only after residents of those communities have protested, visibly and vociferously.

The expectations of visitors and residents, in terms of their demands and behaviour and how they think tourism will benefit them and what impacts it will have, determine whether tourism is seen in a positive or negative light. Clearly, expectations differ from stakeholder to stakeholder and politics are rarely considered. When those who are driving demand consider their own goals rather than what would develop a thriving community, imbalance is bound to result. As the tourism experience is influenced by multiple players (e.g. transport is almost always nationally and/or privately run), it makes it hard for a total governance approach, let alone a complete vision for effective management to be introduced and to be implemented properly. Such a state of affairs would tend to suggest that the steps proposed and taken have not been, and are unlikely to be, successful in their current forms in preventing overtourism. In the discussion below, the most frequently cited measures for dealing with overtourism are briefly outlined.

Dispersal of tourists

Redistribution of visitors over space and over time has been a popular suggestion, but it has not really worked except perhaps at a truly local level. This is because tourism is place specific and attractions usually cannot be changed. For example, iconic tourist attractions such as Big Ben in London or the Eiffel Tower in Paris are located in a specific area, in city centres, and cannot be relocated. Visitors who want to see such attractions will not agree to visit alternatives. There is no other Venice (replicas in hotels in Las Vegas and Macao are not considered to be meaningful substitutes for the real thing), so redistributing tourists who wish to visit Venice does not diminish demand for Venice, it simply generates visitation to other places. As well, many visitors probably would not want to go elsewhere because other attractions and facilities are found at or near the main attractions. Another consideration is that the number of tourists that would have to be dispersed is often too great for any area that is expected to receive them, with the result being that the issue of overtourism is simply spread to other areas. Thus, the redistribution of tourists is rather like moving deckchairs on the sinking Titanic: it doesn't address the underlying issue. Moreover, it possibly antagonizes locals at both destinations. The communities at new destinations may not wish for large numbers of visitors, and some stakeholders in the original destinations may regret losing some of their customers.

Dispersing tourism over time, i.e. tackling the "seasonality problem", is even more difficult. Considerable literature on seasonality exists (see, for example, essays in Baum and Lundtorp, 2001) because many people going to destinations at the same time, in what is known as the "high season", is seen as a problem. This pattern is not accidental; people travel at similar times for various reasons, including the season (e.g. summer), school holidays and special events, and such patterns are extremely difficult to change. It has been shown that trying to stimulate off-season visits to a destination can actually increase visits in the peak season rather than decreasing them because of additional publicity about the destination (Butler,

2001). Moreover, established holiday patterns cannot be changed easily because of institutional constraints, such as fixed dates for school holidays, a factor recognised in tour company pricing mechanisms. While shoulder seasons can sometimes be extended, this may in fact cause overtourism to develop beyond the peak season, thus aggravating the problem rather than resolving it. Destination communities often welcome the shoulder and off seasons as periods free from the pressures of tourism experienced during the peak season and welcome the resulting temporary decline in numbers. One study on seasonality in northern Europe concluded that

> all evidence is against any serious attempt to promote a resort as an off-season destination. [...] The major recommendation is to accept seasonality as a fact – not as a problem (Lundtorp et al., 2001: 103).

Thus, dispersal of tourists, even if the visitors are willing to go to less well-known places at less than optimal times, a doubtful proposition at best, is unlikely to be successful to a significant degree at almost any scale. If a destination wishes to disperse tourists, then considerations should be made for how, when and where these tourists will go. Positive efforts to use sustainable transportation to address areas of congestion are one way and promoting lesser known destinations capable of receiving more tourists is another. Many countries or regions have areas that would benefit from tourism, yet they may be less accessible and therefore transport, infrastructure and the visitor experience must be carefully thought out. In all cases, upstream planning should be undertaken to ensure the problem is not just duplicated in another location.

De-marketing

A softer, less direct approach to tackling overtourism is de-marketing. This is only realistic in areas that can afford to experience a reduction in numbers of visitors or which do not want additional growth. De-marketing requires those stakeholders in a position of power to decide when 'enough is enough', which, given the multiple different positions and ambitions held in destinations, is difficult to determine. Furthermore, de-marketing is difficult to achieve because once demand for a destination has been established, a significantly better alternative must be provided to lure tourists away from the original attraction, otherwise an entire region, rather than just a specific destination, may lose tourists, which may not be a desired outcome.

Well-known places may well be too famous for de-marketing to be effective, as they have often engaged in continuous marketing and reputation building for many years, and consequently feature on travel "bucket lists", which have firmly romanticised such destinations (List Challenges, n.d.). This process of induced fame and desire to visit is reinforced by media inputs, such as from the 2007 movie of the same title (*The Bucket List*), as well as peer pressure from social media, which may well be the most influential factor in a decision to visit a specific destination in the modern era (Chapter 5).

It is vital that de-marketing should not eliminate the overall appeal of a destination, unless the destination has decided to end tourism completely. Replacing a positive image with a negative one is not likely to be well-received or supported by all stakeholders, so de-marketing or de-promoting a destination should only be done with a specific target in mind and probably only for a specific period, so no permanent damage is done to a destination's image and appeal. Additionally, tour operators should take responsibility for taking their clients to different locations and providing education regarding why they are doing so. De-marketing is probably most effective when specific tourist groups or segments are the problem, as action can be focused and clear in terms of target, e.g. large group tours in Lucerne (Chapter 12). The more specific a campaign is, the more likely it is to have success in reducing a particular market segment.

Responsible marketing to attract a different type of visitor

There has been much discussion in destinations such as Amsterdam, Barcelona and Nova Scotia, Canada, of attracting a certain *type* of visitor or niche market segment of "good" travellers. This category is generally comprised of high-yield, longer-stay tourists that are socially and environmentally conscious (see Hansla et al., 2008; Dodds et al., 2010; Cohen et al., 2014; Buffa, 2015; Pulido-Fernandez and Lopez-Sanchez, 2016; Nickerson et al., 2016). Although this segment may exist, it is small relative to total numbers of tourists, and travel behaviour is not the same for each tourist on every trip. Thus, this segment may bring a new set of issues. Furthermore, curbing the numbers of this type of visitor is never highlighted, usually because every destination wants more of these. Therefore, an alternative approach to de-marketing is to market more responsibly. Under this approach, media writers, bloggers, film crews and other influencers have to take responsibility – informed by destinations – for educating both tourists and tourism providers. This is necessary because in many cases films and other media (e.g. *Poldark*, filmed in Cornwall, England; *Harry Potter*, filmed in Scotland; and *The Beach*, filmed in Thailand) have created and boosted demand for visitation to the sites of filming. People go to both the location in which filming took place, as well as what they think is the "real" location (Beeton, 2016; Agarwal and Shaw, 2017), which contributes to too many people visiting places that lack the capacity to handle them. Although there has been no shortage of discussion about making tourists more responsible, there is little focus on marketing responsible behaviour and this needs to change. One such case is Amsterdam's recent "Enjoy & Respect" campaign, which focuses specifically on male visitors between the ages of 18 and 34, making it clear that behaviour like public urination is not only unacceptable, but will also cost them money (Iamsterdam, 2018).

Limiting numbers

Limiting visitor numbers to attractions, and even to entire destinations, is a solution that may be applicable in some situations and can be successful if the steps taken to achieve this are seen to be sensible, transparent and fair. Limits are accepted for many other things, such as sports and music events, so applying the same process to museums and town centres should also be seen as appropriate. Limiting the number of cruise ships and/or passengers is possible in some locations, as is currently practised in Orkney and the Bahamas, and in Dubrovnik, Croatia, where there is a limit of two ships per day and a maximum of 5000 passengers (Simmonds, 2018), which is aimed to address the impact of large ships on a relatively small area (see Fig. 18.1). Such actions need coordination between operators of ports and other relevant agencies and authorities. Sometimes regional or national authorities will have to intervene if there is no agreement between local authorities and the agencies or private operators. For example, in Venice continued hotel development beyond the city boundaries will enable more and more people to visit the city, almost entirely in the form of day trips, and preventing such a process, halting further development and limiting further growth of day-trippers, will need regional government coordination and cooperation between the stakeholders.

Fig. 18.1: Dubrovnik town with cruise ship (photo credit: Rachel Dodds).

Situations in which the numbers of tourists of specific nationalities have increased rapidly often reflect changes in host countries' visa requirements and other policies. For example, one reason Thailand became overwhelmed with Chinese visitors was that Thailand was one of the first countries to relax visa restrictions for them (Chapter 8). The resolution of such cases requires cooperation at both national and international levels. In some cases, if overtourism problems are to be avoided, it may be necessary to impose or reimpose limits or quotas on visitors from specific countries, however politically unattractive such an approach may be.

Designing effective policies to reduce visitor numbers also requires accurate data. As large booking operations such as Booking.com and Airbnb have much better and more comprehensive data on visitor numbers than municipalities, municipalities should work with them to understand trends and visitation patterns. While many DMOs do not consider such booking platforms as tourism stakeholders, this is a mistake. Their data is much more sophisticated than that held by most DMOs and they are often willing to work with municipalities to make data available for local purposes.

Facility provision

An approach to addressing some of the issues associated with overtourism, such as insufficient toilets and parking for tourists, is to simply provide such facilities. This pragmatic approach recognises that it is no longer good enough to assume nothing specific needs to be done to meet the demands of increasing numbers of tourists and to assume that the local residents and the private sector can provide everything. Municipalities need to provide facilities such as public toilets, medical aid, car parks, transport, assistance, security and accessibility installations, in adequate quantities, even if the costs of such provision are considerable. This is the approach taken by Saudi Arabia in Makkah (Chapter 13) and by Boracay following the closure of the island (Chapter 7). To avoid such provision is both short-sighted and eventually expensive, both in terms of lost visitors (as the quality of the tourist experience declines) and because the costs of refitting and adding facilities after development has occurred are always higher than providing the appropriate facilities and services before development takes place. Funding such initiatives, however, can be expensive and using the approach of mandatory contributions towards facility provisions where new hotels or developers fund a portion of these added facilities may be a solution.

Implementation needs to be well organised and any facilities must be purpose built and designed to handle actual and future numbers. Municipalities need to allocate funds for such purposes and ensure tax structures are in place to support the upkeep of these facilities, many of which would be used by local residents as well as tourists. One way of securing such funds is by local bed taxes and similar measures. Such measures, however, need to be implemented with full government support. The "eco tax" imposed in Calvià failed mainly because of poor implementation and lack of support from senior levels of government (Dodds, 2007). Local taxes have been successful in other places, such as Porto, Portugal, for example, where a municipal tourist tax was introduced to "consolidate Porto as an attractive and sustainable city" (Câmara Municipal do Porto, 2018). The rate was set at 2 EUR per person per overnight stay, up to a maximum of 14 EUR (seven nights). Disabled travellers and those travelling for medical reasons are exempt, as are those under the age of 14 (Câmara Municipal do Porto, 2018).

For such schemes to be successful and for the benefits of tourism to reach those who most need it, cooperation between municipalities is essential. In some situations it may be best to avoid providing certain services. For example, Loop Head in County Clare, Ireland, made a conscious decision to not open a café or gift shop when opening the local lighthouse to the public in order that the nearby village of Kilbaha would gain business and employment opportunities. Additionally, deliberate efforts were made to ensure tourism in the area does not cater to the mass market. As outlined in their tourism policy:

> We have also been insistent from the start that the area would not be developed in any way for the mass market such as tour bus operators. We have lobbied the council to ensure that there would be no road widening or passing bays placed along the coast to make coach access easier and at the lighthouse we insisted that the car parking facility would only accommodate car traffic. (Loop Head Tourism, n.d.)

While such actions will not solve the problems of overtourism, they may help avoid new problems or may mitigate them.

Imposition of controls

When excessive numbers of tourists visit destinations, it may be necessary to adopt measures to mitigate the effects of crowding, and thus prevent busy destinations from experiencing overtourism. For example, dynamic pricing and pre-purchasing of tickets, and reserved and timed entry to facilities and galleries may ease congestion. The latter measure has been introduced in Florence and other cities. Other controls may be needed to address problems created by tourists, such as littering and blocking of roads. For example, in 2017 Florence began hosing down cathedral steps to stop visitors eating there and leaving a mess behind them (Ahluwalia, 2017), and Venice plans to limit sitting on bridges because tourists disrupt the flow of foot traffic (Carey, 2018).

Controls need to be appropriate, transparent, justified and explained so that tourists and local residents can understand why they are being imposed. Without such clarity, resentment and less desirable behaviour may result. When controls are implemented, coordination and monitoring must be effective and followed through. Failure in coordination could result in more local initiatives, which may be successful but which may also result in a backlash and eventual economic downturn. Tour operators must be involved in discussions as they are increasingly concerned about the visitor experience. If tour companies feel their customers are being unfairly treated by such measures, they may well remove destinations from their offerings which, while reducing tourist numbers, may not be the result desired by any of the parties involved.

Information/education

Another way of mitigating the impacts of overtourism is to provide tourists with information and education. To be effective, this information must be specifically designed for actual problems and carefully orchestrated, rather than just talked about. However, although education is often put forth as the solution, there are few examples of success. For example, globally, governments spent 413 billion United States dollars in 2011 on tourism marketing and infrastructure (WTTC, 2012) but little was seen in terms of efforts to encourage or require more responsible tourism behaviour. Signs, apps and information pamphlets have little chance of changing tourist behaviour unless they are part of the overall desired tourist experience. That is, unless such education and information contributes to the visitor experience, there is little acknowledgement or buy-in to the desired action (e.g. reuse of hotel towels) and visitors will not cease their problematic behaviour. Iceland has developed the "Iceland Academy", using humour marketing videos to educate visitors on everything from dressing properly for Icelandic weather to how to take "safe selfies" (Jardine, 2016). Nudge marketing has also had some success in the case of environmentally appropriate behaviour. For example, Vanoise National Park in France placed little wooden blocks in tourist accommodation suggesting that viewing the stars at night is more spectacular when the lights are off (see Fig. 18.2). This type of education encourages positive behaviour rather than discouraging negative activities.

When accommodation providers in Tofino, Canada, banned the use of hot tubs during a 2009 water shortage (CBC News, 2009), guests cooperated because the providers explained the reasons for it when guests checked in. In all cases, clarity, focus and transparency are essential if education and information are to be effective in changing the behaviour and expectations of visitors and residents.

Taking a long-term view in planning and management

As discussed in Chapter 2, one of the key enablers of overtourism is a short-term view. A long-term view is therefore essential in preventing overtourism. It needs to be integrated, however, with appropriate action, and the views of all stakeholders must be incorporated in planning. Local residents are well able to appreciate the need for a long-term view, as shown in research on Whistler (Sheppard, 2017) and

Fig. 18.2: Vanoise National Park: Turn out your lights to light up our stars (photo credit: Rachel Dodds).

the Isle of Skye (Chapter 14). Furthermore, plans must be implemented, as atourist plans and sustainability statements and documents are not worth the paper they are written on unless they are implemented.

The TALC model (Chapter 6) is a useful tool for illustrating the potential direction of destinations and the stages of development in which care needs to be taken about further tourism development. While there has been ample work done on determining indicators for sustainable tourism (Laimer, 2017), these can be complex and expensive to monitor, and are therefore often ignored or not applied. Given that most enterprises require business plans with goals and specific objectives, there is no reason why tourism plans cannot also have specific, measurable, realistic and timely objectives and indicators. The failure of governments to produce these is a further cause of resentment and anger amongst residents of tourist destinations, who have to suffer the consequences of inadequate foresight and planning and may have to adjust their own behaviour accordingly (Ap and Crompton 1993).

As almost all expressions of opposition to overtourism involve concerns expressed by local residents, it is clear that any attempts at alleviating or avoiding overtourism (including policies and plans) should include input from residents. It is necessary for decision makers at all levels to support the residents of destination communities to maintain the quality of their lives and their communities when they feel that they are threatened by excessive and inappropriate tourism development, i.e. overtourism. To fail to do so invites the kind of sentiment expressed in graffiti, "Why call it tourist season if we can't shoot them?" (López Díaz, 2017).

Although many destinations conduct visitor exit surveys, residents' views are rarely solicited. Ljubljana, Slovenia, is an exception, and has been collecting data on resident attitudes that have highlighted issues related to visitation growth and disruption (Mihalic and Kuščer, 2018). The University of Ljubljana, in cooperation with the local government, has completed two surveys – one in low season and one in high season (summer). Too often, the only surveys that try to ascertain the views of residents about tourists and tourism in their communities are by academics and the results not widely disseminated to the industry and governments involved. Things may be changing, however, as a consulting company in Brussels is now advertising services to gather information on overtourism via resident surveys (TCI Research, n.d.).

It has been clear for a long time that destination residents vary in their responses and strategies with regard to tourism in their community. Ap and Crompton (1993) identified four types of responses that residents in North American communities have in response to disturbances by tourism: embracing tourism, tolerating tourism, adjusting to tourism and withdrawing from contact with tourism. Similar findings were made by Viero (2003) in the context of the Spanish pilgrimage town of Santiago de Compostela. Butler (1975) identified similar types of responses, but found that when residents experience negative impacts of tourism and tourists they often take what they consider to be appropriate and justified actions, changing their behaviour and, in some cases, trying to change the behaviour of tourists (e.g. removing the tourists' stone cairns in Skye, as noted in Chapter 14).

Resilience rather than sustainability

The arguments in favour of taking a more sustainable approach to tourism have gained great popularity since the publication of *Our Common Future* (WCED, 1987) despite the oft-mentioned point that tourism does not feature in that report. Governments and agencies at all levels have signed up to the concept of sustainable development and much improvement in the operations of services and facilities has undoubtedly taken place as a result. There is, however, no sign that tourism as a whole has become significantly more sustainable over the past three decades. Indeed, mass tourism has continued to grow and remains by far the predominant form of tourism throughout the world. As noted above, while mass tourism and overtourism are not synonymous (overtourism can occur in the absence of mass tourism and mass tourism does not necessarily constitute overtourism), mass tourism is clearly not what is generally meant by sustainable tourism (although mass tourists may be less harmful to the environment on a per capita basis than some niche forms of tourism that involve long haul flights). As admirable and sensible as sustainable tourism is as a concept, its implementation has been limited and flawed. It can therefore be argued that in the context of overtourism prevention and mitigation, it would be much more appropriate to shift the focus to the concept of resilience, and to manage destinations accordingly.

Resilience entered the tourism lexicon relatively recently. Articles on the subject began to appear around a decade ago, with increasing frequency, and in the past year four books were published on the subject (Butler, 2017; Cheer and Lew, 2017; Lew and Cheer, 2017; and Hall et al., 2018). These represent a body of research that argues that improving the resilience of a community to withstand the shock of development (such as from tourism) is probably the most appropriate action to enable communities to survive in the long term. Tourism, when properly designed and managed, can also aid in building resilience in communities against other shocks (such as natural disasters). Many of the issues discussed in the case studies in this volume are the result of communities being poorly prepared for the impacts of tourism, particularly, but not exclusively, large-scale tourism, on their infrastructure, environment and quality of life. Building adaptability to change and resilience to shocks would seem a sensible approach for all destination communities to follow, as this would involve taking positive, proactive steps to prevent overtourism.

Conclusion: we have seen the enemy and it is us

Tourism will not cease; this has been proven time and time again through the resilience of destinations that have faced adversity in many forms. Overtourism is probably here to stay also, at least in a significant number of locations, as tourist numbers overall are going to continue to rise. There is no simple solution for how to mitigate or prevent overtourism and places that have tried by keeping prices high to limit tourism (e.g. Bhutan, Switzerland) have not been entirely successful. Moreover, the belief that dispersing visitors and the use of technology to time visitor entry will solve the problems has proven false.

There is, perhaps, a potential silver lining in the dark cloud of overtourism. If residents are given the chance to express their opinions about tourism and long-term development, they potentially have the power to change the state of affairs by influencing decision makers. The difficulty is, of course, that tourism is often only one of a several issues facing destination communities and it may not always be obvious, or even the case, that tourism is one of or even the single cause of some of these problems. As well, residents are quite as likely to be biased in favour of supporting continued economic development (jobs) which governments insist can only be obtained by increasing the numbers of tourists. It is always much easier to argue for growth than to argue in favour of environmental and social issues, which may be perceived to have significant costs or losses of opportunities. Thus, information and education are not only needed for tourists, but also for residents. Their empowerment through education may well be the only way to elicit community support for a more sustainable and resilient future; one that would avoid the problem of overtourism.

References

Agarwal, S. and Shaw, G. (2017) *Heritage Screen and Literary Tourism*. Bristol: Channel Vie Publications.

Ahluwalia, R (2017) Florence church steps hosed down to deter tourists, *The Independent*, 1 June, https://www.independent.co.uk/travel/news-and-advice/florence-church-tourists-water-wet-hose-santa-croce-basilica-picnics-eating-food-italy-a7767111.html (Accessed 29 November 2018).

Ap, J. and Crompton, J. L. (1993) Residents' strategies for responding to tourism impacts, *Journal of Travel Research*, 32 (1): 47–50.

Baum, T. and Lundtorp, S. (Eds.) (2001) *Seasonality in Tourism*. Oxford: Pergamon.

Beeton, S. (2016) *Film-Induced Tourism*, 2nd edition. Bristol: Channel View Publications.

Buffa, F. (2015) Young tourists and sustainability. Profiles, attitudes, and implications for destination strategies. *Sustainability*, 7 (10): 14042–14062.

Butler, R. W. (1975) Tourism as an agent of social change. In *Proceedings of the International Geographical Union's Working Group on the Geography of Tourism and Recreation*. Peterborough, Ontario: Trent University, pp. 85–90.

Butler, R.W. (1993) Tourism – An Evolutionary Perspective. In J. G. Nelson, R. Butler, and G. Wall (Eds.) *Tourism and Sustainable Development: Monitoring, Planning, Managing*. Waterloo: University of Waterloo. pp. 27–44.

Butler, R. W. (1998) Sustainable tourism – looking backwards in order to progress? In C. M. Hall and A. Lew (Eds.), *Sustainable tourism: A geographical perspective*, Harlow: Longman, pp. 25–34.

Butler, R.W. (2001) Seasonality in tourism issues and implications. In T. Baum and S. Lundtorp (Eds.), *Seasonality in Tourism*. Oxford: Pergamon, pp.5–22

Butler, R. W. (Ed.) (2017) *Tourism and Resilience*. Wallingford: CABI.

Câmara Municipal do Porto (2018) Taxa Municipal Turistica. http://www.cm-porto.pt/assets/misc/documentos/Dire%C3%A7%C3%B5es%20municipais/Comercio%20e%20Turismo/Folheto%20Taxa%20Turistica.pdf (Accessed 29 November 2018).

Carey, M. (2017) Venice asks tourists not to pause too long on bridges, *Conde Nast Traveler*, 26 July. https://www.cntraveler.com/story/venice-asks-tourists-not-to-pause-too-long-on-bridges (Accessed 29 November 2018).

Carey, 2018 Venice is banning tourists from some parts of the city. *CNN Traveller*, https://www.cntraveler.com/story/venice-is-banning-tourists-from-some-parts-of-the-city.

CBC News (2009) Tofino bans outdoor water use, *CBC News*, 20 July. https://www.cbc.ca/news/canada/british-columbia/tofino-bans-outdoor-water-use-1.855725 (Accessed 29 November 2018).

Cheer, J. M. and Lew, A. A. (2017) *Tourism, resilience and sustainability: Adapting to social, political and economic change*. Abingdon, UK: Routledge.

Cohen, S. A., Higham, J. E. S., Peeters, P. and Gössling, S. (Eds.) (2014) *Understanding and governing sustainable tourism mobility: Psychological and behavioural approaches*. Abingdon, UK: Routledge.

Dodds, R. (2007) Sustainable tourism and policy implementation: Lessons from the case of Calvia, Spain. *Current Issues in Tourism*, 10 (4): 296–322.

Dodds, R. and Butler, R. W. (2009). Inaction more than action: Barriers to the implementation of sustainable tourism policies. In S. Gössling, C. M. Hall and D. Weaver (Eds.), *Sustainable tourism futures: Perspectives on systems, restructuring and innovations*. London: Routledge, pp. 63–77.

Dodds, R., Graci, S. R. and Holmes, M. (2010) Does the tourist care? A comparison of tourists in Koh Phi Phi, Thailand and Gili Trawangan, Indonesia. *Journal of Sustainable Tourism*, 18 (2): 207–222.

Gill, A. and Williams, P. (2018) Transitioning towards sustainability in the mountain resort of Whistler, British Columbia. *Tourism Recreation Research*, 43 (4): 528–539.

Hall, C. M., Prayag, G. and Amore, A. (2018) *Tourism and resilience: Individual, organisational and destination perspectives* Bristol, UK: Channel View Publications.

Hansla, A., Gamble, A., Juliusson A. and Gärling, T. (2008) Psychological determinants of attitude towards and willingness to pay for green electricity, *Energy Policy*, 36 (2): 768–774.

Iamsterdam (2018) Amsterdam launches a campaign to stop offensive behaviour, 29 May. https://www.iamsterdam.com/en/our-network/amsterdam-marketing/about-amsterdam-marketing/news/enjoy-and-respect (Accessed 29 November 2018).

Jardine, A. (2016) Iceland's tourist 'academy' will teach you how to not kill yourself taking selfies in treacherous landscapes, 30 Nov. https://adage.com/creativity/work/iceland-academy-how-take-safe-selfie/50036.

Laimer, P. (2017) Tourism indicators for monitoring the SDGs. Presented at the Sixth UNWTO International Conference on Tourism Statistics, Manila, Philippines, 21–24 June. http://cf.cdn.unwto.org/sites/all/files/pdf/laimer_conf2017manila_central_paper.pdf (Accessed 29 November 2018).

Lew, A. A. and Cheer, J. M. (2017) *Tourism resilience and adaptation to environmental change*. Abingdon, UK: Routledge.

List Challenges (n.d.) Places I've travelled to. https://www.listchallenges.com/places-ive-travelled-to (Accessed 29 November 2018).

Loop Head Tourism (n.d.) Responsible tourism policy. www.loophead.ie/responsible-tourism-policy/ (Accessed 29 November 2018).

López Díaz, A. (2017) Why Barcelona locals really hate tourists, *The Independent*, 9 August. https://www.independent.co.uk/travel/news-and-advice/barcelona-locals-hate-tourists-why-reasons-spain-protests-arran-airbnb-locals-attacks-graffiti-a7883021.html (Accessed 29 November 2018).

Lundtorp, S., Rassing, C. R., and Wanhill, S. (2001) Off-season is no season: The case of Bornholm. In T. Baum and S. Lundtorp (Eds.), *Seasonality in Tourism*. Oxford: Pergamon, pp.89–108.

Mihalic, T. and Kuščer, K. (2018) Managing residents' dissatisfaction with tourism: The case of Ljubljana. Presented at the Travel and Tourism Research Association's (TTRA 2018) European Chapter Conference, Ljubljana, 25 April.

Nickerson, N. P., Jorgenson, J. and Boley, B. B. (2016) Are sustainable tourists a higher spending market? *Tourism Management*, 54: 170–177.

Pulido-Fernández, J. I. and López-Sánchez, Y. (2016) Are tourists really willing to pay more for sustainable destinations? *Sustainability*, 8 (12): 1240.

Sheppard, V. A. (2017) Resilience and destination governance. In R. W. Butler (Ed.), *Tourism and Resilience*. Wallingford: CABI, pp.53–68.

Simmonds, L. (2018) Crowds a thing of the past? Dubrovnik will finally limit cruisers. *Total Croatia News*, 1 October. https://www.total-croatia-news.com/lifestyle/31375-crowds-a-thing-of-the-past-dubrovnik-will-finally-limit-cruisers (Accessed October 2018).

TCI Research (n.d.) Resident Sentiment Index. http://tci-research.com/travelsat/resident-sentiment-index/.

Viero, A. G. (2003) *Residents' Opinions of Tourism in Sacred Places: The Case of Santiago de Compostela, Spain*. MSc Thesis, Guildford: University of Surrey.

Waligo, V. M., Clarke, J. and Hawkins, R. (2013) Implementing sustainable tourism: A multi-stakeholder involvement management framework, *Tourism management*, 36: 342–353.

World Commission on Environment and Development (WCED) (1987) *Our common future* Oxford: Oxford University Press.

World Travel and Tourism Council (WTTC) (2012) *The comparative economic impact of travel & tourism*. London and Oxford: WTTC and Oxford Economics. https://www.wttc.org/-/media/files/reports/benchmark-reports/the_comparative_economic_impact_of_travel__tourism.pdf (Accessed October 2018).

Author biographies

Susanne Becken is the Director of the Griffith Institute for Tourism at Griffith University in Australia. She has published widely on sustainable tourism, climate change and tourism resource use and was a contributing author to the Fourth and the Fifth Intergovernmental Panel on Climate Change Assessment Reports. Susanne is a member of the Air New Zealand Sustainability Advisory Panel, PATA's Sustainability and Social Responsibility committee, and the Whitsunday Climate Change Innovation Hub.

Richard W. Butler is Emeritus Professor at Strathclyde University, Glasgow and visiting Professor at the Tourism Academy in NHTV University, Breda (Netherlands). He has taught also at the University of Western Ontario, the University of Surrey, James Cook University (Australia), and CISET (Venice). A geographer by training in the UK with degrees from Nottingham and Glasgow Universities, his research has focused on destination development and its associated impacts, sustainability in tourism, particularly in insular and remote regions, and also links between tourism and political change, and with religion. A past president of the International Academy for the Study of Tourism and of the Canadian Association for Leisure Studies, he has published over twenty books and a hundred papers on tourism. He has acted as advisor to UNWTO and Canadian, Australian and UK governments and in 2016 was awarded the Ulysses medal for excellence in the creation and dissemination of knowledge and named the 2016 UNWTO Ulysses Laureate.

Reil G. Cruz is former Dean of the University of the Philippines Asian Institute of Tourism where he currently heads its tourism and extension division. His research interests are inclusive tourism, tourism regulations, and Filipino travel behavior. He is an active member of the Philippine Association of Researchers on Tourism and Hospitality whose main goals include the publication of a Philippines-focused journal of tourism and hospitality studies.

Rachel Dodds is a Professor in the Ted Rogers School of Hospitality and Tourism Management at Ryerson University in Toronto, Canada. She holds a PhD from the University of Surrey in the UK and also works in the private sector assisting governments, industry and NGO's to help tourism become more sustainable. Rachel is known globally for her work in sustainable tourism and her research encompasses CSR, destination planning and management, environmental management in addition to sustainable/responsible tourism. She was recently appointed a council member for Canada's Jobs and the Visitor Economy Secretariat – a national government council.

Florian Eggli is a PhD candidate in Tourism Studies at the University of Lausanne and simultaneously working at the Institute of Tourism at the Lucerne University of Applied Sciences and Arts. His doctoral research is focused on the current tourism development of Lucerne. He holds a Master degree in International Tourism Management of London Metropolitan University and Bachelor in Social Anthropology of the University of Berne.

Ulrike Gretzel is a Senior Fellow at the Center of Public Relations, University of Southern California and serves as the Director of Research at Netnografica, a market research company that extracts insights from online conversations. She received her Ph.D. in Communications from the University of Illinois at Urbana-Champaign. Her research focuses on the impact of technology on human experiences and the structure of technology-mediated communication. She studies social media marketing and destination marketing, influencer marketing and the emerging reputation economy. She has also researched the design of intelligent systems in tourism, smart tourism development,

https://doi.org/10.1515/9783110607369-019

technology adoption and non-adoption in tourism organizations, tourism in technological dead zones, and the quest for digital detox experiences.

She is frequently acknowledged as one of the most cited authors in tourism and her work has been quoted in major news outlets such as the New York Times and The Australian.

Harold Goodwin is Professor Emeritus at Manchester Metropolitan University and Director of Responsible Tourism in the Institute of Place Management. He chairs a series of International Conferences on Responsible Tourism in Destinations the first of which, in Cape Town in 2002, launched the Responsible Tourism movement. Overtourism is a consequence of paying little more than lip service to sustainability and failing to use tourism, to make better places to live in, because great places to live in are great places to visit. www.haroldgoodwin.info and www. responsibletourismpartnership.org. A directory of resources for "coping with success" is available at www.overtourism.info.

Janto S. Hess is an independent consultant and PhD Researcher at University College London (UCL). His research focus is on exploring the link between tourism and climate change in Thailand, in particular in relation to industry stakeholders' perceptions towards and potential to engage in adaptation finance. As a consultant he provides support for national level adaptation planning, project design, funding proposal development, and climate finance readiness to enable governments to cope with climate change induced hazards and access international climate finance. His expertise is based on several years of experience in international development (for example with UNDP and GIZ), the tourism sector, and think tanks. He enjoys exploring new cultures, debating, and photography.

Walter Jamieson has worked with a number of organisations (ADB, UNWTO, ESCAP, World Bank, UNESCO, JICA and ASEAN). His activities have included heritage, planning and tourism work in Canada, research and consultancy work in China, extensive community-based tourism work in Southeast Asia, and exploration of the power of tourism as a tool for cultural, economic and social development. Jamieson has held high positions in universities in Canada, the United States and Asia. His awards and recognitions include the Queen's Jubilee Medal, the Heritage Canada Lieutenant Governor's Award, and his election to the College of Fellows of the Canadian Institute of Planners. He has authored and contributed to 140 academic publications and over 150 consultancy and research projects. Recent consultancies include participation in the Integrated Tourism Master Plan for Lomboc, ASEAN Tourism Strategic Plan; the ASEAN Tourism Marketing Strategy; Myanmar Tourism Master Plan and the updated Greater Mekong Subregion Tourism Sector Strategy (2016–2025). His most recent co-authored book, *The Planning and Management of Responsible Urban Heritage Destinations in Asia*, was published in late 2018. Currently, Jamieson is an Adjunct Professor at Ryerson University in Toronto, Canada; Distinguished Adjunct Professor at the Asian Institute of Technology, Thailand; and Chief Innovation Officer at Green Door Solutions Ltd.

Michelle Jamieson has a strong background in tourism, change management and communications. Having worked in the tourism and hospitality industry on a global scale and on a number of regional tourism and tourism marketing strategies, including the Association of Southeast Asian Nations (ASEAN) Tourism Marketing Strategy 2017–2020, Michelle has an appreciation and interest in destination and stakeholder management approaches in a variety of capacities through policy and marketing planning. The tourism and hospitality landscape has undergone a significant shift over the past few years and Michelle has a strong focus on exploring creative and innovative solutions to a wide spectrum of industry issues to ensure that tourism is sustainable and responsible.

Marion Joppe is a Professor at the School of Hospitality, Food and Tourism Management, University of Guelph, and President, *Tourism environment*. She received her doctorate in Law and Economics of Tourism from the Université de Droit, d'Economie et des Sciences d'Aix-Marseille III (France), where her research focused on government intervention in tourism, and the approaches taken by different political systems and countries. Marion specializes in destination planning, development and marketing, and the experiences upon which destinations build. She has extensive private and public sector experience, having worked for financial institutions, tour operators, consulting groups and government, prior to joining academia.

Giovanni Francis A. Legaspi is an Assistant Professor at the University of the Philippines, Asian Institute of Tourism. He obtained his Bachelor of Science in Tourism and Master of Industrial Relations at the University of the Philippines. He has been teaching integrated resort management, organization and behavior in tourism enterprise and human resource development. His current research interests are in the areas of human resource management and resort management.

Emma Nolan has 25 years' experience as an event management practitioner and an academic. This includes working in visitor attractions, theatres and local authorities and delivering events for a variety of clients including political parties, the TUC and the NHS. She moved into academia in 2008 and worked as a Senior Lecturer in Project and Event Management at the University of Winchester for several years. She is a Senior Fellow of the HEA, has an MA in Education and is currently working towards her PhD at the University of Chichester. Emma recently published her first book, *Working with Venues for Events* (Routledge, 2018*)*, and her current research interests are centred on the MICE sector. She is specifically interested in exploring the site selection process in the organisation of association conferences.

Timo Ohnmacht is a Sociologist and Professor at the Institute of Tourism at the Lucerne University of Applied Sciences and Arts. His research focuses on the interrelation of tourism mobilities and modernity, leisure, and tourism travel. He studied Transportation and Sociology at the Technical University of Berlin, University of Lancaster (UK), and ETH Zurich.

Jahanzeeb Qurashi achieved his PhD in Tourism at University of Central Lancashire, UK. He obtained his first B.A (Hons) degree from the University of Birmingham in Tourism and Business Administration and his first Master degree in International Hospitality from the University of Birmingham. He obtained a second Master Degree (MBA) from University of Chester in Business & Marketing and a Post Graduate Certificate in research methodology from University of Central Lancashire, UK. His interests include commodification of religious tourism, varying experiences of pilgrim/tourist in tourism, destination management, contemporary hospitality, event management, the role of SMART media technologies in the tourism & hospitality sector and heritage tourism. He is a member of the Scientific Committee and Editorial Board for the International Journal of Religious Tourism and Pilgrimage and a member of Institute for Religious Tourism and Pilgrimage, UK.

Jillian M. Rickly is Associate Professor of Tourism Management and Marketing at the University of Nottingham. She is a tourism geographer with interests in authenticity/alienation in tourism motivation and experience, the ethics of sustainability, and mobilities and wellbeing. She is the Series Editor for De Gruyter Studies in Tourism. She is co-author of *Tourism, Performance, and Place: A Geographic Perspective* (Ashgate, 2014), and co-editor of *Tourism & Leisure Mobilities: Politics, Work, and Play* (Routledge, 2016), *Events Mobilities: Politics, Place and Performance* (Routledge, 2016), and her most recent co-edited book is *Authenticity & Tourism: Materialities, Perceptions, Experiences* (Emerald, 2018).

Miroslav Rončák has more than 25 years' experience in international tourism, research and effective destination promotion. He spent 12 years as director of the Czech Tourist Authority in Frankfurt, Berlin and Moscow. He was awarded the "Tourism Olymp" Prize and Travel industry & Mass media professional Award "Leaders of the Travel industry" for his work as the best foreign representative of tourism for Russia, CIS and the Baltic States. Currently, he is working as a tourism researcher in the Department of Recreation and Leisure Studies at the Palacky University in Olomouc, Czech Republic. His research focuses on overtourism, sustainable development of tourism destinations and impacts of tourism on the host`s community quality of life. Miroslav also represents TCI Research, an independent UNWTO-awarded market intelligence agency in international tourism and travel competitive analysis in Eastern Europe. He is a regular speaker at international forums in Eastern Europe and part of FVW Medien team, the Germany`s leading travel trade media publisher responsible for Russia, CIS, Central Asia and Eastern Europe.

Hugues Séraphin is a Senior Lecturer in Event and Tourism Management Studies. He is also the Programme Leader for Event Management at the University of Winchester. Dr. Hugues Seraphin has expertise and interests in tourism development and management in post-colonial, post-conflict and post-disaster destinations. He has recently published in *International Journal of Culture, Tourism, and Hospitality Research; Current Issues in Tourism; Journal of Policy Research in Tourism, Leisure and Events; Journal of Business Research; Worldwide Hospitality and Tourism Themes, Journal of Hospitality and Tourism Management*; and *Journal of Destination Marketing & Management*.

David G. Simmons is the leader of Lincoln University's tourism programme and a founding staff member of the Department of Tourism, Sport and Society. He is University Principal Research Strategist, and Professor of Tourism. His research career has been focused around one main theme – managing tourism at the destination area. It is informed principally by human geography, resource economics and the social sciences but increasingly adopts a multi or interdisciplinary epistemology. More recently he has examined broader questions of tourism governance and policy, and been a member of the New Zealand Tourism2025 strategy. Current research projects examine social resilience building through the lens of transient populations (including tourists and sector employees) from recent disruptive events in the region surrounding Kaikoura, and the second examines longer term risks around the geospatial and temporal dispersal of tourists as biosecurity, bio-health disease vectors.

Jürg Stettler is Deputy Dean and Head of Research of the Business School and Head of Institute of Tourism at the Lucerne University of Applied Sciences and Arts. He studied Business Administration and Political Economy at the University of Berne. His research focuses on destination management, sustainable tourism and impact studies of mega sport events.

Geoffrey Wall is Distinguished Professor Emeritus, Department of Geography and Environmental Management, University of Waterloo, Canada. His research focuses on the consequences of tourism of different types for destinations with different characteristics, and the planning implications that follow from them. He has long been involved in research and consulting in Asia, formerly in Indonesia and, more recently, in China, including Taiwan. Recent work focuses on indigenous tourism, natural and cultural heritage, and the implications of tourism for those living in and around protected areas.

Fabian Weber is lecturer and project manager at the Institute of Tourism at the Lucerne University of Applied Sciences and Arts. His main research interests are in sustainable tourism development, overtourism, tourism and climate change as well as on quality and environmental management in tourism. He studied geography, sociology and environment protection at the Universities of Basel and Berne, Switzerland.

List of Figures

https://doi.org/10.1515/9783110607369-020

List of Tables

https://doi.org/10.1515/9783110607369-021

Index

https://doi.org/10.1515/9783110607369-022

www.ingramcontent.com/pod-product-compliance
Lightning Source LLC
Chambersburg PA
CBHW081055220326
41598CB00038B/7101